GW00367245

SEEKING RIGHTS FROM THE LEFT

SEEKING RIGHTS FROM THE LEFT

Gender, Sexuality, and the Latin American Pink Tide

ELISABETH JAY FRIEDMAN, EDITOR

DUKE UNIVERSITY PRESS
Durham and London
2019

© 2018 Duke University Press
All rights reserved
Printed and bound by CPI Group (UK) Ltd,
Croydon, CR0 4YY
Typeset in Minion by Westchester Book
Group
Library of Congress Cataloging-in-Publication Data
Names: Friedman, Elisabeth J., [date] editor.
Title: Seeking rights from the left ; gender, sexuality, and the
Latin American pink tide / ed. Elisabeth Jay Friedman.
Description: Durham : Duke University Press, 2018. |
Includes bibliographical references and index.
Identifiers: LCCN 2018016919 (print) | LCCN 2018019937 (ebook)
ISBN 9781478002604 (ebook)
ISBN 9781478001171 (hardcover : alk. paper)
ISBN 9781478001522 (pbk. : alk. paper)
Subjects: LCSH: Women's rights—Latin America. | Gay rights—
Latin America. | Right and left (Political science)—Latin America. |
Latin America—Politics and government—21st century.
Classification: LCC HQ1236.5.L37 (ebook) | LCC HQ1236.5.L37
S44 2018 (print) | DDC 320.5098—dc23
LC record available at https://lccn.loc.gov/2018016919

Cover art: International Women´s Strike in Buenos Aires
on International Women´s Day, March 8, 2017. Photo by
Felicitas Rossi.

TO THE NEXT GENERATION OF SEEKERS

CONTENTS

AMY LIND

When we first began to witness Latin America's shift away from neoliberalism and toward socialism in the late 1990s and early 2000s, so many of us—feminist, queer, antiracist, antiglobalization, decolonial scholars and activists—held high hopes for social transformation in the region. After living through the "lost decade" of the 1980s, which exacerbated long-standing economic and social inequalities through neoliberal policies focused on servicing foreign debt, and after witnessing the deeper, far-reaching institutionalization of the neoliberal logic of "free market" development in the 1990s, with its emphasis on privatization, decentralization, and NGOization, the promise of new left experiments was exhilarating, albeit often combined with a healthy dose of skepticism. As scholars and activists imagined "another world," many assumed that gender and sexual rights, and queer imaginings of economy, nation, citizenship, and sustainable life, would be concretely realized.

To reflect their newly proposed socialist and/or decolonial agendas, some Pink Tide governments passed national referendums to change their constitutions. Ultimately, whether such changes occurred through constitutional reform, broader legal reforms, or changes in public policy, a general aim was to share resources more equitably and increase citizen access to states' socialist-inspired redistributive projects. Through this process, there have been some exciting innovations, some of which are explored in this collection. The shared dissatisfaction among Pink Tide governments with the region's neoliberal legacy, and the global financial architecture that catalyzed and sustained it, led to an array of moderate and more radical antineoliberal and/or socialist projects. Unfortunately, as this volume documents so well, these projects have been incomplete, often fraught with tensions and contradictions. We have learned much since the inception of the Pink Tide, and have perhaps lost some hope. Yet we have also found some key political openings, fissures, and spaces in which to imagine a more just world, thanks to Pink Tide political movements and sometimes despite them as well.

This volume shatters Cold War binaries that many scholars still hold about capitalism versus socialism, and religion versus secularism, as they affect women's and LGBT rights and social movements. Feminists and queers have been attacked by all ideological sides in different historical moments and spaces, but little research has been conducted to analyze how this has occurred within Latin America's Pink Tide. *Seeking Rights from the Left* provides a deeply grounded framework for analyzing gender and sexual rights in Latin America's shift to the left, raising difficult questions about the relationships between ideology and governance, and highlighting how feminists and LGBT/queer people are often scapegoated in broader nationalist, antineoliberal, and antiimperialist struggles. Some chapters in this book take head-on the ways in which Cold War assumptions continue to haunt scholarly work on gender and sexual rights. Indeed, as several contributors point out, what we tend to see is a complex blend of pro- and anti-women's and LGBT rights discourses and practices, often converging in the same state. For example, Ecuadorian president Rafael Correa (2007–17) supported an explicit decolonial queer rights agenda early on in his administration, yet is notorious for his neglect of women's rights and his outright misogyny. A same-sex civil union bill was passed in Chile in 2014, yet despite Chilean president Michelle Bachelet's (2006–10, 2014–to date) leadership on women's and to a lesser extent LGBT issues (as former UN Women executive director, 2010–13), in Chile, indigenous women's rights lag far behind and indeed have at times been directly challenged by the state.

Despite the excitement of imagining a more just world—one that has inspired some Pink Tide states to adopt an intentional "decolonization" agenda, and even a "depatriarchalization" agenda in the case of Bolivia—these persistent paradoxes demonstrate that ideology and party politics do not determine how gender and sexual rights are or are not addressed in Pink Tide contexts. Indeed, in our increasingly globalized world, the transnational flow of resources, labor, and information about family, gender, and (homo)sexuality plays as much into leftist leaders' visions, and leftist states' articulations, of heteronormative socialism as do internal politics and alliances. Right-wing, often religiously inspired discourses claiming that "gender ideology" is "dangerous" to the traditional family are now prominently embedded in political processes in places as diverse as France, the United States, Uganda, and Malawi, as well as Chile, Ecuador, and other Latin American countries. Not surprisingly, some Pink Tide countries are thus more influenced by religion than during earlier waves of socialism, and this greatly affects how women and LGBT people are represented in public policy, law, and state programs.

So, how do we make sense of these contradictions? This volume is the first of its kind to directly focus on these complex relationships, cultural and political movements, and processes as they occur in eight countries. Interestingly, when we analyze gender and sexual rights "after" neoliberalism (remembering that many Pink Tide states still utilize and promote neoliberal development frameworks), we find many inconsistencies across time and within the Pink Tide era: in some countries, for example, more rights were extended to women and/or LGBT people during the neoliberal period than during the more recent socialist period. Women have benefitted more from Pink Tide policy and legal changes in countries such as Uruguay and Argentina than in other nations. Moreover, Pink Tide states often prioritize one set of rights over another. For example, some states have utilized a pro-LGBT rights discourse to defend their modernization projects and brand themselves as "modern" and "civilized," while simultaneously eroding women's and indigenous rights. Such "trade-offs" potentially pit the advances of one group against the losses faced by another and create uneven access to socialist redistributive projects.

I invite you to read this provocative volume, which grounds and transforms our understanding of how gender and sexuality matter to and are represented in forms of Pink Tide governance and development in Latin America. These generative analyses will inspire new conversations about the central place of feminist and queer studies in (post)neoliberal politics and Latin American social movements, and remind us how notions of gender and sexuality are always present, even when unnamed.

ACKNOWLEDGMENTS

This book exists because of the contributors' passionate commitment to critical analysis of the politics, policy, and protagonists of this volume. I thank them for their patience and persistence in bringing this complex collaboration to fruition. Such collaboration is the only way to create the kind of rich and representative insights found in these pages—the only way, indeed, to create meaningful and inclusive change.

I am grateful to Lorraine Bayard de Volo and Gwynn Thomas, who strongly encouraged me to initiate this project, and to Constanza Tabbush for her unflagging enthusiasm, informed understanding, and well-honed networking skills. Antje Wiener, Eric Hershberg, Max Cameron, and Amrita Basu graciously offered presentation and publication opportunities for my early exploration of the regional dynamics of gender and sexuality politics and policy, particularly under the Pink Tide. Bayard de Volo, Pascha Bueno-Hansen, and Esther Rodriguez were crucial contributors to the research effort that resulted in this volume. All of the authors appreciate the time, interest, and hard work they put into it, from which we learned so much. University of San Francisco students Janet Chavez and Alexandra DeFazio provided valuable research and editing assistance, and the university's Faculty Development Fund generously underwrote research and publication processes.

We have had opportunities to present various chapters in a range of settings: the Latin American Studies Association (LASA) Congress in Puerto Rico (2015) and in New York City (2016), the Consejo Latinoamericano de Ciencias Sociales (CLACSO) Congress in Bogotá (2016), the University of San Francisco Global Women's Rights Forum (2017), and the American Political Science Association in San Francisco (2017). We particularly thank the following LASA discussants, who ensured lively, critical, and productive sessions: Sonia E. Alvarez, Amy Lind, Jocelyn Olcott, and Heidi Tinsman.

We deeply appreciate the seriousness with which reviewers Jocelyn Olcott, Maxine Molyneux, and Millie Thayer took the project, and their many detailed and insightful interventions to improve and weave together the individual pieces, even as they recognized the distinct perspectives of the contributors. We are very grateful to Duke University Press editor Gisela Fosado for her enthusiasm, patience, and support. We also thank editorial associates Lydia Rose Rappoport-Hankins and Stephanie Gomez Menzies for their assistance, and project editor Sara Leone for her guidance through publication.

A Spanish-language version of chapter 3 appeared as "Matrimonio igualitario, identidad de género y disputas por el derecho al aborto en Argentina: La política sexual durante el Kirchnerismo (2003–2015)," in *Sexualidad, Salud y Sociedad*, no. 22 (April 2016): 22–55. Centro Latinoamericano de Sexualidad y Derechos Humanos (CLAM/IMS/UERJ).

A Portuguese-language version of part of chapter 6 was published as "Gênero e sexualidade nas políticas públicas: O temor de retrocesso," *Teoria e Debate*, no. 149 (June 17, 2016). https://teoriaedebate.org.br/2016/06/17/%EF%BB%BFgenero-e-sexualidade-nas-politicas-publicas-o-temor-de-retrocesso/.

Contesting the Pink Tide

ELISABETH JAY FRIEDMAN

AND CONSTANZA TABBUSH

The beginning of the twenty-first century promised a profound transformation in Latin American politics. By 2005, the vast majority of the region's citizens were governed by states whose executives, if not their legislatures, identified as being on the left of the political spectrum. Whether inspired by socialist, social democratic, liberal, decolonial,[1] or other ideologies, they sought to challenge deep-seated social, political, and economic inequalities. Such an experience offers students and analysts focused on Latin America as well as on other world regions a unique opportunity to explore and understand the impact of left governance. More than a decade later, with the "Pink Tide"[2] of left-leaning governments ebbing, it is time to take stock.

This collection offers a central, yet largely ignored, contribution: a comparative assessment of the Pink Tide's engagement with feminist, women's, and lesbian, gay, bisexual, and transgender (LGBT) movements and demands. Focusing on eight national cases—Argentina, Bolivia, Brazil, Chile, Ecuador, Nicaragua, Uruguay, and Venezuela—chapter authors map out and evaluate the ways in which the contemporary Left addressed gender- and sexuality-based rights through the state, from roughly 2000 to 2015. They find that while Pink Tide administrations transformed the everyday lives of women and LGBT populations in the region, advancements were highly uneven among the central policy arenas covered in this collection: social welfare, political representation, violence against women, women's bodily autonomy, and LGBT relationship and identity recognition. Beyond "an impact of left governance" approach, the book's focus on state-society relations reveals how gender and sexuality have been fundamental to the political projects of the Latin American Left—but in often unexpected ways.

This focused comparison of the achievements in women's and LGBT rights and the experiences of their proponents departs from a fascinating conundrum. Some have found that inclusion of women and LGBT groups, as well as attention to gender and sexual inequality, is most likely under democracies governed from the Left (Esping-Anderson 1990; Stetson and Mazur 1995). But while previous studies suggested the Pink Tide would offer new opportunities to advance gender and sexual justice, historically, Latin American left and center-left parties, movements, and governments have had a variable record, and state agencies also perpetuated previous policy legacies and institutional practices (Díez 2015; Htun 2003; Htun and Weldon 2010). Moreover, studies of gender and sexuality and the state show that political transformation does not always result in the transformation of gender and sexuality-based inequalities (Dore and Molyneux 2000; Molyneux 2001; Díez 2015; Htun 2016). Instead, continuities in norms and practices across political cycles may be as important as policy changes. Has this period of left governance offered a unified narrative of progress concerning gender and sexuality? To answer this question, we build on comparative analysis that insists that we disaggregate policy arenas based on the degree to which they challenge deeply rooted cultural values and the power of their proponents (Htun and Weldon 2010).

Our comparative analysis demonstrates that the countries of the Pink Tide made a significant difference in the lives of women and LGBT people in the region. Crosscutting results show that most governments improved the basic conditions of poor women and their families. In many cases, they advanced women's representation in national legislatures to high global ranks. Some countries legalized same-sex relationships and enabled their citizens to claim their own gender identity. They also opened up opportunities for feminist and queer[3] movements to articulate and press forward their demands. But at the same time, these governments largely relied on heteropatriarchal relations of power—ones that privilege heterosexual men—ignoring or rejecting the more challenging elements of a social agenda and engaging in strategic trade-offs among gender and sexual rights. Moreover, the comparative examination of such rights arenas reveals that the Left's more general political and economic projects have been profoundly, if at times unintentionally, informed by traditional understandings of gender and sexuality.

This last point highlights the combination of policy change and continuity that this volume uncovers. There is no linear story of progress across these chapters, which as often contest as uphold the transformations promised by left governance. Instead, the possibilities for change seem to depend on institutional contexts as well as the organization and actions of collective actors seeking rights from the Left. On the one hand, the collection highlights that the degree of state institutionalization, particularly the effectiveness of checks on executive power, is critical in determining the ultimate impact of the Left in power. Moreover, the largely underanalyzed alliances between progressive political forces and conservative religious ones play a central role in determining the fate of policy issues that deeply contest traditional or cultural norms in Latin America, such as abortion, same-sex marriage, gender identity recognition, or even gender-based violence. However, these dangerous liaisons have not been an obstacle to achievements in policy arenas that do not challenge deeply rooted norms, such as the advancement of social rights or the political representation of women.

On the other hand, this collection also offers multiple examples of how advocates and movements have fought for gender and sexual justice, and provides insights into their successful strategies. The experiences recounted in this volume underline the relevance of building state-society coalitions that can cut across policy sectors and state institutions, as well as the need for strategically framing demands. These two aspects of state-society relations help us explain the variable outcomes of the Left's governance in Latin America. They also help us explain why looking through the lenses of gender and sexuality erodes any unified notion of the Pink Tide as a common political experience.

To explain its wide spectrum of results, this collection sheds light on the complex, and sometimes contradictory, relationships among governments, left-leaning parties, femocrats,[4] feminist and women's movements, LGBT movements, and opponents as well as proponents of gender and sexual rights. By engendering and queering the study of the Latin American Left, the analyses focus on new social actors, processes, and institutions. Sidelined movements become protagonists: grassroots, Afro-Brazilian, and indigenous movements, feminist and LGBT movements, and their alliances cut across the collection. Chapters bring largely overlooked state bureaucracies, most notably national women's agencies and antidiscrimination institutions, to the forefront, along with the Catholic and Protestant forces that have often sought to impede policy change. The volume covers scenarios of overt conflict between the Left and a feminist agenda, such as those found in Daniel Ortega's Nicaragua and Rafael Correa's Ecuador, with their direct attacks on women's rights and their proponents. It also includes more collaborative scenarios, such as those witnessed during the Frente Amplio administration in Uruguay, when mobilization and alliances between feminist and LGBT movements promoted "emblematic achievements such as same-sex marriage and the decriminalization of abortion, and innovative affirmative action measures for the trans population" (chapter 1). Our analytic comparison enables a display, in productive tension, of national specificities, as well as the regional and subregional trends in policy and politics that are the focus of this introduction.

This volume's objective was to enable comparison while giving authors enough room to tailor their chapters around the distinct experiences and central political struggles of each country. While some authors offer more comprehensive explorations (as in the chapters on Uruguay, Chile, and Venezuela), others have foregrounded a particular conundrum: Why did Argentina succeed in advancing same-sex marriage and gender identity recognition while calls for the right to abortion went largely unheeded? What does a wide-ranging gender and sexuality policy inventory reveal about left versus centrist governance in Brazil? These explorations reflect the distinct political, geographical, analytic, and disciplinary perspectives of their authors.

Taking such variety into account, the remainder of this introduction is organized into two main sections: the first explains the book's common framework, and the second presents the main comparative findings. Taken together, these findings establish how the countries under examination dealt with the issues of social welfare, political representation, violence against women, and the trade-offs between women's bodily autonomy and LGBT identity recognition, as well as offer insights on successful strategies for achieving changes for women and LGBT communities.

Conceptual and Methodological Framework

This section starts by addressing three key analytic choices undergirding this project. The first, and most fundamental, is why we should expect Pink Tide governments to focus on gender and sexual justice. The second considers why these countries should be grouped together at all. What do Pink Tide governments share that allow us to consider them as an expression of a similar political phenomenon? And what are their basic differences? The third moves to methodological concerns, and invites us to explain why we chose to analyze gender and sexuality, two issues that are diverse (and, in some cases, divergent) in their traditions and objects of study, within one analytic frame. Are there similarities in how gender and sexuality are embedded in Latin American states, and in how advocates seek change on these issues? After spelling out these analytic choices, we set out the framework that organizes our comparative findings.

Should We Expect Pink Tide Governments to Fare Better on Gender and Sexual Justice?

One of the conceptual aims of this collection is to unpack the putative association between gender and sexual rights and left governance. Global analysis suggests that while left-wing organizations can play critical roles in advancing the social rights of women and LGBT populations, they are less significant in advancing other dimensions of gender and sexual justice (Htun and Weldon 2010). Moreover, counterintuitive findings from Latin America show that some progressive policies have been promoted by neoliberal, right-wing, or even undemocratic governments (Htun 2003), such as recent efforts by neoliberal Mexican and Chilean presidents to support same-sex marriage. The latest research on the relationship between the Left and gender equality policy in particular finds the Left to be "reactive" rather than proactive on these issues (Blofeld, Ewig, and Piscopo 2017). While taking stock of the uncertain relationship between the Left and gender and sexual justice, this project started from the assumption that the Pink Tide was a period of political opportunity for feminism and queer politics. This hypothesis was based on Latin American presidential commitments, political party platforms, and historical legacies of left-wing politics, as well as previous research on gender, sexuality, and politics.

Pink Tide governments distinguished themselves from previous administrations in their explicit promises to tackle historical inequalities by reshaping relationships among state, society, and the market. First, they mobilized state resources to address class inequality by reversing many of the neoliberal reforms of their predecessors, with increases in public spending, the renationalization of public services and natural resources, a stronger portfolio of social policies, and the expansion of social protection. Second, they focused on the political incorporation of historically excluded or marginalized social groups, such as the urban poor, indigenous populations, LGBT groups, and women.[5]

Third, they sought to alter state-society relations and address historic social inequalities by incorporating a language of rights and well-being to reshape constitutions, state policies, and/or individual programs.[6] These general commitments to furthering equality in economic, social, and political life allow us to assess whether such statements translated into more opportunities for advancing feminist and queer movement demands, and more inclusion of their protagonists. Thus, this collection sheds light on the relationships between these discursive commitments and the lived experiences of women and LGBT people.

In addition to general pledges for redistribution and recognition, leaders and presidents of these administrations called upon the rhetorical link between socialism and women's emancipation (Molyneux 2001). For example, the long-serving presidents Rafael Correa of Ecuador (2007–17) and Hugo Chávez of Venezuela (1999–2013) claimed that their revolutionary projects had "a woman's face." In these cases, women's rights were highlighted as a fundamental dimension of the social transformation sought by the Pink Tide, while women as a constituency were mobilized for revolutionary change.

In terms of the Left's relationship with LGBT populations, Pink Tide governments have ameliorated previous tensions (Corrales and Pecheny 2010, 23). Historically, prejudice and/or fear of losing popular support prevented much of the Left from allying with gay advocates (Brown 2010, 90). Male leaders used macho imagery in the service of nation building, consciousness raising, and guerrilla warfare. This political rhetoric reified heteronormativity and homophobia on the Left, and led scholars to argue that "in relation to sexuality, members of the Left have sometimes been as reactionary as their right-wing counterparts" (Corrales and Pecheny 2010, 24). Yet, some contemporary Left parties offer a newfound support for gay rights (Encarnación 2016, 70–71; Schulenberg 2013).[7] This explicit hailing of women and the opening to LGBT rights issues also set the stage for an evaluation of their gender and sexual politics.

At least rhetorically, the Pink Tide has leaned toward gender and sexual justice. What does the more general literature on gender and the Left lead us to expect about their relationship? Global studies find that left political actors will be more relevant on class-based gender and (by extension) sexuality issues, such as the gendered division of labor and social and economic rights (Htun and Weldon 2010). For instance, left parties and unions drove the expansion of European welfare states (Esping-Anderson 1990), and cross-national analyses highlight their role in the extension of parental leave and day care in Western and Northern Europe (Huber and Stephens 2001; Grey 2002; Weldon 2011). Other research concludes that left parties have helped to advance women's rights and representation, as well as with the creation and consolidation of effective national women's agencies (Stetson and Mazur 1995). In Latin America, left parties have been more central in LGBT rights achievement than those on the right (Schulenberg 2013).

Yet, other scholars assert a weaker association between left-leaning parties and gender redistributive issues. For instance, women's presence in legislatures trumps party ideology in achieving maternity leave in Organisation for Economic Co-operation and Development democracies and Latin America

(Kittilson 2008; Schwindt-Bayer 2006). In Latin America, left governments have extended welfare rights and social income to those working informally as well as the income poor with a particular focus on women. These governments made some progress on reducing gender and class inequalities separately, yet did not address their interactions (Filgueira and Franzioni 2017). And researchers underline the long-standing tensions between women's movements and left parties (della Porta 2003; Mueller and McCarthy 2003).[8] Thus, left parties' role in class-based issues of women and LGBT people might be better characterized as ambiguous and dependent on both context and the issue type addressed.

Globally, left political actors have been less relevant in addressing issues, such as family law and abortion, that focus on women's status as a subordinate group. These demands are more likely to be achieved by autonomous women's organizations whose main agenda is gender equality. For instance, cross-national studies find women's movements to be the central actors in achieving progressive policies on violence against women (VAW) (Htun and Weldon 2012). In Latin America, abortion policy reform exhibits considerable variation under Left governments (Blofeld and Ewig 2017). Left parties' support for LGBT rights is mediated by public opinion, and progress has often come as part of larger political phenomena such as constitutional or criminal code reform (Schulenberg 2013). As with VAW policy dynamics, the protagonistic role of LGBT advocates in achieving same-sex marriage has proved more important than the ideology of the party in power (Corrales 2015). Thus, although the Pink Tide seemed to promise transformation and/or inclusion with respect to gender and sexuality, the larger context of left governance predicts a more contested reality.

How Red Are the Pink Tide's Many Lefts?

Although Pink Tide governments have sought to ameliorate long-standing inequalities, they have offered distinct political projects, and achieved different results. To indicate their commitments to left transformation they have appealed to left-leaning political legacies, rhetorics, parties, or movements to quite dissimilar degrees.[9] For example, while some governments built on long-standing institutionalized or experienced political forces, such as the Partido dos Trabalhadores (Workers' Party) in Brazil, the Frente Amplio (Broad Front) in Uruguay, the Concertación in Chile, or the Partido Justicialista (Justicialist Party, known as the Peronist Party) in Argentina, others have relied on political outsiders and newer parties, such as Hugo Chávez's Partido

Socialista Unido de Venezuela (United Socialist Party of Venezuela), and Evo Morales and the Movimiento al Socialismo (Movement Towards Socialism) in Bolivia. Thus, this section justifies their comparison while bearing in mind their different points of departure, development, and outcomes.

Despite distinctive historical legacies and contemporary political systems, it is analytically meaningful to consider these governments part of a regional political experience. At a time when regional institutions and exchanges intensified, these executives recognized one another as part of a shared process of transformation. In addition, during this period, state policymakers departed from similar definitions of social problems to be targeted, as well as their common advocacy for a stronger role of the state in the market and society more generally. The Pink Tide ushered in a long-awaited period of state attention to social, economic, and political inequality. Given Latin America's notoriety in this regard—it is the world region with the worst income inequality[10]—the shift seemed to herald a much-needed political change through democratic decision making.

As the central point of commonality, the rise of the Pink Tide is considered to be a political response to the negative outcomes of neoliberal policies. During the 1990s, right-wing and centrist incumbents were tarnished by their open support of crisis-prone economic transitions with devastating social consequences for vast sectors of the population. After decades out of power, left-leaning parties responded to the demands of movements challenging inequality through both recognition of their distinct identities—such as indigenous, LGBT, and Afro-Latinx—and social redistribution of the economic resources held tightly in the fists of powerful capitalists and elite classes. Once in power, many of the left and center-left administrations drew on the resources of a sustained commodities boom to fund poverty alleviation and social service expansion, even as they did not follow through on promises for structural economic change (Levitsky and Roberts 2011; Queirolo 2013). This state attention to inequality and exclusion are grounds for comparing the national case studies presented in this book, even as we acknowledge differences among and within countries.

In distinguishing among Pink Tide cases, analysts have focused on two main axes: what governments claim to achieve (their political platforms) and how they do it (their exercise of power). Their distinct political projects have frequently been placed across a spectrum from reformist to revolutionary. The second axis orders these administrations in terms of their institutionalist, charismatic, or individualist modes of doing politics, as well as their degree of authoritarianism and durability in power. Mainstream, institutionally focused analysts offer a normative assessment of the Pink Tide's many lefts, which tends to applaud the projects that come closer to the idealized model of representative liberal democracy and (somewhat) free-market capitalism, as in Chile, dismissing the other experiences as hewing to an outdated populism led by charismatic caudillos seeking to centralize power (Castañeda 2006). They look askance at the constitutional (and extraconstitutional) transformations in those countries at the far end of the spectrum, such as Venezuela, Ecuador, and Bolivia, watching warily at increasing concentrations of power in the executive branch (Levitsky and Roberts 2011; Weyland, Madrid, and Hunter 2010).

They are not alone: echoing the main criticism of previous forms of state socialism, critical left-wing Latin American intellectuals also question the authoritarian traits and moves to perpetuate personal power of some Pink Tide executives, highlighting their mix of democracy, neopopulism, and extractivism (Svampa 2015). Sociological analyses acknowledge the criticism of the authoritarian features of these governments, while also taking into account their inclusive and democratizing aspects and highly polarized political contexts (de la Torre 2013, 2017). They find them to be characterized by the mobilization of popular sectors[11] against elites as well as the fight against poverty, an increase in social spending, and redistribution of the surplus of natural resource extraction upon which they remain deeply dependent.

More sympathetic approaches see incomplete, yet inspirational, transitions to twenty-first-century socialism under way, with committed leadership turning the "constituted power" of the state to the service of the "constituent power" of the masses (Ciccariello-Maher 2014). They seek to illustrate how more radical experiments encouraged and/or responded to the will of those groups previously marginalized on the basis of class, race/ethnicity, and even gender (Ellner 2014). Last, a smaller set of analysts has complicated these dichotomous assessments by exploring similarities across the spectrum or focusing on each country's complex contextual realities (Cameron and Hershberg 2010).

Without hewing to a single perspective, the authors in this volume are careful to contextualize what "left" means in each national context. For example, Constanza Tabbush, María Constanza Díaz, Catalina Trebisacce, and Victoria Keller argue that the political phenomenon of Peronism in Argentina has included not only an (ever-transforming) party, but also worker and grass-roots movements. Given its pre-dominant political influence across other ideologies, the "classical divide between left and right" and "between civil society and representative politics" do not hold there. In Nicaragua, Edurne Larracoechea finds a misalignment between the claims of revolutionary transformation and the reality of the "cynical, pragmatic, and clientelistic way of doing politics" through which former Marxist guerrilla Daniel Ortega and his party, the FSLN, govern.

Finally, a gender and sexuality perspective reminds us to consider the importance of the relationships between the Left and religious institutions or forces. This dimension of analysis has been ignored or downplayed by both mainstream analysis and left intellectual accounts, which seem to assume that left politics by definition challenge conservative religious belief and hierarchies. But by highlighting the relationship between left-leaning governments and traditional religious groups, this book underlines that certain religious institutions could be strategic allies in advancing projects of social equity even as some, such as, prominently, the Catholic Church, are the strongest actors opposing reproductive autonomy and LGBT rights. This is seen most clearly in Nicaragua, Ecuador, and Brazil, where executive alliances with religious forces, or their inability to challenge them legislatively, have become a serious obstacle for these rights-based agendas. For example, Marlise Matos shows that in Brazil a parliamentary *bancada evangélica* (evangelical bloc) has developed that systematically opposes women's and LGBT rights. However, many of this volume's authors highlight the shifting relationship between and among administrations and conservative forces in the same country. The confrontation or alliance between executives and representatives of the Catholic Church around gender and sexual rights laws lead Tabbush, Díaz, Trebisacce, and Keller to distinguish among the three successive administrations of Kirchnerism. In Chile, argues Gwynn Thomas, changing relationships among the Left, religious parties, and the Church have acted as a window of opportunity to question the heteropatriarchal family model during Michelle Bachelet's second term in office. The possibilities for change depend on the strength of religious parties or coalitions and the dynamics of cooperation and conflict between the leadership of the executive branch and conservative or religious actors. A focus on gender and sexuality unearths these understudied dimensions of the Pink Tide that partly explain its heterogeneous performance.

Why Consider Gender and Sexuality Together?

This collection presents an original, and unusual, thematic comparison by bringing together a focus on gender and sexuality. It does so because previous research has established that gender and sexuality have been linked at the foundations and throughout the development of Latin American nation-states. Moreover, political analysis attests that those who challenge heteropatriarchal policy, such as feminist and LGBT movements, build coalitions to address linked demands. This section explains these two central reasons to analyze gender and sexuality together.

Historically, states have promoted both traditional gender roles and heterosexuality. In her review of Latin American state-gender relations, Maxine Molyneux (2000a, 39) argues that states "have largely served to perpetuate and enforce" unequal gender relations, whether deliberately or "through . . . indifference and inaction." They have done so in three ways. First, they have institutionalized men's social, political, and economic power over women. Second, they have established heterosexual relationships, and the families based upon them, as the focus of social policy. Finally, these relationships have been seen as fundamental to nation building. Such normative ideals acquire force because, across the political spectrum, national ideologies have built upon metaphors of nuclear families—generally lighter- rather than darker-skinned—and heterosexual relationships (McClintock 1995; Bernstein 2008). And these ideals continue to have influence, despite their clear contrast with contemporary family arrangements in Latin America[12] and the reality of the racial and ethnic makeup of the region.

This gendering and sexing of the Latin American state, harking back to the colonial era and developing in the nineteenth century,[13] was reinforced throughout the twentieth century. States continued to deploy gender and sexuality as integral aspects of development, although in ways that were "variable and contingent," as political elites grappled with development pressures and an increasingly organized society (Molyneux 2000a, 40, 38). Even as women entered into education and employment as part of national development projects, they largely remained legally subordinated to their husbands and fathers.[14] The heterosexual family remained the ideal, with some state policy openly castigating homosexuality even as women's rights developed (Bejel 2010). Beginning in the late 1960s, the wave of authoritarian regimes that fiercely opposed struggles for political and social inclusion elevated the traditional family as fundamental to their draconian policies of political order. Although the succeeding democratic states, which preceded the Pink Tide, provided more opportunities to transform state policy around gender and sexuality, they also demonstrated an often-unrecognized dependence on women's subordination. The stripped-down neoliberal state of the late twentieth century relied heavily on unpaid women's labor and community activities, such as the communal kitchens poor women established to ensure their families could eat.[15] To claim modern values in the face of real economic hardship, some states offered a trade-off of state recognition of certain gender- and sexuality-based demands for economic benefits.[16] History contests narratives of progress around gender and sexuality that map over political and economic transformations.

Given this reality, demands that contest men's control over women's bodies, such as reproductive autonomy, or reject the heterosexual basis of the family, such as equal marriage rights for gays and lesbians, profoundly challenge political leaders and institutions. Advocates are contesting not only an ideology at the foundation of Latin American state formation but one that continues to be highly relevant. While women's, feminist, and LGBT movements have evinced this contestation in myriad ways, they also have built from intertwined histories of mobilization to strengthen their common causes.

Movements focused on both gender and sexuality have sought to disrupt state institutionalization of patriarchy and heterosexuality through their demands for "sexual citizenship" or "the transformation of public life into a domain that is no longer dominated by male heterosexuals" (Hekma 2004, 4). This deepening of citizenship recognizes that "individual autonomy, partly determined by the control of one's body, is a necessary condition for true citizenship, with all its rights and responsibilities" (Pecheny 2010, 113). It includes free sexual expression, bodily autonomy, institutional inclusion, and even access to public spaces (Hekma 2004). Feminist and queer communities, with their overlapping memberships (such as lesbian and transgender feminists), have built coalitions to make their demands known and improve their strategic capacities.

Feminist and queer movements have common roots in opposition to authoritarian rule and engagement in democratic politics. Both were inspired by the powerfully antiauthoritarian discourse of human rights of the late twentieth century, resulting in "the formation of sexual subjects and social movements around gender and sexuality throughout the region" (Pecheny 2012/2013; Brown 2010). Under conditions of political democracy, these have converted into claims for full citizenship. Thus, unlike the predominantly identitarian claims of movements in many countries of the Global North, in Latin America feminist and, especially, queer movements have often framed their claims as part of larger demands for state responsiveness to protect and expand rights.[17]

The contemporary politics of sexual citizenship often relies upon collaborations among those working to shift traditional norms around gender and sexuality in policy, politics, and society.[18] In some places these coincidences reach back to foundational moments in movement history, as with Argentina's Frente de Liberación Homosexual (Homosexual Liberation Front), begun in the early 1970s, within which an "autonomous movement" sought to challenge Argentina's "discriminatory male hierarchy," according to Omar Encarnación (2016, 89), or in Ecuador, where marginal LGBT organizations "decided to join forces with a variety of feminist groups, which had a stronger, more legitimate presence" in politics (Xie and Corrales 2010, 225). Those united in defense of sexual citizenship were also inspired by international dynamics, such as the norms generated through the UN Conference on Population and Development and the Fourth World Conference on Women of the 1990s as well as more recent international efforts (Corrêa, Petchesky, and Parker 2008, 174). And their work has a vibrant present: for example, in Brazil "the greatest development in the struggle for sexual rights" are the alliances "to strengthen the commitment of gay militants to the abortion cause, and to bring sex workers and feminists together" (Vianna and Carrara 2010, 131). In a vivid recent illustration, women and queer activists joined together to protest the coup against Brazilian president Dilma Rousseff in 2016, and the misogyny and homophobia upon which its leaders relied (Hertzman 2016).

Building sexual citizenship coalitions has not been an easy process; it can be tension-filled and fragile, given the distinct social positions and demands of different sectors (Moreno 2010).[19] For example, feminist and gay movements in some countries resisted the inclusion of lesbians and trans women and men, and their demands, fearing a dilution of their agenda and/ or evincing sexism, lesbo- and trans-phobia. Coalitional efforts depend on the energies and perspectives of particular actors and organizations. Ultimately, despite their struggles for inclusion by both "sides" and consequent demands for political autonomy (Friedman 2007, 794), lesbian feminists have been key actors in bridging their communities (Thayer 2010; de la Dehesa 2010, 150–53); their "vital link . . . has to do with an understanding of obligatory heterosexuality as a social institution" that produces male dominance (Espinosa Miñoso 2010, 403). And transgender organizations in which feminists are active also build bridges to both feminist and gay movements (Vianna and Carrera 2010, 131).

Many coalitions, or the networks that undergird them, follow the pattern in which an earlier generation of feminist activists collaborates with a burgeoning LGBT sector. In Mexico, successful state-directed LGBT activism has been characterized by "an articulation with feminists," particularly through lesbian feminist organizations and elected officials (de la Dehesa 2010, 153). Whether or not they have built extensive coalitions, feminist and LGBT organizations have collaborated around demands for sexual health, predominantly through the fight for just treatment of people with AIDS (Gómez 2010). As they organized around their own health crisis, gay men discovered feminist allies with over a decade of experience, particularly in reproductive health.

As the foregoing suggests, successful coalition building is not limited to non-state actors but also incorporates party cadre and state decision makers. Here again, the inroads feminists have made in such spaces can be fruitful for LGBT sectors. Feminists in left parties are often key allies for LGBT movements, due to their shared struggle against gender oppression (Marsiaj 2010, 207). As individual activists take on higher-profile work in parties or governing institutions, they bring along their commitments to preexisting networks of colleagues and fellow travelers, becoming key allies in policy-making endeavors.

From national identity to many areas of policy and politics, Latin American states have relied upon and promoted the ideal of a heterosexual family with the father at the helm. This ideal has lasted through many state formations, shifting in the service of state development needs. In reaction, feminist and queer activists have built coalitions to defend and promote sexual citizenship at the intersection of their demands. However, there are other issues of fundamental significance to the gendering of the state that are not usually the focus of such citizenship demands, which address the economic status and social rights of women (or poor queers). Poor and working-class women, among whom indigenous and Afro-Latinx women are overrepresented, have repeatedly mobilized in reaction to economic inequality, and the ways it is crosscut by race and ethnic relations.[20] These movements have grown in strength and numbers, informed by—but always in uneasy relation with—the feminist ideals and organizing principles of largely middle- and upper-class white and mestiza women. Due to such movements' importance, they are also considered in this volume.

As the trends detailed below will show, feminist, women's, and LGBT demands, and the communities from which they emerge, are not monolithic: while forging common agendas, they have walked distinct historical paths and face different contemporary challenges. This analysis reveals diverse dynamics in internally differentiated communities. While a feminist analysis might focus on how poor women's reproductive labor is mobilized on the basis of their assumed maternal identity, queering that lens will remind us that they are also assumed to have (had) male partners. Gender itself is interpellated differently: for example, feminist analysis has focused more on the ways male and female genders, and masculine and feminine bodies, are constructed through social processes, whereas queer analysis considers the extent to which individuals have the right to state recognition of their gender identity. Although this volume addresses a range of issues using an intertwined analysis, the chapters tend to reach out from feminist starting points to include queer insights, rather than the other direction. This is based on the analytic grounding of the authors as well as the earlier development of both feminist analysis and mobilization.

Our Framework for Analyzing Gender and Sexuality Policy

Because Latin American states have built patriarchal heteronormativity into their historical foundations and contemporary functions, and the real-world politics of sexual citizenship show actors coming together to confront common challenges, the chapters in this volume address issues of both gender and sexuality. As they do so, they depart from the understanding, underlined by previous studies, that countries can become leaders in some areas of gender and sexual equality, and laggards in others (Franceschet 2010). The actors involved, the relevance of left governance, and the priorities, strategies, and effectiveness of defenders and critics of these changes are conditioned by the type of issue being debated (Htun and Weldon 2010). In addressing gender and sexuality policy, a focus on political context is crucial.

In order to determine to what extent left governance has made a difference on issues of gender and sexuality, we offer an analysis that focuses on the key demands of those seeking sexual citizenship rights, alongside the long-time feminist focus on ameliorating the gendered division of labor through state redistribution. We characterize those demands using a typology that builds on Mala Htun and Laurel Weldon's (2010) delineation of policies that aim to shift gendered systems of power. Thus, as the Intro.1 table below displays, one axis of the typology differentiates among gender status policies, which challenge men's power and privilege; we also break out LGBT status policies, which focus on the institutionalization of heterosexuality and cisgender privilege, as well as policies that confront class and gender inequality with a focus on women's subordination in the gendered division of labor.

However, again with reference to Htun and Weldon's analysis, it is not sufficient to differentiate policies based on whether they focus primarily on gender, LGBT, or class status. As shown on the other axis, some of these policies are "countercultural" demands (Goetz and Jenkins 2016) because they directly challenge "religious doctrine or codified cultural traditions" (Htun and Weldon 2010, 209). As highlighted above, traditional or religious authorities are deeply invested in particular understandings of gender relations, sexuality, or gender identity that uphold their moral and social ideals. Thus, the fate of policies that challenge those understandings depends on the existence of religious political parties or coalitions and the dynamics between the political leadership and religious leaders. However, other policies that promote women's and LGBT equality may not be perceived as acting against such authorities' power or values.

Table Intro.1 illustrates the placement of central examples such as abortion, a policy that affects women's gender status and invokes clear opposition by morally and religiously inspired authorities, and same-sex marriage, which similarly invokes opposition but on LGBT status. However, the gender status policy of gender candidate quotas is not often perceived as challenging the structure of society, and gender identity recognition may be seen as a realignment of an individual into her or his "correct" status, although there is considerable variability in these policy dynamics.

As the foregoing suggests and the authors in this volume make clear, although policies may at first blush seem to fit only in one area, there is no "inherent" placement. Table Intro.1 shows that policies initially proposed as gender equitable may then be adopted in ways that do or do not challenge gender inequality, for example by giving antigender violence legislation a family-unification orientation rather than one that protects women from male aggression. Or the implementation of antidiscrimination policy with respect to sexual orientation, such as civil union registration, may be so weak as to effectively uphold heteronormativity. However, the targets of such policies may themselves shift their meaning through use, as when low-income mothers develop their leadership capabilities by managing poverty alleviation funds.

TABLE INTRO. I Typology of gender and sexuality policies

	Culturally acceptable (nondoctrinal)	Countercultural (doctrinal issues)
Gender status *Challenge power hierarchies that "privilege men and the masculine"*	Quotas Violence Against Women policy that foregrounds the family	Abortion Violence Against Women policy that foregrounds women's human rights
LGBT status *Contest "institutionalization of normative heterosexuality" and cisgenderism*	Gender identity recognition	Same-sex marriage
Class-based *Ameliorate division of labor that "devalues women and the feminine"*	Conditional Cash Transfer policies that rely on poor women's reproductive labor	Conditional Cash Transfer policies that incorporate poor women as central protagonists

Source: Authors' elaboration of concepts/table from Htun and Weldon 2010, 208–9.

The rest of the introduction uses this framework to critically evaluate the difference Pink Tide governments have made with respect to gender and sexual justice, relying on comparative insights gleaned from the collection's case studies. We organize our explorations by addressing the issues of social welfare, political representation, violence against women, and the trade-offs between women's and LGBT rights. We then turn to an evaluation of the more successful strategies through which advocates have advanced their demands under Pink Tide governments.

Comparative Findings

Welfare, Social Redistribution, and Poverty Alleviation

One of the most important claims of Pink Tide administrations was their explicit promise to fight poverty and, to a lesser extent, inequality in order to redress the neoliberal legacy of historic class divisions and subsequent marginalization of the poor. Initially, and as described by the figures below, these governments offered some remarkable achievements in reducing extreme poverty and deprivation. Yet, in many cases, the socioeconomic gains of the

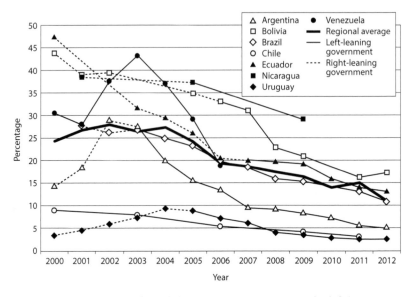

Figure Intro.1 Percentage of people living in extreme poverty under left-leaning governments, 2000–2012. Source: Socio-Economic Database for Latin America and the Caribbean (CEDLAS and the World Bank), http://sedlac.econo.unlp.edu.ar/.

Pink Tide, which could have challenged the gendered division of labor and empowered women economically, were overshadowed by the one-third of the regional female population who still lacked their own income in 2015 (ECLAC 2015). In addition, poor women's unpaid work was the backbone of social programs that reduced extreme poverty, as well as central to the entire political project of the Left in power. Such overall findings were generally upheld in this volume.

When considering social indicators, all countries in this collection attest to the material gains for poor women under left administrations.[21] As figure Intro.1 indicates, extreme poverty declined, sometimes precipitously, in all cases, with half at or below the regional average. Countries with a significant population living in acute deprivation experienced the most positive outcomes. For example, in Ecuador this population declined from 47.5 percent in 2000 to only 13.1 percent in 2012; and Bolivia brought down its extreme poverty rates by more than 25 percent.

Poverty levels in female-headed households experienced a similar decline. Figure Intro.2 shows that when considering these households, the Pink Tide countries of this volume had very different points of departure. Yet,

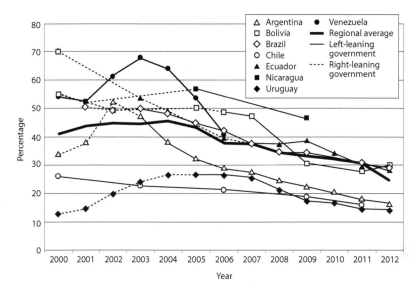

Figure Intro.2 Percentage of female-headed households living in poverty under left-leaning governments, 2000–2012. Source: Socio-Economic Database for Latin America and the Caribbean (CEDLAS and the World Bank) http://sedlac.econo.unlp .edu.ar/.

between 2000 and 2012, they all converged close to or below the regional average. Although clearly other factors besides political ideology (such as rising commodity prices) are at play in achieving these positive results, the figures demonstrate the definitive impact that left-leaning governments had on the situation of poor people and, in particular, poor women who were solely responsible for their children.

While the data on extreme poverty is very positive, the following figures attest to a more troubling picture. First, as presented in figure Intro.3, in the 2000s women were more likely than men to still be living in poverty. The countries with socioegalitarian traditions, such as Argentina, Chile, and Uruguay, are the ones with significantly higher ratios of poor women compared to poor men. Many countries are considerably above the regional average and point out the persistence of gender poverty gaps even in the most developed welfare states of the region. This is partially explained by the fact that women in the lowest two quintiles of income distribution are disproportionately unlikely to have their own source of income, emphasizing women's continued dependency (see figure Intro.4). Beyond the implementation of poverty

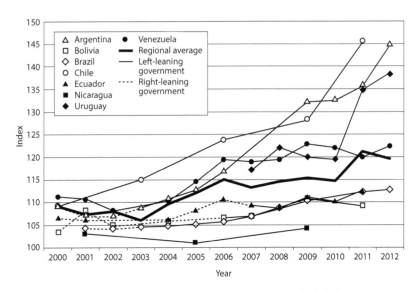

Figure Intro.3 Femininity index of indigence and poverty under left-leaning governments, 2000–2012. Source: CEPALSTAT Economic Commission for Latin American and the Caribbean, http://estadisticas.cepal.org/cepalstat/web_cepalstat /Portada.asp?idioma=i.

alleviation measures, this signals that women's economic autonomy remained an important challenge to the Pink Tide's narrative of social transformation.

Turning to the welfare policy arena, this collection affirms other studies of gender and left politics (Htun and Weldon 2012). Pink Tide administrations, left-leaning political parties and coalitions of movements, and unions played an important role in advancing a social rights agenda, including state funding for social policies, programs, and transfers. With little participation of feminist movements and national women's agencies, these left-leaning parties promoted state-led social protection policies, which included the expansion of social transfers, such as noncontributory pensions and poverty alleviation in the form of conditional cash transfers given directly to women (Molyneux 2008; Lavinas 2013; Tabbush 2009).

While recognizing this positive development, the chapters reveal an unsettling series of continuities between Pink Tide social programs and previous neoliberal policies. The chapters uphold other critical analyses in identifying similarities in how gendered assumptions undergird policy formulation as well as the models of economic development that financed such policy. Both left-leaning and neoliberal policy regimes have relied on poor women's

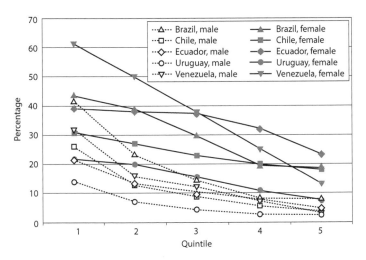

Figure Intro.4 Percent of men and women without own income under left-leaning governments, 2013. Source: CEPALSTAT Economic Commission for Latin American and the Carribean, http://estadisticas.cepal.org/cepalstat/web_cepalstat /Portada.asp?idioma=i.

various forms of work and traditional notions of the family, environmentally unsustainable extractivist industries, and poverty alleviation, rather than addressing the structure of gender and class inequalities.

The country studies focus particularly on the widespread implementation of "Conditional Cash Transfer" (CCT) policies and their links with broader social policies and schemes. As a central policy through which Pink Tide governments have reduced poverty, the chapters analyze CCT policies that provided monetary support to mothers on the condition that they send their children to school and get regular medical checkups. Initiated in Brazil (1995) and Mexico (1997), by 2011, CCTs were adopted by nearly every Latin American country, covering almost 20 percent of the regional population (Cecchini and Madariaga 2011, 11). They have been quite successful in reducing extreme poverty, meeting health and education targets, and overall positive outcomes for poor women and their families (Johannsen et al. 2008; Molyneux and Thompson 2011; Molyneux with Jones and Samuels 2016).

In this sense, the chapters indicate that the policy of giving cash directly to women is an important acknowledgment of feminist scholars' advocacy and development practitioners' awareness that adult males tend to undervalue (and underfund) family budgets and reproductive responsibilities. It also redresses the historic segregation of women, who were considered by social insurance contributions (such as social security or other retirement benefits) as part of the family wage of formally employed male heads of household. Such programs, promoted by practitioners to support the unpaid labor of poor women, have the potential to challenge the gendered division of labor.

Yet, our comparative findings suggest that, to various degrees, Pink Tide administrations have designed and implemented CCT programs as culturally acceptable policies that target poor mothers and vulnerable families. Moreover, feminist activists and national women's agencies have played mostly a secondary role, when compared to their salience in the other policy arenas analyzed in this introduction.

One of the key findings of this volume is that across the Pink Tide, social policies relied on poor women's unpaid labor in different ways and with various intensities. Between 2000 and 2015, countries implemented a wide spectrum of CCT policies and social programs that largely reproduced, and only under certain circumstances challenged, the gendered distribution of power, labor, and resources available for women from popular sectors. Three groups of national administrations can be identified: those that maximized the use of poor women's unpaid reproductive, community, and political labor; a second group that naturalized women as intermediaries of the human development of their children; and finally a smaller third cluster that attempted to redistribute gendered tasks and responsibilities.

The first group of governments included programs in Argentina implemented just after the economic crisis during the presidency of Néstor Kirchner (2003–7), and the redder administrations of Bolivia, Ecuador, Nicaragua, and, most notably, Venezuela under President Chávez's administrations. As Annie Wilkinson writes in her chapter on Ecuador, there is an "unquestioned centrality of the heteropatriarchal family" in both policy and the discourse used to justify it. These countries maximized the use of women's unpaid work and attempted to renegotiate the "reproductive bargain" through which the state supports poor women and their families.[22] They combined and intensified the use of various forms of women's labor in the areas of social reproduction and care, community development, and grassroots political activism in popular neighborhoods. Written prior to Venezuela's political and socioeconomic crisis, including widespread shortages of food and medicine, Rachel Elfenbein's critical analysis of the social welfare "missions" of the 2000s provides a paradigmatic example of the combined use of all these forms of work. Her chapter underscores how, through this intensification, "popular women became the backbone of the revolutionary process."

In these countries, women have continued to manage reproductive and productive tasks, even as they have taken on the lion(ess)'s share of managing various targeted poverty alleviation policies, and become politically mobilized at the local level. As with their neoliberal variants, these policies work because poor women have made them work (Lind 2009). The Pink Tide administrations seeking profound social transformations either by tackling deep economic crisis or by revolutionizing state-society relations did so by supporting social programs that embody conservative ideals of the family. They aimed to secure the support of poor urban households for their political parties through their heavy dependence on women's unpaid work, time, and commitment.

In the middle of the spectrum, a second group of countries follow the guidelines of international organizations that link poverty alleviation with the human development of children. In contrast to the previous group, in these cases the political labor of women to sustain a left-leaning political project of social transformation is reduced. These country experiences support and nuance feminist findings that stress CCTs' focus on poor women as intermediaries of their children's welfare or with other developmental goals in mind, rather than as full citizens in their own right (Molyneux 2007). Argentina after 2009 (with the implementation of the CCT program Asignación Universal por Hijo [Universal Child Allowance]), the implementation of CCT program Bolsa Família (Family Income) in Brazil, and the lighter pink Chilean Concertación government until 2014 (through the Puente [Bridge] program and Chile Solidario [Solidarity] are all examples that follow the overall regional trend in poverty reduction that targets mothers (Molyneux 2007). These maternalistic—or, as our analytic framework labels them, "culturally acceptable"—policies provide a potent, yet inegalitarian, recipe that largely naturalized the gendered division of labor, accomplishing little gendered and class redistribution of work, power, and resources (Molyneux 2008; Lavinas 2013; Tabbush 2010).

Finally, there is a smaller third set of Pink Tide administrations in which social policies challenged traditional cultural or religious beliefs about the family and women's role in it. These "countercultural" social policies attempted to alter the unequal gendered division of labor within households. At this end of the spectrum, we find most notably the cases of Uruguay and the Chilean administration after 2014. During the José Mujica government in

Uruguay, Niki Johnson, Ana Laura Rodríguez Gustá, and Diego Sempol describe how feminists in midlevel ministerial positions were critical actors in taking on women's movements demands to create a National System of Care for the elderly, children up to the age of five, and the disabled. In Chile, Gwynn Thomas describes how President Michelle Bachelet's vision of social provision as a right provided state-funded child and elderly care for low-income groups. The Chile Crece Contigo (Chile Grows with You) program oversaw the construction of hundreds of day care centers for children under the age of five, and other supports for low-income working women (Staab 2017).

But to be sure, as Shawnna Mullenax observes in Bolivia, CCTs have different meanings for various factions of women's and feminist movements, pointing toward some of the challenges in building coalitions among popular women's movements, middle-class feminists, and women's indigenous organizations. Overall, popular and grassroots women's movements tend to look favorably on these programs, whereas feminists are more outspoken critics of their heteropatriarchal basis. Feminists battling for social justice across the Pink Tide promote an agenda of universal, unconditional, expanded transfers to women within a framework that links social redistribution with gender justice.[23]

Women's indigenous movements, for their part, often welcome the extra resources, while remaining critical of the cultural disciplining of indigenous mothers (Cookson 2016). In a more trenchant critique of the economic model, their political organizations focus on the fact that the social programs responsible for the precipitous drop in extreme poverty in their countries are, by and large, based on funding that is tied to unsustainable and environmentally degrading extractivist industries. Indigenous and peasant women's mobilizations strongly linked to the defense of their territories and natural resources open a much-needed debate on the Pink Tide's future developmental models and sustainability. For example in Ecuador, Wilkinson finds that "Correa's neoextractivist model puts economic inclusion and gender equality at odds." As decolonial feminists insist, and the chapters on Chile, Bolivia, and Ecuador demonstrate, such economic policies run roughshod over indigenous rights to land and livelihoods. These various standpoints on social policies mark the still-sharp class and ethnic divisions between feminists and women's organizations.

In summary, even though the results of this comparison indicate a historical continuity of state policy under the Pink Tide with earlier neoliberal governments, in some countries femocrats have incorporated movement de-

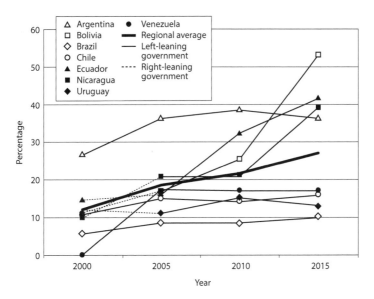

Figure Intro.5 Percent of women in single or lower house of national legislature under left-leaning governments, 2000–2015. Source: Inter-Parliamentary Union, "Women in National Parliaments," http://www.ipu.org/wmn-e/ classif.htm.

mands in promoting a countercultural agenda of redistribution of care. In this way they have sought to challenge the conservative ideals of the family underpinning policy formulation.

Political Representation: Fighting for Presence and Substance

Turning to a key global measurement of women's empowerment, the percentage of women in national legislatures, the Pink Tide governments covered in this volume are generally, but not universally, leaders in women's descriptive representation. Figure Intro.5 above shows that these governments have high rates of women's inclusion: half of them have national legislatures that are more than one-third female, and a quarter are 40 percent or more female. The redder governments tend to have the highest rates, particularly Bolivia, Nicaragua, and Ecuador. However, this movement is not uniform. Half of the countries are considerably below the regional average, with socialist Venezuela being close to the bottom—along with lighter pink Brazil. Finally, and notably, during its progressive policy explosion Uruguay has had low levels of women's representation.

The major mechanism for the dramatic developments in descriptive representation is the use of candidate gender quotas.[24] These did not originate with the Pink Tide but were already on the agenda, and, in some cases, were implemented beforehand.[25] With the return to largely democratic politics in the 1980s, demands to improve women's formal representation through gender-based quotas for electoral office diffused across the region. Inspired by the lessons from European advocates from social democratic and socialist parties (Krook 2009, 166–67), women both outside and inside of the state organized to advance the adoption of quotas in individual parties and through national legislation. Quota advocates organized at a propitious moment; in the 1990s, Latin American governments were eager to adopt measures seen as legitimating their nascent democracies. Although some male elites proved resistant, such as Concertación leaders in Chile, others, such as then-president Carlos Menem of Argentina, took it on as another symbol of modern, democratic inclusion. The highly successful demand for quotas eventually made Latin America a global standout, with the highest regional average of women in national legislatures.[26]

The Pink Tide governments that have pulled ahead in descriptive representation have varied in their approach to quota adoption. In regional leader Argentina, quotas were adopted, and, after a difficult battle in which proponents were forced to appeal to the Inter-American Commission on Human Rights for redress, were implemented, just before the Kirchners came to power. Since that time, left-leaning governments have overseen quota fulfillment, with between 36 and 38 percent of Congress made up of female representatives. In Bolivia, pressure for quotas from organized women during and after the institutional foundation of the plurinational state through the 2009 constitution resulted in Bolivia having the second-highest percentage of female legislators in the world. In this case, quotas took place within a larger context of demands for inclusion, particularly for the constitutional recognition of indigenous peoples. Similarly, with Ecuador's "Citizen Revolution" positive action was enshrined in the constitution in a context of widening inclusion. Its parliament is now not only over 40 percent women but boasts a female president and vice presidents. Moreover, the Constitutional Court is also characterized by gender parity. Although not constitutionally mandated in Nicaragua, women's representation has shot up over 40 percent under the leadership of President Daniel Ortega, and the dominance of his party in the National Assembly. Moreover, executive ministries and mayoralties have reportedly reached gender parity.

The international emphasis on office holding as a key measurement of gender equality is undergirded by an assumption that female representatives will devote more attention to women's issues, equating descriptive with substantive representation. As Latin American cases such as Argentina and Bolivia have shown, the demand for female candidates has enabled coalition building across parties and other sources of difference (Htun and Ossa 2013). However, analysts of the impact of descriptive representation find considerable variation. While some observe that having more women in office does lead to a shift in both the discussion and implementation of new policies, others find that barriers remain "to the articulation of women's concerns" (Krook and Zetterberg 2014, 288). Quotas may even "reduce women's collective influence" (Htun 2016, 140). Women who are bound to their leaders' or parties' dictates have less room for maneuver; and all women must contend with male-dominated power networks beyond the floor of the legislature (and on it) that prevent gendered agendas from going forward (Franceschet and Piscopo 2013). Such findings are generally upheld by this volume.

The countries under study here reveal a lack of correlation between high levels of women's descriptive representation and positive outcomes for women's rights. Having more women in office can lead to the introduction of more gender-focused legislation, as the case of Argentina attests. But as the paradigmatic case of Uruguay manifests, progressive achievements on gender and sexuality, including the extraordinarily difficult feat of decriminalizing abortion as well as same-sex marriage and gender identity recognition, have come about with women's representation below 13 percent. In Brazil, with even lower levels of representation, left-leaning administrations made substantially more policy interventions on gender and sexuality. And, as the three chapters that focus on the countries with the highest numbers of women in office make clear, higher descriptive representation can be inversely correlated with substantive representation. Mullenax suggests that in Bolivia, high numbers may be "a strategic move by the government to appear that they were working on women's issues," although she also makes clear that indigenous women's organizations have had demands implemented by their government. In Nicaragua and Ecuador, Larracoechea and Wilkinson find high numbers to be a cynical symbol in the face of the denigration or outright repression of feminist activism, and the weakening of national women's agencies. External validation of such "window dressing" is the focus of these last two leaders, rather than the material situation of women in their countries.

When power is concentrated in the hands of executives, legislative representation may be less than salient in terms of real change. When those executives are wooing supporters from among conservative religious movements or hierarchies, or adopt a discriminatory agenda for other reasons, women's presence in congress is far from the answer to ensuring women's substantive representation. As with other demands from organized women, the implementation of this policy shows how difficult it is to pin down a particular measure as being inherently countercultural. Once the quota has been implemented, under certain circumstances high numbers of women may, paradoxically, be used to mask an antifeminist agenda.

Violence against Women

At first glance, the Latin American region as a whole offers a remarkable diffusion of legislation on violence against women. Between 1993 and 2000, nearly every country passed a law prohibiting domestic violence; several have since reformed and strengthened their laws. But what made the reformist "wave" of legislation necessary was the notable reinscription of gender hierarchies in the first one. Advocates had pressured their governments to comply with the path-breaking Inter-American Convention on the Prevention, Punishment, and Eradication of Violence against Women (known as Belém do Pará after the city where it was adopted in 1994). Belém do Pará takes a feminist perspective in drawing attention to the many ways gender hierarchies undergird violence against women in the home, on the street, and in the state, and— finding it to be a violation of women's human rights—holds the state responsible for its prevention. But the majority of first-wave legislation prohibited "intrafamilial" violence, simultaneously ignoring the particular ways women are victims of gender-based violence within the home, and the kinds of violence they face outside of it. In a final indication of this legislation's protection of the family, rather than women, the legal sanction for intrafamilial violence was usually not criminal; mediation was promoted instead. As a result of these developments, advocates pushed for the second wave of revised laws that followed the spirit of Belém rather than ran counter to it (Friedman 2009). This second wave largely overlapped with Pink Tide governance, but, as the following discussion demonstrates, debates continued over how—or whether—to challenge the gendered power relations inherent in gender-based violence.

These chapters evince a spectrum of approaches to violence against women ranging from feminist to heteropatriarchal. At one end are those countries that have successfully advanced legislation, institutionalization, and, to a certain extent, implementation of robust policies. In Uruguay, feminist work to transversalize attention to violence against women across multiple ministries has had significant institutional success, particularly in terms of its support through the national women's agency Inmujeres. Chile's parallel agency also had a central role in achieving revisions to their initial legislation, resulting in the criminalization of domestic violence and an increase in state responsibility for preventing gendered violence.

In the middle of the spectrum are countries that have advanced adequate policy but faltered on implementation. The chapters on Venezuela and Bolivia show that, while women's movement pressure has resulted in reforming legislation to focus on preventing violence against women in all its forms, rather than centering on the family, it is largely unenforced. Although Argentina's revised law widened the ambit of violence prevention beyond the family, eliminated reconciliation between spouses as a legal resolution, and offered victims guaranteed services, the weak institutional position of its national women's agency, the Consejo Nacional de la Mujer (National Council on Women), has meant less support for implementation. The obvious impunity for perpetrators inspired a massive outcry across Argentina and elsewhere in the region: in 2015 and 2016, hundreds of thousands of protestors from all walks of life took to the streets mobilized by the slogan #NiUnaMenos (Not One Less) (Goñi 2015; Friedman and Tabbush 2016).

Most disturbing, Ecuadoran and Nicaraguan governments, in close collaboration with the Catholic hierarchy in their countries, have gutted legislative efforts to combat gender-related violence. As Wilkinson explains, the Ecuadorean Penal Code reform of 2013 returned to first-wave approaches: "The paradigm of 'violence against women' that women had fought for was changed to 'intrafamily violence,' placing violence against women once again in the private sphere of the heteropatriarchal family." The change also stripped the victim protections afforded to women. The antifeminist president and first lady of Nicaragua have overseen the evisceration of antiviolence legislation, which now is committed to strengthening the Nicaraguan family through mandates such as having women attend church- and community-led family mediation sessions instead of reporting abuse to women's police stations. Moreover, Larracoechea details, the executive regulation redefined "femicide" in order to halve the number of reported murders of women.

Htun and Weldon (2012) argue in their global analysis of the genesis of anti-VAW policies that left parties are not the major protagonists for change on this issue; the strongest efforts depend on the collaboration between autonomous women's movements and national women's agencies. This collection confirms and extends these findings. When women have successfully mobilized to demand stronger VAW legislation in many countries, robust state support is essential, as the cases of Chile and Uruguay demonstrate. However, Htun and Weldon characterize antiviolence work as "nondoctrinal," or as we call it here, "culturally acceptable" policy, that is less objectionable to religious forces. But as the first regional wave of legislative reform, alongside the dramatic shifts in Ecuador and Nicaragua, indicate, some elements of the Catholic Church and religiously inspired leadership have perceived feminist VAW as an attack on the family, and have promoted conservative policies in its stead.

Trade-offs between Feminist and LGBT Demands for Bodily Autonomy and Recognition: Variations in "Pinkwashing"

As the chapters on Argentina, Chile, Ecuador, Nicaragua, and Venezuela detail, some states have focused their attention on the most challenging issues of sexual citizenship in paradoxical ways that we, following increasingly popular usage, term "pinkwashing." Although the term has migrated to focus on the ways in which states advance LGBT policies to claim progressive or modern status in the face of other areas of repression or neglect, it was originally coined by breast cancer activists in critique of corporations' "pink-ribbon" marketing initiatives supporting women's health despite their contributions to unhealthy lifestyles and environmental contamination (Lind and Keating 2013, 5). As such, "pinkwashing" can also be used to consider how states trade off different gender-based rights, for example offering evidence of women's political leadership to distract from the rejection of women's right to control their own bodies.

Pink Tide governments have made strategic or unintentional trade-offs between and among the policy issues central to feminist and LGBT communities. Some governments have intentionally pinkwashed their failure or rejection of women's substantive rights, such as reproductive autonomy or the implementation of effective antiviolence policies, by promoting their tolerance of the LGBT community, often to an international community eager to see this latest sign of modernity. In our cases, governments also display improvements in particular women's rights to mask other problems. In this sense, what is being "washed" varies in different national contexts.

The intentional pinkwashing trade-off between LGBT and women's rights is most starkly presented in Nicaragua and Ecuador, where presidents have cemented alliances with religious leaders and distanced themselves from feminist movements and demands. Under the leadership of former revolutionary Daniel Ortega, Nicaragua criminalized therapeutic abortion in the same Penal Code reform that decriminalized homosexuality. The president and first lady have declared war against the feminist movement even as they have attempted to build support among younger LGBT people. In Ecuador, Correa also used cooptation to undermine the more challenging aspects of the sexual citizenship agenda. He elevated the work and profile of a single trans leader, relying on her to publicly denounce criticisms from the broader LGBT movement. At the same time, he undermined proposed gender identity legislation, held the conservative line against same-sex marriage and abortion, and shuttered a successful teenage pregnancy prevention program.

It is worth noting that some countries on the red side of the Pink Tide engage in trade-offs in which, as Rachel Elfenbein signals, LGBT issues were peripheral. The Venezuelan constitutional reform of 1999 met almost all the rights demands of the women's movement, except the right to abortion. And, while the constitutional national assembly presented a political opportunity to "contest and set a framework for restructuring gender power relations, it did not signify an opening to contest heteronormativity and advance LGBTTI interests." Elfenbein's analysis concludes that the marginalization of LGBT and sexual diversity demands in Venezuela was tied to the maternalistic and heteronormative governmental approach to gender issues, and to explicit homophobia within government ranks.

Another variation in the processes of pinkwashing is the audience to whom the clean laundry is displayed. Sometimes domestic audiences are the target, for example, by presidential candidates seeking to build coalition support, as in Argentina and Ecuador. Argentina demonstrates the significance of shifting executive-church relations: moments of tension allowed for presidential support for same-sex marriage, while phases of cooperation consistently held off abortion rights, despite growing public and legislative support for long-delayed decriminalization. But nearly always lurking not so distantly in the background are the global audiences—from philanthropists to Western governments to the United Nations Development Program—upon which some governments are heavily dependent for program funding and international recognition. Larracoechea finds that Ortega strategically positioned his partial acceptance of the "sexual diversity" community "in order to improve [his] international credentials as a modern leftist leader"; these credentials were burnished when the World Economic Forum ranked Nicaragua sixth in its influential *Global Gender Gap Report* of 2014, "leaving first lady Murillo overjoyed and [the] feminists startled."

As the foregoing suggests, the (in some cases, hyper-) presidentialist systems of Latin America leave a great deal of policy direction in the hands of individual leaders. Sometimes this worked in sexual citizenship advocates' favor, when executives decided to promote issues in the face of legislative recalcitrance, or offer state resources. Marlise Matos shows how much supportive executive action grew under the Partido dos Trabalhadores, and Gwynn Thomas sees some hope in President Bachelet's promotion of quotas, improved state services, and advocacy of therapeutic abortion in her second term. But as this section suggests, executive support is often inconsistent, nonexistent, or instrumentalized. President Cristina Fernández de Kirchner's support for marriage equality was crucial; she even took two intransigent legislators from her party out of the country during the vote. But she was similarly persuasive to her supporters in the legislature to throw up roadblocks to legal abortion, despite the increase in bill signatories and popular approval. Following their executive's orders, state women's organizations in Venezuela have largely mobilized popular women to support revolutionary transformation, rather than transforming revolutionary regimes to support popular women. Correa and Uruguay's Tabaré Vázquez threatened to resign in the face of abortion decriminalization bills (and the former saw expanding exemptions as "treason"). As Wilkinson argues, "The heteropatriarchal family . . . became as entrenched at the center of the state as Correa did himself." Moreover, reliance on the executive often results in unsustainable policies—such as Matos tracks in Brazil, where the removal of Dilma Rousseff negatively affected rights gains.

The chapters in this volume offer additional insights with regard to executive power. To begin with, not all presidential systems concentrate power and compromise accountability mechanisms to the same degree. Furthermore, the political opportunities for feminist and LGBT movements may shift between different administrations in a given national context. The contrasts marked by Bachelet's two terms, the distinctions between Vázquez's and Mujica's administrations in Uruguay, between Kirchner and Fernández de Kirchner in Argentina, and Chávez and Nicolás Maduro in Venezuela, bring out such differences. In an often-neglected dimension of executive analysis, the Nicaragua chapter illuminates the role of the first lady, who has strengthened her husband's conservative Catholicism and is becoming equally powerful. And finally, Thomas reminds us of the importance of party systems even within presidentialism: she finds that coalition dynamics have moderated the impact of conservative religious forces.

This comparative analysis of trade-offs between women's and LGBT rights under Latin American left governance offers a complex picture with regard to the two demands most often categorized as "countercultural." The chapters suggest significant variations between countries and administration in terms of political opportunities and policy issues. They also suggest that there are various audiences to which these trade-offs are directed.

In terms of advances in sexual rights for women and LGBT constituents, this collection distinguishes three main groups of countries. Crosscutting findings reveal that the Pink Tide administrations with a strong rights platform, such as Uruguay, have pushed for the most progressive demands for legal abortion, same-sex marriage, and provisions for the recognition of gender identity. Whereas a second set of countries, including Argentina, Bolivia, and Brazil, have advanced considerably in aspects of LGBT rights while largely holding the line on abortion decriminalization. The most extreme cases of pinkwashing are in Nicaragua and Ecuador. They suggest that the intensity of pinkwashing depends on the degree of hostility between the executive and the feminist movement; the links between the executive and religious conservative forces; and their desire to be reviewed well internationally.[27] Left administrations seeking religious support have downplayed feminist demands and presented their support for LGBT rights to an international audience as a beacon of modernity.

The foregoing sections summarize the multifaceted challenges to gender and sexual justice under Pink Tide governments. In many cases, a more generous social policy has treated women as the center of their families,' and often countries,' well-being, rather than as individuals deserving of rights beyond their roles in the gender system. Our case studies frontally contest the assumed equivalence between women's descriptive representation and their ability to advance a gender justice agenda in politics. On the issue of violence against women, these chapters echo the global analysis that left parties are not the central protagonists, and that other forces—organized women and femocrats—are more deeply committed to making change. But perhaps most discouraging to their protagonists, concerted efforts for sexual citizenship may be thwarted by governments eager to trade LGBT recognition for a firm rejection of reproductive choice.

Successful Contestation through Strategic Framing and State/Society Collaborations

In addition to the considerable challenges that remain, these chapters also analyze how advocates have successfully articulated, organized, and achieved some of their demands. Their activities transform the arena of social and political activism, as well as the relationships between social movements and Pink Tide administrations. Confirming previous studies, chapter authors find that effective crosscutting movement work has depended on two major factors: savvy narrative framing and strategic coalition building across state/society boundaries.

In terms of the first factor, Uruguay stands out: according to chapter authors, LGBT organizations "reconfigured the master frame of the sexual diversity movement," expanding their agenda to include other potent sources of discrimination based on class, race-ethnicity, and gender. In a vivid illustration of their coalitional perspective, they changed the name of the Gay Pride Parade to the "Diversity March"; its numbers then soared. Firmly embedding demands within previously legitimated human rights frames helped Argentine proponents successfully lobby for the first same-sex marriage legislation in the region and one of the most progressive gender identity recognition laws in the world. Failure to sync frames with dominant sources of legitimacy is clearly a challenge to movements; as the Argentina chapter also recounts, the frame of women's rights to their own bodies has been unsuccessful in promoting abortion decriminalization. In Ecuador and Venezuela, feminist and LGBT activists seized the political opportunity of constitutional conventions to advance a common agenda and repel common opponents. Here again, framing was crucial: in Venezuela, activists reappropriated revolutionary concepts to join in the Bolivarian revolution even as they critiqued it.

To achieve policy successes, movements have worked closely with allies inside the state. In Brazil, for example, Matos claims that women's and LGBT movements advanced their agenda significantly under the Partido dos Trabalhadores by working through institutional engagement and close relations with sympathetic state actors. Similarly in Uruguay, feminist and women's movements have been the motor behind "a multinodal policy network" of feminists throughout the state which "has facilitated the entry of central feminist demands onto the government agenda" and ensured their policy adoption when executives have been less than supportive. As the chapters on Uruguay and Chile make clear, national women's agencies provide the potential for effective state-society coalition building. In the case of Argentina, successful state collaboration was not central on abortion legislation but was extended to the LGBT community: same-sex marriage proponents received robust support for their demands from the antidiscrimination institute. This finding helps to put into perspective how damaging it is for sexual and gender rights when actors within these state agencies turn their backs on movements, as has happened in Ecuador and Nicaragua, or when the agencies have few resources or capabilities.

However, intersectional alliances are highly dependent on the broader political context. For instance, conflictive contexts such as military dictatorships or economic crises tend to unite movements under broad political objectives, such as democratization or social inclusion. In contrast, in the context of progressive governments, disagreements have arisen over the specific policies to achieve gender or sexual justice; priorities, interpersonal rifts, and competition over resources; politics shaped by deep gender, class, and ethnic or racial inequalities; and relationships to political parties and the state. Wilkinson's analysis of Ecuador indicates that the fracturing of social movements has been exacerbated by a context of extreme polarization, and clientelistic state politics that divide feminist and LGBT movements even as they may co-opt elements of their communities. This fragmentation and divide-and-rule approach to feminist, women's, and LGBT movements is also strong in Nicaragua, and where indigenous women have found more support from Evo Morales's administration than other women in terms of their demands for recognition and redistribution.

Conclusion

By exploring distinct elements of a gender and sexual rights agenda, this volume contests the narrative of the Pink Tide's uniform experience and transformative impact. As with other historical periods, this one manifests continuities in heteropatriarchal structures and practices of state power even as such power has been dramatically or mildly altered in other ways. Reflecting back on table Intro.1, through which we categorized gender- and sexuality-related policy, we see that there is no fixed understanding of the extent to which a given issue challenges deep-seated cultural values and their proponents. Across these arenas, the largely underanalyzed but ever-stronger alliances between putatively progressive political forces and conservative religious ones play a central role in determining the degree to which these policies promote transformation.

As this volume attests, the impact of the Pink Tide cannot be understood without reference to the politics of and policy on gender and sexuality. At first glance, restoring such references might seem to indicate that the more radical attempts at reorienting social, political, and economic development have been, paradoxically, more dependent on traditional gender ideology and its institutional manifestations. Instead, the countries with a less radical framework for change have been more effective in challenging traditional sexuality norms and male privilege. Indeed, feminists seem to have greater possibilities to exert influence within institutionalized partisan left governments (Blofeld, Ewig, and Piscopo 2017, 362).

But it is precisely by refocusing our view through the lenses of gender and sexuality that we can see that neat bifurcations between "bad" and "good" Lefts lead to erroneous conclusions. It is not Ortega's, Correa's, Chávez's, or, periodically, Fernández de Kirchner's ideological radicality that are at issue here, but their hyperpresidentialism and strategic alliances with conservative actors, particularly the Catholic Church, to maintain their holds on power and develop electoral or ruling coalitions. It is not Chávez's, and now, Maduro's, attempt to mobilize popular sectors to support a socialist project that has exploited popular women's unpaid labor, but their eagerness to perpetuate their support and power in the face of legislative opposition, use of police repression against mass protests, and unexamined reliance on gendered social and economic structures in doing so. And it is not Morales's claim to decolonize the Bolivian state that has alienated many indigenous women—and men—but his administration's continuing dependence on extractivist economic development. At the other end of the spectrum, progress in Uruguay has depended on the shrewd actions of multisectoral coalitions rather than on institutionalized political processes alone. The concentration of power and its continued reliance on gendered and sexual relations of power undermine transformative political projects.

However, revolutionary rhetorical commitments and their embodiment through new constitutions have provided political opportunities by which movements have articulated and demanded the diverse changes they seek. They have built conjunctural coalitions and shared platforms, or at least shared resistance to common foes. They have also connected with allies inside the state; such state-society collaboration proves central to the successes movements have achieved. And they have advanced distinct ways of staking their claims that resonate with domestic contexts.

As nearly all of the countries profiled in this collection experience the growth of the center-right and the decline of commodity-fueled growth, the reliance on poor women's unpaid labor will doubtless continue as a fundamental, yet invisibilized, element of shifting economic and social relations. It remains to be seen whether the kind of coalitions that have been successful in challenging less material elements of the heteropatriarchal social order, such as demanding action on gender-based violence and relationship and gender identity recognition, can be turned to the work of lightening the burdens placed on those mothers' shoulders.

To make progress in shifting political contexts, movements can build on the lessons learned under Pink Tide governance—since trends such as hyperpresidentialism, alliances with conservative religious forces, and dependence on extractive industries are bound to continue under right-wing rule. Enhanced descriptive representation, as attractive as it may appear to global audiences, does not seem to be the lynchpin to achieving gender and sexuality justice, particularly when such representation is subject to the control of centralizing executives and hamstrung by the pressure of conservative actors. Instead, effective substantive representation has to be achieved through strategically connecting movement actions to legitimized frames of understanding and institutional spaces at many levels, including the judiciary. Movement actors must fight to maintain spaces such as state women's agencies and anti-discrimination institutions and demand that allies fill them. They should also continue to exploit opportunities to "judicialize" their demands, such as those mentioned in the chapters on Argentina and Brazil, especially where independent supreme courts attempt to hold other powers accountable.

We invite readers to consider these findings as they explore the chapters that follow. In order to make the comparisons as clear as possible, we have organized the rest of the volume to reflect countries' relative progressivity on the policies challenging the heteropatriarchal organization of society: women's reproductive autonomy, LGBT recognition, and the empowerment of poor women. Challenging a key global measurement for women's equality, we interrogate but do not organize the chapters according to the vexed question of women's representation, given the contested relationship and lack of correlation between women's descriptive and substantive representation. The complexities of the cases belie a smooth analytic trajectory, but the endpoints are clear. The more that feminist and queer movements have seized the political opportunities opened by left governance and been able to count on state allies within a framework of institutionalized political interactions, the more successful they have been at seeking rights from the Left. The more control that executives have had, and the more tightly bound they have been to conservative religious hierarchies and ideas, the less a gender and sexual justice agenda has been realized by its proponents.

Notes

We would like to thank the reviewers of this volume for their insightful feedback on earlier drafts, as well as participants at the CLACSO Congress of 2016. We are grateful for the work of Janet Chavez and Maegan Hoover in collecting data and creating figures.

1. This worldview challenges the power hierarchies embedded in Western social, political, and economic frameworks and their appropriateness for formerly colonized peoples.

2. The color pink refers both to the global association of the color red with the Left, and to the spectrum of political projects, from light-pink reformist to deeper-red radical, included in this period. The countries in which left-leaning executives were in power for at least one term between the mid-1990s and the present are Argentina, Bolivia, Brazil, Chile, Costa Rica, Cuba, Dominican Republic, Ecuador, El Salvador, Guatemala, Honduras, Nicaragua, Paraguay, Peru, Uruguay, and Venezuela.

3. In this introduction we use the adjective "queer" and the acronym "LGBT" as synonyms, following increasingly common usage in the United States, even as we acknowledge that the former is often used as a way to acknowledge the blurred boundaries among nonheteronormative and gender-nonconforming identities, and the latter is often expanded to take into account more specific identities, such as transsexual, intersex, and asexual. Although they have different histories and contemporary valences, both terms reference individuals and communities whose lived experience and identities in some way challenge heterosexual, cisgender, and patriarchal norms. However, because the communities we reference in Latin America use a range of terms to self-identify that are relevant to their own contexts, the authors of the country studies also use a range of different terms.

4. Feminists who work inside state institutions.

5. The modes of incorporation varied from executive cabinet placements to legislative action to shifting the entire constitutional framework toward more mass-based participation.

6. These entailed broad-based legal reforms such as constitutional modifications, revisions of civil and penal codes, and the passing of laws regulating gender and sexuality; writing national plans based on social inclusion and indigenous notions of *buen vivir* (this concept roughly translates to "living well"; in context, it

suggests placing community needs above those of the individual); and creating new "imagined political communit[ies]" (Anderson 1983, 6).

7. This is due to three main reasons: the expansion of the agenda beyond economic issues; a desire to reconnect with an anticlerical history; and the use of social liberalism to restore a sense of radicalism (Encarnación 2016, 70–71).

8. Previous experiences of state socialism in Eastern Europe, Russia, and Latin America show the distance between discursive affirmation of gender equality and the lived experiences of citizens (Molyneux 2001).

9. There is an abundant political science and sociological literature that attempts to characterize these governments. For example, see Castañeda and Morales 2008; Cameron and Hershberg 2010; Weyland, Madrid, and Hunter 2010; Levitsky and Roberts 2011; de la Torre and Arnson 2013; Queirolo 2013; and Ellner 2014.

10. This is according to income distribution as measured by the World Bank through the Gini index (Roser and Ortiz-Ospina 2017).

11. There is no English translation of the widely used term *sectores populares*. According to the translators of Elizabeth Jelin's 1990 edited collection, *Women and Social Change in Latin America*, "working class" is not an accurate definition since the poor do not often work for a regular salary. Instead, they perform the most precarious informal and temporary work and also experience high unemployment. Although they have political citizenship, they do not have social rights, and are segregated in neighborhoods in remote suburbs or marginal urban areas. Jelin uses the term "popular sectors" as a synonym for the Latin American urban poor to reflect their substantial presence as well as their social and political protagonism (Jelin 1990a, 10–11; 1990b).

12. In practice, the nuclear family is becoming less and less common, as the numbers of female-headed households and people living alone increase (Arriagada 2002).

13. In colonial times, Elizabeth Dore (2000, 12, 11) explains, "officials drew on legal and cultural norms of patriarchal authority to lend legitimacy to the authority of the state"; as a result "men's gender privileges and obligations were regarded as natural law," and women's legal autonomy determined by their relationship to men, as well as their race and class. Catholic teachings reinforced the male-dominated family as the basic building block of society, and, as Jordi Díez (2015, 33) notes, "excluded any sexual expression other than heterosexuality." After independence and the rise of the liberal state, both social and political organization continued to privilege light-skinned, propertied men; secular liberalism reinforced, rather than challenged, heteropatriarchal norms. Moreover, new laws and constitutional frameworks institutionalized the male-dominated family as the basis of citizenship and began to outlaw homosexuality (Díez 2015, 34). Even after it was decriminalized with the adoption of Napoleonic codes, homosexuality moved from sin to a sickness, pathologized by its medicalization (Bejel 2010, 48).

14. Maxine Molyneux (2000a) explains that corporatist governments, while more inclusive of the working class, privileged men through party-union relations. Their openness to women's political participation, if not mobilization, was largely

to support state projects; the expansion of women's social rights were awarded through their roles as daughters, wives, and mothers.

15. Although this reliance is not new, it became especially marked where the state shed responsibility for social programs and services.

16. As Mario Pecheny argues (2012/2013), "advances in gender and sexual rights facilitate a regional self-image of modern societies, modern politicians, and modern political systems. The enlightened middle classes that support individual values of sexual freedom find in these measures (divorce, sex education, and even equal marriage) a sort of compensation for the unjust economic policies and attacks on social rights that have occurred simultaneously."

17. Such frames are also adapted to distinct contexts. In Mexico City, framing of both abortion and marriage equality as part of a secular society, harkening back to the revolutionary promise of a separation of church and state, helped to broaden the coalition supporting these demands and win legislative victories. Moreover, claims for "sexual diversity" connected queer theory to the idea of cultural diversity, a particularly relevant idea given Mexican indigenous demands for well-being and recognition of their cultural heritage (Díez 2015, 97).

18. This is not to imply that such movements operate in a mobilizational vacuum; other social change movements, such as those focused on race, ethnicity, and territory, interpenetrate these efforts, resulting in other forms of collaboration.

19. For a careful critique of the tensions implicit in the use of a liberal notion of rights to demand inclusion on the basis of sexuality in national and international institutions, see Corrêa, Petchesky, and Parker (2008, part 3).

20. For instance, the period of economic decline and political repression that characterized the region from the late 1960s through the 1980s was a particularly fertile time for such organizing, as popular women formed soup kitchens and neighborhood organizations (Jelin 1990b; Schild 1994).

21. Although this section offers what are often considered objective measurements of socioeconomic progress based on gender, manipulation of official statistics is not unknown. For governments whose legitimacy depends on improving social indicators, the temptation is strong to produce indicators that demonstrate an even more improved situation than what is actually happening. (See, for example, the Nicaraguan government's approach to femicide in chapter 7.) This could have a straightforward impact on women's status, such as reporting higher-than-actual educational enrollment. Or it could have a more indirect effect. Consider inflation statistics: if they are underreported, governments can claim that the prices of necessities upon which poverty rates are based are low enough that those rates are correspondingly low. But if the reality of inflation is much higher, those necessities are also more expensive—and the economic and social status of the women often responsible for purchasing them is then worse than reported.

22. The "reproductive bargain" focuses on the state-society relations that ensure the continuity of goods and services for social reproduction in its widest sense, as

well as expectations of how such reproductive responsibilities are distributed and a moral economy of welfare is legitimated (Pearson 1997, 680).

23. In the Pink Tide, CCT coverage is quite variable, ranging from countries such as Argentina, Brazil, Chile, and Uruguay, where coverage reaches all those living in extreme poverty, to Bolivia and Peru, where it is significantly lower (50 and 60 percent) (Gender Equality Observatory of Latin America and the Caribbean 2012, 56). There is also a sharp variability in the amount of cash provided to women between programs and countries (Gender Equality Observatory of Latin America and the Caribbean 2012).

24. Some countries have replaced earlier minimum quotas with parity (50 percent) requirements for party lists.

25. Recent work argues that ideology, in fact, is not as important an explanatory factor as parties' "decision environments" in explaining female candidacy. Parties nominate more women when facing public distrust, and more men in times of economic weakening or higher partisan competition (Funk, Hinojosa, and Piscopo 2017).

26. This holds true if Europe is taken as a single region (of OSCE member countries). If Nordic countries are broken out into their own region, the Americas form the region with the second highest average (IPU 2017).

27. With respect to LGBT rights, Javier Corrales (2015, 28) also points to the legislative branch: "The veto power of religion is most strongly felt where Protestants and Evangelicals are dominant, growing, or have a strong presence in Congress. By contrast, in predominantly Catholic countries, religion tends to be decisive where church attendance is high or where strong historical ties exist between the clergy and at least one dominant political party."

References

Anderson, Benedict. 1983. *Imagined Communities: Reflections on the Origin and Spread of Nationalism*. London: Verso.

Arriagada, Irma. 2002. "Cambios y desigualdad en las familias latinoamericanas." *Revista de la CEPAL* 77: 143–161. http://archivo.cepal.org/pdfs/revistaCepal/Sp/077143161.pdf.

Bejel, Emilio. 2010. "Cuban CondemNation of Queer Bodies." In *The Politics of Sexuality in Latin America: A Reader on Lesbian, Gay, Bisexual, and Transgender Rights*, edited by Javier Corrales and Mario Pecheny, 44–59. Pittsburgh, PA: University of Pittsburgh Press.

Bernstein, Lisa, 2008. "Introduction: Mothers and Motherlands." In *(M)Othering the Nation: Constructing and Resisting National Allegories through the Maternal Body*, edited by Lisa Bernstein, 1–9. Newcastle: Cambridge Scholars.

Blofeld, Merike, and Christina Ewig. 2017. "The Left Turn and Abortion Politics in Latin America." *Social Politics* 24 (4): 481–510.

Blofeld, Merike, Christina Ewig, and Jennifer M. Piscopo. 2017. "The Reactive Left: Gender Equality and the Latin American Pink Tide." *Social Politics* 24 (4): 345–69.

Brown, Stephen, 2010. "'Con discriminación y represión no hay democracia': The Lesbian and Gay Movement in Argentina." In *The Politics of Sexuality in Latin America: A Reader on Lesbian, Gay, Bisexual, and Transgender Rights*, edited by Javier Corrales and Mario Pecheny, 86–101. Pittsburgh, PA: University of Pittsburgh Press.

Cameron, Maxwell, and Eric Hershberg, eds. 2010. *Latin America's Left Turns: Politics, Policies, and Trajectories of Change*. Boulder, CO: Lynne Rienner.

Castañeda, Jorge G. 2006. "Latin America's Left Turn." *Foreign Affairs* 85: 28–43.

Castañeda, Jorge G., and Marco A. Morales, eds. 2008. *Leftovers: Tales of the Latin American Left*. New York: Routledge.

Cecchini, Simone, and Aldo Madariaga. 2011. "Conditional Cash Transfer Programmes: The Recent Experience in Latin America and the Caribbean." *Cuadernos de la CEPAL* 95.

Ciccariello-Maher, George. 2014. "Constituent Moments, Constitutional Processes: Social Movements and the New Latin American Left." *Latin American Perspectives* 40 (3): 126–45.

Cookson, Tara P. 2016. "Working for Inclusion? Conditional Cash Transfers and the Reproduction of Inequality." *Antipode* 48 (5): 1187–205.

Corrales, Javier. 2015. "LGBT Rights and Representation in Latin America and the Caribbean: The Influence of Structure, Movements, Institutions, and Culture." UNC Chapel Hill/USAID/Victory. Accessed October 15, 2016. https://globalstudies.unc.edu/files/2015/04/LGBT_Report_LatAm_v8-copy.pdf.

Corrales, Javier, and Mario Pecheny. 2010. "Introduction: The Comparative Politics of Sexuality in Latin America." In *The Politics of Sexuality in Latin America: A Reader on Lesbian, Gay, Bisexual, and Transgender Rights*, edited by Javier Corrales and Mario Pecheny, 1–30. Pittsburgh, PA: University of Pittsburgh Press.

Corrêa, Sonia, Rosalind Petchesky, and Richard Parker. 2008. *Sexuality, Health, and Human Rights*. London: Routledge.

de la Dehesa, Rafael. 2010. *Queering the Public Sphere in Mexico and Brazil: Sexual Rights Movements in Emerging Democracies*. Durham, NC: Duke University Press.

de la Torre, Carlos. 2013. "El populismo latinoamericano, entre la democratización y el autoritarismo." *Revista Nueva Sociedad* 247 (September–October): 120–37.

de la Torre, Carlos. 2017. "Los populismos refundadores: Promesas democratizadoras, prácticas autoritarias." *Revista Nueva Sociedad* 267 (January—February): 129–41.

de la Torre, Carlos, and Cynthia J. Arnson, eds. 2013. *Latin American Populism in the Twenty-First Century*. Baltimore, MD: Johns Hopkins University Press.

della Porta, Donatella. 2003. "The Women's Movement, the Left and the State: Continuities and Changes in the Italian Case." In *Women's Movements Facing the Reconfigured State*, by Lee Ann Banaszak, Karen Beckwith, and Dieter Rucht, 44–69. New York: Cambridge University Press.

Díez, Jordi. 2015. *The Politics of Gay Marriage in Latin America: Argentina, Chile, and Mexico*. Cambridge: Cambridge University Press.

Dore, Elizabeth. 2000. "One Step Forward, Two Steps Back: Gender and the State in the Long Nineteenth Century." In *Hidden Histories of Gender and the State in Latin America*, edited by Elizabeth Dore and Maxine Molyneux, 3–32. Durham, NC: Duke University Press.

Dore, Elizabeth, and Maxine Molyneux, eds. 2000. *Hidden Histories of Gender and the State in Latin America*. Durham, NC: Duke University Press.

ECLAC (Economic Commission for Latin America and the Caribbean). 2015. CEPALSTAT. Accessed November 21, 2015. http://estadisticas.cepal.org/cepalstat /web_cepalstat/Portada.asp?idioma=i.

Ellner, Steve, ed. 2014. *Latin America's Radical Left: Challenges and Complexities of Political Power in the Twenty-First Century*. Lanham, MD: Rowman & Littlefield.

Encarnación, Omar G. 2016. *Out in the Periphery: Latin America's Gay Rights Revolution*. New York: Oxford University Press.

Esping-Andersen, Gösta. 1990. *The Three Worlds of Welfare Capitalism*. Princeton, NJ: Princeton University Press.

Espinosa Miñoso, Yuderkys. 2010. "The Feminism-Lesbianism Relationship in Latin America: A Necessary Link." In *The Politics of Sexuality in Latin America: A Reader on Lesbian, Gay, Bisexual, and Transgender Rights*, edited by Javier Corrales and Mario Pecheny, 401–5. Pittsburgh, PA: University of Pittsburgh Press.

Filgueira, Fernando and Juliana Martínez Franzoni. 2017. "The Divergence in Women's Economic Empowerment: Class and Gender under the Pink Tide." *Social Politics* 24 (4): 370–98.

Franceschet, Susan. 2010. "Explaining Domestic Violence Policy Outcomes in Chile and Argentina." *Latin American Politics and Society* 52 (3): 1–29.

Franceschet, Susan, and Jennifer Piscopo. 2013. "Equality, Democracy, and the Broadening and Deepening of Gender Quotas." *Politics & Gender* 9 (3): 310–16.

Friedman, Elisabeth Jay. 2007. "Lesbians in (Cyber)Space: The Politics of the Internet in Latin American On- and Off-line Communities." *Media, Culture and Society* 29 (5): 790–811.

Friedman, Elisabeth Jay. 2009. "Re(gion)alizing Women's Human Rights in Latin America." *Politics & Gender* 5 (30): 349–75.

Friedman, Elisabeth Jay and Constanza Tabbush. 2016. "NiUnaMenos: Not One Woman Less, Not One More Death!" Nacla.org. Accessed February 14, 2018. https://nacla.org/news/2016/11/01/niunamenos-not-one-woman-less-not-one -more-death.

Funk, Kendall D., Magda Hinojosa, and Jennifer M. Piscopo. 2017. "Still Left Behind: Gender, Political Parties, and Latin America's Pink Tide." *Social Politics* 24 (4): 399–424.

Gender Equality Observatory of Latin America and the Caribbean. *Annual Report 2012: A Look at Grants, Support and Burden for Women*. ECLAC.

Accessed February 22, 2018. https://www.cepal.org/publicaciones/xml/5/50235 /GenderEqualityObservatory.pdf.

Gioconda Espina. 2007. "Beyond Polarization: Organized Venezuelan Women Promote Their 'Minimum Agenda.'" NACLA *Report on the Americas* 40 (2): 20–24.

Goetz, Anne Marie, and Rob Jenkins. 2016. "Agency and Accountability: Promoting Women's Participation in Peacebuilding." *Feminist Economics* 22 (1): 211–36.

Gómez, Eduardo J. 2010. "Friendly Government, Cruel Society: AIDS and the Politics of Homosexual Strategic Mobilization in Brazil." In *The Politics of Sexuality in Latin America: A Reader on Lesbian, Gay, Bisexual, and Transgender Rights*, edited by Javier Corrales and Mario Pecheny, 233–50. Pittsburgh, PA: University of Pittsburgh Press.

Goñi, Uki. 2015. "Argentine Women Call Out Machismo." *New York Times*, June 15. Accessed November 17, 2015. http://www.nytimes.com/2015/06/16/opinion /argentine-women-call-out-machismo.html.

Grey, Sandra. 2002. "Does Size Matter? Critical Mass and New Zealand's Women MPs." *Parliamentary Affairs* 55 (1): 19–29.

Hekma, Gert. 2004. "Sexual Citizenship." GLBTQ Archive. Accessed July 26, 2016. http://www.glbtqarchive.com/ssh/sexual_citizenship_S.pdf.

Hertzman, Marc. 2016. "'To Love without Fear': Feminist and LGBTQ Mobilizations in Brazil." *Notches*, September 15. Accessed June 28, 2017. http://notchesblog.com /2016/09/15/to-love-without-fear-feminist-and-lgbtq-mobilizations-in-brazil/.

Htun, Mala. 2003. *Sex and the State: Abortion, Divorce, and the Family under Latin American Dictatorships and Democracies.* Cambridge: Cambridge University Press.

Htun, Mala. 2016. *Inclusion without Representation in Latin America: Gender Quotas and Ethnic Reservations.* Cambridge: Cambridge University Press.

Htun, Mala, and Juan Pablo Ossa. 2013. "Political inclusion of marginalized groups: indigenous reservations and gender parity in Bolivia." Politics, groups, and Identities 1 (1): 4–25.

Htun, Mala, and Laurel S. Weldon. 2010. "When Do Governments Promote Women's Rights? A Framework for the Comparative Analysis of Sex Equality Policy." *Perspectives on Politics* 8 (1): 207–16.

Htun, Mala, and Laurel S. Weldon. 2012. "The Civic Origins of Progressive Policy Change: Combating Violence against Women in Global Perspective, 1975–2005." *American Political Science Review* 106 (3): 548–69.

Huber, Evelyn, and John Stephens. 2001. *Development and Crisis of the Welfare State: Parties and Policies in Global Markets.* Chicago, IL: University of Chicago Press.

Inter-Parliamentary Union (IPU). 2017. "Women in National Parliaments." Accessed June 26, 2017. http://www.ipu.org/wmn-e/world.htm.

Jelin, Elizabeth. 1990a. "Introduction." In *Women and Social Change in Latin America*, edited by Elizabeth Jelin, 1–11. London: UNRISD and Zed Books.

Jelin, Elizabeth. 1990b. *Women and Social Change in Latin America*. London: UNRISD and Zed Books.

Johannsen, Julia, Luis Tejerina, and Amanda Glassman. 2008. "Conditional Cash Transfers in Latin America: Problems and Opportunities." Inter-American Development Bank Paper. Accessed June 16, 2017. https://publications.iadb.org/handle/11319/2530.

Kampwirth, Karen. 2011. *Latin America's New Left and the Politics of Gender: Lessons from Nicaragua*. New York: Springer Publishing.

Kittilson, Miki Caul. 2008. "Representing Women: The Adoption of Family Leave in Comparative Perspective." *Journal of Politics* 70 (2): 323–34.

Krook, Mona Lena. 2009. *Quotas for Women in Politics: Gender and Candidate Selection Reform Worldwide*. Oxford: Oxford University Press.

Krook, Mona Lena, and Pär Zetterberg. 2014. "Introduction: Gender Quotas and Women's Representation—New Directions in Research." *Representation* 50 (3): 287–94. Accessed June 23, 2017. DOI:10.1080/00344893.2014.951168.

Lavinas, Lena. 2013. "21st Century Welfare." *New Left Review* 84 (November–December): 5–40.

Levitsky, Steven, and Kenneth M. Roberts, eds. 2011. *The Resurgence of the Latin American Left*. Baltimore, MD: Johns Hopkins University Press.

Lind, Amy. 2012. "Family Norms, Constitutional Reform, and the Politics of Redistribution in Post-Neoliberal Ecuador: Revolution with a Woman's Face?" *Rethinking Marxism: A Journal of Economics, Culture & Society* 24 (4): 536–55.

Lind, Amy, and Christine (Cricket) Keating. 2013. "Navigating the Left Turn: Sexual Justice and the Citizen Revolution in Ecuador." *International Feminist Journal of Politics* 15 (4): 515–33.

Marsiaj, Juan P. 2010. "Social Movements and Political Parties: Gays, Lesbians, and *Travestis* and the Struggle for Inclusion in Brazil." In *The Politics of Sexuality in Latin America: A Reader on Lesbian, Gay, Bisexual, and Transgender Rights*, edited by Javier Corrales and Mario Pecheny, 197–211. Pittsburgh, PA: University of Pittsburgh Press.

McClintock, Anne. 1995. *Imperial Leather: Race, Gender, and Sexuality in the Colonial Contest*. New York: Routledge.

Molyneux, Maxine. 2000a. "Twentieth-Century State Formations in Latin America." In *Hidden Histories of Gender and the State in Latin America*, edited by Elizabeth Dore and Maxine Molyneux, 33–81. Durham, NC: Duke University Press.

Molyneux, Maxine. 2000b. "State, Gender and Institutional Change: The Federación de Mujeres Cubanas." In *Hidden Histories of Gender and the State in Latin America*, edited by Elizabeth Dore and Maxine Molyneux, 291–321. Durham, NC: Duke University Press.

Molyneux, Maxine. 2001. "State Socialism and Women's Emancipation: A Continuing Retrospective." In *Women's Movements in International Perspective Latin America and Beyond*, 99–139. London: Palgrave Macmillan UK.

Molyneux, Maxine. 2006. "Mothers at the Service of the New Poverty Agenda: Progresa/Oportunidades, Mexico's Conditional Transfer Programme." *Social Policy and Administration* 40 (4): 425–49.

Molyneux, Maxine. 2007. "Change and Continuity in Social Policy in Latin America: Mothers at the Service of the State?" UNRISD *Programme on Gender and Development*, Paper 1. Geneva: UNRISD.

Molyneux, Maxine. 2008. "Conditional Cash Transfers: A 'Pathway to Women's Empowerment'?" Pathways Working Paper 5. Sussex: IDS.

Molyneux, Maxine, and Marilyn Thompson. 2011. "CCT Programmes and Women's Empowerment in Peru, Bolivia and Ecuador." CARE Policy Paper. Accessed February 21, 2018. https://insights.careinternational.org.uk/media/k2/attachments/cct-progs-and-womens-emp-peru-bolivia-ecuador.pdf.

Molyneux, Maxine, with Nicola Jones, and Fiona Samuels. 2016. "Can Cash Transfer Programmes Have 'Transformative' Effects?" *Journal of Development Studies* 52 (8): 1087–98.

Moreno Aluminé. 2010. "'The Gay Pride March? They're Not Talking about Me': The Politicization of Differences in the Argentine GLTTTB Movement." In *The Politics of Sexuality in Latin America: A Reader on Lesbian, Gay, Bisexual, and Transgender Rights*, edited by Javier Corrales and Mario Pecheny, 387–400. Pittsburgh, PA: University of Pittsburgh Press.

Mueller, Carol McClurg, and John D. McCarthy. 2003. "Cultural Continuity and Structural Change: The Logic of Adaptation by Radical, Liberal, and Socialist Feminists to State Reconfiguration." In *Women's Movements Facing the Reconfigured State*, by Lee Ann Banaszak, Karen Beckwith, and Dieter Rucht, 219–41. New York: Cambridge University Press.

Pearson, Ruth. 1997. "Renegotiating the Reproductive Bargain: Gender Analysis of Economic Transition in Cuba in the 1990s." *Development and Change* 28:671–705.

Pecheny, Mario. 2010. "Sociability, Secrets, and Identities; Key Issues in Sexual Politics in Latin America." In *The Politics of Sexuality in Latin America: A Reader on Lesbian, Gay, Bisexual, and Transgender Rights*, edited by Javier Corrales and Mario Pecheny, 102–21. Pittsburgh, PA: University of Pittsburgh Press.

Pecheny, Mario. 2012/ 2013. "Sexual Politics and Post-Neoliberalism in Latin America." Special issue, *S&F Online* 11.1–11.2, edited by Elizabeth Bernstein and Janet R. Jakobsen. Fall /Spring. Accessed July 26, 2016. http://sfonline.barnard.edu/gender-justice-and-neoliberal-transformations/sexual-politics-and-post-neoliberalism-in-latin-america/.

Queirolo, María del Rosario. 2013. *The Success of the Left in Latin America: Untainted Parties, Market Reforms, and Voting Behavior*. Notre Dame, IN: University of Notre Dame Press.

Roser, Max, and Esteban Ortiz-Ospina. 2017. "Income Inequality." Our World in Data. Accessed June 16, 2017. https://ourworldindata.org/income-inequality/.

Schild, Veronica. 1994. "Recasting 'Popular' Movements: Gender and Political Learning in Neighborhood Organizations in Chile." *Latin American Perspectives* 21 (2): 59–80.

Schulenberg, Shawn. 2013. "The Lavender Tide: LGBT Rights and the Latin American Left Today." In *Same-Sex Marriage in Latin America*, edited by Jason Pierceson, Adriana Piatti-Crocker, and Shawn Schulenberg, 23–39. Lanham, MD: Rowman and Littlefield.

Schwindt-Bayer, Leslie A. 2006. "Still Supermadres? Gender and the Policy Priorities of Latin American Legislators." *American Journal of Political Science* 50 (3): 570–85.

Staab, Silke. 2017. *Gender and the Politics of Gradual Change: Social Policy Reform and Innovation in Chile.* London: Palgrave Macmillan.

Stetson, Dorothy McBride, and Amy G. Mazur. 1995. *Comparative State Feminism.* Thousand Oaks, CA: Sage.

Svampa, Maristella. 2015. "América Latina: De nuevas izquierdas a populismos de alta intensidad." *REVISTA Memoria*, Mexico 12. Accessed October 15, 2016. http://revistamemoria.mx/?p=702.

Tabbush, Constanza. 2009. "Gender, Citizenship and New Approaches to Poverty Relief: The Case of Argentine CCT Strategies." In *The Gendered Impacts of Liberalization: Towards Embedded Liberalism?*, edited by Shahra Razavi, 290–326. Routledge/UNRISD Series in Gender and Development. London: Routledge.

Tabbush, Constanza. 2010. "Latin American Women's Protection after Adjustment: A Feminist Critique of Conditional Cash Transfers in Chile and Argentina." *Oxford Development Studies* 38 (4): 437–59.

Thayer, Millie. 2010. "Identity, Revolution, and Democracy: Lesbian Movements in Central America." In *The Politics of Sexuality in Latin America: A Reader on Lesbian, Gay, Bisexual, and Transgender Rights*, edited by Javier Corrales and Mario Pecheny, 144–72. Pittsburgh, PA: University of Pittsburgh Press.

Vianna, Adriana R. B., and Sérgio Carrara. 2010. "Sexual Politics and Sexual Rights in Brazil: A Cast Study." In *The Politics of Sexuality in Latin America: A Reader on Lesbian, Gay, Bisexual, and Transgender Rights*, edited by Javier Corrales and Mario Pecheny, 122–34. Pittsburgh, PA: University of Pittsburgh Press.

Weldon, S. Laurel. 2011. *When Protest Makes Policy: How Social Movements Represent Disadvantaged Groups.* Ann Arbor: University of Michigan Press.

Weyland, Kurt, Raul L. Madrid, and Wendy Hunter, eds. 2010. *Leftist Governments in Latin America: Successes and Shortcomings.* Cambridge: Cambridge University Press.

Xie, Selina, and Javier Corrales. 2010. "LGBT Rights in Ecuador's 2008 Constitution: Victories and Setbacks." In *The Politics of Sexuality in Latin America: A Reader on Lesbian, Gay, Bisexual, and Transgender Rights*, edited by Javier Corrales and Mario Pecheny, 224–29. Pittsburgh, PA: University of Pittsburgh Press.

CHAPTER I

Explaining Advances and Drawbacks in Women's and LGBTIQ Rights in Uruguay

Multisited Pressures, Political Resistance, and Structural Inertias

NIKI JOHNSON, ANA LAURA RODRÍGUEZ GUSTÁ,
AND DIEGO SEMPOL

In Latin America, Uruguay is considered a "country of firsts." In the early twentieth century, important legal precedents were set in defense of women's rights in the family, the education system, and the workplace. In 1932, Uruguay became the first country in the region to grant women full political rights to vote and stand for election, and civil equality followed in 1946. The constitution of 1917 also formally separated the state from the Catholic Church, and since then Uruguayan society has become increasingly secular, now registering very low levels of religious belief and practice compared to the rest of Latin America (World Values Survey 2017). In contrast, the second half of the twentieth century, which was marked by economic stagnation and a civil-military dictatorship (1973–84), witnessed no further significant advances in terms of women's rights.

In the postdictatorship period, Uruguayan politics has seen the sustained electoral growth of the left-wing Frente Amplio (Broad Front, or FA), founded in 1971. In 1989, the FA gained control of the subnational government in the capital, and in 2004 won the presidential elections for the first time, a victory repeated subsequently in 2009 and 2014. Since coming to power, the FA has pursued public policies that include human rights and social equality as core principles. In this context, Uruguayan social movements, including feminist and LGBTIQ (Lesbian, Gay, Bissexual, Transgender, Intersex, and Queer); pushed forward new policy issues relating to gender

equality, sexuality, autonomy and antidiscrimination, and sexual and reproductive rights.

The FA proved to be more open than the "traditional" Uruguayan political parties to incorporating such demands in their policy agenda. Nevertheless, women's and LGBTIQ rights did not become constituent elements of the
FA's government program, nor did they figure prominently in the electoral
speeches of the coalition's presidential candidates. In the FA's official discourse, the classic class divide and inequalities deriving from gender, sexual
diversity, and racial difference were not brought together within a single comprehensive emancipatory framework.

Despite this, between 2005 and 2015, the FA government promoted gender
equality and respect for diversity from a rights perspective, including emblematic achievements such as same-sex marriage and the decriminalization
of abortion, and innovative affirmative action measures for the trans population. In order to understand the scope of gender equality and LGBTIQ rights
policies under the Left in Uruguay, this chapter's first objective is to characterize these policies and describe the process by which they came about. In
particular, we highlight how the feminist movement, women's organizations,
and LGBTIQ collectives used a range of mobilization and alliance-building
strategies to successfully press for issues to be included in the policy agenda.

In the case of the women's movement, one of its foundational features is
the dense network among feminist NGOs, grassroots women's groups, women
in trade unions and political parties, and female legislators. The multinodal
nature of feminism became truly multisited (in the sense of "multiinsti-
tutional politics," as proposed by Armstrong and Bernstein 2008) with the
coming to power of the FA, the subsequent appointment of feminists in state
positions, and the expansion and strengthening of gender institutions. This
facilitated the formation of strategic feminist policy "triangles" (Holli 2008)
among women in elected office, feminist and women's movement actors, and
"femocrats" (Sawer 1995) in women's policy offices, which Amy Mazur (2002,
4) identifies as one of the "most important conditions for feminist success."

In contrast, in the period under study, the LGBTIQ movement remained
primarily "social" in nature, with its key agents located in movement organizations. It took advantage of the window of opportunity created by the rise
to power of the FA by "reframing" (Benford and Snow 2000) its demands
within a broader social justice agenda. Given the weak and incipient nature of
antidiscrimination institutions, the LGBTIQ movement then pursued its goals
by developing alliances in the legislature and executive arenas with "critical

actors," that is "those who are able to bring resources [to give] leverage in the process of building alliances, and influencing gender policy outcomes" (Macaulay 2005, 5; Childs and Krook 2009).

Drawing on recent discussions in the literature on feminist policies (Htun and Weldon 2010; Mazur 2002), in this chapter we argue that, despite the advances, many policies fall short of their objectives, and implementation gaps exist regarding the rights frameworks that inform them. In certain cases "framing contests" (Bacchi 1999; Charles and Mackay 2013) around policy issues have resulted in the marginalization of feminist frames in the process of policy development. In others, setbacks or stagnation when it comes to guaranteeing rights through public policies are due to a lack of effective "state capacity" (Htun and Weldon 2010, 211–12). Under the FA governments there does not appear to have been a true "paradigm shift" (Hall 1993) in the regulation of gender relations and sexuality. Rather, we observe more piecemeal and incomplete advances while patriarchal and heteronormative ideas of social relations and rights persist. A second objective of the chapter, therefore, is to provide some preliminary explanations about why this has occurred.

The chapter is based on qualitative research specifically conducted for this project during 2014 and 2015, including an exhaustive review of legislation and policy documents, and in-depth interviews with key informants. It also draws on the findings of previous research undertaken by the authors and is informed by their personal experience, through their links with the Uruguayan feminist and LGBTIQ movements, as scholars and/or activists.

The structure of the chapter is as follows. Following this first section, the second section provides an overview of the rise to power of the Left in Uruguay and a general evaluation of its openness toward gender equality and LGBTIQ rights agendas. The third section focuses on the feminist/women's and LGBTIQ movements—their origins, organizational and mobilizing dynamics, and political lobbying strategies. The fourth and fifth sections review progress in gender equality and sexual diversity policies respectively under the two consecutive FA governments, between 2005 and 2015. In these two sections we review the gains made, highlighting the role and interaction between different actors making gender equality or LGBTIQ rights claims, as well as identifying continuing sites of resistance and ongoing challenges. In the final section we reflect on the insights the Uruguayan case offers for understanding the articulation of gender and LGBTIQ agendas under left-wing governments, and the challenges and possibilities for advancing further under the third FA government that took office in March 2015.

Uruguay's Frente Amplio

The Nature and Rise of the Left

For most of the twentieth century, Uruguayan politics were dominated by the two "traditional" parties until, in the run-up to the 1971 elections, the FA was founded: a center-left coalition bringing together all left-wing parties behind a single presidential option for the first time. Following the return to democracy, the FA steadily increased its share of the vote. In 1989, it won control of the local government in Montevideo, the capital city and home to half the country's population, where it has since retained power. The Montevideo government was seen as a laboratory for implementing social policies within a rights framework and aspired to be a demonstration of what the FA could do were it to reach national government. In 2004, in the aftermath of one of the severest economic crises to hit the country for decades, the FA won the presidential elections, and was triumphant again in 2009 and 2014, securing a small overall parliamentary majority in all three periods.

The FA has a multiclass electoral and activist base. It is a coalition of left parties and factions, spanning a wide ideological spectrum from radical left to center-left groups, and including long-standing parties and newer factions founded in the postdictatorship period. One factor in the FA's electoral growth was its gradual shift to the political center and the development of a "progressive politics" based on gradualist and reformist processes of social transformation (Yaffé 2005).

This shift had two important consequences. First, it left behind traditional goals of the Uruguayan Left, such as agrarian reform and the nationalization of the means of production. It also implied a shift in economic policy, including its position on foreign investment and public-private partnerships. Second, the broadening of the Left's ideological and policy platform allowed feminists and youth sections in various FA factions to put new issues on the agenda, such as human rights, gender equality, sexual and reproductive rights, and antidiscrimination. These actors questioned the privileged position that class was afforded in the Left's traditional emancipatory discourse and sought to open up discussion around multiple crosscutting forms of exploitation and social domination. However, these ideological and strategic changes did not ultimately produce a new integrated left discourse and agenda. Traditional actors within the Left were unwilling to acknowledge the intersection between class and other forms of inequality, and the FA's strategies for social transformation continued to be marked by the false dilemma between recognition and redistribution (Fraser 1997).

The Left's Commitment to Gender Equality and Sexual Diversity

Nonetheless, the FA proved much more open than other parties to including gender equality policy proposals in its official government programs. This was primarily due to successful internal lobbying by feminist FA militants, who in 1997 formed the Unidad Temática de los Derechos de las Ciudadanas (Female Citizens' Rights Committee, or UTDC) within the FA. Yet, generally speaking, the FA's gender equality policy commitments were prominent neither in the coalition's electoral platforms nor in its presidential candidates' discourses. Thus, during the 2004 electoral campaign, despite the care taken by the FA's presidential candidate, Tabaré Vázquez, to use gender-inclusive language, his speeches did not include substantive references to gender issues (Johnson 2005). Moreover, the policy document drawn up by the UTDC, which analyzed existing gender inequalities and formulated policy proposals in the six areas covered by the FA's government program, was not treated as an integral part of the FA's program, thus effectively relegating gender rights to the margins of government action.

In the run-up to the following elections, the UTDC sought to avoid this marginalization by pursuing a different strategy and ensuring participation by its members in all the key committees contributing to the elaboration of the FA's government program of 2009. As a result, gender equity was defined as one of the governing principles and central crosscutting concepts that should frame national development policy ("programa de gobierno"). Specific gender policy proposals were present in three sections of the program and included key feminist demands: parity political representation; a national care system for dependents (infants, the elderly, and the disabled); strengthening of the national women's agency; and legalization of abortion. As before, however, these proposals were not foregrounded by the FA's 2009 presidential candidate, José Mujica, nor were they included as priority measures in the Left's electoral platform and discourse (Johnson and Pérez 2010).

Although certain feminist policy proposals—such as the legalization of abortion—were undoubtedly "silenced" for strategic electoral reasons, it is also clear that there is no institutional, party-wide commitment to substantive gender equality measures. The fact that these policy issues were not voluntarily espoused, or even openly rejected, by the FA's presidential nominees also reflects the high degree of autonomy these figures enjoy, as will be signaled in specific cases below. In short, the advances in engendering the FA's government program can rather be seen to reflect the capacity of gender-aware party activists (UTDC) to influence the agenda-setting process.

In contrast, neither the 2004 nor the 2009 FA government program included sexual diversity issues, and none of the demands formulated by the LGBTIQ movement in those years appeared among the priority measures defined by the Vázquez and Mujica administrations. In fact, in 2013, while the parliamentary debate on same-sex marriage was taking place, Mujica declared that "part of the Left has given up discussing the struggle for power, and now entertains itself discussing same-sex marriage" (*El País* 2013), implying that the democratization of marriage was irrelevant to power relations and that it was "distracting" the Left from the "real" issues. Also illustrative is the fact that the only antidiscrimination measure sponsored directly by Vázquez was an executive decree in 2009 prohibiting discrimination based on sexual orientation in recruitment to the armed forces. This was an issue that the LGBTIQ movement had never pursued, and the decree had no real practical effect, since it was not accompanied by measures designed to deepen understanding of the issue within the armed forces. As will be shown below, without the growing political pressure and mobilization capacity of the LGBTIQ movement, it would have been impossible to achieve the advances that were eventually made in terms of the expansion and recognition of sexual diversity rights.

Although the Left's presidential candidates—and, in fact, most faction leaders within the coalition—showed little more than rhetorical support for the new rights agenda, as will be shown below, other figures from the FA played a crucial role in pushing laws and policies through.

Women's and LGBTIQ Representation in the FA Governments

It is true that since 1995 the FA has been the party with the most women elected to parliament, accounting for more than half of total female legislators (Johnson 2013, 9–11). Nonetheless, it is only following the application of the quota law in the 2014 elections that women account for just over 20 percent of the FA's bench in parliament. Similarly, while the FA was historically the party that most actively supported quota bills in parliament (Johnson and Pérez 2011), this has not been accompanied by the adoption of voluntary quotas within the left coalition as a whole or within its factions. In fact, only the

Partido Socialista (Socialist Party) has adopted an effective voluntary quota, which since 1992 is applied both in elections to internal decision-making bodies and in the selection (by vote) of its parliamentary candidates.

Despite long being a demand of both the feminist movement[1] and female party members, the descriptive representation of women was not considered in the designation of cabinet or other top executive posts (CNS Mujeres 1999, 2000, 2004). These are appointed (and changed) at the discretion of the president, and both Vázquez and Mujica used left factions' electoral performance as the primary criterion for defining the distribution of these posts. Nevertheless, both FA governments included more female ministers than had previous administrations.[2] Moreover, during Vázquez's first term (2005–10) the appointment of women to head the Ministerio de Defensa Nacional (National Defense Ministry) and the Ministerio del Interior (Interior Ministry) undoubtedly contributed to deconstructing the traditional image of "hard" politics as "men's business" and to "normalizing" women as legitimate political leaders. Still, it is also true that only one of the female ministers or vice-ministers under the first two FA national administrations had a history of sustained gender activism,[3] and in fact, the health minister in the first FA government shared Vázquez's opposition to the legalization of abortion.

Sexual diversity has been even less of an issue in executive appointments. However, in November 2011 the public coming out of Andrés Scagliola, head of the Dirección Nacional de Política Social (National Directorate of Social Policy) in the Ministerio de Desarrollo Social (Ministry for Social Development, or MIDES), marked a milestone in terms of the visibility and legitimacy of sexual diversity. As will be seen below, Scagliola was a critical ally in promoting feminist and LGBTIQ claims in social policy. In 2015, Scagliola was not only removed from the post of director of social policy but was not given another position in Vázquez's second administration, although he did head up the new Secretaría de la Diversidad (Diversity Secretariat) in the Montevideo local government starting in 2016.

The Feminist/Women's and LGBTIQ Movements in Uruguay: Organizational Dynamics and Lobbying Strategies

Feminist Activism in Uruguay: A Multisited Movement
As in several other Latin American countries, the second-wave Uruguayan women's movement has its roots in the resistance to the dictatorship in the early 1980s (Johnson 2000, chap. 3). As a result it developed as a dynamic

"multinodal" movement, spanning different spaces within civil society and extending across different spheres of public life. On the one hand, it includes organizations that espouse overtly feminist agendas as well as grassroots women's organizations that pursue "practical gender interests" (Molyneux 1985). The latter participate in national-level actions around demands central to the feminist agenda, on a case-by-case basis, and feminist actors pursue a permanent strategy of forging of ties with local women's organizations and grassroots women. On the other hand, in the early years of the postdictatorship period, many women's rights activists were active simultaneously in both social and institutional spheres, as members of political parties, civil society organizations, and/or the trade union movement. The 1990s saw a greater separation between these spheres of activism, with feminists opting to concentrate their militancy either within political parties or in the sphere of civil society. However, the links among them remained, whether on a formal or personal basis, and more or less intensively, depending on the specific issues being addressed and windows of political opportunity.

The 1990s also produced a greater NGOization (Alvarez 1999) and professionalization of the feminist movement. The lack of effective state structures and government policy on gender issues led many feminist organizations to fill this gap by providing advice and support services in the areas of domestic violence, reproductive health, and women's legal rights within the family and workplace. The specialist nature of these organizations was consolidated through their participation in issue networks at national and regional levels, and in transnational activism linked to events in the international gender rights agenda.[4] In parallel, feminists within political parties formed the Red de Mujeres Políticas (Political Women's Network, 1992), a cross-party coordination that aimed to strengthen women's political participation and promote attention to gender issues in parties and policy arenas. Following the Fourth United Nations (UN) World Conference on Women in Beijing in 1995, feminist and women's groups formed the Comisión Nacional de Seguimiento: Mujeres por Democracia, Equidad y Ciudadanía (National Follow-up Committee: Women for Democracy, Equity and Citizenship, or CNS Mujeres), to monitor government compliance with the international and regional agreements on women's rights endorsed by the Uruguayan state.

Under pressure from the women's movement to fulfill the commitments laid out in the Beijing Platform for Action, the Uruguayan government began to implement basic policies in areas such as employment, sexual and reproductive health, and gender-sensitivity and domestic violence training for police operators, very often funded by international cooperation. Given the neoliberal framework of state policy at the time, many of these services were outsourced to specialized women's NGOs. In contrast, a more articulated relationship developed between feminist organizations and the women's commission of the FA subnational government in Montevideo, under Mariella Mazzotti's leadership (Johnson 2004).Working jointly with women's NGOs, the commission's strategy aimed at promoting local-level organizing by poor women in neighborhoods with scarce resources through the Comuna Mujer (Women's Commune) program (Rodríguez Gustá 2012).

The Lesbian, Gay, Bisexual, and Transgender Movement

As in Argentina and Brazil, the LGBTIQ movement in Uruguay emerged only once the dictatorship was over.[5] The first gay organization was founded in 1984 during the transition to democracy. During the 1980s and 1990s, there was a token LGBTIQ movement, which in 1993 began to gain visibility with the annual Gay Pride March. The history of the Uruguayan LGBTIQ movement has been one of cooperation between single-identity organizations, although mixed organizations (with lesbian, gay, and transgender members) have been more successful in creating a public presence and achieving legal reforms and institutional change, due to the fact that local political culture tends to be less receptive to exclusively identity-based demands.

The electoral triumph of the FA in 2004 created a window of opportunity for collective action on LGBTIQ issues. New organizations emerged that politicized the struggle against discrimination in areas as yet unexplored, such as culture, academia, sports, and the cooperative movement (Sempol 2013). At the same time, the interpretative frames of the movement shifted. Led by members of Ovejas Negras (Black Sheep), an organization founded in 2004 that campaigns for LGBTIQ rights, the movement debated the need to situate their demands within the context of broader social struggles, in order to build a more just and equal social system. Thus, the LGBTIQ movement began to adopt an intersectional approach, based on the notion of equivalence between different types of discrimination and the understanding that Uruguayan society manifested a "phobia of diversity" in general. This innovative framework reconfigured the master frame of the sexual diversity movement. Its agenda broadened to include discrimination on the basis of gender and race-ethnicity, as well as sexual orientation and gender identity, and to explore the complex interaction with other structures of subalternity and the social class system.

The LGBTIQ movement believed that the FA should introduce a more complex vision of inequality if it were to elaborate a truly progressive agenda. The dispute between the movement and the FA over the meaning and scope of categories such as equality and social justice generated a cultural climate favorable for social mobilization during the successive FA national governments. This, together with the change in name from Gay Pride to the Diversity March in 2005, considerably strengthened the LGBTIQ movement's ability to mobilize support. Attendance at the march rose from an average 120–200 people between 2000 and 2004 to 20,000 in 2012 (*El Observador* 2012), and related activities extend throughout September. These innovations, which received extensive media coverage, began to produce social shifts and transformations in subjectivities. Participation in demonstrations and antidiscrimination actions was no longer limited to LGBTIQ people, and these spaces became highly integrative.

Movement Allies in Social and Political Arenas

In the twenty-first century, both the feminist and LGBTIQ movements prioritized a strategy of alliance building with other social movements with whom they could articulate agendas and coordinate mobilization and lobbying actions. CNS Mujeres became a node of coordination for social activism beyond the women's and feminist movement, including among its members development, human rights, union, LGBTIQ, environmentalist, and research organizations that shared gender equality as a dimension of their social struggle. Feminists also sought to build issue networks in support of specific policy claims. Thus feminists campaigning for the legalization of abortion forged an alliance with other progressive social actors to broaden their lobbying base, resulting in 2002 in the Coordinación Nacional de Organizaciones Sociales por la Defensa de la Salud Reproductiva (National Coordination of Social Organizations in Defense of Reproductive Health). This included feminist and women's organizations, influential social collectives (the union movement and some protestant churches), and institutional actors (such as the state university) (Johnson et al. 2015, 61).

Similarly, in 2007, non-LGBTIQ organizations began participating in the organizing committee of the Diversity March. In the same year, the slogan of the march embodied the two principal legislative campaigns on which LGBTIQ and feminist actors were coordinating at the time: sexual and reproductive health, including abortion, and consensual unions, including between same-sex couples. The consolidation of the articulation among different social movement agendas was reflected in the inclusion of demands not relating solely to the LGBTIQ population in the proclamations read during the Diversity Marches. For example, the 2009 Diversity March proclamation included affirmative actions for the Afro-Uruguayan and trans populations; the legalization of abortion and of marijuana cultivation for personal use; the annulment of the law preventing prosecution of human rights violations committed during the dictatorship; and the passing of a media regulation law.

The process of articulation among the sexual diversity, feminist, student, trade union, Afro-Uruguayan, and other social movements involved extensive dialogue, coordination, and mutual recognition, as well as the negotiation of agendas and political priorities. Although this process was not free from tensions, it did prove to be a successful strategy for making these movements' struggles more visible and opening up public debate, and especially for effective lobbying for legal change on specific issues. As part of their lobbying strategies, particularly after the FA came to power, feminist and LGBTIQ organizations developed alliances with critical actors in the legislative and executive arenas, often within the context of programs sponsored by UN agencies.

The growing presence of "gender-aware" legislators in the Uruguayan parliament represented a key point of access for the feminist movement. This was consolidated in 2000, when the three founders of the Red de Mujeres Políticas were all elected to the Chamber of Representatives, where they created the Bancada Femenina (Women's Bench), a cross-party women's caucus. The aim of the caucus was to represent women's interests in parliament, primarily through the promotion of bills on gender issues (Johnson 2014). Many important legislative gains resulted from strategic alliances between this caucus and feminist and women's movement activists (Johnson and Moreni 2011). The Bancada Femenina also intervened on several occasions in budgetary discussions to promote the strengthening of the national women's agency. In 2005, the caucus expanded to include female senators, becoming the Bancada Bicameral Femenina (Bicameral Women's Bench), and with the FA in government was dominated by left legislators. As a result, an effective multinodal policy network took shape, including the feminist movement, the women's caucus, and the national women's agency, as well as feminists who took up political posts in other state arenas.

Those female legislators who defined themselves as feminist also proved to be strategic allies, along with several male legislators, in the struggle to achieve legal recognition of LGBTIQ rights during the first ten years of FA government.

Although a few Partido Colorado (Colorado Party, or PC) or Partido Nacional (National Party or PN) legislators voted in favor of some bills, the main active allies of the LGBTIQ movement within parliament were FA legislators. LGBTIQ organizations also had access to midlevel executive officers, several of who proved to be open to dialogue and collaboration on the diversity agenda. As a result, the dynamics in this case took the form of alliances between the LGBTIQ movement and these critical actors in the legislative and executive branches to advance the diversity agenda from 2005 to 2015.

The fact that the FA feminists and other rights-friendly actors within the Left came from a number of different FA factions helped to overcome internal resistance and to sustain political discussion of these issues. However, these strategic allies, while present right across the FA, did not represent official party- or faction-wide positions. Rather they operated on the basis of their own personal convictions that these issues should be addressed, and in doing so constituted key nodes within a wider network of social and institutional actors.

Opposition to the Feminist and LGBTIQ Agendas: Religious Groups

As in many other Latin American countries, the greatest resistance to gender equality and sexual diversity agendas has come from the Catholic Church, which has maintained channels of influence over the political system despite the early secularization of the Uruguayan state. The Catholic hierarchy has repeatedly condemned the promotion of "gender ideology" in public policy and systematically opposed all legal advances on LGBTIQ rights. In 2003, the archbishop of Montevideo publicly declared that homosexuality was a "contagious disease" and "deviant," and that gays should be "isolated" from the rest of society (Brecha 2003). In recent years, a grassroots movement led by Pentecostal churches has emerged in support of "traditional family values" and against feminist and LGBTIQ rights issues, spearheading the "prolife" movement against the legalization of abortion.

These religious actors have close ties to the most conservative sectors of the Partido Colorado and in particular the Partido Nacional, which not only opposed all the legal gains in the new rights agenda over the last decade but also presented initiatives to roll back the rights won or to limit the legal conditions for establishing new rights. In the 2009 elections these religious actors began to pursue a dual strategy to win political leverage, either backing like-minded conservative candidates or fielding their own. However, it was not until 2014 that three evangelical deputies were elected within the ranks of the PN, leading to the formation of an official "evangelical caucus" (Schneider 2015).

However, it is not only with the traditional parties that we find evidence of "elective affinity" (Weber 1992) with Catholic beliefs or the Church hierarchy. Vázquez first publicly announced that he would veto any law legalizing abortion as he was leaving a meeting with the archbishop of Montevideo, and, as will be discussed below, other FA figures have attempted to block legislative advances in the new rights agenda on the basis of their religious convictions.

Institutional Structures

Under the FA governments institutional structures responsible for planning and overseeing gender policy were revitalized or created, and new antidiscrimination institutes were also put in place. While in the first case this process significantly strengthened the participation of institutional actors as part of the multinodal feminist network, in the second the initiative and scope of action of these institutions proved to be rather limited in the defense of LGBTIQ rights.

National Women's Agency

A national women's agency was first created in Uruguay in 1986, which in 1991 was assigned statewide responsibility for overseeing gender policy development and implementation. However, its low status and lack of budget left it with very limited potential for action. When the FA came to power, the women's agency was transferred to the newly created MIDES as the Instituto Nacional de las Mujeres (National Women's Institute, or INMUJERES). This move was welcomed by feminists as a more appropriate site from which to influence the social policies that the FA had announced would be the center of its government program. However, INMUJERES still lacked ministerial status and its own budget, raising doubts about its capacity to influence other state institutions or advance concrete measures itself.

INMUJERES' institutional weaknesses were partly offset in the first period by the capacity for political negotiation of its director, Carmen Beramendi, who had been national deputy from 1990 to 1995 and headed a FA think tank from 1997 to 2001. She also had a long history of activism on gender issues both within the FA and in social women's organizations, enabling successful articulation with women's movement organizations in policy implementation. In Mujica's administration, Beramendi was replaced by Beatriz Ramírez, an Afro-Uruguayan feminist who was active in both movements but who had less political capital and therefore less political leverage within the FA. Finally, in 2015 Vázquez appointed Mariella Mazzotti, who also had strong links to the feminist movement, had headed the women's commission in the Montevideo subnational government from 1995 to 2004, and occupied political posts in areas relating to citizen participation in first the MIDES and later the Montevideo subnational government from 2005 to 2014.

A critical advance in gender institutionalization was the passing in 2007 of law 18104 on "equal opportunities and rights," and the elaboration of the National Plan for Equal Opportunities and Rights (PIODNA), which provided a clear normative framework for gender policies. Under the leadership of INMUJERES, gender policy mechanisms were created in all ministries (see INMUJERES 2011, 2014). While these mechanisms were considered a crucial step toward statewide gender mainstreaming, some of these structures remained practically inoperative over the next ten years, lacking the status and capacity to influence organizational reform or development of gender policies in their respective sector (Guzman et al. 2014, 38). In contrast, those that were headed by feminists who had transferred to the state with the installation of the FA government—such as in the Ministerio del Interior and the Ministerio de Salud Pública (Public Health Ministry)—proved to be effective focal points for advancing gender policy aims.

The FA governments also strengthened existing or created new interinstitutional mechanisms to develop and monitor policy in specific areas. These mechanisms included participation by civil society representatives, in line with the Left's policy of promoting "social dialogue" and "citizen participation." While these spaces provided openings for social movements to participate formally in the policy-making process as valid political interlocutors, evaluation of these spaces by social activists is not completely favorable. Although in some cases they are considered key points of access for making policy claims, in others they are seen to be lacking real influence and badly managed, or as an attempt by government to co-opt support and defuse criticism from social movements (Pérez 2007; MYSU 2014).

Antidiscrimination Institutes

In August 2004, six months before the FA came to power, the parliament had passed law 17817 "against racism, xenophobia and discrimination," including for reasons of sexual orientation and identity. Over the following ten years, offices were created in three state bodies to receive complaints of discrimination:

the Comisión Honoraria de Lucha contra el Racismo, la Xenofobia y Toda Forma de Discriminación (Honorary Committee for the Fight against Racism, Xenophobia and All Forms of Discrimination) in the Ministerio de Educación y Cultura (Education and Culture Ministry, or MEC), founded in 2007; the Área de Denuncias e Investigación (Complaints and Investigation Section) of the Institución Nacional de Derechos Humanos y Defensoría del Pueblo (National Institution for Human Rights and Ombudsperson, or INDDHH), founded in 2012; and the Oficina de Denuncias y Asesoramiento (Complaints and Counselling Office) of the Inspección General del Trabajo y de la Seguridad Social (General Inspectorate of Work and Social Security) in the Ministerio de Trabajo y Seguridad Social (Work and Social Security Ministry, or MTSS), founded in 2010.

These offices have received few complaints of discrimination in general (249 over six years), and while the aggregated data from the three sources show that discrimination on the basis of sexual orientation and gender identity is the second most numerous category (19.2 percent) after racial discrimination (38.5 percent), by 2014, LGBTIQ organizations had identified just twelve cases of legal action taken on these grounds. Considering the visibility of the sexual diversity movement and the legislative and policy gains made in the period when these institutions have been functioning, and the resulting public politicization of sexuality and gender identity (Sempol 2013), the number of complaints received seems rather low.

This gap between the pervasiveness of discrimination on the basis of sexuality and gender identity and the low rate of denunciations registered in the specialized state offices may partly be due to the existence of social and economic barriers to access for the affected populations. However, it is also clearly the result of a lack of diffusion by these antidiscrimination institutes of the recently acquired rights, or of the procedures for registering complaints. Complainants have often confronted a lack of a response from the service, or have been represented by lawyers who do not have adequate training, or their claims have been dismissed on legal or administrative technicalities. These negative experiences may well deter other potential complainants from coming forward.

Two paradigmatic legal cases call into question the efficacy of the antidiscrimination law and the adequacy of institutional responses by both the antidiscrimination institutes and the judiciary. In July 2011, a member of a gay couple who had been thrown out of a bar for kissing filed a complaint with the police. When the case came to court, the district attorney requested that the case be shelved as there was "no evidence of criminal liability" or that discrimination had taken place (*La Diaria* 2011). A year later, Mercedes Rovira, the future rector of the Opus Dei–run Universidad de Montevideo (University of Montevideo) stated in a press interview that homosexuality was an "anomaly" that was "naturally taken into account" when employing teaching staff at the university (Draper and Peralta 2012). Her declarations were strongly repudiated—by Ovejas Negras, who threatened to take legal action against Rovira; by a six-hundred-strong demonstration that marched to the doors of the university; and in condemnatory statements by the Education and Labor ministers, as well as by the INDDHH. As a result, the Universidad de Montevideo decided not to appoint Rovira and publicly apologized, and Ovejas Negras therefore decided not to take legal action. The district attorney did, however, press charges, but in the end the judge absolved Rovira.

These cases reflect the growing denaturalization of acts of discrimination in that the denunciations made received strong social support, something that a decade ago was unheard of (Sempol 2013). However, it is also clear that the antidiscrimination laws and institutions are far from achieving their objectives in practice, despite offering a framework of guarantees.

Women's Rights and Gender Equality Policies

Implementing Women's Right to Be Elected

A legal milestone achieved at the end of the first FA administration was the passing of the quota law 18476, twenty-one years after the first quota bill was presented in parliament. While the law was strong in that it included a position mandate and sanctions for noncompliance,[6] its implementation at the parliamentary, departmental, and municipal level was restricted to a one-off application in the 2014–15 elections, thereby contradicting the basic principle of affirmative action. Furthermore, analysis of how parties applied the quota in the 2014 elections reveals how the effectiveness of the law was undermined (Johnson 2015). While the FA's overall performance was better than that of the PN or the PC, once the data are disaggregated by sector, we find that this is the result of one or two sectors presenting parity lists, while the Left's majority sectors replicate the same minimalist pattern as the traditional parties.

Ending Violence against Women

By the time the FA won the 2004 national elections, violence against women was already on the policy agenda. Following many years of lobbying by the women's movements and an intense campaign by the Bancada Femenina, in 2002 the Uruguayan parliament passed law 17514 on "prevention, treatment and eradication of domestic violence," which provided a basic normative framework for policy design. The FA also had experience in developing policies on violence against women in the Montevideo government, where it introduced legal and psychological support for low-income victims of domestic violence and installed a helpline that later provided country-wide coverage.

In the first FA national government, violence against women was given top priority by INMUJERES. Its director, Carmen Beramendi, had presented in 1991 the first bill on domestic violence during her term in parliament, and was also active in the NGO Mujer Ahora, which provides support to battered women. INMUJERES implemented a program of integral support services for female victims of domestic violence, and extended psychological and legal counseling beyond the capital city, often in partnership with specialist NGOs. In the second FA government, under the directorship of Beatriz Ramírez, INMUJERES continued to prioritize violence against women. The number of support centers increased, including a mobile unit, and a protocol was introduced to guarantee the use of a unified human rights perspective in attention to victims. In terms of policy governance, the Consejo Nacional Consultivo de Lucha contra la Violencia Doméstica (National Advisory Council to Combat Domestic Violence) is the interinstitutional body responsible for developing and evaluating policy in this area. The council is chaired by INMUJERES and provides a formal channel of participation for civil society actors; initially it functioned rather erratically, but in the FA's second term it began to play a more effective role (Herrera et al. 2012).

However, the main determinant of advances in policy development on violence against women was the presence of feminists in middle-management positions in different ministries. In the Ministerio de Salud Pública, the Programa Nacional de Salud de la Mujer y Género (National Women's Health and Gender Program) introduced a protocol on domestic violence for all health service providers, including prevention and attention in cases of sexual abuse, as part of the reform of the national health system. Gender-based violence also was included as a topic in teacher training, through the Programa de Educación Sexual Integral (Integral Sex Education Program), created in 2006. The normative frame of these policies determined that women's physical integrity was a basic human right; that male aggressors should take responsibility for their actions; and that the state ought to provide full guarantees to enable women to effectively exercise their rights.

Undoubtedly the greatest policy advances in violence against women took place in the Ministerio del Interior. Here the person responsible for policy development from 2007 until the end of the Mujica administration was Marisa Lindner, another feminist with a long history of activism in NGOs combating violence against women. She had also worked in the Montevideo government's Comuna Mujer program and in INMUJERES on the development of the PIODNA. Using the strategic support of UN agencies, Lindner successfully achieved the institutionalization of the ministry's policy on violence against women.

Crucial elements in her success were the creation of an institutional space specifically dedicated to the development of gender policy within the Ministerio del Interior; the fact that Lindner's policy actions were positively valued by other movement and state feminists; the legitimacy deriving from the support of the UN; and the incorporation of the language of human rights by the ministry. Feminist organizations commend the fact that data on domestic violence are systematically gathered and published by the ministry, and that the institutional discourse on security now recognizes that women are at greatest risk "at home and that that is a problem that cannot be resolved simply by assigning more police."[7]

Overall, then, the FA government's policies on violence against women advanced thanks to an active women's movement and the leadership of state femocrats with roots in the feminist movement. While they were appointed to these posts for their record as party activists (rather than feminists), they came with a clear feminist agenda and aimed to design and implement multidimensional policies. Another key element in the success of policy development in this area was the Uruguayan government's successful application in 2012 for funding from the UN Trust Fund to eradicate violence against women, which gave it resources to execute in partnership with specialist NGOs. This strengthened the multisited feminist "triangle" that emerged around this policy issue and provided resources and tools for policy implementation.

Nonetheless, shortcomings persist in this policy area, relating to loopholes in the human rights framework informing the law on domestic violence and to limited state capacities. Despite the fact that state feminists have sought to introduce a conceptual shift centered on the notion of gender-based violence and violence against women, the law refers explicitly to "domestic" violence, which constrains political discourse and policy actions. Another obstacle is the lack of adequate infrastructure, with insufficient counseling centers, refuges, and housing and employment opportunities for victims of violence, a situation that leaves women unprotected, particularly in less-populated areas. Feminists and NGOs that work with female victims of violence have also criticized the lack of a committed judiciary, which often revictimizes women, leaving them without due protection and failing to provide an effective response. In June 2012, over one hundred organizations presented a petition demanding that the Suprema Corte de Justicia (Supreme Court of Justice, or SCJ) respond to unacceptable legal and forensic practices. Almost six months later, the SCJ acknowledged the legitimacy of a large part of the petition, and ordered legal operators to align their practices with the law (Mujer Ahora 2017). Despite this important victory, feminist and women's organizations insist on the need for a new law on gender violence and the transformation of the judiciary's treatment of such cases.

Sexual and Reproductive Rights and Health

Uruguay was one of the first Latin American countries to develop policies in sexual and reproductive (SR) health. Though initially these policies had a strong maternalist focus, they began to be framed in terms of SR rights following the UN Conferences in Cairo (1994) and Beijing (1995) (López Gómez and Abracinskas 2009). Under the FA governments the SR rights perspective was deepened within the context of the global reform of the national health system (2007), the main purpose of which was to guarantee universal access to quality services on the grounds that health is a fundamental human right. Nonetheless, changes in this area did not come smoothly, and at certain junctures tensions surfaced between the officially adopted rights framework and continuing resistance among some of the FA leadership, in particular around the feminist demand for safe and legal abortion.

By the time the FA came to power in 2005, the legalization of abortion had been transformed from an exclusively feminist issue into a broader citizen claim (Abracinskas and López Gómez 2007). This was partly the result of feminists' strategic reframing of the demand in terms of women's right to abort without placing their lives in danger, as part of their broader SR rights and within a wider conceptual framework of social justice and democratic consolidation (Johnson et al. 2015, 60), which enabled them to build a broad-based alliance with other social organizations. Also crucial in consolidating the issue on the public agenda was the fact that early in the twenty-first century, a group of doctors from the country's main public maternity hospital (who later formed the Iniciativas Sanitarias [Health Initiatives]), joined in the abortion debate due to their concern with the high rates of maternal mortality caused by unsafe abortions.

These medical actors proved to be critical in giving added visibility to the abortion debate and legitimacy to the demand for state action on this issue. They also allied with feminists to promote the SR rights focus in other policy initiatives, but they did not join the broad social front campaigning for the legalization of abortion. In fact, although the discourses of both collectives—feminists and doctors—overlapped, the fact that the medical discourse was restricted to sanitary aspects generated tensions between them at certain junctures (Johnson et al. 2015, 65–69). In 2004, Iniciativas Sanitarias made a successful bid to institutionalize pre- and postabortion attention for women (ministerial decree 369/04), which drastically cut maternal mortality rates. This led one of the collective's members (who was later appointed vice-minister of Health in Mujica's government) to conclude that there was no longer any need to legalize abortion, effectively dismissing the legitimacy of the other dimensions of the feminist movement's discursive framing of the issue.

Nonetheless, in the first FA national administration, the broad social front of feminists and their allies, together with key feminist representatives, in particular FA senator Mónica Xavier and deputy Margarita Percovich, successfully pushed through a bill "in defense of the right to SR health," which included the decriminalization of abortion as one of a comprehensive series of policy actions. This victory was short-lived, however, as Vázquez immediately vetoed the articles on abortion. He based his veto on his personal convictions, disregarding not only the favorable position on the issue held by his own political party and by parliament but also the majority (63 percent) of public who were in favor of the law (Johnson et al. 2011).

In the run-up to the next presidential election, in 2009, the UTDC ensured that the legalization of abortion was explicitly included in the FA's government program, while feminist civil society activists used a campaigning event organized by the FA's presidential formula to oblige Mujica to publicly state his position on abortion. In contrast to Vázquez, Mujica declared that he would not veto an abortion law passed by parliament. By the end of 2011, the Senate had passed a new bill, presented by thirteen FA senators. However, there were not enough votes to get it through the lower house because—in addition to opposition from the PN and PC—four FA deputies opposed the bill, two of them on grounds of religious beliefs.

Faced with this impasse, feminist left senators Mónica Xavier and Constanza Moreira, together with male allies in the FA's bench in both houses, set out to convince their fellow party members, and were successful with all but one of the religious objectors. They then negotiated the final vote that was needed with one of just two deputies from the small Partido Independiente, who had himself presented a bill to decriminalize abortion. This negotiation, while successfully ensuring the passing of the law, resulted in the loss of the original initiative's clear feminist frame. Abortion was no longer defined in terms of women's right to decide; rather it remained a crime, with the penalty suspended under specific circumstances. In addition, women's autonomous decision making was limited by the introduction of a compulsory process of counseling and "reflection" before the abortion could be performed. The complex process leading to the decriminalization of abortion clearly illustrates the ambiguous attitude of the Left toward key feminist policy claims.

The conservative opposition (Catholic and Evangelical Churches and some sectors of the PN and PC) immediately sought to overturn the law. They managed to gather sufficient signatures to support a plebiscite (set for June 2013), which would decide whether a referendum on derogation should be held. Again, the FA sent out mixed signals. Although the Plenario Nacional (National Plenary) of the FA resolved that it should undertake a campaign in support of the law, in practice the idea prevailed that campaigning would just give the issue visibility (something to be avoided since the plebiscite was voluntary). President Mujica signed the petition in support of the plebiscite as the "most democratic" way of resolving the issue, while ex-president Vázquez went a step further and actually turned out to vote in June. Only in the final run-up to the plebiscite did the FA's prominent feminist activists—Constanza Moreira, the UTDC, and Mónica Xavier, by then president of the FA—come out publicly in support of the law. Again, it was the feminist movement and other social organizations (including LGBTIQ collectives) that campaigned most actively against the plebiscite. In the end, the plebiscite fell well short of the mark,[8] with only 8 percent of voters supporting the initiative.

The policy record of the two FA governments on SR rights in other areas is also patchy. Among the achievements was a restructuring of the institutional architecture responsible for SR health, first with the creation of the Programa Nacional de Salud de la Mujer y Género in the Ministerio de Salud Pública, which was headed by Cristina Grela, a feminist gynecologist who had founded the Latin American branch of Catholics for a Free Choice in the 1980s. Under the leadership of Grela and other committed medical professionals in mid-level state management positions (many from Iniciativas Sanitarias), a "Plan for Sexual and Reproductive Health" was created in 2010, which made provision of SR health services an obligation for all health care providers country-wide. The plan institutionalized training for medical staff in human rights, gender, and sexual diversity perspectives, and gender-sensitive protocols and guides to health care became part of regular medical practice. It also guaranteed universal access to contraceptive methods in both public and private health care services, thus achieving an unprecedented level of coverage. In the same year, the programs for women's health and gender, violence and health, men's health, and STD-AIDS were brought together under the umbrella Área de Salud Sexual y Reproductiva (Sexual and Reproductive Health Area).

In terms of policy governance, the Comisión Nacional Asesora en Salud Sexual y Reproductiva (National Advisory Committee on Sexual and Reproductive Health), created in 2004 a space for state and civil society actors to debate policy initiatives and follow up on state actions, was weakened after Vázquez vetoed the decriminalization of abortion, when most social organizations withdrew. By contrast, the Comisión Nacional de SIDA (National AIDS Committee), created in 2005, started functioning regularly in 2008, due to the active engagement of social collectives pursuing diversity issues.

In addition, SR policies face implementation difficulties. For example, smaller rural locations do not have access to SR health services. Also, many medical professionals continue to reproduce the maternalist paradigm or are openly antiabortion, in direct contradiction to official policy. With respect to abortion provision, overall there is a 30 percent rate of "conscientious objection" among gynecologists (the only professionals authorized to perform abortions), which in one department in the north of the country rises to 100 percent, and two health care providers have claimed "ideological objection" (MYSU 2014). Thus, even once these policies are in place, stumbling blocks remain at the micro level due to actors' resistance, and limited state capacities to regulate and provide services.

Employment and Unpaid Care Work

Redistributive policies have been a central pillar of the FA's social policy, though they have generally been informed by traditional conceptions of gender roles and the family. One policy issue that originated in the women's movement and was presented by the FA as a priority for the Mujica administration as part of the overhaul of Uruguay's welfare system was the creation of a Sistema Nacional Integrado de Cuidados (Integrated National Care System, or SNIC) for the elderly, children from zero to five years old, and the disabled.

Since the end of the 1990s, feminists in the women's movement and at the state university (who formed the Red Género y Familia [Gender and Family Network] in 1996) have insisted on the need for the Uruguayan state to design policies to deal with the consequences of the second demographic transition,[9] and once the FA was in power they redoubled their efforts to lobby for action on this issue (Johnson et al. 2009).

This time the critical actors allied with the feminists were the policy team in the Dirección Nacional de Política Social of the MIDES, headed by Andrés Scagliola, who led a far-reaching dialogue among state and civil society actors on the issue in 2010–11. Underlying the debate on the SNIC was a framing contest between, on the one hand, the feminist movement and their allies within the state, and on the other hand, other civil society and political actors who were resistant to recognizing gender equality as a central issue in the design of the SNIC (Aguirre and Ferrari 2014, 37–38). However, the policy design document that emerged from this process stated that the system would strengthen social welfare and "address one of the many bases of inequality among people, in this case, between women and men: the sexual division of labor" (Grupo de Trabajo Interinstitucional 2012, 8). In 2011, a similar "Dialogue for Employment" produced a policy document highlighting the need for measures promoting work-life balance and joint parental responsibility (Salvador 2013).

At least initially, then, the blueprint for care policies was attuned to feminist claims. However, in subsequent years the implementation of this reform has been piecemeal and come up against important obstacles. In July 2013, top government authorities stated that for budgetary reasons the SNIC would not be implemented according to the policy design document. Funds were instead channeled to "priority" programs originally aimed at "poverty reduction" but subsequently reframed in government discourse as "care policies." However, gender analyses of these programs indicate that they are based on maternalist principles, lack a gender equality perspective, and do not promote women's empowerment or shared responsibility between women and men for child care (Balsa Ruella 2014). New legislation passed in 2013 did no more than extend parental leave in line with International Labor Organization (ILO) standards. Rosario Aguirre and Fernanda Ferrari (2014, 56–61) conclude that the implementation of a truly integrated and coordinated SNIC has come up against the lack of an earmarked budget, institutional fragmentation and inertia, the lack of top-level political will and leadership, and tension between the SNIC's universalist goal and the implementation of targeted programs focused on poverty reduction.

In terms of labor market regulation, the most significant advance was the 2006 law to regulate domestic work, an initiative of INMUJERES and allies at the MTSS. Domestic workers gained basic labor and collective negotiation rights, and union liberties (Márquez Garmendia 2011). INMUJERES and feminist organizations, particularly Cotidiano Mujer (Everyday Woman), engaged in a multisited campaign to inform domestic workers of their newly acquired rights and get employers to register them. In 2011, legal advice and litigation support were made available to unionized domestic workers through the state university and social insurance authority. However, despite these efforts, it is calculated that 48.2 percent of domestic workers were still working informally in 2013 (Bené 2014), a situation that exceeds the Ministerio de Trabajo limited inspection capacity.

LGBTIQ Rights Policies

Legal Advances: Consensual Unions, Adoption by Same-Sex Couples, and Same-Sex Marriage

In December 2007, Uruguay became the first country in Latin America to pass a national-level law governing consensual unions including between same-sex couples.[10] The law was passed with the votes of the FA and some PC legislators, while almost all PN legislators in both chambers opposed the bill on the grounds that it undermined traditional visions of the family. The law responded to the profound transformations that had been taking place in Uruguayan society. The number of couples choosing not to get married had tripled in less than twenty years (from 10 percent in 1987 to 30 percent in 2004), and this tendency was especially marked among younger age groups (Cabella 2006, 57).

The original bill, presented by FA deputy Margarita Percovich, did not cover same-sex couples, who were subsequently included as a result of the pressure brought to bear by LGBTIQ activists. While Percovich managed to build unanimous backing for the bill among FA legislators—despite the fact that it did not figure among the Left's policy commitments—the growing mobilization by LGBTIQ organizations demanding legal protection for same-sex couples ensured the issue entered the public agenda.

The strategy to push through laws on consensual unions and the reform of the Children's and Adolescents' Code, which would allow same-sex couples to adopt, was devised by Percovich in 2007. Once same-sex couples could legally formalize their unions, the reform of the Children's Code was presented, which included modifying the adoption system to allow all couples—both married and in consensual unions—to adopt children. The reform thus gave same-sex couples the right to adopt by extension, even though they were not named explicitly in the new code. The promoters of the new code strategically framed the reform in terms of the right of all children to legal parity, regardless of what kind of family they came from. This strategy preempted the argument offered by opponents of the reform counterposing children's rights to the rights of same-sex couples to adopt, as had occurred in Spain.

From 2009 on, the growth of the LGBTIQ movement and the expansion of its wider social base of support further increased its capacity to wield political influence and instigate legal reforms. Despite it being an electoral year, in 2009 LGBTIQ activists successfully lobbied FA legislators to push through a law allowing trans people to change their name and sex in the civil registry. Originally presented by Percovich, the bill was not considered a priority by the rest of the FA bench, who considered that the two laws already passed covered the most pressing issues for the LGBTIQ population, and were also reluctant for a potentially polemical issue to gain public attention during the electoral campaign. However, members of Ovejas Negras exploited informal channels of contact with FA deputies, managing ultimately to convince them of the urgency of this measure to ensure the social integration of the trans population. The law was finally passed in October, just thirteen days before the national elections.

Following this victory, the movement took the initiative and proposed a reform of the civil code that would legalize same-sex marriage. The bill was drawn up by Dr. Michelle Suàrez, Uruguay's first trans lawyer, and Ovejas Negras led efforts to promote social and political debate on the issue between 2010 and 2013. A broad coalition of social organizations (including non-LGBTIQ) emerged in support of the reform. These actors organized hundreds of events throughout the country to explain the scope of the bill, with an emphasis on the principle of legal and symbolic equality underpinning the proposal. They also carried out public information campaigns with participation by leading figures from the cultural sphere, which had a crucial impact on public opinion: while in 2005, 58 percent of Uruguayans were against same-sex marriage, by 2013, 54 percent of the population were in favor of the law (Centro de Estudios de Género y Diversidad Sexual n.d.) In parallel, LGBTIQ activists held countless meetings with FA representatives in parliament, thus securing the votes needed to get the bill passed. The success of the public campaign in support of the law and the backing of the entire FA bench also convinced several legislators from other parties to support the bill, and it was voted through by a large majority in April 2013.

Public Policies for Trans People

Beyond legislating a gender identity recognition law, Uruguay is the first country in the world to develop affirmative action policies for the trans population. These too resulted from the alliance forged between LGBTIQ organizations and critical actors in the MIDES, in particular Scagliola, the director of social policy. The first measures adopted were designed to raise awareness among the ministry's employees and generate data on the situation of trans people in Uruguay.[11] Subsequently, a ministerial resolution was signed in September 2012 granting all trans people unconditional access to the Tarjeta Uruguay Social (Uruguay Social Card) program (which gives beneficiaries a monthly subsidy to spend on food and cleaning products), on the grounds of the "extreme social exclusion" that trans people suffer in Uruguayan society (MIDES 2012).

This was the first time that the MIDES applied an affirmative action criterion in its social redistribution policies. The decision to implement a targeted policy of this kind implied recognizing that different forms of social inequality exist that cannot all be measured by the same instruments. By October 2014, 786 trans people were receiving this benefit. This measure was further consolidated by a package of affirmative actions for the trans population adopted between 2012 and 2014, including a quota in various work training and labor market insertion programs implemented by the MIDES and the Instituto Nacional de la Juventud (National Youth Institute) in which critical actors also held posts during the Mujica administration.

Sex Education

However, dialogue between the LGBTIQ movement and the state was not fruitful in all areas, especially where there were no critical actors with real political power within the bureaucracy. For example, LGBTIQ activists made few inroads into the education sector, where the Catholic Church maintains a good degree of influence due to its strong presence in the private education sector, and where educational actors sustained conservative attitudes toward the issue of sexuality and particularly sexual diversity. Although a sex education program introducing this subject in public high schools and technical education centers was created in 2006, three years later the program lost its funding. Although the program has continued working, the lack of staff and resources has significantly delayed any transformation of the system.

Meanwhile, both feminist and sexual diversity organizations have tried to help strengthen sex education by producing manuals for teachers to introduce issues of sex and sexuality in the classroom. However, some school authorities in the public education system and the Consejo Directivo Central (Central Governing Council, or CODICEN) itself have put up strong resistance. The CODICEN blocked distribution of a sex education kit in 2012, and a guide to education and sexual diversity in 2015—both of which had been requested and approved by midlevel educational authorities, revealing the persistence of strong ideological and political disputes in this area.

Bodily Autonomy and Health Policies

Advances and setbacks have also been registered in the area of LGBTIQ health issues. Despite civil society–based advocacy, sex-reassignment surgery has become less accessible than when it first became available in 1991 at the university hospital. With an average delay of eight years for operations, by 2010 a total of only fifteen had been performed, and many transsexuals had resorted to going to Chile. In 2010, Ovejas Negras initiated a dialogue with the directors of the hospital to propose drafting a protocol that would reduce waiting time to two years and guarantee male transsexuals the prosthesis they need to make the sex-reassignment operation functional. They also requested the creation of a special health center to concentrate and coordinate all the services required in health care for transsexuals. Unfortunately, in the end the protocol was never applied, and in 2012 the hospital stopped performing sex reassignment surgery, because the hospital director considered that both these operations and mastectomies were "not a priority" (Aparicio 2013).

In view of the fact that LGBTIQ people continued to confront problems of access and misdiagnoses (since doctors assume heterosexual behavior), pilot projects, involving state, academic, and LGBTIQ movement actors, and with funding from the UN Population Fund, were set up to create homophobia-free health care centers at the primary level. This experience is now being institutionalized throughout the entire network of primary health care centers in the country.

Conclusions

This review of the first two left national governments in Uruguay has shown that the rise of the FA to power provided openings for significant gains in key areas of both the feminist and sexual diversity agendas.

In the first case, advances were made in legislation and in executive policy development on SR rights, including abortion, some aspects of violence against women, and domestic workers' rights. However, these advances are not simply the result of a convergence between the Left's agenda and feminist claims. In fact, on occasion some feminist demands have been directly rejected or more subtly resisted by powerful actors within the Left. The blocking of the legalization of abortion—a measure approved by the FA's maximum authority, the Congress—by individuals within the Left raises questions about the strength of the commitment of the Left as a whole to the new rights agenda, and also about how it functions internally in terms of democratic practices. Nonetheless, the consolidation of a multinodal policy network of feminist actors in the legislature and within key state institutions, as well as a stronger national mechanism for the advancement of women, has facilitated the entry of central feminist demands onto the government agenda. It is also clear that it is highly unlikely that these advances would have been made were it not for the active feminist and women's movements, which have pushed first to get certain issues debated in the public arena, and then to ensure that they do not later "slide off" the agenda and that the emphasis on gender equality does not dissipate during their translation into policy issues.

Similar conclusions can be drawn about the advances in LGBTIQ rights. Perhaps even more so in this case, gains in new legislation were first presented by activists who subsequently engaged in targeted lobbying of key legislators who would accompany the bills, ensuring a favorable vote by the rest of the left parliamentary bench as well as allies in other parties. While advances in policy design and implementation have been more limited, partly because the normative framework was established much more recently, once again key actors, for example, in the MIDES, have promoted policy measures such as affirmative actions. This has changed the face of the political agenda on sexual diversity over the last ten years. As has happened with advances on feminist issues, the challenge for the LGBTIQ movement will be to monitor closely future state actions to ensure that the legal gains effectively translate into policy advances on the ground and that the institutional structures in place to combat discrimination become effective mechanisms of redress.

While the third FA administration came to office in March 2015 with a slightly smaller parliamentary majority and the consolidated presence of more conservative religious actors among the democratically elected opposition, feminist and LGBTIQ actors have also gained organic spaces within the left coalition. This is particularly the case of the new sector that has emerged under the leadership of the feminist senator Constanza Moreira, who in 2014 became the first woman to compete for the presidential nomination within the FA. Her candidacy won the support of many nonaligned FA members who were disillusioned with the hegemony of certain large factions within the left coalition, the lukewarm commitment to the new rights agenda, and the lack of renovation in the ranks of the FA's main leadership and candidates. Moreira's programmatic platform included feminist priorities (such as parity in political representation and the creation of a national care system) and the expansion and consolidation of LGBTIQ rights, as well as other issues from the more radical left agenda (for instance, reduction of the armed forces, increase in the education budget, and sustainable development). Moreover, the factions that supported her included among their candidates many feminist and LGBTIQ activists, as well as a high proportion of young party militants. Despite the sustained opposition of the main FA factions to Moreira's candidacy and her clear disadvantage in terms of campaigning resources, she won 18 percent of the FA vote in the internal elections and went on to retain her seat in the Senate, while the supporting factions also won two seats in the lower house. This novel presence of an FA sector that foregrounds gender equality and LGBTIQ rights issues and actors may signal the beginning of a truly renewed left politics in Uruguay.

Notes

We would like to thank the discussants and participants at the LASA Congress of 2016 for their feedback on our chapter.

1. See the "Political Agenda" presented by CNS Mujeres to presidential candidates in 1999, 2000, and 2004. In 2004, the feminist collective Cotidiano Mujer launched the "50/50 Campaign," demanding a parity cabinet, and in 2014, together with CNS Mujeres and Ciudadanías en Red (Citizens' Network), presented political leaders with over 4,000 signatures supporting a parity law for parliamentary elections.

2. Before 2005 only one female minister had held office at any one time (out of a total of thirteen portfolios); Vázquez's first administration included a maximum of four, and Mujica's government a maximum of two (Johnson 2013, 19).

3. This was the socialist Daisy Tourné, Minister of the Interior from 2006 to 2007.

4. For participation at national levels, see Red Uruguaya contra la Violencia Doméstica y Sexual (Uruguayan Network against Domestic and Sexual Violence or RUVDS, created 1992); Red Género y Familia (Gender and Family Network, 1994); and Mujer y Salud en Uruguay (Women and Health in Uruguay or MYSU, 1996). For participation at regional levels, see Red de Salud de las Mujeres de América Latina y el Caribe (Women's Health Network of Latin America and the Caribbean

or RSMLAC), Red Feminista de América Latina y el Caribe contra la Violencia hacia la Mujer (Feminist Network of Latin America and the Caribbean against Violence Against Women), and Articulación Feminista Marcosur (Marcosur Feminist Articulation or AFM).

5. For a history of the LGBTIQ movement in Uruguay, see Sempol (2013).

6. The law requires that candidates of both sexes be included in every three consecutive places on all electoral lists; lists that do not comply will not be registered by the electoral authorities.

7. Feminist social activist, interview with authors, October 15, 2014, Montevideo.

8. The support of at least 25 percent of the electorate was needed to call the referendum.

9. This was producing an aging population with a low fertility rate and high levels of women's workforce participation.

10. The regional precedents had been much more limited: in Argentina civil unions were legalized in the city of Buenos Aires and the province of Río Negro, while in Mexico gay marriage had been approved only in the federal capital.

11. In 2012, six hundred MIDES employees attended training courses on discrimination and sexual diversity, and all the forms used by the ministry to gather information included the categories "male trans" and "female trans."

References

Abracinskas, Lilián, and Alejandra López Gómez. 2007. "El aborto en la agenda social: El involucramiento de la ciudadanía a favor del cambio legal." In *Aborto en debate: Dilemas y desafíos del Uruguay democrático*, 11–29. Montevideo: MYSU/IWHC.

Aguirre, Rosario, and Fernanda Ferrari. 2014. *La construcción del sistema de cuidados en el Uruguay: En busca de consensos para una protección social más igualitaria*. Santiago, Chile: CEPAL.

Alvarez, Sonia. E. 1999. "Advocating Feminism: The Latin American Feminist NGO 'Boom.'" *International Feminist Journal of Politics* 1 (2): 181–209.

Aparicio, Anabella. 2013. "Clínicas ya no hace mastectomías por falta de presupuesto." *El Observador*, May 17. Accessed June 27, 2017. http://www.elobservador.com.uy/clinicas-ya-no-hace-mastectomias-falta-presupuesto-n250965.

Armstrong, Elizabeth A., and Mary Bernstein. 2008. "Culture, Power, and Institutions: A Multi-Institutional Politics Approach to Social Movements." *Sociological Theory* 26 (1): 74–99.

Bacchi, Carol. 1999. *Women, Policy, and Politics: The Construction of Policy Problems*. London: SAGE.

Balsa Ruella, Silvana. 2014. "La igualdad de género: La bandera ausente en el buque insignia del gobierno de Mujica: Análisis del caso de 'Uruguay Crece Contigo.'" Unpublished BA diss., Instituto de Ciencia Política, Facultad de Ciencias Sociales, Universidad de la República (ICP-FCS-UDELAR).

Bené, Nicolas. 2014. "Evasion en puestos de trabajo: Año 2013." *Comentarios de Seguridad Social* 46 (October–December): 137–48.

Benford, Robert D., and David A. Snow. 2000. "Framing Processes and Social Movements: An Overview." *Annual Review of Sociology* 26:611–39.

Brecha. 2003. "Alerta: El 'virus' gay es 'contagioso.' Iglesia Católica y homosexualidad." *Semanario Brecha*, August 22: 14.

Cabella, Wanda. 2006. "La demografía de las uniones consensuales en Uruguay en la última década." In *El proyecto de ley de unión concubinaria*, 57–62. Montevideo: Trilce-Red Género y Familia.

Centro de Estudios de Género y Diversidad Sexual. N.d. "Archivo de encuestas sobre la opinión de la ciudadanía uruguaya acerca de el reconocimiento de los derechos de la diversidad sexual." Accessed February 26, 2018. http://www.generoydiversidad.org/estadisticas.php.

Charles, Nickie, and Fiona Mackay. 2013 "Feminist Politics and Framing Contests: Domestic Violence Policy in Scotland and Wales." *Critical Social Policy* 33 (4): 593–615.

Childs, Sarah, and Mona L. Krook. 2009. "Analysing Women's Substantive Representation: From Critical Mass to Critical Actors." *Government and Opposition* 44 (2): 125–45.

CNS Mujeres. 2009. *Agenda 2009. Una propuesta política de las mujeres organizadas.* Montevideo: CNS Mujeres.

CNS Mujeres. 2004. *Agenda. Una propuesta política de las mujeres.* Montevideo: CNS Mujeres.

CNS Mujeres. 1999. *Agenda de las mujeres.* Montevideo: CNS Mujeres.

Draper, Guillermo, and José Peralta. 2012. "La homosexualidad es una 'anomalía' y es 'obvio que juega' al designar docentes, dice la rectora de la Universidad de Montevideo." *Semanario Búsqueda*, July 12: 52.

El Observador. 2012. "Miles de personas marcharon por la diversidad." September 28. Accessed June 28, 2017. http://www.elobservador.com.uy/miles-personas-marcharon-la-diversidad-n233622.

El País. 2013. "El FA se entretiene con unión igualitaria." January 30. Accessed June 27, 2017. http://historico.elpais.com.uy/13/01/30/pnacio_692127.asp.

Fraser, Nancy. 1997. *Justice Interruptus: Critical Reflections on the "Postsocialist" Condition.* New York: Routledge.

Grupo de Trabajo Interinstitucional. 2012. *Hacia un modelo solidario de cuidados.* Montevideo: Consejo Nacional de Política Social-MIDES, Gabinete Social.

Guzman, Virgina, Carla Frías, and Ana Agostino. 2014. *Evaluación del "Primer plan de igualdad de oportunidades y derechos, 2007–2011."* Montevideo: INMUJERES-MIDES.

Hall, Peter. 1993. "Policy Paradigms, Social Learning, and the State: The Case of Economic Policymaking in Britain." *Comparative Politics* 25 (3): 275–96.

Herrera, Teresa (coord.). 2012. *Evaluación del plan nacional de lucha contra la violencia doméstica. Informe final.* Montevideo: Aire.uy Asociación Interdisciplinaria.

Holli, Anne M. 2008. "Feminist Triangles: A Conceptual Analysis." *Representation* 44 (2): 169–85.

Htun, Mala, and S. Laural Weldon. 2010. "When Do Governments Promote Women's Rights? A Framework for the Comparative Analysis of Sex Equality Policy." *Perspectives on Politics* 8 (1): 207–16.

INMUJERES. 2011. *Rendición de cuentas 2010 en la implementación del "Plan nacional de igualdad de oportunidades y derechos entre hombres y mujeres."* Montevideo: INMUJERES-MIDES. Accessed June 10, 2017. http://www.inmujeres.gub.uy /innovaportal/file/18217/1/rendicion_2010_de_los_avances_en_la_ejecucion_del _piodna.pdf.

INMUJERES. 2014. *Proceso institucional del "Primer plan de igualdad de oportunidades y derechos (PIODNA)."* Montevideo: INMUJERES-MIDES. Accessed June 10, 2017. http://www.inmujeres.gub.uy/innovaportal/file/25958/1/proceso -institucional.pdf.

Johnson, Niki. 2000. "'The Right to Have Rights': Gender Politics, Citizenship and the State in Uruguay, 1985–1996." Unpublished PhD diss., Queen Mary University of London.

Johnson, Niki. 2004. "Mecanismos Estatales para el Avance de las Mujeres en el Uruguay." En *Perspectivas de género en las políticas públicas*, 43–54. Montevideo: Cotidiano Mujer.

Johnson, Niki. 2005. *La política de la ausencia: Las elecciones uruguayas (2004/2005), las mujeres, y la equidad de género*. Montevideo: CNS Mujeres/ ICP-FCS-Udelar.

Johnson, Niki. 2013. *Mujeres en cifras: El acceso de las mujeres a espacios de poder en Uruguay*. Montevideo: Cotidiano Mujer.

Johnson, Niki. 2014. "La Bancada Femenina en Uruguay: Un 'actor crítico' para la representación sustantiva de las mujeres en el parlamento." *América Latina Hoy* 66:145–65.

Johnson, Niki. 2015. "Parte I: El impacto de la cuota en la representación descriptiva de las mujeres en las elecciones uruguayas 2014." In *¿Renovación, paridad? Una mirada feminista sobre género y representación política en las elecciones uruguayas 2014*, 21–103. Montevideo: Cotidiano Mujer/ICP-FCS-UDELAR.

Johnson, Niki, Florencia Cabrera, and Noelia Maciel. 2009. *Los cuidados de la niñez: Un desafío para la transversalidad de género en el estado uruguayo, 2005–2009*. Montevideo: FESUR.

Johnson, Niki, Alejandra López, and Marcela Schenck. 2011. "La sociedad civil ante la despenalización del aborto: Opinión pública y movimientos sociales." In *(Des) penalización del aborto en Uruguay: Prácticas, actores y discursos: Abordaje interdisciplinario sobre una realidad compleja*, 237–263. Montevideo: CSIC-UDELAR.

Johnson, Niki, and Alejandra Moreni. 2011. *De una pequeña minoría a una masa crítica: 10 años de la Bancada Bicameral Femenina en el parlamento del Uruguay*. Montevideo: BBF-Parlamento del Uruguay-AECID-PNUD-ONU Mujeres.

Johnson, Niki, and Verónica Pérez. 2010. *Representación (s)electiva: Una mirada feminista a las elecciones uruguayas 2009*. Montevideo: Cotidiano Mujer/ UNIFEM/ICP-FCS-Udelar.

Johnson, Niki, and Verónica Pérez. 2011. "From Vanguard to Straggler: Women's Political Representation and Gender Quotas in Uruguay." In *Diffusion of Gender Quotas in Latin America and Beyond: Advances and Setbacks in the Last Two Decades*, edited by Adriana Piatti-Crocker, 151–72. New York: Peter Lang.

Johnson, Niki, Cecilia Rocha, and Marcela Schenck. 2015. *La inserción del aborto en la agenda político-pública Uruguaya, 1985–2013: Un análisis desde el movimiento feminista*. Montevideo: Cotidiano Mujer.

La Diaria. 2011. "Más que beso." July 19. Accessed June 3, 2017. https://ladiaria.com .uy/articulo/2011/7/mas-que-beso/.

López Gómez, Alejandra, and Lilian Abracinskas. 2009. *El debate social y político sobre la ley de defensa del derecho a la salud sexual y reproductiva*. Montevideo: Cuadernos de UNFPA.

Macaulay, Fiona J. 2005. "Cross-party Alliances around Gender Agendas: Critical Mass, Critical Actors, Critical Structures or Critical Junctures?" Paper presented at the Expert Group Meeting on equal participation of women and men in decision-making processes, UN-DESA-DAW, ECA, IPU, December 12.

Márquez Garmendia, Martha. 2011. "El trabajo doméstico: La ley uruguaya y su representación en la normativa internacional (proyecto de convenio y recomendación de la OIT): Una mirada desde el género." Paper presented at the seminar organized by the Law and Gender Group, Universidad de la República, Uruguay, May 1.

Mazur, Amy. 2002. *Theorizing Feminist Policy*. Oxford: Oxford University Press.

MIDES. 2012. Resolución ministerial 1160/012, September 28.

Molyneux, Maxine. 1985. "Mobilization without Emancipation? Women's Interests, the State, and Revolution in Nicaragua." *Feminist Studies* 11 (2): 227–54.

Mujer Ahora. 2017. "Un gran avance de la justicia, un logro de las mujeres organizadas para todas las mujeres uruguayas." Accessed June 3. http://www.mujerahora .org.uy/content/un-gran-avance-de-la-justicia-un-logro-de-las-mujeres -organizadas-para-todas-las-mujeres.

Mujer y Salud (MYSU). 2014. *Plataforma ciudadana en salud y derechos sexuales y reproductivos*. Montevideo: MYSU.

Pérez, Verónica. 2007. *Ir a más: Monitoreo de lo actuado por el Instituto Nacional de las Mujeres (período 2005–2006)*. Montevideo: CNS Mujeres-UNFPA.

"Programa de gobierno del Frente Amplio 2008." Frente Amplio 5th Extraordinary Congress, December 13–14, 2008.

Rodríguez Gustá, Ana Laura. 2012. *La transversalización de género en la Intendencia de Montevideo: Evaluación del "Segundo plan de igualdad de oportunidades y de derechos" de la Intendencia Departamental de Montevideo*. Montevideo: AECID / Intendencia de Montevideo / ONU Mujeres.

Salvador, Soledad. 2013. *Análisis de costos y posibles impactos de diferentes modelos de licencias por maternidad, paternidad, y parentales*. Montevideo: UNFPA.

Sawer, Marian. 1995. "Femocrats in Glass Towers? The Office of the Status of Women in Australia." In *Comparative State Feminism*, edited by Dorothy McBride Stetson and Amy G. Mazur, 22–39. Thousand Oaks, CA: Sage.

Schneider, Iglesias. 2015. "Mucho más que dos." *La Diaria*, August 11.

Sempol, Diego. 2013. *De los baños a la calle. Historia del movimiento lésbico, gay, y trans Uruguayo, 1984–2013*. Montevideo: Debate.

Weber, Max. 1992. *The Protestant Ethic and the Spirit of Capitalism*. London: Routledge.

Weldon, S. Laurel. 1998. "Feminists, Femocrats and Institutions: Explaining Cross-National Variations in Government Responses to Violence against Women." Paper presented at the Conference for Women's Progress, Institute for Women's Policy Research, Washington, DC, June.

World Values Survey. 2017. "Online Data Analysis." Accessed July 1. http://www.worldvaluessurvey.org/WVSOnline.jsp.

Yaffé, Jaime. 2005. *Al centro y adentro. La renovación de la izquierda y el triunfo del Frente Amplio en Uruguay*. Montevideo: Linardi y Risso.

CHAPTER 2

LGBT Rights Yes, Abortion No

Explaining Uneven Trajectories in Argentina under

Kirchnerism (2003–15)

CONSTANZA TABBUSH, MARÍA CONSTANZA DÍAZ,

CATALINA TREBISACCE, AND VICTORIA KELLER

The Pink Tide of the Southern Cone has had a mixed record in advancing legal reforms that promote women's and LGBT rights. Sexual politics in Argentina between 2003 and 2015 were marked by the tension between the advancement of LGBT rights, particularly the passing of legislation on gay marriage and gender identity, and the frustrated efforts of feminists to legalize women's rights to abortion.[1] This chapter focuses on this tension, presenting a comparative study of these three attempts to promote legal change under the Frente para la Victoria (Front for Victory or FpV[2]) party, led by Néstor Kirchner (2003–7) and Cristina Fernández de Kirchner (2007–11 and 2011–15). This analysis allows us to highlight the points of convergence, rupture, and tension between these successive Kirchner administrations—which described themselves as "progressive"—and the rights of women, gays, lesbians, and transgender persons.

The empirical results identify four main dimensions that—combined—promoted or resisted legal advances in gender and sexual policies: the links between the executive branch and the church, parliamentary party politics in a presidential system, the framing of demands, and both the organizing and strategies of the movements supporting the above-mentioned legal reforms.

While this volume signals that center-left administrations have had a positive impact on the lives of women and queer populations, it also shows that the relationships between these administrations and movements are variable, complex, and contradictory, ranging from direct confrontation to experiences of active collaboration (Friedman and Tabbush, Introduction). The concept of pinkwashing is used to highlight that, with the objective of being seen as progressive, Pink Tide administrations made trade-offs between advances in some LGBT rights and setbacks or stagnation in policies central to feminism or human rights (Lind and Keating 2013).

Within this regional context of center-left administrations, the Argentine experience gains relevance due to its notable normative advances in human and LGBT rights. Argentina was a pioneer and legalized same-sex marriage in 2010, before it became a marker of modernity in Latin America (Corrales and Pecheny 2010).[3] Two years later, Argentina passed a law that, even though maintaining a binary gender distinction, decriminalized and depathologized the right of gender identity and is internationally viewed as progressive (Cutuli and Keller 2015; Farji Neer 2013). But even though laws advocating women's rights were also promoted during the period studied, Argentine feminists did not advance women's reproductive rights (Ariza and Saldivia 2015; Belgrano 2012).

What are the reasons for this tension? Was it the order in which these rights were attained? Is Argentina an example of "pinkwashing"? Was the Argentine tension the result of pressure from conservative forces and the Catholic Church, or was it that the Argentine people simply did not support these demands? Was it because "progressive" legislators did not fully support women's demands (Pecheny 2013) or because of differences between the movements behind each bill (Ariza and Saldivia 2015)? Over the course of this chapter, we will take up these questions by way of a comparative analysis, relying on interviews with key actors (activists, lawmakers, academics), draft legislation and other legislative documentation, and the current literature on these three political issues.[4]

An initial motivation for writing this chapter was the many times we witnessed heated arguments on the Left—in the Global North—in which intellectuals were surprised to find in Argentina a reverse trajectory in sexual and gender rights as compared to Western Europe, where abortion was first legalized and only decades later gay marriage and transgender rights debated. However, such surprise presupposes a linear, one-way progression, a kind of necessary order among the multiple demands that make up the sexual and gender rights agenda.

In this chapter, we take an opposite path–dependent approach. We consider the political processes of each demand as dependent on the historical legacy of each policy issue and on its political and institutional context. Our

analytical framework is largely based on Mala Htun's (2003) and Camilla Reuterswärd et al.'s (2011) disaggregated view of policy issues, also advanced in
the introduction to this volume, which allows us to analyze the tensions and/
or contradictions in the state's regulation of gender and sexuality. This literature has the advantage of combining two perspectives on legal changes: one
that emphasizes structural and institutional elements (the formal and informal rules of such processes) and the structures of opportunities they offer to
collective actors, and the other that underscores the organizing, resources,
and interpretive frameworks used by the activists who push these demands
forward. Thus, our objective is to analyze the institutions, political processes,
and main political actors who have been able to turn the key demands of
LGBT organizations into law, while feminist demands for legal abortion encountered greater resistance.

This chapter is divided into five sections. In the first section, we describe
the Argentine political context. In the remaining sections, we present the results of our comparative research, identifying four core dimensions that, in
combination, open up opportunities for, or generate resistance to, changes
in sexuality and gender policies. In sections two and three, we take up the
formal and informal rules of institutions as they pertain to the relationship
between the executive branch of government and the church, and to the legislative activities of political parties working within a presidential system. In
sections four and five, we turn the spotlight on collective actors, comparing
the interpretive frameworks used in formulating these demands and the organizational and action strategies used by social movements in promoting the
various demands under review here.

Kirchnerism, Feminisms, and LGBT Movements

Argentina is a middle-income country with a presidential system, an eroded
two-party structure, and a welfare system that is quite well developed for the
region. The neoliberal policies enacted in the 1990s drove the country into a
social and political crisis in 2001. Néstor Kirchner's first administration, and
the successive administrations of Cristina Fernández de Kirchner, opposed
such policies and defined themselves as representatives of a center-left Peronism (see below) that sought to redefine the state's relationships with the
market and society to ameliorate poverty and reduce inequality. They forged
an active role for the state in providing social and economic rights based on
an extractive agro-export economic model, persecuting crimes against hu-

manity, and advancing a rights-based governance agenda. This period, characterized as a decade of progress, has had a mixed record of social indicators. Following the initial gains made, social conditions have stagnated or declined since 2012 (Kessler 2014). The final Kirchner administration (2011–15) has been harshly criticized for its top-down, personality-driven governance style, and (as in other Latin American countries) members of that administration have faced highly mediatized prosecutions for corruption.

For political scientists, Kirchnerism is characterized by its Peronist legacy, which harks back to the powerful political movement initiated by Juan Domingo Perón and his wife Evita in the late 1940s. Peronism is often linked to the notion of populism, which distinguishes Argentina from other programmatic left parties swept up in the Pink Tide. Peronism stands out for its ever-changing ideological breadth (Acha 2013, 9), for its constant appeal to popular sectors, and for alternating between resistance and integration (James 1988). Within Peronism, there are groups that align with the Left and others that tilt to the Right or even tend toward hard-line conservatism. Peronism, in addition, is not based only in institutionalized politics; it is also part of unions, territorial social movements, and communities (see Casullo 2015). In this sense, neither the classical divide between left and right nor the separation between civil society and representative politics is present in the Argentine case.

A second observation about the period studied (2003–15) is that, as a result of the 1991 quota law promoting women's political participation in Congress (Public Law 24.012), a growing number of women in Congress have favored the passage of laws promoting and protecting the basic rights of women (Borner et al. 2009; Franceschet and Piscopo 2008). Among these laws, the following stand out: Sexual Health and Responsible Reproduction (Public Law 25.673/2002), Comprehensive Sex Education (Public Law 26.150/2006), Comprehensive Protection for Preventing, Punishing, and Eradicating Violence against Women (Public Law 26.485/2009), Universal Assistance for Children (Executive Order 1602/2009 and Public Law 24714), and Fertility Treatment (Public Law 26.862/2013).[5]

In this period, the state took an active role in social policies and directed conditional cash transfers to women living in poverty. Through a maternalistic framing, these policies seek to safeguard the human development of children and protect households against economic shocks. However, these antipoverty policies sidelined the gender-equality demands of adult women. Moreover, the positive effects the policies had on the lives of women were eroded over this period due to the high rate of inflation and the manipulation—or lack— of government statistics on poverty (Tabbush 2015).

The legal changes we will analyze are part of this set of regulations aimed at promoting women's rights, ending discrimination, and advancing gender equality. The 2009 bill to amend the Argentine civil code that specified marriage must be between a man and a woman, known as the Marriage Equality Law, was introduced by Vilma Ibarra, Member of Parliament (MP), for the Nuevo Encuentro (New Encounter) party. The law was passed the following year, in 2010, after months of public debate that included street marches and demonstrations for and against the law, as well as widespread media coverage and a lengthy session of Congress with repercussions across the country. The Federación Argentina de Lesbianas, Gays, Bisexuales y Trans (Argentine Federation of Lesbian, Gay, Bisexual, and Transgender Persons or FALGBT) became the mouthpiece for those in the LGBT community who demanded the right of marriage equality.[6] The bill was approved in the Chamber of Deputies (lower house) on May 5 with the explicit support of the ruling party (FpV): it received 126 yeas and 110 nays, with a few abstentions. On July 15, 2010, the bill was passed in the Senate with thirty-three votes in favor, twenty-seven against, and three abstentions.[7]

Shortly after the Marriage Equality Law was passed, the Gender Identity Law came up (May 9, 2012). Apart from FALGBT, another main backer of this law was the Frente Nacional por la ley de Identidad de Género (National Front for the Gender Identity Law, FNLIG).[8] In spite of being a law that many experts agreed was one of the most progressive in the world, it did not garner media attention. Though the law perpetuates a binary definition of gender, it does provide for changes to identity registries and documents without judicial or medical authorization, and it affirms health rights for transvestites, transsexuals, and transgender people vis-à-vis surgical procedures and/or hormone treatments for those who seek them. This law was passed in the Chamber of Deputies with 168 in favor, seventeen against, and six abstentions. In the Senate, only fifty-six lawmakers showed up for the vote, and they passed the law unanimously, with one abstention.

In that same period, feminists whose demands that had, in the 1990s, included political participation and economic rights, came together in the struggle to legalize or decriminalize abortion (Tarducci and Rifkin 2010). They organized themselves into the Campaña Nacional por el Derecho al Aborto Legal, Seguro y Gratuito (National Campaign for Legal, Safe and Free Abortion, known as the Campaign), which at the time of writing comprised

338 organizations from across the country.[9] This is the main collective actor behind the bill for the Voluntary Termination of Pregnancy (la interrupción voluntaria del embarazo or IVE), introduced before the Chamber of Deputies on four consecutive occasions, in 2007, 2010, 2012, and 2014, as Bill 2249-D-2014. Even though it was debated on more than one occasion in the Criminal Law Committee, it was never brought up for a vote in Congress. The number of members of Congress endorsing the bill increased over the years, including many from the ruling FpV party. However, Cristina Fernández de Kirchner, the most recent FpV president, spoke publicly against decriminalizing abortion, in contrast to her eventual support for the marriage and identity laws. Over the period studied, new activists have joined the cause, adding strategies of direct action and court litigation to this legislative battle.

Before analyzing these comparative processes, we should make one final distinction between the demands of feminists and those of LGBT organizations: the caliber of the executive institutions supporting their proposals. In working to pass gay marriage legislation, FALGBT was able to gain the support of a state institution that challenged discrimination, the Instituto Nacional contra la Discriminación, Xenofobia y el Racismo (National Institute against Discrimination, Xenophobia, and Racism, INADI). Several members of FALGBT belonged to INADI's sexual diversity division, and at the time of writing this chapter, they were working as FpV legislators in the Autonomous City of Buenos Aires (as was the case for María Rachid, the former president of FALGBT). Feminists, however, witnessed budgetary cutbacks and a persistent lack of relevance to the national women's agency—the then-Consejo Nacional de las Mujeres (National Women's Council, CNM)—subsumed under the Ministry of Social Development with the mandate to advance and defend women's rights (CEPAL 2017). For instance, Mariana Gras Buscetto, CNM's president from 2011 to 2015, was a politician with a history of participation in territorial social movements within Kirchnerism, with no links to feminism.

In the following sections, we examine those aspects of the relationship among activists, the state, and political processes that are most essential for our comparative analysis of the Argentine case.

Splits between the Catholic Church and the Executive Branch in Argentina

In Latin America, legislative advances on issues of gender and sexuality are often met with institutional resistance, such as that of the Catholic Church and political parties of the religious right. Argentina stands as an exception to this, in that it does not have any religious parties or coalitions in its national legislature. And for their part, Argentine religious leaders have no significant influence on how the public votes.[10] But in spite of the country's social and political secularism, the Church does have a heavy influence on the decisions of the executive. In this section, we examine the role of the Church as a political actor, and examine the windows of opportunity opened by the periods of conflict between the president and the Catholic Church, in a national context that has an independent Supreme Court.

Relations between top levels of the government and the Church were mostly conflictual under the first two Kirchner administrations (2003–7 and 2007–11). And those divisions created a window of opportunity for positive policy reforms in sexual rights. However, cooperation was prevalent during Kirchnerism's final years (2011–15), which thwarted measures that caused the Church's unease—such as legalizing abortion.

From the very outset of the first Kirchner administration, in May 2003, human rights policies and the pursuit of judicial prosecution for the human rights violations during the former military dictatorship (1976–83) were a source of profound disagreement. The Catholic Church and Cardinal Jorge Bergoglio (later Pope Francis) have been accused of collaboration and involvement with that dictatorship (Verbitsky 2010a, 2010b). This first Kirchner administration continued to oppose the Church by advancing the legal rights for women, gays, and lesbians listed in the previous section. Those measures, which were harshly criticized by the Church, were backed by the then-national minister of Health, Ginés González García, and widened the gulf between the executive and the local episcopate.

Compounding the split, the first Kirchner administration (2003–7) nominated an avowedly feminist and atheist judge, Carmen María Argibay, to the Supreme Court (Yusseff 2013). It is that court that years later, in 2012, would issue a groundbreaking ruling called the "FAL ruling"[11] that is seen as a huge victory for the women's movement. As we will see, this ruling on the right of an adolescent who was raped to terminate her pregnancy establishes the grounds for Non-Punishable Abortion (Abortos No Punibles, ANP) and prohibits practices that delay or block access to the right to ANP, such as unnecessary judicialization, and intuitional delays in access.[12] We will return to this court ruling in the final section of this chapter.

These divisions between the Church and the head of state coincided with a period of high government popularity, and thus, they became a facilitating context for advancing the Marriage Equality Law in 2010. Let us recall that Cardinal Bergoglio openly denounced the bill as "a war against God," calling on the people to stand with the Church in that fight (Noticia Cristiana 2011). In turn, President Cristina Fernández de Kirchner seized the opportunity to emphasize her support for the bill, publicly appealing to the cardinal to leave behind "the Middle Ages and the Inquisition" (Gallego-Díaz 2010, 1). As for the Gender Identity Law of 2012, the Church played a more passive role and did not resist it with the same energy or resources that it deployed against marriage equality or abortion.

During Cristina Fernández de Kirchner's first term (2007–11), the Church continued to show opposition to the government's main policies, for example, in regard to Public Law 26.522 on Audiovisual Communications, or Resolution 125, which proposed to increase taxation on the agricultural sector. Yet, this conflict with the Church ended when Jorge Bergoglio was elevated to become Pope Francis. At that point, the president began drawing closer to the Church, and that rapprochement was facilitated by her opposition to legalizing abortion (Yussef 2013). Most of the activists and lawmakers interviewed pointed out the president's commitment to the pope not to advance with this feminist demand as a barrier to the parliamentary review of the bill on Voluntary Termination of Pregnancy during that final Kirchner administration (2011–15).[13]

Strictly speaking, though, only the final hearing on the bill to legalize abortion, presented by the Campaign in 2014, was conducted in such an adverse scenario. The Campaign had presented the bill on three prior occasions—in 2007, 2010, and 2012—a period in which marriage equality and gender identity achieved positive results.

Figure 2.1 shows the Church's position and its effects on the three legislative processes studied here.

This figure shows two things. First, the Church did not maintain the same resistance to all of the legal reforms examined here. While it fervently opposed gay marriage and the voluntary termination of pregnancy, the Church did not wage such opposition against the Gender Identity Law, a law that was passed without meaningful resistance in terms of resources and labor invested. Furthermore, it can be inferred from the table that the divisions between the head of the executive and the head of the Church is a necessary factor but not a determining one. Even though the Church, to varying degrees of intensity, came out against all three reforms, it is only on the matter of abortion that the Church succeeded in keeping the practice criminalized.

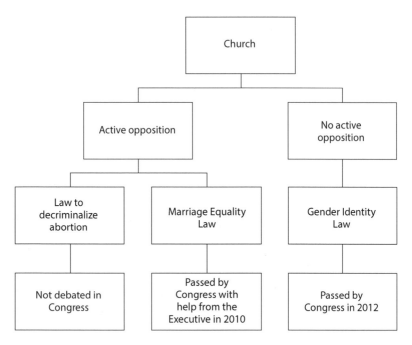

Figure 2.1 The Church's position and its effects on the three legislative processes studied.

The Legislature and Its Protagonists: The Power of Committees, "Progressive" Legislators, and Presidential Influence

In addition to the splits between the Church and the executive, the uneven trajectories that we are examining are strongly dependent on institutional factors, such as party politics within the legislature and the use of parliamentary rules.[14] This section highlights three elements of the legislative process: using committee powers to block or enable bills in Congress; left-leaning legislators' assumptions about the costs of supporting these controversial bills; and the influence that the president has, in a presidential system, over the behavior of congress members (in this case, from her own majoritarian FpV party).

As for the powers that committees had over the advancement of bills, two committees oversaw the bill on marriage equality, which was introduced in parliament in 2010 by Vilma Ibarra (Encuentro Popular y Social [Popular and Social Encounter]): the General Legislation Committee, led by Ibarra herself, and the Family, Women, and Childhood Committee, headed by Claudia Rucci (Peronismo Federal [Federal Peronism]).[15] According to the legislators interviewed, Ibarra's office was transformed into a FALGBT activist bunker.[16] At first, Rucci showed support for the bill; but later, she ended up supporting the "Civil Union" proposal instead (this proposal did not recognize the possibility of LGBT persons having or adopting children).

Members of the House and Senate enjoyed "freedom of conscience" on these issues, as the FpV party did not hold a roll-call vote. But the president's express support of the bill, though late in coming, helped win over the more tepid legislators within the FpV's majority bloc by presenting gay marriage as an equal-rights issue (Hiller 2013). Peronism has a vertical structure and political culture; as Casullo argues, "it is governed by a center whose main slogan is 'the one who wins commands, and the one who doesn't plays along with it'" (2015, 23). Interviews show just how shocked some of the congresspeople were, when they stated, "Can you believe it, we're going to vote for those fags?"[17] Another way in which the president influenced the final voting, which was by a razor-thin margin, was by inviting two FpV legislators who were against the bill to an official trip to China, causing them to miss the vote.[18]

Two years later, the Gender Identity bill was passed, as a consequence of both successful LGBT activism and the good public image enjoyed by Kirchnerism. The administration still had the support of large segments of the population, and good social indicators. As legislators stated in their interviews, that was a time when they felt that "anything was possible."[19]

In that favorable climate, and thanks to the advocacy and lobbying of the coalition of organizations (FNLIG), a unified bill was proposed with the support of many representatives. This bill brought together four competing bills written by activist groups.[20] The behavior of legislators on this bill was influenced by the minimal Church resistance and the support of the president, whose FpV party also headed up the two oversight committees.[21] As with marriage equality, "the personal leadership of the chief, typically, the head of the Executive power" was again paramount (Casullo 2015, 25). The path forward had already been laid out by the earlier activist success on marriage equality. Our interviews with legislators confirm that, at the time, "No one could go against the sexual diversity agenda."[22] This combination of (relative) Church indifference, executive leadership, and activist success is how the review and passage of this bill, introduced by Silvia Augsburger of the Partido Socialista (Socialist Party, PS), was—according to activists and lawmakers—"torpedoed through"[23] with fifty-five "yeas" and only one abstention.

In studying Congress' review of the bill on voluntary termination of pregnancy, the stance of committee leaders, "progressive" legislators, and the president

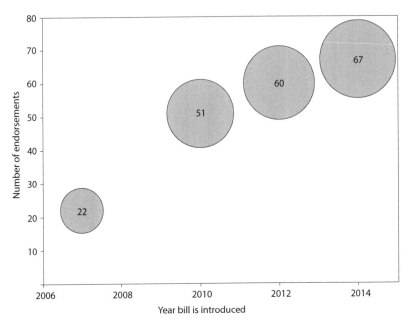

Figure 2.2 The number of lawmakers endorsing the bill, by year (2006–14). Source: Data provided by the direction of parliamentary information, National Lower Chamber, Argentina. Accessed June 7, 2017, http://www1.hcdn.gov.ar /dependencias/dip/indexvo.html.

stands in sharp contrast to those of the sexual rights bills previously analyzed. Figure 2.2 shows the increased endorsement the bill received, from twenty-two votes in 2006 to sixty-seven in 2014. This represents a tension between a sustained increase in legislative endorsement of the bill and the barriers the bill faced when being brought to Congress for a vote.

Considering that this bill was presented four times, with increasing support each time, congressional rules and the party politics at play have functioned as obstacles rather than as facilitators of this policy change. The first two times the bill was presented, it was "filed away" without even passing out of committee, causing it to lose all standing. In 2012 and 2014, the bill was debated in committee, but there it met with obstacles placed by committee leaders, and also suffered from the negative impact the lack of presidential backing had on the behavior of "progressive" legislators.

The female lawmakers behind the bill had a history of strategizing across party lines to overcome such obstacles. For example, in 2011, female representatives from different parties, such as the Unión Cívica Radical (The Radical Civic Union, UCR) and FpV, were able to get the bill heard by the Criminal Law Committee, by negotiating with the president of that committee, Juan Carlos Vega, of the Coalición Cívica (Civic Coalition) party, who wanted to bring international NGOs into the discussion. These female politicians were able to bring representatives of Human Rights Watch and Amnesty International to come testify at the hearings.[24] These politicians were able to use that first public hearing as a strategy for getting the bill heard, but in the end, they were not able to win the committee ruling that was needed to move the bill forward, and it lost its congressional standing.

The activists interviewed indicated that congressional rules, which are streamlined at times when the political will commands it, got log-jammed in the case of abortion.[25] The events of 2014 are illustrative. Presented by Adela Segarra of the FpV party, the abortion bill was introduced into Congress by the Criminal Law Committee, chaired by Patricia Bullrich of the UNION-PRO coalition (a fervent opponent of the bill) (*Infobae* 2014) and by vice-chair Diana Conti of the FpV party (a sponsor of the bill).[26] These leaders' behavior proved decisive in stalling the bill. The committee met on November 4 of that year, and that meeting devolved into a public debate marathon, with nine speaking on behalf of the Campaign, and another nine speaking out against it.[27] The committee chair was successful in ensuring that no ruling on the bill could be made, resulting in its loss of parliamentary standing. Well into the parliamentary debate, she argued that a quorum had not been reached at the exact time when the meeting began (3:00 PM, with nine of the eleven required representatives in attendance), even though the bill had not even been under discussion when the meeting started. Committee Vice-Chair Conti, who had endorsed the bill, did not register any objection to that administrative decision.[28] These examples show that committee leaders are capable of stalling a bill in Congress using bureaucratic rules and procedures, even when the majority of the committee formed of various parties and factions sponsored the bill.[29]

One central factor in securing legal change is the ruling party's support. In the period studied here, the FpV held the presidency and majorities in both houses of parliament (Calvo 2005; Tagina and Varetto 2013), and was pursuing a rights-based policy agenda. The politicians interviewed felt that supporting certain feminist projects carried political costs for those leading the charge, especially at a time of cooperation between the president and the Church. However, studies of previous legislative periods do not support this claim. They show that such costs do not seem to affect the political careers of legislators who pushed through women's rights (Piscopo and Caminotti, 2015) or LGBT rights (Pecheny 2003).

Yet, this lack of impact on their careers does not mean legislators do not face costs within their political parties, particularly in cases such as the FpV, which are characterized by high internal competition (Casullo 2015). The qualitative evidence shows that feminist causes tend to be devalued by a party that also directs various forms of discrimination, marginalization, and harassment toward its female legislators (Borner et al. 2009). For these reasons, "progressive" female legislators from the FpV who sponsored this bill were disincentivized when the active lobbying began. They reported weariness at having to pay these internal costs within the FpV for sustaining their position to legalize abortion in the face of internal power struggles over nominations for the presidential elections of 2015, in a context that combined Church collaboration with a devalued public image of the president and her administration (Tagina and Varetto 2013).[30] The same did not occur with female legislators from the smaller non-Peronist, traditional left-wing parties, which included legal abortion in their platforms.

Activists and female legislators from these left-wing parties consider the bill's failure to pass out of committee as partly the result of the behavior of FpV legislators. These legislators had sponsored the bill—and held a majority on the committee—but did not lobby actively for it to avoid any friction with the president, who was against abortion.[31] "Let's stay out of this, to keep us from hurting Cristina," is how several FpV legislators described it. At the same time, parliamentarians and activists from left parties stated, "The bill failed because Cristina did not want it to pass."[32] In this way, party tensions between FpV and left parties within the Campaign were a factor in driving a wedge in the main coalition on this issue and weakening its advocacy in Congress. In the words of one congresswoman and activist, "The Trotskyists sometimes don't want a bill to pass, so they can keep criticizing us (the FpV). And Kirchnerist supporters within the Campaign try to stifle debate to keep from contradicting the president. The bill can only pass with the support of both of these sectors. As long as Kirchnerism is in power, this bill will pass only if there is an open conflict with the Church."[33]

Framing of Demands

When considering collective actors, Htun (2003) suggests that two crucial elements are needed for successfully advancing gender- and sexuality-based demands. These include the framing activists use in advancing their causes, and the reliance on an issue network, the organizational model most effective in influencing institutional politics. These elements will be analyzed in the following sections.

Previous research suggests that the way in which a demand is communicated determines the institutional paths that are most effective for achieving normative changes. If a topic is framed as a technical problem, the debate tends to be limited to a small number of experts, jurists, and consultants. However, if it is presented as a clash of worldviews or value systems, the policy debate takes on an emotive tone. Then a broad-based public discussion in the legislature and society is needed in order to achieve policy change (Htun 2003). In the latter case, when the main actors are social movements, any proposed changes will be met by public opposition from across the political spectrum, including active resistance from the religious hierarchy (Carbonelli et al. 2011). Any of the three legal reforms studied here could be construed either as a technical problem or as a problem of worldviews, because such characterizations are not inherent in the policy issues themselves but rather are a feature of their political framing.

The marriage equality bill triggered an emotional debate, widely covered in the media, about value systems (Hiller 2013). As table 2.1 shows, this emotional component had an impact on the behavior of legislators: in both chambers we observe a high participation rate and a polarized voting outcome.[34] Faced with an unavoidable clash of worldviews, the social movements first used a strategy of reappropriating several of the pillars of the Kirchnerist discourse on human rights that centered on notions of equality, diversity, and inclusion. In addition, FALGBT excluded those talking points that focus groups had shown to cause moral outrage among conservatives—the adoption and raising of children—from public debate and congressional hearings. The organization then went viral with a slogan that focused on equality as a right: "Same love, same right," and expanded the familialism embedded in Peronism by showcasing the lives of "diverse families."[35] Using these elements in provincial public hearings, with the participation of parents and siblings of gays and lesbians talking in "the first person," this legal change was presented as further expanding democracy and the Kirchners' social project. Finally, this successful legislative outcome was aided by the fact that it represented an entirely technical modification to a provision of the civil code, which recognized a de facto situation and would not incur any financial costs for its implementation. As a result of these factors, even though the bill sparked a

TABLE 2.1 Percentages of participation and voting for Marriage Equality Law and Gender Identity Law in the Chamber of Deputies and the Senate

CHAMBER OF DEPUTIES				
	Participation	Yes	No	Abstain
Marriage Equality	93.7%	52.2%	45.6%	2.2%
Gender Identity	74.7%	87.5%	8.8%	3.1%

SENATE				
	Participation	Yes	No	Abstain
Marriage Equality	87.5%	52.3%	42.8%	4.7%
Gender Identity	77.7%	98.2%	0%	1.7%

Source: Data provided by the direction of parliamentary information, National Lower Chamber, Argentina. Accessed June 7, 2017, http://www1.hcdn.gov.ar/dependencias/dip/indexvo.html.

wide social debate on sexual values and cultures, during legislative debate it was successfully presented as an initiative that "benefited all" (Hiller 2013).

The Gender Identity Law of 2012 benefited from its proximity to the success of the Marriage Equality Law of 2010, which had strengthened the state's recognition of sexual diversity rights. It also benefited from a communication strategy based on the right to identity recognition, a cornerstone of the government's own discourse on human rights (Cutuli and Keller 2015). In this way, the bill benefited from three decades of human rights movement work done by organizations such as Madres de Plaza de Mayo (Mothers of the Plaza de Mayo), Abuelas de Plaza de Mayo (Grandmothers of the Plaza de Mayo), and H.I.J.O.S. (Hijos e Hijas por la Identidad y la Justicia contra el Olvido y el Silencio, Sons and Daughters for Identity and Justice and against Silencing and the Loss of History) in connection with the crimes against humanity of the last Argentine dictatorship. The framework used in presenting this law to Congress underscored the transgender community's inclusion in Kirchnerism's discourse on the right to identity, but left out of the debate the more vanguard aspects of transgender rights (Cutuli and Keller 2015).

Accordingly, the legislative review that this bill received was reduced to a group of experts, activists, and political consultants. It did not make a splash in the mass media, nor did it require any public opinion polling. This enabled, for instance, the bill to pass with the support of more than 98 percent of the

Senate, shielded from the media spotlight and spared the outrage of society's most conservative groups.[36] This speed and the incipient public consciousness raising on the topic led its proponents to conclude that "the bill remained on a much higher plane than the public's understanding of it."[37]

Table 2.1 compares the differential behavior of legislators on both bills, in terms of both debate participation (much higher in the gay marriage bill) and voting polarization (the gender identity bill is approved without any polarization).

Interpretive frameworks in the struggle for women's reproductive rights, and abortion in particular, vary according to the political goals that are being pursued. For instance, the differences between a "sanitary position" and an "emancipatory stance" present an obstacle for unifying feminist claims (Ariza and Saldivia 2015).[38] And these tensions crystallize in the multiple ways of naming this demand: "free abortion," "voluntary abortion," "decriminalization of abortion," and "abortion as a legitimate form of contraception" (Ariza and Saldivia 2015, 191n16). Within this frame conflict, the Campaign mobilized its groups for "legal, safe, and free" abortion on the basis of the slogan "Sex education to be able to choose, contraceptives to keep from aborting, legal abortion to keep from dying." Even though the Campaign brings together voices from across the political spectrum, there is a consensus view of abortion as a disruptive practice. It is considered challenging to a maternal understanding of femininity and to stress the right of women to make choices over their own bodies. Olga Grau Duhart states, "Abortion has established itself as an area of constant and perverse struggle; a struggle in which women are forever squaring off against patriarchal authority, and, at the same time, are silenced and excluded by that authority" (Duhart 2013, 25). In this sense, the political debate for passing the bill on voluntary termination of pregnancy was framed as a bid to usher in a new worldview on sexuality and the female body. This framing has dominated the debates in politics and in the media, with opposition legislators levying counterarguments that are based on when life begins, and arguing, from their interpretation of certain principles of human rights and international law, that the rights of the most vulnerable among us—"unborn children"—would be denied (CELS 2015).[39]

In recent years, women's organizations have tried reframing the debate, placing abortion within a human rights framework and locating it within Argentina's international treaty obligations (Sutton and Borland 2013). The Campaign has drawn on the field of public health in its efforts to justify this cause (Ciriza 2013). It must be noted that the majority of the country—64 percent—supports the decriminalization of abortion in certain circumstances, and this percentage is on the rise among Catholics, at 68.4 percent (CEIL-CONICET 2008).

In spite of the arduous work of feminists, the legislative debate in 2014 continued to be organized as a battle of worldviews or value systems.[40] This has foreclosed the possibility of having a sober political debate among experts, one based on empirical evidence and on a jurisprudential and epidemiological examination of the facts. It highlights the difficulty of incorporating women's reproductive capacity into public debates on sexuality.[41] As a departure from the other bills (and the best efforts of feminists notwithstanding), the frameworks used for advancing this policy change continued to fall outside of the discourse on inclusion, nondiscrimination, diversity, and identity that was championed by three Kirchner administrations. The Campaign focused instead on the notion of inequality—in this case, the inequality faced by women with poor access to abortion—and the consequences of having to resort to illegal abortions.

The second framework used to justify abortion is one that seeks to broaden the availability of Non-Punishable Abortions (ANPs) based on a broad psychological, social, and physical definition of women's health. In this case, ANP is framed as a technical matter that is circumscribed to the judicial actors. This has been accepted gradually, though not without resistance, in some provincial health care systems, in local child health and welfare councils, and among some provincial justice systems. This framework focuses on the medical aspect, stressing the duty to lower mortality and morbidity rates in mothers, and the duty to comply with existing laws on the sexual and reproductive rights of women. This set of actions makes it less likely that ANP is framed as a moral controversy. Instead, it is kept within the judicial sphere, where it has been upheld by the Supreme Court's FAL ruling that clarified the grounds for legal abortions and called for the elimination of any judicial or institutional barriers on women's access to it.

All the legal changes on gender and sexuality profiled here modify the status quo on matters of relationships and sexuality. Even though the demands fostered strong public debate, our analysis shows that successful claims not only benefited from translating their policy issues into technical, evidence-based issues and/or legalistic argumentation, as suggested by Htun (2003), but also when they were framed within the central narrative of the national project behind Kirchnerism. In contrast, and despite activist efforts, when legislative proposals are framed as a clash of values or worldviews, policy transformation becomes more difficult, and in particular, the possibility of capitalizing on moments of conflict between the executive and the Catholic Church is unlikely.

Movement Strategies and Resources

In this section, we illustrate two features of movement activism that are needed in order to push gender and sexual justice demands forward in institutional politics: (1) issue networks that bring together activists, professionals, and government representatives (Htun 2003); and (2) judicial activism (Reuterswärd et al. 2011). This section will focus on these two dimensions.

Issue Networks in Legal Reforms

Part of the marriage equality and gender identity advocacy took the form of issue networks. These networks are defined as small groups of professionals, government actors, journalists, lawyers, and activists whose goal is to bring about regulatory changes (Htun 2003).

Although it later expanded its geographic reach, FALGBT started out as a small group of professionals, lawyers, and journalists with a strong presence in the nation's capital, who proposed an action plan: to start out by pursuing marriage equality and later move on to getting gender identity recognized. FALGBT received financing and expertise from Spanish activists, based on their success in promoting marriage equality legislation in their home country (Friedman 2012). FALGBT also used social research tools and marketing methods, such as focus groups and public opinion surveys, to test out its arguments on public opinion. In addition, it relied on communication strategies that were in line with the national narrative of Kirchnerism, which popularized the term "marriage equality"[42] instead of "gay marriage."

The National Front for the Gender Identity Law backed the most ambitious of the four bills introduced in parliament. FNLIG functioned as an issue network for drafting the bill and for the negotiations in achieving a unified bill, which fostered links between activists and lawyers who were committed to the cause. Though not quite fitting the profile of "aseptic experts," these lawyers answered the call of transgender organizations to "translate into law" their social demands or needs, drafting a bill that contemplated decriminalizing and depathologizing trans identity.[43] During their negotiations to bundle together these preexisting bills, lawyers, politicians, and activists met in the representatives' own offices and worked together on a joint project that won support for the FNLIG-backed bill.[44]

Marriage and gender identity proponents presented a unified front. This is more challenging for women's and feminist movements to do with respect to abortion.[45] In our research we observed three avenues of political organization for the right to abortion: movement activism to legalize abortion; judicial activism to expand the scope of ANP; and guidance and direct action provided on the issue of medically induced abortions by organizations such as Lesbians and Feminists for the Decriminalization of Abortion and Socorristas en Red—Feministas que Abortamos (network of First Responders—Feminists who have abortions; affiliated with the Campaign).[46]

The historical makeup of the Campaign—the core actor behind this legal transformation effort—differs from that of FALGBT or FNLIG. It grew out of the neighborhood assemblies and grassroots movements that cropped up during and after the socioeconomic crisis of 2001, and was consolidated through the Encuentros Nacionales de Mujeres (National Women's Encounters, ENM).[47] The women interviewed echoed the existing literature (Alma and Lorenzo 2009; Sutton and Borland 2013), which finds that the ENM held in Rosario in 2003 was key to building up mass support within the women's movement for the demand for abortion rights and for the creation of the Campaign. This organizational trajectory brings the Campaign much closer to the modes of organization of popular social movements that stress federal representation and horizontal relations than to issues networks that brought together small professional groups of professionals, as described by Mala Htun (2003).

From its very beginning, the Campaign employed a federated structure and promoted, with mixed results, a decision-making process that relies on participatory democracy. The main benefit of this is that within the Campaign, multiple political positions coexist, with differing opinions on how to engage, and work with, state institutions. At the same time that this federal-style, multiparty participation is one of the most relevant achievements of the Campaign, it is, on occasions, perceived by some activists as causing delays or creating barriers for legislative action. For example, several of the activists interviewed shared the opinion that the drafting of the bill was a slow process, requiring two years of consultations and plenaries of the membership. On this question of time, certain left-leaning sectors within the Campaign believed that politics should bend to the movement's time lines, not vice versa.[48] Finally, women activists of various political stripes cite another barrier to their legislative effort: the increasingly sharp divisions between Kirchnerists and activists on the left (at least until 2015). The Campaign was permeated by the tensions of the election campaign of 2015 and by an increasingly polarized politics that led to situations in which party loyalties were, at times, placed above feminist priorities. This had a significant impact on how the Campaign was able to lobby the FpV.[49]

Beyond advocacy, the Campaign's activities are directed at increasing public awareness on the issue of illegal abortion—mainly the deaths of women living in poverty—as well as at increasing the Campaign's visibility as a political actor through staging protests, panels, performance art, and conferences in different parts of the country and outside Congress. Thanks to their public signature gathering and the support received in public opinion surveys, the Campaign's activists aver that this issue is now firmly part of the national political debate (CEIL-CONICET 2008). "The destigmatizing of abortion has been achieved," they proclaim.[50] Such activist affirmations are echoed in academic studies on the issue, undermining the argument by conservative and progressive lawmakers that society is not ready for such a debate—or for the legislation that could stem from it.

Judicial Activism for Legal Reforms

This chapter's comparisons also highlight the role that judicial activism plays in legal change, particularly in countries with an independent supreme court (Reuterswärd et al. 2011), such as Argentina. Key actors within the LGBT movements established legal precedents as a way of pressuring the system and paving the way for legal reforms. For example, in the case of marriage equality, FALGBT developed its judicial activism by targeting judges who would set a favorable legal precedent in the city charter of Buenos Aires. One case that garnered tremendous media coverage was the request for a marriage permit filed by lesbian activists María Rachid and Claudia Castro in February 2007.[51] Other couples then engaged in similar judicial process in Buenos Aires, Rosario, and other cities (Bimbi 2017).

And as for gender identity recognition, the case of transvestite actress Florencia de la V set a new legal precedent. With FALGBT support, she petitioned for a court order allowing her to change her name without the request or commitment to undergo any genital reassignment surgery. That petition, which became known as the "Florence Trinidad Doctrine," was granted without the need for any expert-witness testimonies by medical experts or any social workers' background investigations. In turn, FNLIG's lawyers supported similar petitions, offering pro bono support to people from the transgender community who wanted to change how they were listed in the civil registry (Farji Neer 2013).

These judicial actions highlight another difference between FALGBT, FNLIG, and the abortion rights Campaign. Until 2012, the Campaign's historical trajectory was not known for using litigation as a tool for triggering legislative debates, despite having relied on lawsuits on several occasions in its demands for ANP. Prior to the FAL ruling, judicial activism on abortion cases came mainly from religious organizations (for example, Portal de Belén, or Gates of Bethlehem), whose intention was to block legal abortions from being carried out. During that period, feminist judicial activism rose in reaction. It consisted of responding to, researching, and debunking the anti-abortion-rights claims made in appeals and injunctions brought by religious groups that were in violation of Article 1921 of the Penal Code. In this sense, that period of activism was defensive in nature.[52]

However, after that Supreme Court ruling in 2012, a network of feminist lawyers consolidated, bringing together professionals working in different areas—from academia to the justice system to women's groups to human rights organizations—with ties to the Campaign. This loose network strategizes within the justice system to expand the use of ANP. Among their achievements is the Supreme Court's FAL ruling of 2012, mentioned above.[53] After 2012, this network acquired many of the features described by Htun's issues networks (2003), and its actions transitioned from defensive to proactive litigation based on the theory that, by judicial reasoning, nearly any circumstance for terminating a pregnancy can be included under the rubric of legal abortions.

This intergenerational network provided training and education to lawmakers, government officials, and legal departments at health institutions and enabled abortion to be established as a human rights issue on the agenda of NGOs, women's groups, and human rights organizations. The strategy bore fruit in the collaboration built among organizations with feminist lawyers and professionals—such as the Asociación por los Derechos Civiles (Association for Civil Rights, ADC), Amnesty International Argentina, the Centro de Estudios Legales y Sociales (Center for Legal and Social Studies, CELS), and the Equipo Latinoamericano de Justicia y Género (Latin American Team for Justice and Gender, ELA)—to bring judicial proceedings against provincial governments and the national administration when they were out of compliance with the FAL ruling (Gebruers and Gherardi 2015).[54] In combination with strategic litigation, this network together with women's organizations carried out legislative advocacy, such as a public debate series and the publication of briefings for legislators that set the judicial foundation for legalizing abortion as a matter of advancing human rights (CELS 2015).

This loose professional network is a central piece in actions seeking to hold Argentine governments accountable on women's rights issues through judicial procedures as well as popular mobilizations. In this sense, as the experiences of LGBT activism signals, the approaches—actions focused on the public sphere and litigation strategies—can be complementary. The evidence collected here shows they can work well hand in hand, or even sequentially. Although it may seem as if judicial activism is paramount, without raising consciousness, it may result in legal changes with no societal acceptance, and thus always open to ongoing opposition. Actions focused on the public sphere, such as those described in this chapter, have the potential to develop a wide base of support.

Conclusion

At the beginning of this chapter we wondered whether we could consider Argentina an example of pinkwashing, noting a mismatch between the advance of LGBT rights and those of women. The chapter reveals that the Argentine case lacks two central elements of this concept. On the one hand, the period under review stands out precisely for its advances in human rights, rather than for human rights violations in need of hiding through pinkwashing (Ariza and Saldivia 2015). In addition, we found no direct or sharp opposition between Kirchnerism and the feminist movement (even though parts of the movement were critical of the latter administrations), as in the case of Ecuador and Nicaragua. Nor was there an explicit reversal in the rights women had achieved, as under these other Latin American left-leaning administrations. In the case of Argentina, obstacles to reproductive rights persisted rather than worsened.

In Argentina, the tensions between LGBT and reproductive rights were based on domestic rather than the international factors evident in other cases. Our comparison explains the discontinuities between LGBT and women's rights as a product of the interactions between institutions, political processes, and central actors in the four dimensions described. The central dimension that explains these tensions is executive-church relations. These had much to do with supporting the same-sex marriage, while consistently holding off abortion rights, despite growing public and legislative support for long-delayed decriminalization. This marks a qualitative difference with the extension of the LGBT rights regarding inclusion in the legal right of marriage and the recognition of self-determined gender identity. Thus, Argentina's distinctiveness in this regard refers to the audience, which is clearly more domestic than international, and its executive-church relations, which are more malleable than in other cases.

These results indicate that there is no single factor that serves as the key to unlocking the door to legal and institutional change. Through empirical analysis, we have identified combinations of institutional conditions and movement features; combinations that, in a specific political moment and context, open up opportunities for positive change in gender and sexuality policies. These uneven trajectories lead us to caution against treating this process as a homogeneous or tightly packaged political agenda that rolls out in predictable stages.[55] Moreover, the tensions revealed by the Argentine case suggest the need to approach each policy on gender and sexuality as its own special area of study, taking pains to distinguish policies that are more focused on inequality from others that focus on the concept of diversity.

Our results show that political timing played a role in the success enjoyed by proposals that were backed by LGBT movements. Both FALGBT and FNLIG found windows of opportunity during Kirchnerism's greatest popularity (2003–7 and 2007–11). In those periods, Kirchnerism enjoyed high positive ratings and a better public image, and it advanced a human rights agenda that was open to the demands of sexuality politics. Likewise, the conflictive relations between the executive and the Catholic Church during the first two Kirchner governments (2003–7 and 2007–11) opened up new opportunities, during both administrations, for LGBT activists to achieve progressive reforms on issues that were sensitive for the Church. In Argentina, the Church's involvement in these kinds of progressive reforms was not based on directly influencing the vote of the people or on religious parties in the legislature. Instead the top Church leadership influenced the behavior of the president.

By contrast, the timing of the political moment was not a significant factor for the feminist bill introduced into Congress on four occasions. During the period of conflict between the government and the Church, the bill did not garner the signatures needed for a vote in Congress (it got just twenty-two signatures in 2007). While the bill was still gathering signatures (sixty-seven lawmakers endorsed it in 2014), the executive branch actively began to overhaul its ties to the Church when Pope Francis assumed the papacy.

In that milieu, various institutional barriers came into play. Given the lack of support from committee leaders and the behavior of the majoritarian FpV party in the Chamber of Deputies, the legislators considered "progressive" (Pecheny 2003), or those who endorsed the bill, were reluctant to actively lobby for it. Such behavior is explained to a large extent by the lack of support from President Cristina Fernández de Kirchner, and from government spokespersons who did not come out in favor of the bill to legalize abortion.[56] Argentina's presidential system, combined with the top-down organizational style of Peronism, caused the executive branch to take on extra relevance, creating costs and benefits within the FpV that have conspired to derail this feminist cause. Thus, despite a growing number of legislators endorsing the bill—in a legislature where, we repeat, the FpV held the majority—it was not able to pass out of committee to be heard in Congress.

This point underscores the informal effects of this political system. In the context of Latin American presidential systems, the president's influence over legislators of her own party—a party that is considered center-left—which held a majority in both houses of Congress, was a defining variable that set the conditions on the ground, under which social movements tried to achieve positive legal changes. This point shows the need to go beyond legal reform analysis focused only on the internal dynamics within the legislature.

Similarly, there were some aspects, in the case of marriage equality, and, in some respects, in the gender identity law (specifically, the change to the civil registry), that favored their passage due to low implementation costs. This explains why hormone treatments or free surgeries for those who needed them were written into the regulations at a later stage under the gender identity law. Such treatments, like providing free legal abortions, have substantial financial implications. They also require a negotiation process with public agencies and prepaid medical providers, whereas a marriage filing or a registry change do not (see also note 20).

Given these institutional conditions, differences can be seen in how framing is crafted, and what communication strategies these three movements used to win over public opinion and to gain the support of the media and of Congress. We have witnessed a greater capacity for drawing together the Kirchnerist narrative on inclusion, embracing diversity, and expanding human rights, with the activist discourse on marriage equality and gender identity. The right of identity and the use of a familiaristic logic served as a conduit between these national projects and the key referents within the LGBT community. We did not find a similar alignment between the government and activist discourses on the right to abortion, where different framings and value systems compete. In this case, the framings are deployed in the form of a powerful struggle of worldviews regarding women's autonomy over their own bodies, and stresses the conditions of class inequality that put poor women at further risk. Moreover, it represents a challenge to the family-oriented ethos that has historically marked Peronism.

In terms of the organizational differences between activist groups, we have focused on identifying the development of issue networks that are effective in getting laws passed (Htun 2003), as well as on the ways in which judicial activism is used as a prelude to legislative advocacy, considering that Argentina has an independent supreme court (Reuterswärd et al. 2011). In the case of marriage equality and gender identity, the formation of issue networks and the pursuit of favorable court rulings happened prior to, or in tandem with, these legal demands. And while the demand for the right to abortion started out as a traditional social movement, only recently has it been bolstered by issue networks and litigation strategies. The Campaign's record of activism has focused on gaining ground for the women's movement and for raising consciousness in the public sphere to build support for legal changes. But the level of professionalism recently seen in the judicial activism and lobbying—areas in which it faces the institutional obstacles previously noted—must also be underscored.

Thus, we conclude with the hypothesis that, in the face of the historical and institutional particularities examined throughout this chapter, the feminist movement is responding by gradually diversifying its strategies and its multiple lines of attack. And while one segment of the feminist movement continues moving forward with its demand to legalize abortion and its effort to increase visibility for the problems connected with illegal abortion, other contemporary strategies are also consolidating. Organizations linked to or outside of the Campaign are pursuing local pre- and postabortion counseling and other forms of direct action to offer women access to medical abortions. For their part, issue networks that are focused on judicial activism and strategic litigation are now up and running, and they are poised to expand the availability of ANPs and increase women's access to abortions. Such multiplicity, coordination, and porosity are going to be needed to meet the challenges of post-2015 politics, where conservative wins in the general election and changes to the composition of the Supreme Court do not favor feminist causes.

Notes

We would like to thank the anonymous reviewers for their helpful comments, and our interviewees for their time and insights.

1. For more on the passing of legislation on gay marriage and gender identity, see the Marriage Equality Act (Public Law 26.618/2010) and the Gender Identity Act (Public Law 26.743/2012). For more on efforts to legalize women's rights to abortion, see Bill 2249-D-2014.

2. In this chapter, acronyms are based on Spanish names.

3. As is the case in Nicaragua (see Larracoechea, chapter 7).

4. In this chapter, we draw heavily from our own doctoral research and master theses. In addition, we carried out thirty-six interviews with activists, politicians, and state officials during 2014–15. For an example of current literature, see Ariza and Saldivia (2015), Belgrano (2012), Cutuli and Keller (2015), Hiller (2013), Farji Neer (2013), Gutiérrez (2004), and Pecheny (2001).

5. In the period studied, the following laws were also passed: Female Representation in Labor Unions (Public Law 25.674/2002), Prevention and Punishment of Human Trafficking and Support for Victims (Public Law 26.842/2012), and Special Rules on Employment Contracts for Domestic Workers in Private Residences (Public Law 26.844/2013).

6. For further information see the FALGBT website http://www.falgbt.org/ (accessed June 28, 2017).

7. Of the positive votes it received, 37 percent were from the FpV, without taking into consideration provincial Peronist parties or other allied parties such as Nuevo Encuentro.

8. FNLIG was formed in 2010 for the purpose of endorsing a law that would guarantee the right of identity for transgender persons. FALGBT comprises the following groups and organizations: ALITT, the Nadia Echazú Cooperative, Trans Men of Argentina, the Anti-Discrimination and Liberation Movement, Futuro Trans (Trans Future), United for Diversity (Córdoba), MISER, Antroposex (Anthroposex), Perlongher's Widows, Youth for Diversity, Escénika Art and Diversity, Zero in Conduct (based in Santiago del Estero), ADISTAR-Salta, the Homosexual Community of Argentina, Apid, Chrysalis (based in Tucumán), AMMAR Córdoba, and individual activists (FNLIG 2010)

9. The Campaign was founded in 2005; for further details see the campaign's website http://www.abortolegal.com.ar/ (accessed June 24, 2017).

10. The Argentine population considers itself religious, but most Argentines are nonobservant. In this sense, they stand apart from, say, Brazilians.

11. The acronym of the ruling is based on the name and surname of the mother of the rape victim who was seeking a legal abortion.

12. The FAL ruling clarifies the judicial interpretation of ANP guaranteed under Article 86 of the Penal Code (as a legal practice in all cases of rape or sexual abuse, and when there is risk to the woman's life or health). It reaffirms the legal bases nec-

essary for putting an end to unnecessary judicialization and obstructions carried out by public health and justice systems. It clarifies that the right of access to ANP is guaranteed under Article 86 of the Penal Code. "This is aimed at putting an end to *practica contra legem* (unlawful practices)" (CELS 2015, 13). For an analysis of ANP in Argentine law, see Bergallo and Michel (2009).

13. The Campaign activist, interview with authors, December 9, 2015, Buenos Aires.

14. Argentina does not have religious parties such as those in Brazil's evangelical legislative caucus, nor does it have highly conflictive parties—as in Chile, for example—and this is favorable to bills on sex and gender issues (Reuterswärd et al. 2011).

15. This bill was treated in the House of Deputies (lower house) by the General Legislation Committee and the Family, Women, and Childhood Committee, and in the Senate by the General Legislation Committee.

16. FALGBT activist, interview with authors, December 5, 2014, Buenos Aires.

17. FpV congresswoman, interview with authors, December 16, 2014, Buenos Aires. Former congresswoman, interview with authors, December 5, 2014, Buenos Aires.

18. Senators Marina Riofrío (San Juan) and Anda Iturrez (Santiago del Estero).

19. FpV congresswoman, interview with authors, December 16, 2014, Buenos Aires.

20. For a description of the various bills presented prior to the unified bill, see Farji Neer and Castro (2011). The most controversial points were provisions of the law dealing with health matters, and there was some fear that these might become sticking points when it came time to tally up a voting majority, because the health provisions required investments from government coffers, public insurance, and prepaid healthcare providers. In March 2015, a letter signed by dozens of groups was sent to the Ministry of Health; it requested rulemaking in this area and was eventually carried out.

21. This project was debated in the House of Deputies by the General Legislation Commission, and in the Senate by the General Legislation Commission and the Population and Human Development Commission.

22. FALGBT attorney, interview with authors, December 5, 2014, Buenos Aires.

23. FNLIG attorney, interview with authors, December 16, 2014, Buenos Aires.

24. Former congresswoman of the Frente Grande party, interview with authors, December 5, 2014, Buenos Aires.

25. FALGBT attorney who participated in the Campaign, interview with authors, December 5, 2014, Buenos Aires. Campaign activist, interview with authors, December 5, 2014, Buenos Aires.

26. In the House of Deputies the project was assigned to the Penal Law Commission, the Social Action and Public Health Commission, and the Family, Women, Children and Adolescents Commission.

27. Stenographic Congress Report Record of the Session of the Committee on Criminal Law of November 4, 2004. Official document accessible through the

Directory of Parliamentary Information at http://www.hcdn.gob.ar/secparl/dgral _info_parlamentaria/dip. Accessed June 3, 2017.

28. FpV congresswoman, interview with authors, December 16, 2014, Buenos Aires.

29. This majority included Conti (FpV), Victoria Donda (Libres del Sur), and Manuel Garrido (UCR).

30. FpV congresswoman, interview with authors, December 16, 2014, Buenos Aires. Conti's conduct in the committee debate is paradigmatic of such reasoning.

31. Former congresswoman for the Córdoba Nueva (New Córdoba) Front in the Frente Grande party, interview with authors, December 5, 2014, Buenos Aires.

32. On this point, there is agreement between a female union activist and Campaign member who was interviewed in January 2015, and a congresswoman, formerly representing the Partido Justicialista (Justice Party), who was interviewed that same month.

33. Activist from the Campaign, interview with authors, December 5, 2014, Buenos Aires.

34. The vote in the House of Deputies was carried out by 241 legislators (of a total of 257).

35. "Same love, same right"; FALGBT activist and attorney, interview with authors, December 5, 2014, Buenos Aires. According to Acha (2013), part of Peronism's appeal is its sentimental support for the family and image of the president as a father figure.

36. The voting in House of Deputies took place with 192 legislators (of a total of 257), and in the Senate with fifty-six legislators (of a total of seventy-two).

37. FNLIG attorney, interview with authors, December 16, 2014, Buenos Aires.

38. The sanitary stance stresses that unsafe abortion causes deaths and serious consequences for women, especially the poorest women. The emancipatory stance sees abortion as a way of revealing/resisting the heterosexual/capitalist patriarchal regime (Ariza and Saldivia 2015, 191n16).

39. These groups acknowledge that they are "adding 'fertilization' to the term 'conception.'" In their defense, they cite outdated research or various studies lacking in consensus or scientific rigor, or representing the opinions of individual academicians, scientists, or social scientists" (CELS 2015, 15).

40. Congress transcribed record, Criminal Law Committee, November 4, 2004.

41. A point also highlighted by Ariza and Saldivia (2015).

42. FALGBT activist and attorney, interview with authors, December 5, 2014, Buenos Aires.

43. Activist and attorney, interview with authors, December 5, 2014, Buenos Aires.

44. Diana Conti's office played a crucial role in the effort to join these bills together; FNLIG attorney, interview with authors, December 16, 2014, Buenos Aires.

45. Despite their differences, LGBT movements have historically agreed on the need for depathologizing and strongly questioned medicalization, whereas with

respect to the right to abortion, the demand for demedicalization is more recent and has been driven only by some sectors of the movement (Ariza and Saldivia 2015).

46. For further information of these organizations refer to their websites. http://www.abortoconpastillas.info/ and http://socorristasenred.org/ (accessed June 25, 2017).

47. Since 1986, these annual meetings have brought together the women's movement in Argentina and are unique to this national context. They stand out for their national appeal, mass participation, and historical continuity.

48. The Campaign activist, interview with authors, December 18, 2014, Buenos Aires.

49. The Campaign activist, interview with authors, December 5, 2014, Buenos Aires.

50. Former congresswoman for Frente Córdoba Nueva (New Córdoba Front) of the Frente Grande party, interview with authors, December 5, 2014, Buenos Aires.

51. The city registrar denied their request and they then filed an appeal that was sponsored by FALGBT's lawyers and was based on the Family Law provisions of the Civil Code of Argentina. That appeal made it all the way to the Supreme Court.

52. Feminist lawyer, interview with authors, December 11, 2014, Buenos Aires.

53. Feminist lawyer, interview with the authors at a network of feminist lawyers for sexual and reproductive rights, December 11, 2014, University of Palermo. Feminist activist lawyer, interview with authors, December 2, 2014, Buenos Aires.

54. For example, in 2012 a class-action petition for injunctive relief was filed against the city government of Buenos Aires; *Association for Civil Rights et al. v. the City Government of Buenos Aires* (Article 14, City Charter of Buenos Aires), Case No. 46062, Second Civil Administrative and Tax Court, Department 4, CAYT Hall, Court Room 3. In 2014, a class-action suit was filed against the national administration; *Center for Legal and Social Studies et al. v. Ministry of Public Health* (not heard), Case No. 71865/2014, Eighth Federal Civil and Commercial Court, Department 16.

55. Examples of this are the ways in which the concept of sexual citizenship is sometimes expressed (Sabsay 2013).

56. To a large extent, this is due to the current period of cooperation with Church leadership.

References

Acha, Omar. 2013. *Crónica sentimental de la Argentina peronista: Sexo, inconsciente e ideología, 1945–1955*. Buenos Aires: Prometeo.

Alma, Amanda, and Paula Lorenzo. 2009. *Mujeres que se encuentran: Una recuperación histórica de los Encuentros Nacionales de Mujeres en Argentina, 1986–2005*. Buenos Aires: Feminaria Editora.

Ariza, Sonia, and Laura Saldivia. 2015. "Matrimonio igualitario e identidad de género sí, aborto no." *Derecho y Crítica Social* 1 (1): 181–209.

Belgrano, Milagros. 2012. "Ley de matrimonio igualitario y aborto en Argentina: Notas sobre aborto una revolución incompleta." *Estudos Feministas* 20 (1): 173–88.

Bergallo, Paola, and Agustina Ramón Michel. 2009. "El aborto no punible en el derecho argentino." In *Hoja Informativa 9*. Argentina: CEDES, FEIM, IPPF.

Bimbi, Bruno. 2017. "El matrimonio gay, en manos de la Corte." *Página/12*. Accessed June 25, 2017. https://www.pagina12.com.ar/diario/elpais/1-99810-2008-02-28.html#arriba.

Borner, Jutta, Mariana Caminotti, Jutta Marx, and Ana Laura Rodríguez Gustá. 2009. *Ideas, presencia, jerarquías políticas: Claroscuros de la igualdad de género en el Congreso Nacional de Argentina*. Buenos Aires: PNUD-Prometeo.

Calvo, Ernesto. 2005. "Argentina, elecciones legislativas 2005: Consolidación institucional del kirchnerismo y territorialización del voto." *Revista Ciencia Política* 25 (2): 153–60.

Carbonelli, Marco, Karina Felitti, and Mariela Mosqueira. 2011. "Religión, sexualidad y política en la Argentina: Intervenciones católicas y evangélicas en torno al aborto y el matrimonio igualitario." *Revista del Centro de Investigación* 9 (36): 25–43. Journal of the Research Center, University of La Salle.

Casullo, María Esperanza. 2015. "Argentina: Del bipartidismo a la 'democracia peronista.'" *Nueva Sociedad* 257 (July–August): 16–28.

CEIL-CONICET. 2008. *Estructura social, creencias e identidades religiosas: La perspectiva de las personas*. CEIL, Buenos Aires. Accessed on June 25, 2017. http://www.ceil-conicet.gov.ar/wp-content/uploads/2013/08/BCN-Creencias.pdf.

Centro de Estudios Legales y Sociales (CELS). 2015. "Aportes del CELS a los debates legislativos sobre derechos sexuales y reproductivos." CELS, Buenos Aires. Accessed July 10, 2017. https://www.cels.org.ar/web/publicaciones/aportes-del-cels-a-los-debates-legislativos-sobre-derechos-sexuales-y-reproductivos/.

Ciriza, Alejandra. 2013. "Sobre el carácter político de la disputa por el derecho al aborto: 30 años de luchas por el derecho a abortar." In *El aborto como derecho de las mujeres: Otra historia es posible*, compiled by Campaña Nacional por el Derecho al Aborto Legal, Seguro y Gratuito, 63–83. Buenos Aires: Herramienta Ediciones.

Comisión Económica para América Latina y el Caribe (CEPAL). 2017. "Observatorio de Igualdad de Género de América Latina y el Caribe." Accessed June 27, 2017. http://www.cepal.org/oig/ws/getCountryProfile.asp?language=spanish&country=ARG.

Corrales, Javier, and Mario Pecheny. 2010. "Six Reasons Argentina Legalized Gay Marriage First." *Americas Quarterly*, July 29. http://www.americasquarterly.org/node/1753.

Cutuli, Soledad, and Victoria Keller. 2015. "At the Forefront of Sexual Rights? Notes on Argentinean LGBT Activism." In *The Global Trajectories of Queerness: Rethinking Same-Sex Politics in the Global South*, 213–28. Boston: Rodopi Press.

Farji Neer, Anahí. 2013. *Fronteras discursivas: Travestismo, transexualidad y transgeneridad en los discursos del Estado argentino, desde los Edictos Policiales hasta la Ley de Identidad de Género*. PhD diss., Universidad de Buenos Aires.

Farji Neer, Anahi, and Guillermo Castro. 2011. "Entre la academia, el movimiento y 'la ley.' 'Ley de identidad de género': Categorías en debate." *X Congreso de Antropología Social* (November 29–December 2). Buenos Aires: Facultad de Filosofía y Letras (UBA).

FNLIG (Frente Nacional por la Ley de Identidad de Género). 2010. "Histórico: Argentina tiene Ley de Identidad de Género." *Frente Nacional por la Ley de Identidad de Género*, May 10. http://frentenacionaleydeidentidad.blogspot.be.

Franceschet, Susan, and Jennifer Piscopo. 2008. "Gender Quotas and Women's Substantive Representation: Lessons from Argentina." *Politics & Gender* 4 (3): 393–425.

Friedman, Elisabeth Jay. 2007. "How Pink Is the 'Pink Tide'?" *NACLA Report on the Americas* (March–April): 16–44.

Friedman, Elisabeth Jay. 2009. "Gender, Sexuality, and the Latin American Left: Testing the Transformation." *Third World Quarterly* 30 (2): 415–33.

Friedman, Elisabeth Jay. 2012. "Constructing 'The Same Rights with the Same Names': The Impact of Spanish Norm Diffusion on Marriage Equality in Argentina." *Latin American Politics and Society* 54 (4): 29–59.

Gallego-Díaz, Soledad. 2010. "'Guerra de Dios' contra las bodas gays en Argentina." *El País*, July 14. Accessed June 27, 2017. http://internacional.elpais.com/internacional/2010/07/14/actualidad/1279058406_850215.html.

Gebruers, Cecilia, and Natalia Gherardi. 2015. "El aborto legal en Argentina: La justicia después de la sentencia de la Corte Suprema de Justicia en el caso 'F.A.L.'" *Serie documentos REDAAS* (2). Accessed July 15, 2017. http://clacaidigital.info:8080/xmlui/bitstream/handle/123456789/792/DocumentosRedaas2015%282%29.pdf?sequence=1&isAllowed=y.

Grau Duhart, Olga. 2013. "Hay nudos que no se desatan: El nudo gordiano patriarcal como materia dura de resistencia al aborto legal." In *El aborto como derecho de las mujeres: Otra historia es posible*, compiled by Campaña Nacional por el Derecho al Aborto Legal, Seguro y Gratuito, 119–36. Buenos Aires: Herramienta Ediciones.

Gutiérrez, María Alicia. 2004. "Silencios y susurros: La cuestión de la anticoncepción y el aborto." In *Ciudadanía sexual en América Latina: Abriendo el debate*, edited by Carlos Cáceres et al., 129–40. Lima: Universidad Peruana Cayetano Heredia.

Hiller, Renata. 2013. "Same-Sex Marriage and the Public Sphere in Argentina." In *Sexuality, Culture and Politics—A South American Reader*, 152–73. Rio de Janeiro: CLAM. (Latin American Center on Sexuality and Human Rights) Accessed June 20, 2017. http://www.clam.org.br/uploads/publicacoes/book2/09.pdf.

Htun, Mala. 2003. *Sex and the State*. Cambridge: Cambridge University Press. Accessed on June 27, 2017. doi:10.1017/CBO9780511615627.

Infobae. 2014. "La despenalización del aborto no es un tema para debatir en esta Argentina dividida." November 3. Accessed June 27, 2017. http://www.infobae .com/2014/11/03/1606192-la-despenalizacion-del-aborto-no-es-un-tema-debatir -esta-argentina-dividida/.

James, Daniel. 1988. *Resistance and integration: Peronism and the Argentine working class, 1946–1976*. Cambridge; New York: Cambridge University Press.

Kessler, Gabriel. 2014. *Controversias sobre la desigualdad: Argentina, 2003–2013*. Buenos Aires: Fondo de Cultura Económica.

Lesbianas y Feministas por la Descriminalización del Aborto. 2012. *Todo lo que querías saber sobre cómo hacerse un aborto con pastillas*. Buenos Aires: Ediciones Madres de plaza de mayo. Accessed on June 25, 2017. http://www .abortoconpastillas.info/.

Ley de Identidad de Género (Ley 26.743/2012). Sanctioned in May 9, 2012 and promulgated in May 23, 2012. Senate and Deputes houses of Argentina. Buenos Aires, Argentina. Accessed May 20, 2017. https://www.tgeu.org/sites/default/files /ley_26743.pdf

Ley de Matrimonio Igualitario (Ley 26.618/2010). Sanctioned in July 15, 2010 and promulgated in July 21, 2010. Senate and Deputes houses of Argentina. Buenos Aires, Argentina. Accessed May 23, 2016. http://servicios.infoleg.gob.ar /infolegInternet/anexos/165000–169999/169608/norma.htm.

Lind, Amy, and Christine (Cricket) Keating. 2013. "Navigating the Left Turn." *International Feminist Journal of Politics* 15 (4): 515–33.

Noticia Cristiana. 2011. "Iglesia Catolica en Argentina matrimonio homosexual es una movida del diablo." Accessed July 15, 2016. http://www.noticiacristiana .com/sociedad/iglesiaestado/2010/07/iglesia-catolica-en-argentina -matrimoniohomosexual-es-una-movida-del-diablo.html.

Pecheny, Mario. 2001. *La construction de l'avortement e du sida en tant que questions politiques: Le cas de l' Argentine*. Lille, France: Presses Universitairs du Septentrion.

Pecheny, Mario. 2003. "Yo no soy progre, soy peronista: ¿Por qué es tan difícil discutir políticamente sobre aborto?," 1–16. Instituto Gino Germani. Accessed June 27, 2017. http://www.ciudadaniasexual.org/reunion/M5%20 Pecheny.pdf.

Piscopo, Jennifer, and Mariana Caminotti. 2015. "¿De dónde vienen y a dónde van las legisladoras feministas? Género y carreras políticas en Argentina." July 22–24. 8th Congreso ALACIP, Lima.

Proyecto 2249-D-14. 2014. Honorable Cámara de Diputados de la Nación, Diputada Nacional Segarra y otros sobre. Interrupción voluntaria del embarazo. Régimen. Modificación del código penal.

Reuterswärd, Camilla, Pär Zetterberg, Suruchi Thapar-Björkert, and Maxine Molyneux. 2011. "Abortion Law Reforms in Colombia and Nicaragua: Issue Networks and Opportunity Contexts." *Development and Change* 42 (3): 805–31. Accessed June 27, 2017. doi:10.1111/j.1467-7660.2011.01714.x.

Sabsay, Leticia. 2013. "Dilemas queer contemporáneos : ciudadanías sexuales, orientalismo y subjetividades liberales Un diálogo con Leticia Sabsay." *Iconos, Revista de Ciencias Sociales*, 47, 103–18.

Sepúlveda Zelaya, Carmen. 2014. *The Legal and Political Battles behind the Distribution of Emergency Contraception in Chile under Ricardo Lagos (2000-2005) and Michelle Bachelet (2006-2010)*. PhD diss., University College London.

Stenographic Congress Report Record of the Session of the Committee on Criminal Law of November 4, 2004. Official document accessible through the Directory of Parliamentary Information at http://www.hcdn.gob.ar/secparl/dgral_info_parlamentaria/dip/.

Sutton, Barbara, and Elizabeth Borland. 2013. "Framing Abortion Rights in Argentina's Encuentros Nacionales de Mujeres." *Feminist Studies* 39 (1): 194–234.

Tabbush, Constanza. 2015. "Marcos de justicia: Secretos secreto a voces en los estudios sobre género y pobreza en Argentina."

Tagina, María Laura, and Carlos A. Varetto. 2013. "Argentina: Del apogeo electoral a la inminencia de la crisis sucesoria." *Revista Ciencia Política* 33 (1): 3–34.

Tarducci, Mónica, and Deborah Rifkin. 2010. "Fragmentos de historia del feminismo en Argentina." In *Las palabras tienen sexo 2*, compiled by Sandra Chaher and Sonia Santoro, 18–39. Buenos Aires: Artemisa Comunicación Ediciones.

Verbitsky, Horacio. 2010a. "El pasado me condena." *Página/12*, April 11.

Verbitsky, Horacio. 2010b. "Jalics y Yorio dijeron que Bergoglio los entregó." *Página/12*, April 18.

Yussef, Nabih. 2013. "La iglesia, el Papa y el Kirchnerismo." *Contexto Internacional, Publicación del Centro de Estudios Políticos e Internacionales de la* FUNIF 37 (December 2013), 9–15.

CHAPTER 3

Working within a Gendered Political Consensus

Uneven Progress on Gender and Sexuality Rights in Chile

GWYNN THOMAS

In March 2014, Michelle Bachelet began her second presidential term cementing Chile's position as the most enduring of the democratically elected Pink Tide governments of Latin America. In 2018, Chile will have been governed by center-left coalitions for twenty-four of the twenty-eight years since Chile's return to democracy in 1990. The Concertación de Partidos por la Democracia (Coalition of Parties for Democracy, known as the Concertación), a political coalition of parties from the center (Partido Radical [Radical Party] and the Partido Demócrata Cristiano [Christian Democratic Party, or PDC]) and the left (Partido por la Democracia [Party for Democracy] and Partido Socialista [Socialist Party]) emerged during Chile's democratic transition and governed through four successive presidencies (1990–2010). Having lost the presidency in 2010 to Sebastián Piñera and his right coalition (Alianza por Chile [Alliance for Chile]), the center-left returned to power in 2014 with the Nueva Mayoría (New Majority), a coalition that included all parties of the Concertación as well as the Partido Comunista (Communist Party) and a number of independent legislators who emerged from the student protests. In addition to this impressive political longevity, Chile's center-left governments have been lauded for governmental stability, sustained economic growth, the expansion of social welfare programs, and poverty alleviation. For example, in 1990, almost 40 percent of the Chilean population was living in poverty, with roughly 13 percent categorized as indigent. By 2010, poverty levels had decreased to just a little over 11 percent, and indigent poverty had dropped to just over 3 percent (CEPAL 2015).[1]

However, Chile remains one of Latin America's most unequal countries in terms of wealth distribution and economic inequality. While in power, the

Concertación did not pursue fundamental changes to either the neoliberal economic model or the political system (including the constitution) inherited from the military dictatorship of Augusto Pinochet (1973–90) (Weeks and Borzutky 2012; Sehnbruch and Siavelis 2014). Citizens' discontent over privatized education systems, income inequality, lack of democratic transparency, and political corruption was partly responsible for the end of the Concertación and the emergence of the Nueva Mayoría with its stronger representation of leftist parties and greater willingness to push for more radical change.

The record of Chile's center-left governments in promoting gender equality and women's and sexual minority rights is equally mixed. The Concertación made gradual progress, particularly in terms of legal reforms around violence against women and in improving women's socioeconomic position. Chile now has strong antiviolence laws, has greatly expanded state support for childcare and community development, and has passed pension reforms that partly addressed gender inequality in retirement security. Chile has twice elected the most feminist of Pink Tide presidents, socialist Michelle Bachelet, who in her first term appointed Latin America's first gender parity cabinet and promoted a "gender agenda" within the state (Thomas 2016). Chile has arguably Latin America's strongest national women's agency, the Servicio Nacional de la Mujer (National Women's Service known as SERNAM), now part of the Ministry of Women and Gender Equality created in 2016. However, women's representation in the lower house of Congress in 2014 was 15.8 percent, one of the region's lowest. Laws and policies promoting women's reproductive rights (such as access to abortion and contraception) or addressing discrimination against the LGBTQ community have often languished without political support from the government (Díez 2015; Franceschet 2005; Haas 2010; Ríos 2009). Until 2017, Chile was one of only three countries in Latin America with a complete ban on abortion as attempts to liberalize access had been mired in political conflict. And while Bachelet's policies went the farthest in recognizing the intersectional needs of indigenous women concerning issues of poverty and economic access, her government maintained the previous emphasis on multicultural incorporation rather than recognizing the growing indigenous demands for land sovereignty and cultural survival (Richards 2013).

This mixed record captures the broader paradox of the Pink Tide governments central to this collection. As Friedman and Tabbush note in the introduction, Chile fits the model of Latin America's left governments that have produced marked improvements in women's socioeconomic position by supporting poverty alleviation programs, but have not consistently addressed demands by women's and sexual minority movements around political representation, bodily autonomy, and identity recognition (see also Friedman 2010). Despite the centrality of the women's movements in Chile's democratic transition and in bringing the Concertación to power, demands for gender equality and women's rights have not been a political priority. Given Chile's uneven progress, why has the expansion of social-welfare programs and poverty alleviation (which often require significant investment of state resources) generated greater political support and change than demands for policies promoting political representation, bodily autonomy, and identity recognition?

In this chapter, I argue that in Chile this pattern of uneven outcomes reflects the role played by heteropatriarchal norms, particularly an idealized vision of the family,[2] in constructing the political compromises needed to maintain a governing political coalition. While many scholars have discussed how the stability and success of the Concertación depended upon the coalition's "politics of consensus" (Siavelis 2009; Sehnbruch and Siavelis 2014; Weeks and Borzutky 2012), the gendered foundations of this political strategy have been overlooked. I place gender at the center of my analysis of Chile's politics of consensus by analyzing how political actors used heteropatriarchal norms to generate compromises and policies around state welfare programs and poverty alleviation. However, a politics of consensus also depends on avoiding political conflict. Thus, I also examine how feminist and sexual minority demands that directly challenged heteropatriarchal norms were marginalized from the Concertacion's political priorities because they threatened the coalition's politics of consensus. Laws and policies that promoted women's, and increasingly sexual minorities,' bodily autonomy, political representation and identity recognition, were often seen as too contentious and thus not worth the political risks to the coalition despite their support by women's and feminist movements.

To develop this argument, I begin by briefly discussing the politics of consensus and how its maintenance was central to the political projects of the Concertación governments from 1990 to 2014. Unlike other scholars, I show how this politics of consensus was partly crafted through a shared, idealized vision of the heteropatriarchal family and its historical importance to Chilean politics. In the second section, I trace how the relationship between center and left political parties and between political parties and the broader women's movements and increasingly lesbian and gay organizations often reflected areas of both consensus and conflict over heteropatriarchal norms. In the third section, I analyze how the gendered politics of consensus helped determine the scope and timing of policy changes around political representation, socioeconomic redistribution, bodily autonomy, and identity recognition. I include a discussion of the creation of the Nueva Mayoría and Bachelet's second presidency, focusing on what the new coalition might signify in terms of progress toward gender equality and sexual minority rights. I then conclude with the broader comparative lessons of Chile's Pink Tide governments. For this chapter, I draw heavily on the archival research found in my book *Contesting Legitimacy in Chile* (2011) and on interviews conducted over the last ten years with feminist activists, elected political leaders, and appointed civil servants.

The Development of Chile's Politics of Consensus

The exigencies of the transition back to democracy indelibly marked the development of Chile's center-left governments and women's, feminist, and sexual minority movements. The Concertación emerged during the 1988 plebiscite on the continuance of Pinochet's military dictatorship, when a broad coalition of center and left political parties and social movements came together to organize the winning "NO" vote that ushered in the transition. Assuming office in 1990, Patricio Aylwin (PDC), the Concertación's first president, faced a number of "authoritarian enclaves" protected by the continuing political power of Pinochet (who remained in charge of the armed forces) and the 1980 constitution (Collier and Sater 2004; Garretón 2003). The Concertación's ability to embark on radical change was hindered by Chile's unique binominal electoral system designed to overrepresent the right-wing minority in elections, constitutionally required supermajorities for passage of laws (particularly constitutional reforms), and the provision for designated senators originally appointed by the armed forces, the Supreme Court, and the president (Collier and Sater 2004; Garretón 2003; Siavelis 2009). Thus, the Concertación not only had to continue to work to marginalize a deposed, but not powerless, past dictator, but also had to contend with powerful legislative opponents found in the two main parties of the right, the Renovación Nacional (National Renovation) and the Unión Demócrata Independiente (Independent Democratic Union). Even with small legislative majorities, the Concertación often had to find support from right party members for passage of bills that sought legal changes to areas requiring supermajorities, such as laws on education, the armed forces, mining concessions (which regulated Chile's nationalized copper industry), and electoral reform.

Within this challenging context, the leaders of the Concertación emphasized the importance of maintaining its governing coalition, coalition cohesion, and political stability rather than radical change. They created power sharing mechanism between the political parties, and focused on areas where broad agreements could be forged. To diminish areas of political divisiveness, party elites also sought to limit the involvement of the broader social movements that had played critical roles in the transition (Collier and Sater 2004; Garretón 2003). The Concertación's need to minimize conflict and generate broad consensus limited the types of reforms party elites were willing to support, while also cementing the political power of party elites (the mostly male party members active at the time of the transition) (Siavelis 2011; Sehnbruch and Siavelis 2014). Unlike the more definitive breaks of president Hugo Chávez's "Bolivarian Revolution" in Venezuela or Rafael Correa's "Citizen Revolution" in Ecuador, which were driven by populist rhetoric combined with economic and political crisis, Chile's political parties pursued a politics of consensus that has since become the hallmark of Chile's center-left governments (Siavelis 2009; Sehnbruch and Siavelis 2014). This development has shaped how presidents in Chile govern, limiting the development of hyperpresidentialism found in other left governments such as Argentina, Ecuador, and Venezuela. To govern effectively, Chilean presidents must forge consensus first within their own center-left political coalition, thus limiting their ability to pursue purely strategic alliances with more conservative actors.

The uniquely Chilean development of this politics of consensus within Pink Tide countries had long-term consequences for both political reforms around rights for women and sexual minorities, and the relationships between the Left and societal actors, including the broader social movements. In particular, the Concertación was generally unwilling to support political demands that could be seen as challenging one of Chile's foundational political beliefs: that an idealized heteropatriarchal family is the basis of a well-ordered society and the state has the responsibility of protecting and promoting this vision of family (Thomas 2011). As shown below, political projects that were seen as threatening to the heteropatriarchal family created dissent. Further, policy demands addressing women's inequality were much more likely to succeed if the demands could be framed as supporting either women's traditional roles as wives or mothers, or as being generally "profamily" (Blofield and Haas 2005; Franceschet 2005; Haas 2010). The political weight of this gendered political consensus, however, did not arise simply from the posttransition needs of the governing Concertación. Instead, both the ability to build consensus by invoking the state's responsibilities to promote and protect an idealized heteropatriarchal family, and the dissent and conflict that could be generated by criticizing or questioning gendered familial norms, have shaped the development of Chile's political parties and its social movements since Chilean Independence (Thomas 2011). In the next section, I briefly trace the historical development of this gendered political consensus, particularly with respect to the Left, and how it came to shape the politics of the democratic transition and the Concertación period.

The Heteropatriarchal Family and a Gendered Political Consensus

The political belief in the importance of the heteropatriarchal family as the key to political stability and a well-ordered society emerged as a foundational political ideology during Chile's revolutionary founding (Thomas 2011; Felstiner 1983). As in other newly independent Latin American nations, creole elites refashioned the colonial ideology of patriarchalism to help naturalize their rule within the emerging liberal republics (Dore 2000). In Chile, the political importance of the ideological tie between the heteropatriarchal family and the state was maintained throughout the nineteenth and twentieth centuries. These normative ideals proved politically useful for elites in managing the political demands of nonelite men, including from indigenous communities, and all women. Starting in the early 1900s, political reformers also increasingly invoked state responsibility for heteropatriarchal families to push for the creation of Chile's welfare state and social welfare policies. Historians have documented how left political parties and the disparate groups of the first wave of the women's movement drew on familial beliefs to push for a range of political reforms, including early labor legislation (Hutchinson 2001); the social welfare policies of Chile's first center-left political coalition, the Popular Front (Rosemblatt 2001); the development of maternal health programs (Pieper Mooney 2009); and the agrarian reform projects of the 1960s and 1970s (Tinsman 2002).[3] Throughout the twentieth century, women's groups turned to maternalism to argue for such diverse goals as increasing women's access to education, improving the health of mothers and children, and reforming civil codes to give married women greater control over property and wages. Suffrage activists argued for women's citizenship by connecting civic duty to women's familial roles as wives and mothers (Lavrin 1995).

While such maternalist justifications were present elsewhere in the region—appearing in women's rights struggles in places such as Brazil, Argentina, and Mexico—in Chile the use of heteropatriarchal ideals in crafting legislative and policy compromises strengthened their political salience. Left parties and women's groups often found common ground in their shared beliefs about the societal importance of family. Different visions, however, especially of the extent of men's patriarchal privileges within family, could also generate conflict (Kirkwood 1986; Lavrin 1995). Further, very little space for any discussion of either women's sexuality or homosexuality existed. Religious, legal, and medical discourses in Chile during this time presented homosexuality as deviant behavior that needed to be controlled and punished by the state (Contardo 2011). Similarly, women who broke societal norms about women's sexuality by engaging in prostitution were also the targets of legal, medical, and religious control. Prostitution was used politically to advance arguments about either the evils of capitalism (Left) or the danger of moral and religious decay within the society (Right) (Candina 2013). Given this context, Chile's early radical women's groups had difficulties in opening a space to discuss women's sexuality and sexual desire—even inside the confines of the traditional marriage (Hutchinson 2001).

The consensus around the heteropatriarchal family as the basic institution of society and central to political stability and national development continued to shape the politics of Chile during the decades of the 1960s and 1970s. The left political parties in Salvador Allende's Unidad Popular (Popular Unity, or UP) coalition used this consensus to argue for their broader reform agenda (Shayne 2004; Thomas 2011). Allende and the UP supported increasing the wages for working-class men, expanding family allowances (most often also paid to men as the head of household), and improving working-class women's ability to mother by either staying home (because of men's better wages) or by managing conflicts between their roles as workers and mothers (Shayne 2004; Thomas 2011). Pushed by feminist activists, the UP did support attempts to equalize women's relative position within the family, such as granting women "full civil capacity" and making community property the default marital property arrangement, rather than simply recognizing the husband as the "chief of the conjugal society" (Htun 2003, 73–74). While the changes promoted by the UP produced material gains for working-class and poor women, Allende's programs posed virtually "no threat to the patriarchal structures at either the micro or macro levels . . . [and] Allende and the UP coalition felt no need to expand their gendered programs beyond the nuclear family" (Shayne 2004,

88). Questions of homosexuality were also denigrated or completely marginalized. Male homosexuality was positioned as antithetical to the robust masculinity of the Left's iconic male worker. Rather, as in the leftist propaganda against the Right's presidential candidate in 1970, Jorge Alessandri, even the possibility of male homosexuality (Alessandri was unmarried and childless) was portrayed as resulting from the decadence of the bourgeois elite or the perversity of capitalism (Thomas 2011, 73).

The current relationship between the political parties on the Left and the progressive women's movements was forged in their shared resistance to the military government. Women were the backbone of the human rights and popular movements, as well as the women's and feminist movements (Hardy 1987; Chuchryk 1994; Valdés and Weinstein 1989; Baldez 2002; Franceschet 2005). In their struggle against the military dictatorship of Pinochet (1973–90), both left political activists and women's movements often invoked protecting and promoting familial welfare to frame and justify their actions, directly contesting pro-Pinochet propaganda lauding family security (Thomas 2011). Human rights groups such as the Agrupación de los Familiares de los Detenidos y Desparecidos (Association of Relatives of the Detained and Disappeared, AFDD) emphasized the damage and the suffering inflicted by the military on their families (Thomas 2011). Popular women's groups contrasted the idealized family life presented in governmental propaganda with their quotidian experiences of poverty, unemployment, and state neglect (Thomas 2011). While certainly reflecting deeply held personal beliefs and commitments, the explicitly familial framing of these claims also served a number of strategic needs. First, the opposition's invocation of family directly challenged regime propaganda that positioned Pinochet as the father figure dedicated to the welfare of Chilean families and who had saved families from political chaos and the threat of communism. Second, emphasizing family provided a clear connection with the values and priorities of the Catholic Church, which was providing essential material and political support to many women's groups through the Vicaría de la Solidaridad (Vicariate of Solidarity). Finally, the activists could draw on a history of family-based claims from women's and left organizing in order to build coalitions within the broader prodemocracy movement (Thomas 2011).

Providing a more critical lens, feminist activists worked to expose the centrality of patriarchal ideology to the dictatorship. They analyzed how Pinochet was using the connections between patriarchal and authoritarian beliefs to justify his rule (Kirkwood 1986; Valenzuela and Marshall 1986; Bunster 1988).

Indeed, given the gendered power relations that had governed the lives of Chilean women, some Chilean feminists argued that women had never experienced true democracy. Pioneering feminist theorists such as Julietta Kirkwood, Maria Elena Valenzuela, Ximena Bunster, Maria Teresa Marshal, and Teresa Valdés, and organizations such as the Centro de Estudios de la Mujer (Center for Studies of Women, or CEM), El Movimiento Feminista (Feminist Movement), and the Casa de la Mujer La Morada (The Sanctuary: A Home for Women) placed their analysis of gendered power relations at the center of their critique, demanding that political democratization must also contain a radical commitment to democratizing the private world of the family. The idea was captured in the famous slogan that became emblematic of the Chilean women's movement: "Democracy in the home and in the country." Feminist groups thus put forward a political analysis that revealed and critiqued the centrality of the heteropatriarchal consensus in Chilean politics and its political implications for women (Thomas 2011).

The work being done by feminists in exposing the heteropatriarchal roots of Chilean society and politics helped spur activism by sexual minorities. The first explicitly lesbian organization, Colectivo Lésbico Feminista Ayuquelén (Ayuquelén Lesbian Feminist Collective), was founded by Susana Peña, Cecilia Riquelme, and Carmen Ulloa in 1984. The Colectivo Ayuquelén provided critical analysis of compulsory heterosexuality within Chile, hoping to create a space to "open a debate over the space of lesbianism within the social movement of women" (Robles 2009). While transnational lesbian and gay mobilization within Latin America grew throughout the 1980s, in Chile, sexual minority organizations maintained a low profile, mostly meeting in the houses of individual members and not participating in broader public demonstrations (Riquelme 2004; Díez 2015). Even in 1987, when for the first time, the Colectivo Ayuquelén published an anonymous group interview in the opposition magazine *Apsi*, members noted, "It was very difficult to begin a process of opening in Chile . . . because this country is highly homophobic. . . . We are living in a ghetto, we are living a double life" (Robles 2009).

The return of democratic governance dramatically altered the political context for activists. The increasing power of political parties vis-à-vis social movements, and the lack of robust political support on the part of the Concertación for women's rights, exacerbated ongoing tensions within the broader women's movement. In Chile, the debate between those who argued against working with political parties and the state, the *autonomas* (autonomous), and those who participated in both political parties and the women's activism, the *doble militantes* (double militants), was particularly intense during the early 1990s. Many female activists experienced the reluctance of the Concertación to respond to feminist demands as a betrayal of the ideals of democratization and the immense work done by the women's movements in both delegitimizing the military government and in bringing back democracy (Haas 2010). The transition also provided new forms of employment and opportunities for many activists as the Concertación took control of the state. Feminist leaders become femocrats by taking positions in the newly created national women's agency SERNAM, as well as in other ministries. As in Brazil, Uruguay, and, initially, Argentina and Ecuador, this process helped to provide important allies within the state and to create a group of career civil servants committed to feminist goals.[4] But it also helped to demobilize the broader women's movements (Schild 1998).

As Chilean democracy consolidated, many women's organizations also lost previous sources of support from foreign governments and international aid agencies as these organizations either shifted their support to the state or left Chile to focus on other areas (Waylen 2000). This again shifted power toward the state as a source of funding. However, not all women's organizations or feminist NGOs had equal access. State institutions often favored groups that were more moderate, less critical, and those that provided sophisticated technical services, a process understood as "NGOization" (Alvarez 1998; Schild 1998). Critics have noted a consistent class and ethnic bias in the types of groups receiving state support, with popular women's and indigenous groups excluded both from state funding and the access needed to shape policy (Richards 2004). The lack of broader participation on the part of indigenous women has been particularly problematic in terms of policies pursued by the Concertación, which viewed indigenous demands as arising from poverty, while ignoring the history of colonial dispossession, lack of cultural recognition, and effective representation (Richards 2013). This has meant that policies directed toward indigenous communities tend to focus on increasing economic productivity through resource extraction and social integration. Indigenous communities often reject the economic and cultural model promoted in these policies and see the policies as in conflict with their demands for the restitution of land rights, cultural recognition, and community control (Richards 2013).

By the end of the 1990s, some researchers argued that Chile no longer had *a* women's movement and what existed instead was a fragmented proliferation of neighborhood organizations, feminist organizations, and feminist

NGOs (Tobar et al. 2004). Throughout the 2000s, newer organizations often focused on specific issues and sought to be sites for networking at national and international levels, such as the Asociación Nacional de Mujeres Rurales e Indígenas (National Association of Rural and Indigenous Women) and the Foro Salud de Derechos Sexuales y Reproductiva (Sexual and Reproductive Rights Health Forum). Past participants in the women's and feminist movements became embedded in an array of different societal institutions, including universities, international organizations (including the UN and the Ford Foundation), transnational feminist networks, and a growing number of feminist NGOs.

While the movement had fractured, there was continued activism on the part of many women around women's inequality, lack of rights, and the cultural dominance of the gender roles prescribed within a heteropatriarchal ideology. Increasingly, women's political equality, the existence of discrimination against women and sexual minorities, and a more egalitarian understanding of gender roles within the family were being recognized and embraced by Chilean society. Societal support for gender equality and the recognition and rights of sexual minorities often advanced far more quickly than the needed legal changes, posing challenges to the politics of consensus embraced by the Concertación.

Democratic Governance and the Limits of a Policy Change

The Concertación's prioritization of political stability, consensus within the coalition, economic growth, and state-led social welfare affected how they governed and interacted with social movements and their political opposition. For women's, feminist, and LGBTQ groups, the intersection of the Concertación's politics of consensus and the strong heteropatriarchal norms of Chilean society shaped the political opportunities for advancing women's political representation, redistribution, bodily autonomy, and identity recognition. Conforming to existing heteropatriarchal norms was often a useful way to craft needed political consensus for policy changes, but open challenges to these norms risked generating the types of political conflicts that the Concertación and its presidents sought to avoid in order to pursue their broader legislative agenda. This general political dynamic partly explains the limited openings for activists demanding gender equality and LGBTQ rights. Below, I discuss how this dynamic became part of the demands concerning political participation, redistribution, bodily autonomy, and identity recognition during the first twenty years of Concertación rule (1990–2010).

While democracy returned to the country in 1990, women's equality was not assured. Divorce was illegal; men were automatically granted greater rights to manage conjugal property in marriage and the legal authority over children; legal distinctions existed between legitimate and illegitimate children in terms of paternal responsibility for support and inheritance; no legislation existed on domestic violence; all abortion was illegal; pregnant students could be expelled from schools; and rape was not recognized within marriage (Haas 2010, 2). To address these issues, activists formed an umbrella organization, the Concertación Nacional de Mujeres por la Democracia (Women's National Coalition for Democracy, or CDM), which pushed for greater representation of women in elected office, the creation of a women's policy agency, and the ratification of CEDAW,[5] among other demands (Chuchryk 1994, 84–85).

Even with this explicit activism promoting political representation, women made slow progress. In the first posttransition election in 1990, only five women total (5.8 percent) were elected to the Chamber of Deputies and just one woman was elected to the Senate, numbers that were actually smaller than the number of women elected before the coup in 1973.[6] During the first two decades of Concertación governments, women's representation remained below 16 percent in both the Chamber of Deputies and the Senate (IPU 2017). The lack of progress in increasing women's elected political representation in particular reflected the ambivalence of powerful (male) party elites and the conflict generated by mechanisms to address women's marginalization (Franceschet and Thomas 2015).[7] The first three presidents of the Concertación did not push for any national gender quota legislation. Bachelet's government introduced a gender quota law in 2007, but it died in committee, lacking broad support among the Concertación.[8] Women have also made few gains in terms of party leadership, despite ongoing activism of doble militantes. Women's exclusion from leadership positions has meant that very few women have been part of the negotiations among political parties to determine electoral lists and executive appointments. The need for political consensus and the complex negotiations required to compete electorally as a coalition meant that internal party quotas were never enforced (Hinojosa and Franceschet 2012).

Feminist activists eventually had more success in promoting women's representation within the executive branch and state bureaucracy. During the first Concertación government, President Aylwin appointed only one woman to his cabinet, SERNAM head Soledad Alvear. Alvear was granted ministerial status, even though the newly created SERNAM was a service and not a ministry, as a response to protests over the lack of women in the initial cabinet. President Eduardo Frei Ruiz-Tagle (1994–2000) appointed three women to cabinet positions, and President Ricardo Lagos (2000–2006) appointed five. President Bachelet, as part of her government's explicit commitment to gender equality, appointed Chile's, and Latin America's, first gender parity cabinet in 2006.

The most important institutional change within the state was the creation of SERNAM by legislation in 1990 under President Aylwin. SERNAM is tasked with a double mandate: (1) to design and promote policies and laws to address women's inequality in Chilean society; and (2) to coordinate the gender equality programs and policies within the state's other ministries and agencies (Franceschet 2005; Haas 2010). The focus on inter-agency coordination specifically responded to activists' concerns that women's issues would be ghettoized, and instead promoted a transversal mandate for SERNAM (Richards 2004; Haas 2010).

The ability of SERNAM to fulfill its mandate, however, has been limited by the Concertación's need to maintain political consensus and the resistance generated by any attempt to change the centrality of heteropatriarchal gender relations. Chile's right political parties saw the creation of SERNAM as promoting an unacceptable emphasis on women's equality and undermining women's traditional roles within the family as wives and mothers (Franceschet 2005; Haas 2010). Within the parties of the Concertación, there was also disagreement over SERNAM. More socially conservative members, often from the PDC, sought to limit SERNAM's agenda to issues that generated less political conflict. However, working within these limitations, SERNAM grew from a small, understaffed agency into the largest and best-funded women's policy agency in Latin America (Ríos 2009). SERNAM was involved in almost every successful piece of legislation passed promoting women's rights, gender equality, and LGBTQ rights, and played a central role within the executive branch in promoting gender mainstreaming policies.[9] Particularly under Bachelet, SERNAM served as a key institutional advocate on gender equality, an advantage nearly unique to Chile among the cases analyzed in this volume (although Brazil offers a close comparison).

In contrast to the careful management of possible conflicts around women's political representation, there was widespread consensus for expanding state services to the poor. The general priority given to poverty alleviation within the Concertación also benefited women, who are overrepresented among the poor (Staab 2012, 2016). Chile's Left has long recognized that women are economically disadvantaged and exploited in capitalism because of lower rates of workforce participation, the unpaid care-taking responsibilities assigned to women by society, and gender discrimination. This basic analysis has guided the historical attempts discussed above by left political parties that often strengthened both the male-breadwinner bias and the maternalist provisions of state social welfare policies (Staab 2012). During the first four governments of the Concertación, programs that focused specifically on improving women's socioeconomic status, particularly the conditions of women-headed families, were supported and expanded. In 1990, the Concertación created the Mujeres Jefas de Hogar (Women Head of Household) program, a wide-ranging initiative to address the gendered causes of women's poverty and to help women overcome obstacles to labor force participation. Overseen by SERNAM, the national plan originally included legal changes to establish married women's full legal capacity to manage family resources and to establish men's legal responsibility for all their children (regardless of the marital status of the couple); policies that promoted education and training for women; childcare assistance; and housing assistance (Franceschet 2005, 125). While this program has been criticized for prioritizing women's participation in the workforce and for problems coordinating between the ministries and agencies involved in delivering services, it has also been a mainstay of SERNAM's mandate and a significant program directed at women's socioeconomic well-being.[10]

The intersectoral approach to poverty reduction that characterized this program was a model for later programs, particularly Chile Solidario (Solidarity Chile) and Chile Crece Contigo (Chile Grows with You). Chile Solidario was designed and implemented under President Lagos in 2002 as a direct response to the continuing intractability of extreme poverty in Chile (Larrañaga et al. 2012). It targeted families and conceptualized extreme poverty as a result of multiple factors, not just low income but also the marginalization from social networks and state services, and low levels of psychosocial assets. While this broader approach differentiated Chile Solidario from conditional cash transfer programs in other countries, critics point out that women, who are often the focus of benefits, are also the ones expected to shoulder the burden of maintaining participation in the program (Borzutzky 2009). In addition, even though women headed almost 40 percent of the enrolled families, the program did not directly address issues of gender inequality and did not embrace a gender analysis of poverty (Borzutzky 2009).

Under Bachelet, gender equality, as opposed to simply poverty alleviation, did become an explicit part of social programs.[11] This focus on gender equality was unique among left administrations throughout Latin America. In addition, Bachelet embraced a vision of social provision that focused on social protection "from cradle to old age" and saw social provision as a "right" (Staab 2012, 307). These ideals guided the development of the Chile Crece Contigo program designed to provide integrated state support for both children and mothers, particularly from disadvantaged sectors, through programs to address issues of health, preschool education, familial conditions, and neighborhood development. The best-known aspect of Chile Crece Contigo was the construction of at least eight hundred child-care centers by 2010 run by the state through JUNJI (La Junta Nacional de Jardines Infantales [National Board of Preschools]). The legislation provides a right to a place in state-supported child-care centers or kindergartens for households in the lowest two-thirds of income distribution. Full-time spots are provided where the mothers are working, looking for work, or pursuing an education. Right to part-time placement is provided regardless of the mother's activities. The program also contains significant support for pregnant women, including access to prenatal care, protection of adoptive parents' rights, and working women's right to breastfeed their children.[12] Bachelet's government advocated for this program on the basis that it would provide high-quality childcare, early education to poor children, and better access for lower-class women to educational and employment opportunities. Supporters of the program praised the state's recognition of the barriers placed on women because of care work and the state's shared responsibility for childcare as examples of Bachelet's commitment to promoting women's equality.[13]

Bachelet's government also paid special attention to gender inequality in pension reforms passed in 2008. Chile's pension system had been radically privatized in 1980 to create individual capital accounts financed solely by the worker through defined contributions and managed by private insurance companies that were allowed to charge hefty commission fees (Staab 2012). The failures of this system to provide retirement security for many Chileans and its abusive high fees were widely recognized. Bachelet campaigned on reforming the system, and in 2008 passed legislation that expanded governmental provision through a means-tested noncontributory minimum pensions and through subsidies for low pensions up to a set maximum contribution. Women are among the main beneficiaries because many have either no or very small retirement accounts due to low salaries, interrupted working lives, or lack of work in the formal economy (Staab 2012). Bachelet also highlighted the issue of gender equality in the pension reforms through specifically targeted reforms. In particular, Chile now provides a *bono por hijo* (child credit) to all mothers that accumulates in their account until they retire. These reforms went farther than other proposals in guaranteeing a basic pension for women and in recognizing the social costs borne by women because of their role as family caretakers (Staab 2012). They also offer a marked contrast with the fate of the homemakers' right to social security that was enshrined in Venezuela's constitution but never fully implemented.

Bachelet's pension reform and Chile Crece Contigo went the furthest in promoting the concept of the rights of all citizens, including women, to access childcare, health care, and retirement within the Concertación's programs.[14] These programs improved women's economic security by addressing areas where women suffer economic inequality because of gendered responsibilities for care work. However, Bachelet's flagship reforms ultimately did not present a radical challenge to women's traditional gender roles in providing care or in the long-standing emphasis on families as the main target of poverty reduction programs. Her reforms operated within the general neoliberal consensus by focusing on expanding state services, rather than, for example, radically questioning the basic precepts of an economy dependent on insecure and flexible labor, and as care work as ultimately women's private responsibility rather than a social responsibility shared between the state and business.

Within the Concertación, there was strong support for policies directed toward decreasing poverty and expanding state provision of social services for families. Women's demands for bodily autonomy and identity recognition, however, have often generated greater political conflict. Reforms in these areas more directly questioned heteropatriarchal norms. To make advances in these areas, feminist, and increasingly LGBTQ, activists, faced not only strong opposition from political parties on the right, the Catholic Church, and the growing importance of religious Evangelical conservatives but also within the Center and Left. Within the category of bodily autonomy, policy areas that have seen the most advances are, not surprisingly, focused on antiviolence legislation (Haas 2010; Ríos 2009). The strength of the heteropatriarchal consensus to place limits on legislation, however, can be seen in the political struggles involved in passing the 1994 domestic violence law. The original version, proposed by feminist legislators and supported broadly by the women's movement, stressed women's rights and the need to protect victims of abuse. However, as indicated by its title, the "Intrafamily Violence" law that passed promoted conciliation, and family unity and cohesion (Haas 2010, 104–5). The watering down of the original proposal resulted from not only strong opposition from parties on the Right to the original proposal but also uneasiness within the Concertación over the more feminist framing of the bill and the possibility of conflict that this created within the coalition and with the Catholic Church (Haas 2010). Feminist organizations immediately criticized the limitations of the law and began working on reforms. It took ten years before a 2005 law "explicitly criminalize[d] domestic violence," allowed the aggressor to be removed from the home (rather than seeking to maintain family unity), and increased funding for enforcement (Haas 2010). During Bachelet's first presidency, the issue of violence against women was again taken up in terms of strengthening laws on rape and sexual assault originally reformed in 1993, and with legislation that specifically recognized femicide.

Changing laws and policies to allow women to control their reproduction has also been difficult. Until 2017, Chile was one of only three Latin American countries (along with Nicaragua and El Salvador) that completely banned abortion without exception. As one of his final acts, Pinochet prohibited all abortion in 1989, replacing a law (in place since 1931) that allowed for therapeutic abortion. Despite how recent the change was, there was limited willingness on the part of the Concertación to pursue even reinstating the previous law when they assumed power in 1990. Abortion was an issue that generated conflict not only among the parties of the Concertación but also within the individual parties of the coalition, particularly the Partido Demócrata Cristiano (PDC). In addition, the two largest right parties, the Renovación Nacional and the Unión Demócrata Independiente, were quick to frame any support for liberalization as an attack on Chilean families and traditional values, and to use this framing to increase tension between the governing Concertación and the Catholic Church (Brito et al. 2012). The Catholic Church had been an ally of the prodemocratic social movements, and the political elite of the Concertación was often unwilling to pursue issues that might damage this relationship. Thus, while individual feminist legislators have consistently introduced bills to decriminalize abortion, these bills never gained the support of the executive during Concertación presidencies, almost guaranteeing failure (Haas 2010). Even Bachelet was unwilling to publicly support liberalizing abortion during her first presidency, a position critiqued by feminist activists.[15]

The conflict generated by promoting women's bodily autonomy was apparent in the political response to Bachelet's policy expanding women's access to the morning-after pill by making pills available in state-run clinics that serve poor and working-class women. After a Supreme Court ruling prohibiting distribution on the grounds of protecting "life," Bachelet pushed through the "fertility regulation" law that provided legal protections to access contraceptive information and methods, except methods that may cause abortion (Brito et al. 2012; Stevenson 2012).

Legal changes that equalize men and women's position within the family have also generated political conflict, delaying their passage. For example, ending the legal distinction between legitimate and illegitimate children passed only in 1998, and pregnant students were not legally guaranteed equal rights to education until 2000. Currently, changes to marital property laws mean that while married couples can choose to share the management of property or to manage property separately, the default property state entered into upon marriage remains for the husband to manage all property. Thus, issues that challenged heteropatriarchal norms had to be carefully negotiated within the Concertación because of their potential to generate conflict, often delaying or removing from the political agenda policy changes demanded by feminists and women's groups.

The slow progress around issues of bodily autonomy and identity recognition for sexual minorities also reflects the overall dynamic between heteropatriarchal norms and the politics of consensus. The growth of publicly visible gay and lesbian groups in Chile often lagged behind that in other Latin American countries (Díez 2015). The few groups that existed during the dictatorship, such as Colectivo Ayuquelén or the Corporation for AIDS Prevention, founded in 1987, had limited presence or visibility in the broader democratization movement. In the 1990s and 2000s, most LGBTQ organizing took place within either a broadly liberal human rights framework or on issues of public health (MUMS Chile 2015). During this time there were growing divisions among activists over whether to focus on AIDS or combatting homophobic discrimination. The lack of unity and their general isolation from other social movements, particularly the women's movement, limited LGBTQ group's ability to push for legal rights and recognition for sexual minorities (Díez 2015, 103–4). Although Chile finally decriminalized homosexuality in 1999, this success was a product not of concerted activism but of the individual actions of certain committed legislators, the technical work of SERNAM, and a broader desire on the part of the Concertación to bring Chile in line with international norms, particularly as it pursued agreements with the European Union (Díez 2015, 197–202).

However, during the 2000s, groups such as MOVILH (Movimiento de Integración y Liberación Homosexual, Movement for the Integration and Liberation of Homosexuals) and MUMS Chile (Movimiento por la Diversidad Sexual, Movement for Sexual Diversity) began a strategy of publicly denouncing cases of discrimination in order to press for greater societal recognition and legal protection (Díez 2015, 207). In 2003, MOVILH and committed feminist deputy María Antonieta Saa introduced a bill to legalize civil unions in Chile. However, neither Lagos nor Bachelet prioritized the issue during their presidencies. In 2005, Lagos submitted a general antidiscrimination bill to Congress that included antidiscrimination protection for sexual orientation and gender identity. These inclusions generated significant opposition on the part of conservative legislators, who cast the bill as an attack on the ability of people to express opposition to homosexuality grounded in religious belief (Díez 2015, 215). While Bachelet had voiced her support for this proposal during her first presidency, opposition to the measure by the Right and lack of consensus in the Concertación meant it was not a priority for her presidency and no legislative action was taken.

Both issues were unexpectedly taken up by Sebastian Piñera in his 2010 presidential campaign as part of a broader strategy to present an image of a "renewed, liberal and non-threatening Right" (Díez 2015, 227). Piñera's support of civil unions in his campaign platform, while supported by his Renovación Nacional party, had not been agreed to by the more conservative party of the Alianza coalition, the Unión Demócrata Independiente (UDI), which saw civil unions as a threat to marriage as the central institution of Chilean society (Díez 2015, 227–28). Once in office, Piñera's government faced continuing disagreement within his governing coalition on this issue. However, activism around LGBTQ issues also grew with the foundation of a new group, Fundación Iguales (Equality Foundation, formed in 2011) and the public support of Pablo Simonetti, a popular author, and Luis Larraín Steib, a member of a prominent conservative family (Díez 2015, 231–33). Fundación Iguales quickly developed a broad network among feminist, human rights, and academic groups to push for the antidiscrimination law. Finally, in 2012, after the brutal killing of a young man because of his sexual identity, demands for action gained greater political weight. With the support of Piñera, key legislators (mostly on the Left), and the lobbying activity of Fundación Iguales, MOVILH and MUMS, a law prohibiting discrimination against sexual minorities passed in both the Chamber of Deputies and the Senate with significant support (Díez 2015, 226–38). However, progress on the civil union bill during Piñera's presidency remained stalled because of the conflict it generated within his coalition and opposition by religious conservatives.

Bachelet's Second Term:
The End of the Heteropatriarchal Consensus?

In 2014, Bachelet won the presidency for a second time, bringing back center-left government. Chile's political context, however, was radically different from that of 2006. While Bachelet had garnered a fourth presidency for the Concertación by promising both "continuity" and "change," in 2014 Chileans were not interested in continuity, just change. Piñera's presidency was widely perceived as a failure because of his struggles in advancing his agenda and governing effectively. Across the political spectrum, Chile's political parties were in deep crisis because of their inability to address ongoing problems with political corruption and growing demands for greater democratic transparency and accountability. Many Chileans, particularly the activists leading the sustained student mobilization under Piñera and the Mapuche indigenous movement against the despoiling of traditional lands, were increasingly critical of both the extractivist, neoliberal socioeconomic model and the basic political system inherited from the military dictatorship but maintained by the Concertación's consensus politics. LBGTQ groups were organizing to demand marriage equality, the expansion of sexual minority rights, and the recognition of transgender identities. Feminists were advocating for not only a liberalization of Chile's total ban but also women's right to freely decide to have an abortion and the safe provision of abortions, including in public medical facilities. More and more organizations and activists were explicitly pushing for policies that questioned long-standing heteropatriarchal norms and the centrality of the traditional family to Chilean politics.

In responding to this new political context, Bachelet and her Nueva Mayoría coalition promised radical reforms to the political system. Bachelet's platform included three basic pillars: reforms to the neoliberal educational system designed to increase state support and improve quality; an overhaul of the tax system designed to generate more income for social programs and greater redistribution of income; and a new constitution that would include the end to the binomial electoral process in favor of a more proportional system (Chile de todos, 2013). While not overlooked, issues of gender equality and LGBTQ rights were certainly secondary in the 2013 campaign. Proposals directed towards women focused on strengthening existing laws and provisions concerning pay equity in employment, gender discrimination in the workforce, and further attention to women's needs in health care and retirement, rather than radical new initiatives. Bachelet's platform also included the creation of a Ministry of Women and Gender Equality (thus strengthening SERNAM), parity in governmental appointments, the expansion of women's reproductive rights—including the liberalization of abortion—and the inclusion of gender quotas in political reforms. For the LGBTQ community, the platform promised to raise the subject of marriage equality and reforms to allow for the legal change of names and gender identity on state documents (Chile de todos, 2013). Many of these promises would not be kept.

As with the previous Concertación governments, the Nueva Mayoría was faced with the need to build broad political consensus to address the difficulties of governing through a large and disparate political coalition. In addition, Bachelet's political capital, personal reputation, and public support were damaged early in her presidency by a corruption scandal involving a real-estate deal by her son and daughter-in-law and charges of influence peddling on their part. Political crisis generated by political scandals around campaign financing affecting all of Chile's traditional political parties also diminished the ability of Bachelet and the Nueva Mayoría to pursue their ambitious reform agenda.

Within this context, successful reforms either had widespread support in the coalition or, at minimum, did not generate much conflict. Bachelet backed legislation that created a Ministry of Women and Gender Equality, expanding SERNAM's institutional weight and further insulating it from political attack. While this change was widely supported, the legislation did not dramatically increase the budget of the new ministry. Chile's first quota law requiring that no gender could represent more than 60 percent of all candidates was passed as part of the larger reform of Chile's binomial system and with the personal support of the president (Vargas 2015). However, without further legislation the gender quota will end after four elections (in 2029), and while radical for Chile in the context of the previous political struggle, much of Latin America is moving towards mechanisms for electoral parity for women. Bachelet also did not carry through with her promises to increase women's representation in executive office. Unlike her first term in office, she did not name a gender parity cabinet (women held 39 percent of seats in the first cabinet), and even fewer women were appointed at the level of subsecretaries and regional governors. Observers believed that Bachelet was unwilling to spend her political capital on gender parity appointments given the continued resistance to gender parity within coalition parties and her other political priorities.[16]

The contrast between the political reception of civil unions and the liberalization of abortion is instructive in showing the continuing power of familial norms even amid change. In April of 2015, Bachelet signed the very first law to recognize same-sex couples, creating civil unions that provide legal protections to couples who choose to register with the state. While parts of the political Right and conservative religious groups opposed civil unions as dangerous to the foundational role played by heterosexual marriage and the nuclear family, proponents defended the law as a way to recognize and protect different forms of families. For example, during the signing ceremony Bachelet noted that the law "recognized the right of all people to form a family." In general, civil unions received broad support within the Nueva Mayoría. In June of 2016, barely a year into the new law, Bachelet and the Nueva Mayoría signed an agreement to promote marriage equality in response to a petition that MOVILH had filed with the Inter-American Court of Human Rights (MOVILH 2016). In this way, civil union and marriage equality might be following the Left's pattern of willingness to recognize diverse family forms, without necessarily meaning the end of strong normative support for patriarchal gender norms.

The continuing power of heteropatriarchal norms to limit reform can also be seen in the political response to Bachelet's attempts to expand women's rights to access safe abortion. While in her first term Bachelet had studiously avoided legislation on abortion, in January of 2015 Bachelet proposed a law that would legalize abortion during the first twelve weeks of pregnancy in three cases: 1) the life of mother is endangered; 2) the pregnancy is the result of rape; or 3) the fetus is unviable. Her action marked the first time the executive has proposed and backed abortion reform. However, even with strong public support for these modest liberalizations, change was politically fraught. Conservative opposition, particularly in the Catholic Church, among Evangelicals, and from the most right political party, UDI, was quite strong. The centrist PDC granted their parliamentary members freedom to vote their conscience rather than making it a party-line vote (Cooperativa 2015). Soledad Alvear, a leader of the PDC and a past minister of SERNAM, actively campaigned against the law, while Laura Albornoz, also PDC member and SERNAM's minister during Bachelet's first government, discussed publicly her own therapeutic abortion and called for PDC support (Marín 2015). The intense debate—even within the Nueva Mayoría—over a moderate liberalization of Chile's complete ban on abortion reflects how controversial issues of women's bodily autonomy remain. After twenty-seven years of legislative debate and political activism, Bachelet's moderate reforms to abortion policy passed in 2017.

Conclusion

Above, I argued that the politics of consensus within Chile's center-left governing coalition politics have shaped the differences found in the type and timing of reforms on socioeconomic redistribution, political representation, bodily autonomy, and identity recognition. Upon assuming power in 1990, the Concertación incorporated into their political platforms and legislative agenda support for women's equality and, after 2000, for the rights of sexual minorities. The greater openness to these demands within center and left political parties partly reflected the shared experience of resistance to the military dictatorship and the ongoing and sustained activism by women, feminists, and LGBTQ activists both within and outside of the Concertación. However, to maintain its coalition and pass legislation, the Concertación often relied upon normative beliefs about appropriate gender roles and the centrality of the family to generate political consensus. Thus, widespread agreement around these norms provided support for reforms such as providing economic support for families; helping poor women and their children; protecting women from violence; and even extending state protection to newer, more diverse families formed out of same-sex unions. Policies that challenge heteropatriarchal norms, particularly advancing women's bodily autonomy and political power, have been more difficult. However, even there, continual pressure has resulted in some hard-fought victories such as the inclusion of gender quotas in the electoral reforms passed in 2016 and the liberalization of abortion in 2017. The exigencies of maintaining a political coalition dependent on consensus is one reason that, even after nearly three decades of center-left governments, the relationship between Chile's Left and women's movements, feminist activists, and the growing LGBTQ groups in Chile remains contradictory.

The dynamic of the politics of consensus has also mitigated the power of factors identified in other cases in explaining the paradoxes of Pink Tide government policies on women's and sexual minority rights. While granted extensive executive and legislative powers, Chile's center-left presidents never displayed the hyperpresidentialism of more populist left leaders who were willing to sacrifice ideological commitments to gender equality to make strategic deals with key conservative actors, such as Daniel Ortega's willingness to ban abortion in Nicaragua to gain the support of powerful conservative actors for his election and governing agenda (see chapter 7). Unlike in Argentina, where the fate of certain gender and sexuality policy reforms clearly depended on the dynamic between the executive and the Catholic Church, in Chile the power of the Church was mediated through the contingencies of coalition politics (see chapter 2). Continuing resistance from the Catholic Church to the recognition of sexual minority rights, for example, has not stopped the passage of civil unions and progress toward marriage equality and transgender rights because of the increasing inclusion of these issues in the parties of the Nueva Mayoría. The type of blatant homophobia that is still sometimes voiced by left leaders in other countries, such as Ortega in Nicaragua or Rafael Correa in Ecuador, is not seen in Chile (see chapters 7 and 8). Public homophobia on the part of party leaders on the Nueva Mayoría would be roundly condemned within their coalition, and politically costly.

With respect to the other cases discussed in this volume, the center-left coalition governments in Chile have also given comparatively more institutional weight to women's rights and gender equality within the state through the creation of SERNAM. SERNAM avoided the fate of the women's policy agencies in places like Argentina, Bolivia, and Ecuador, where they ceased to function because of lack of consistent support and funding, or in cases like Venezuela, where women's policy agencies were largely directed toward supporting Chávez and his goals. While recognizing SERNAM's real institutional limitations and its often vexed relationships with social movements, the stability and growing institutional power of SERNAM within the executive has meant the existence since 1990 of a state organization explicitly tasked with women's rights, gender equality goals, and now the rights and inclusion of sexual minorities. Though not always successful, SERNAM, particularly under Bachelet, was more willing to directly challenge the heteropatriarchal consensus to push for more radical change. That support for SERNAM is now integral to the politics of the center-left in Chile can be seen in the resistance generated by Piñera's unsuccessful attempt during his first presidency to replace SERNAM with a Ministry of the Family. It was partly in response to this attack on SERNAM and its mission within the state that Bachelet in her second presidency was spurred to pass legislation creating the Ministry of Women and Gender Equality, further insulating Chile's women's policy agency from attack from future governments.[17] The question for both feminists and the Left in the twenty-first century is whether support for gender equality and the rights for women and sexual minorities can replace heteropatriarchal norms as the basis for a new political consensus for Chile's center-left coalitions.

Notes

I would like to thank Elisabeth Jay Friedman for her leadership on this project and great editorial comments. I am also grateful for the thoughtful and thought-provoking feedback from the reviewers from Duke University Press and the discussants and participants at both the 2015 and 2016 LASA Congress panels, all of which helped me to refine my argument. The Baldy Center for Law and Social Policy at the University at Buffalo has provided sustained support for my research.

1. There is ongoing debate about the methodology of the measurement and what it captures, but there is consensus around the steep decline since 1990 as a result of state programs.

2. By this I mean the normative commitment to a definition of the family as based on a married heterosexual couple and prescribed differences in gender roles, identities, and power between men and women in the family.

3. Given the focus of this chapter and space limitations, I cannot adequately discuss the role of heteropatriarchal norms within the political development of the Chilean Right and its relationship to other political actors and powerful institutions, including the Catholic Church. But see Blofield 2006; Power 2002; and Thomas 2011.

4. Many feminist civil servants I have interviewed over the last ten years first entered the state through their prodemocracy activist work with the women's movements in the 1980s. These women have been part of the slow process of institutional change promoting women's inclusion and gender equality mechanisms in the state.

5. The Convention for the Elimination of All Forms of Discrimination Against Women, the international women's rights treaty.

6. All information on elections is from the web pages of the Senado de la Republica de Chile (www.senado.cl) and the Camara de Diputados de Chile (www.camara.cl), accessed June 1, 2017.

7. In 2005, 2006, 2008, and 2009, I conducted over forty interviews with party activists, elected representatives, and femocrats appointed by Bachelet. Interviewees repeatedly discussed the resistance within the political parties of the Concertación to demands for greater equality between men and women in both appointed and elected office.

8. Feminist activist, interview with author, July 1, 2016, Santiago, Chile.

9. Carmen Andrade (subdirector of SERNAM), interview with author, December 16, 2008, Santiago, Chile; SERNAM official in Department of Legal Reforms, interview with author, December 28, 2009, Santiago, Chile.

10. SERNAM civil servants, interview with author, December 29, 2009, Santiago, Chile.

11. Carman Andrade (Subdirector, SERNAM), interview with author, December 16, 2008, Santiago, Chile SERNAM official in Department of Legal Reforms, interview with author, Santiago, Chile, December 28, 2009.

12. See www.crececontigo.gob.cl (accessed March 2, 2018).

13. María Estela Ortiz (director, Junta Nacional de Jardines Infantiles), interview with author, December 2, 2008, Santiago, Chile.

14. For the most extensive review of the gender policies of Bachelet's government, see Waylen 2016.

15. Feminist activist, interview with author, December 2, 2008, Santiago, Chile.

16. Former minister, interview with author, July 26, 2016, Santiago, Chile.

17. Ministerio de la Mujer y la Equidad de Género official, interview with author, July 13, 2016, Santiago, Chile.

References

Baldez, Lisa. 2002. *Why Women Protest: Women's Movements in Chile*. Cambridge: Cambridge University Press.

Blofield, Merike. 2006. *The Politics of Moral Sin: Abortion and Divorce in Spain, Chile and Argentina*. New York, NY: Routledge.

Blofield, Merike, and Liesl Hass. 2005. "Defining a Democracy: Reforming the Laws on Women's Rights in Chile, 1990–2002." *Latin American Politics and Society* 47 (3): 35–68.

Borzutzky, Silvia. 2009. "Anti-Poverty Politics in Chile: A Preliminary Assessment of the ChileSolidario Program." *Poverty and Public Policy* 1 (1): 1–16.

Brito Peña, Alejandra, Beatriz E. Cid Aguayo, and Carla Donoso Orellana. 2012. "Ruling the Womb: The Sexual and Reproductive Struggle during the Bachelet Administration." *Latin American Perspectives* 39 (4): 145–62.

Bunster, Ximena. 1988. "Watch Out for the Little Nazi Man That All of Us Have Inside." *Women's Studies International Forum* 11 (5): 485–91.

Candina, Azun P. 2013. "Cuerpo, comercio y sexo: Las mujeres públicas en Chile del siglo XX." In *Historia de las mujeres en Chile, Tomo 2*, edited by Ana María Stuven and Joaquín Fermandois, 241–280. Santiago, Chile: Taurus Historia.

CEPAL. 2015. "Panorama regional de América Latina y el Caribe data." Accessed May 10, 2016. http://estadisticas.cepal.org.

"Chile de todos: Programa de gobierno Michelle Bachelet, 2014–2018." October 2013. Comando Michelle Presidenta, Santiago, Chile.

Chuchryk, Patricia. 1994. "From Dictatorship to Democracy in Chile." In *The Women's Movement in Latin America: Participation and Democracy*, edited by Jane S. Jaquette, 65–109, 2nd ed. Boulder, CO: Westview Press.

Collier, Simon, and Willian F. Sater. 2004. *A History of Chile, 1808–2002*. Cambridge: Cambridge University Press.

Contardo, Óscar. *Raro: Una historia gay de Chile*. Santiago, Chile: Vergara.

Cooperativa. 2015. "La postura de los diputados de la DC ante el aborto de tres causales." July 29. Accessed August 31, 2015. http://www.cooperativa.cl/noticias

/pais/salud/aborto/la-postura-de-los-diputados-de-la-dc-ante-el-aborto-en-tres
-causales/2015-07-29/082853.html.

Díez, Jordi. 2015. *The Politics of Gay Marriage in Latin America*. Cambridge: Cambridge University Press.

Dore, Elizabeth. 2000. "One Step Forward, Two Steps Back: Gender and the State in the Long Nineteenth Century." In *Hidden Histories of Gender and the State in Latin America*, edited by Elizabeth Dore and Maxine Molyneux, 3–32. Durham, NC: Duke University Press.

Felstiner, Mary Lowenthal. 1983. "Family Metaphors: The Language of an Independence Revolution." *Comparative Studies in Society and History* 25 (1): 154–80.

Franceschet, Susan. 2005. *Women and Politics in Chile*. Boulder, CO: Lynne Rienner.

Franceschet, Susan, and Gwynn Thomas. 2015. "Resisting Parity: Gender and Cabinet Appointment in Chile and Spain." *Politics & Gender* 11 (4): 643–64.

Friedman, Elisabeth J. 2010. "Gender, Sexuality and the Latin American Left: Testing the Transformation." *Third World Quarterly* 30 (2): 415–33.

Garretón, Manuel Antonio. 2003. *Incomplete Democracy*. Chapel Hill, NC: University of North Carolina Press.

Haas, Liesl. 2010. *Feminist Policymaking in Chile*. University Park, PA: Pennsylvania State University Press.

Hardy, Clarisa. 1987. *Organizarse para vivir: Pobreza urbana y organizacion popular*. Santiago, Chile: Programa Economía del Trabajo.

Hinojosa, Magda, and Susan Franceschet. 2012. "Separate but Not Equal: The Effects of Municipal Electoral Reform on Female Representation in Chile." *Political Research Quarterly* 65 (4): 758–770.

Hutchinson, Elizabeth Quay. 2001. *Labors Appropriate to Their Sex: Gender, Labor, and Politics in Urban Chile, 1900–1930*. Durham, NC: Duke University Press.

Htun, Mala. 2003. *Sex and the State: Abortion, Divorce, and the Family under Latin American Dictatorships and Democracies*. New York, NY: Cambridge University Press.

Inter-Parliamentary Union (IPU). 2017. "Women in Parliaments: World Classification (Statistical Archive)." Accessed June 1, 2017. http://www.ipu.org/wmn-e/classif-arc.htm.

Kirkwood, Julieta. 1986. *Ser política en Chile: Las feministas y los partidos*. Santiago, Chile: FLACSO.

Larrañaga, Osvaldo, Dante Contreras, and Jaime Ruiz-Tagle. 2012. "Impact Evaluation of Chile Solidario: Lessons and Policy Recommendations." *Journal of Latin American Studies* 44 (2): 347–72.

Lavrin, Asunción. 1995. *Women, Feminism, and Social Change in Argentina, Chile, and Uruguay, 1890–1940*. Lincoln, NE: University of Nebraska Press.

Marín, Veronica. 2015. "Ex-ministra Laura Albornoz DC confeso que se realize un aborto terapeutico." *Emol*, July 29. Accessed August 26, 2016. http://www.emol

.com/noticias/Nacional/2015/07/29/742561/Ex-ministra-Laura-Albornoz-DC
-confeso-que-se-realizo-un-aborto-terapeutico.html.

MOVILH. 2016. "Estado desarrolla primera mesa de trabajo para cumplir acuerdo
por el matrimonio igualitario." August 9. Accessed June 1, 2017. http://www
.movilh.cl/estado-desarrolla-primera-mesa-de-trabajo-para-cumplir-acuerdo
-por-el-matrimonio-igualitario/.

(MUMS) Chile. 2015. "Historia de MUMS." Accessed May 8. http://www.mums.cl
/sitio/mums/historia.htm.

Pieper Mooney, Jadwiga E. 2009. *The Politics of Motherhood: Maternity and
Women's Rights in 20th Century Chile.* Pittsburgh, PA: University of Pittsburgh
Press.

Power, Margaret. 2002. *Right-Wing Women in Chile: Feminine Power and the Struggle against Allende, 1964–1973.* University Park, PA: Pennsylvania State University Press.

Richards, Patricia. 2004. *Pobladoras, Indígenas, and the State: Difference, Equality
and Women's Rights in Chile.* New Brunswick, NJ: Routledge.

Richards, Patricia. 2013. *Race and the Chilean Miracle: Neoliberalism, Democracy,
and Indigenous Rights.* Pittsburgh, PA: University of Pittsburgh Press.

Ríos Tobar, Marcela. 2009. "Feminist Politics in Contemporary Chile: From the
Democratic Transition to Bachelet." In *Feminist Agendas and Democracy in
Latin America,* edited by Jane S. Jaquette, 21–44. Durham, NC: Duke University
Press.

Ríos Tobar, Marcela, Lorena Godoy Catalán, and Elizabeth Guerrero Caviedes, eds.
2004. *¿Un nuevo silencio feminista? La transformación de un movimiento social
en Chile postdictadura.* Santiago, Chile: LOM.

Riquelme, Cecilia. 2004. "Apuntes para la historia del movimiento lésbico en
América Latina." CEME, November. Accessed May 15, 2015. www.archivochile
.com.

Robles, Víctor Hugo. 2009. "AYUQUELÉN." BANDERA HUECA, May 29. Accessed
May 9, 2015. http://banderahueca.blogspot.be/2009/05/ayuquelen.html.

Rosemblatt, Karin Alejandra. 2000. *Gendered Compromises: Political Cultures and
the State in Chile, 1920–1950.* Chapel Hill: University of North Carolina.

Schild, Verónica. 1998. "New Subjects of Rights? Women's Movements and the Construction of Citizenship in 'New Democracies.'" In *Cultures of Politics / Politics
of Cultures: Re-Visioning Latin American Social Movements,* edited by Sonia E.
Alvarez, Evelyn Dagnino, and Arturo Escobar, 93–117. Boulder, CO: Westview
Press.

Sehnbruch, Kirsten, and Peter M. Siavelis, eds. 2014. *Democratic Chile: The Politics
and Policies of a Historic Coalition, 1990–2010.* Boulder, CO: Lynne Rienner.

Shayne, Julie D. 2004. *The Revolution Question: Feminism in El Salvador, Chile, and
Cuba.* New Brunswick, NJ: Rutgers University Press.

Siavelis, Peter M. 2009. "Enclaves de la transición y democracia chilena." *Revista de
Ciencia Política* 29 (1): 3–21.

Siavelis, Peter M. 2011. *The President and Congress in Postauthoritarian Chile: Institutional Constraints to Democratic Consolidation.* University Park, PA: Pennsylvania State University Press.

Staab, Silke. 2012. "Maternalism, Male-Breadwinner Bias, and Market Reform: Historical Legacies and Current Reforms in Chilean Social Policy." *Social Politics* 19 (3): 299–332.

Staab, Silke. 2016. "Opportunities and Constraints on Gender Egalitarian Policy Change: Michelle Bachelet's Social Protection Agenda." In *Gender, Institutions and Change in Bachelet's Chile,* edited by Georgina Waylen, 121–47. New York, NY: Palgrave McMillan.

Stevenson, Linda S. 2012. "The Bachelet Effect on Gender-Equity Politics." *Latin American Perspectives,* 39 (4): 129–44.

Thomas, Gwynn. 2011. *Contesting Legitimacy in Chile: Familial Ideals, Citizenship, and Political Struggle, 1970-1990.* University Park, PA: Pennsylvania State University Press.

Thomas, Gwynn. 2015. "Promoting Gender Equality: Michelle Bachelet and Formal and Informal Institutional Change within the Chilean Presidency." In *Gender, Institutions, and Change in Bachelet's Chile,* edited by Georgina Waylen, 95–120. New York: Palgrave McMillan.

Tinsman, Heidi. 2002. *Partners in Conflict: The Politics of Gender, Sexuality, and Labor in the Chilean Agrarian Reform, 1950-1973.* Durham, NC: Duke University Press.

Valdés, Teresa, and Marisa Weinstein. 1989. *Mujeres que sueñan: Las organizaciones depobladoras en Chile, 1973-1989.* Santiago, Chile: FLACSO.

Valenzuela, María Elena, and María Teresa Marshall. 1986. *La mujer y el gobierno militar.* Santiago, Chile: Facultad Latinoamericana de Ciencias Sociales-Santiago y la Asociación Chilena de Investigaciones para la Paz (ACHIP).

Vargas, Felipe. 2015. "Senado aprueba histórica reforma que pone fin al sistema binominal." *El Mercurio,* January 14. Accessed May 8, 2016. http://www.emol.com /noticias/nacional/2015/01/14/699030/senado-aprueba-en-particular-reforma-al -sistema-binominal-en-historica-votacion.html.

Waylen, Georgina. 2000. "Gender and Democratic Politics: A Comparative Analysis of Consolidation In Argentina and Chile." *Journal of Latin American Studies* 32 (3): 765–93.

Waylen, Georgina, ed. 2016. *Gender, Institutions, and Change in Bachelet's Chile.* New York, NY: Palgrave McMillan.

Weeks, Gregory, and Silvia Borzutzky. 2012. "Michelle Bachelet's Government: The Paradoxes of a Chilean President." *Journal of Politics in Latin America* 4 (3): 97–121.

CHAPTER 4

Gender and Sexuality in Brazilian Public Policy

Progress and Regression in Depatriarchalizing and Deheteronormalizing the State

MARLISE MATOS

This chapter offers a critical, analytical review of key Brazilian government initiatives on issues of gender and sexuality under the Partido dos Trabalhadores (Workers Party, or PT) administrations (2003–16), which decisively marked Brazil's participation in the Pink Tide of left-leaning governance that swept across Latin America. To put their achievements and challenges in context, these initiatives are compared to developments under the first fourteen-year period of democracy following the adoption of the new Brazilian constitution in 1988, with a focus on the initiatives and proposals originating from the legislative, executive, and judicial branches, and, to a lesser extent, proposals put on the agenda by external and social actors. These proposals include depatriarchalization initiatives, which address gender-based hierarchies, especially aspects connected to the oppression of women; deheteronormalization initiatives, which address sexuality hierarchies that are ruled by heteronormativity[1] and that focus on the oppression suffered by diverse segments of the LGBTI*[2] community; and intersectional initiatives, which address gender, sexuality, class, and/or generation or age, among other identifiers.

I start with the hypothesis that these initiatives were relevant goals of the administrations that followed the adoption of the Federal Constitution of 1988 (referred to by its Portuguese acronym, CF/88). These administrations expanded civil and social rights, in some cases through judicial action, but at the same time advanced a neoliberal government agenda that often resulted in obstacles to the fulfillment of such rights. I argue that during the more recent PT administrations, the initiatives were broadened and enhanced, including the development of a raft of public policies recognizing new rights, fighting discrimination, and creating more inclusion for subaltern groups. This was a function, above all, of how effectively movements of women, feminists, and the LGBTI* community seized upon a window of opportunity for dialogue with the Brazilian state. Even more than in countries such as Uruguay and Argentina, much of this progress was made possible when PT administrations appointed professionals with activist commitments to ministries, which then had varying success at incorporating civil society demands into public policy. While progress also stemmed at times from legislative action, this body was also responsible for significant roadblocks.

As this chapter shows, Brazil's still-unfinished redemocratization has been marked by an extensive process of bringing the state and civil society together in order to expand political participation through myriad new institutions and creative methods of civic engagement (Avritzer 2002; Avritzer and Pereira 2005). At the same time, progress on the initiatives that grew out of the pressure exerted by women's and LGBTI* movements, and our democracy itself, are threatened by enormous setbacks. This longitudinal study will enable us to understand where and how such regressive initiatives have occurred.

Throughout the chapter, I rely on an analytic framework that lays out a range of state-society relationships in the Brazilian case. As Marina Brito Pinheiro (2010) and Rebecca Abers, Lizandra Serafim, and Luciana Tatagiba (2014) have explained, there are several kinds of possible relationships that can be forged between the Brazilian state and social movements. One typology delineates four approaches. The first is *protest and direct action*, in which state actors are pressured into negotiating through a demonstration of the movement's capacity for mobilizing. The standard protest method is marching, but there are other ways to draw public attention to the conflicts that serve to reinforce the activists' identities and level of commitment and show the power of numbers (Abers et al. 2014, 332). The second is *partnerships* between nongovernmental organizations (NGOs) and the state, in which civic groups enter into a contract or agreement for carrying out public policies or completing government projects (Pinheiro 2010, 69). The third is *institutional engagement* (Abers et al. 2014, 332), which in Brazil is done particularly when civil society organizations take part in state-sponsored projects of participatory budgeting, public policy councils, and conferences. And finally, the fourth is *hybrid relationships* or *close relationships*, in which activists who show *multiple affiliations* (in movements, parties, universities, etc.) (Pinheiro 2010, 72) move close to or even enter the state and advance their agendas on the basis of personal contacts between state actors and civil society movements and organizations.[3] Finally, it is possible to identify, during the two periods studied here, the existence of a fifth type of interaction not found in the literature: *judicializing*, when organizations approach the judicial branch to secure rulings that will resolve a dispute or secure a right that cannot be achieved by other means or through interacting with other state institutions.

This chapter begins by contextualizing the bumpy road of Brazil's recent, and longest-lasting, redemocratization, a process that has been under way for just three decades. I briefly discuss structural elements that favored this process, and describe the zenith that the redemocratization reached with the PT's assumption of the presidency. Following that, I analyze the ways in which women's, feminist, and LGBTI* movements have taken part in Brazil's anti-discrimination struggle. In different ways and to varying degrees, the movements and organizations examined here ended up collaborating with the state on issues of political inclusiveness in an effort to have more of their needs and viewpoints included in the policy decision-making process. Therefore, I observe not only a dynamic of social inclusion but also the beginnings of a process to transform state structures and practices, with new processes and initiatives being instituted to depatriarchalize and deheteronormalize the Brazilian state. I also offer some critical and context-specific reflections on the kinds of interactions that have emerged among the state, society, and these two movements. Then, I present and analyze data on government initiatives. Finally, I return to the debate over democratizing the state and the goal of political inclusion for subaltern groups.

The original research in this study was based on gathering and analyzing a range of governmental actions from the time periods considered: laws passed, bills introduced (whether approved, set aside, or still under review), proposals for constitutional amendments, public policy assessments, regulations, public policy action plans, and public policy conferences, among other items.[4]

The Brazilian Context of Redemocratization

From the election of president Luiz Inácio "Lula" da Silva at the end of 2002—and later, with his reelection and the subsequent two-term elections of Dilma Rousseff—Brazil has been part of Latin America's Pink Tide. But their party, the PT, was founded in 1980, early on during the transition to democracy. Under trade union leadership, the PT became a political, ideological, and partisan reference point for workers—male and female, urban and rural alike—and appealed to social movements of every stripe. Democratization was a complex and difficult process, marked by notable social and institutional limitations (O'Donnell 2004), but it opened a space for the eventual emergence and structuring of sustainable political opposition. Soon, regular elections were being held, and these opposition forces began consolidating themselves both in party structures and in government. Reaching out to traditionally under–represented sectors, including the working class, poor, Afro-Brazilians, rural landless, and organized women, the PT gained ever more ground in local government in key cities across the nation, such as Porto Alegre, Belo Horizonte, and several of the cities within the greater metropolitan area of São Paulo. The PT kept expanding its political power, growing as a party and moving forward with a set of democratizing political and institutional innovations. These include processes and spaces of state-society interaction such as participatory budgeting, civic consultative councils, and public policy conferences at the national, state, and local levels.

The PT benefitted from the emergence of a new kind of class pluralism, and an attempt to forge an agenda that transcended class. With the corresponding expansion of social groups that had originally found themselves, if only temporarily, on the Left, this transformation began to include the middle class and intellectuals, as well as certain segments of the "productive" bourgeoisie, such as development- and export-oriented industrialists. This was accompanied by notable growth in what came to be known in Brazil as "new" social movements (Doimo 1995; Gohn 2011), such as land-rights movements, feminist movements, women's movements, LGBTI* movements, black or Afro-Brazilian movements, rural peasant movements, and urban housing movements.

The Left, including the PT and other self-proclaimed socialist, labor-oriented, and communist parties, adapted so well to the redemocratization under way in Brazil that they were able to seize multiple opportunities, and explicitly accept the rules of democratic liberalism that were instituted with the adoption of the 1988 constitution. They moved ever deeper into the democratic fray, eventually being accepted as adversaries by their competitors. This led some parties of the left to become comfortable with other, less democratic but still quite institutionalized, aspects of the system, such as pay-to-play, favoritism, clientelism, and corruption.

Finally, another structural feature of Brazil's new left parties was their antineoliberal character. It was this feature that enabled some parties, at least initially, to maintain their position as alternative or opposition parties amid the extensive economic reforms that came alongside democratization. However, the prominent Partido da Social Democracia Brasileira (Social Democratic Party of Brazil, or PSDB), although more ideologically aligned with the center or the center Left, adopted an even more neoliberal orientation. With their success in the presidential elections of their standard bearer, Fernando Henrique Cardoso, they implemented those ideas during his two terms, from 1995 to 1999 and from 1999 to 2002 (the "FHC years").

The Pink Tide swept over Brazil during its transition from the neoliberalism of the FHC years to the democratic-engagement project of the PT. Thus, the country's emergence from dictatorship led Brazilians to pursue a winding path as they moved from one tumultuous transition—to neoliberalism—and then to another project: this time, a more popular and democratic one, but closer to the reformism of social democracy than to the structural transformations sought by the Left. Today, more than at any other time since the dictatorship, authoritarianism has once again stirred up a deep crisis within Brazilian politics and institutions, culminating in the 2016 impeachment of the first woman president.

In Brazil's current crisis, undemocratic and corrupt approaches to rule are intensifying and affecting the entire political and party system. Nonetheless, it seems undeniable that redemocratization brought social victories, and that especially in the PT years it left a legacy of public attention to overcoming income, gender, racial, and sexual inequality in Brazil based on social democracy-oriented reforms. Along with other public policies adopted by PT administrations in the areas of national economic redistribution—led mainly by the innovative Bolsa Família (Family Income) program—these administrations also promoted social justice, affirmative action, and state recognition of racial, gender, and sexuality-based demands. It is this entrenchment of reforms, in comparison to developments in the post-CF/88 period and FHC years, to which this chapter now turns.

"New" Social Movements: The Politicizing of Gender and Sexuality, and Forms of Interaction in Crafting a New Democratization Agenda for the State

This section discusses the transformations experienced by two of the new social movements that emerged during the transition to democracy. These movements shifted from civil and political rights struggles to demanding social rights and respect and recognition in their daily and civic life. The scope of this new action agenda has expanded to include not only the current political system (Alvarez et al. 2003), but also the eradication of deep and historic forms of social inequality—such as those based on race, gender, and sex—as it attempts to confront machismo, racism, homophobia, lesbophobia, and transphobia, among other forms of discrimination that are profoundly rooted in cultural and social practice.

From the 1980s through the end of the century, gender- and sexuality-focused movements in Brazil followed a common regional pattern in terms of their composition. The first wave of activism, not covered here, was more internationalist in nature, and rather elitist. It was championed by women and homosexuals who tended to be more educated and who were predominantly white and urban. The second wave, which intersected the democratization process, was more identity-driven and focused on direct struggle. It was championed by multiple groups: black women, rural women, lesbians, and myriad new actors from the LGBTI* community. The third wave was characterized by the processes of institutionalizing and professionalizing some women's, feminist, and LGBTI* movements' organizations.

Through a new stage in the relationship between Brazilian state and society, these movements, together with the corresponding strategic movement to de-racialize the state, reached a fourth wave. Working from a playbook provided by state mediators, the feminist/women's movements and LGBTI* movements transformed themselves. The former eagerly sought, though not without tensions, to establish processes for depatriarchalizing the Brazilian state. Those processes are rooted in a core action strategy of working with allies, particularly in the executive branch. The latter built up some activism focused on the legislative branch, and especially on the judiciary, in their bid to achieve a substantial portion of their demands to deheteronormalize the Brazilian state. These movements' expansion beyond protest and direct action to other types of state-society relations, set out in the introduction, are summarized in table 4.1.

In the 1980s and into the 1990s, the main strategies of the second-wave movements were *protest and direct action*, whose composition and targets would expand over time. At first, movements shaken by the painful memory of the prior period of dictatorship either rejected the government or did little to organize against it from the outside. Women's, feminist, and LGBTI* movements, among others of the period, were characterized by cultural and identity demands and focused on societal changes. Their strategies were not overtly meant to influence the actions of the government "by way of

TABLE 4.1 Types of state-society relations

I. *Protest and direct action* from outside the state
II. *Partnerships* between civic organizations and state agencies
III. *Judicializing* demands
IV. *Institutional engagement* in state spaces
V. *Hybrid relationships* through activists with multiple affiliations

defending or contesting laws or public policies" (Abers and von Bülow 2011, 55). Compared with how the "old" (workers') movements had operated from an economic or Marxist perspective of social class (Laclau 1986; Young 1989; Alonzo 2009), these new movements were characterized by the independent and autonomous way in which they sought to bring traditional norms in line with new ways of structuring the family (married people living apart, female heads of households, same-sex relationships, and the like). At the same time, these movements experienced enormous internal disagreements, such as the contestation mounted by black women, lesbians, and rural and indigenous women in feminist movements, and the struggles of transsexuals, transvestites, and transgender persons in LGBTI*-identified movements. Over time, these movements have been able to work together, achieving group synergies around their common efforts to democratize the Brazilian state.

Black women's organizing offers a central example of how such intersectional activism has gone forward without neglecting the reality and perspectives of particular communities. Afro-descendant women have been "at the forefront of feminist, antiracist and human rights/social justice activism in Brazil" (Alvarez and Caldwell 2016, vii) even as they have persistently organized for the "basic survival of black communities," including housing and land rights (Perry 2016, 117). As democratization took hold, black women established their own organizations to respond to the neglect of race in feminist movements and gender in black movements—omissions that effectively left out black women's specific experiences of intersecting oppressions (Alvarez and Caldwell 2016, vii). As the prominent historical leader Lélia González argued, "Latin American feminism loses much of its strength by abstracting from reality an extremely important fact: the multiracial and multicultural character of the societies of the region" (as quoted in Pons Cardoso and Adelman 2016, 7). "Blackening feminism" would lead to "broadening the meaning of democracy, equality, and social justice" (Carneiro and Camargo 2016, 33, 47). The hard-fought struggles to expand and deepen feminist movements finally lead to Brazilian feminism largely defining itself as antiracist. Such intersectional work continues to be done through coalitions rather than mixed-race organizations (Bairros et al. 2016, 60–61).

Under such pressure, the women's movement not only grew and became more diverse but also included new arenas of action. It got involved in political parties, unions, church communities, and community organizations. Movement pressure began to have an impact on public policies affecting women, especially in the area of health and ending violence against women. That impact in turn led to the creation of the first government agencies specializing in women's issues. By the 1990s, some of these groups had not only translated their demands into public policy but had also redefined aspects of citizenship and female representation, such as, for example, the funds made available to women's political campaigns, first approved in 1993 and revised in 1995.

The rise of neoliberalism in the 1990s marked a third wave of mobilization, as some social movements moved toward specialization and the professional-development initiatives, consultancies, advocacy, financing, and project management characteristic of NGOs. At the same time, the Brazilian state, which was employing bold strategies of structural and fiscal adjustment, tried to undermine national public policies, substituting them with government initiatives that were more targeted and did not reach as many people. It was in this moment that NGOs took on a larger role through a second type of state-society relationship: *partnerships.* Acting essentially as private contractors, they signed agreements with different state agencies to "implement or cooperate with activities that reinforce the actions of the state" (Pinheiro 2010, 69).

Deeply affected by the HIV/AIDS epidemic, LGBTI* movements sought to make inroads on the state agenda in order to tackle this urgent problem. This was the genesis of their turn toward a third type of strategy: *judicializing* their grievances as a way of securing their rights through legal victories. The National STD and AIDS Program of the Ministry of Health began as far back as 1986. But with the unfolding of medical-scientific discoveries, especially the anti-AIDS cocktail that controlled the progression of the symptoms of the syndrome,[5] many movements, NGOs, and people with AIDS used the justice system to successfully demand that the health system provide treatment free of charge. This intense experience reinforced the way LGBTI* movements came to relate to the state: appealing to the courts to claim rights.

It was also in the closing years of the 1990s that some experiences in local and participatory democracy started to gain currency in Brazil, though that dynamic had begun as far back as the adoption of CF/88.[6] The women's movement was heavily involved in the highly participatory 1986–88 constitutional reform process, with their efforts not only resulting in an astonishing 80 percent of their demands being included in the new constitution but also achieving "a radical change in the legal status of women in Brazil" (Carneiro and Camargo 2016, 30). Building on this and other experiences, the women's and LGBTI* movements were ready to press for and take advantage of public policy and institutional oversight bodies within some Brazilian municipalities, including participatory budgeting processes and consultative councils.

This in turn led to the development of a fourth state-society relationship, *institutional engagement*, in state spaces whose leaders recruited or engaged advocates, especially from the women's movement, in certain areas of governance (Avritzer 2007; Santos 2002).[7] Women's rights councils cropped up around the country, beginning in São Paulo in 1982 and in Minas Gerais in 1983. Responding to direct pressure from women's movements, the Conselho Nacional dos Direitos da Mulher (National Council on Women's Rights, or CNDM), part of Brazil's national women's agency, was eventually established (Carneiro and Camargo 2016, 31). Black women were particularly active on this front, insisting on inclusion in the CNDM and eventually helping to persuade the first PT administration to establish the Brazilian Secretariat of Public Policies for the Promotion of Racial Equality, "the first cabinet-level government agency of its kind in Latin America" (Alvarez and Caldwell 2016, viii).

This moment of democratic deepening in Brazil in the early 2000s culminated in extensive and decentralized conferences and public-policy processes, as well as public hearings on key issues in women's rights and LGBTI* rights. These activities served as veritable open forums within the government—particularly in the legislature, but also with the participation of the executive branch—alongside rights-consolidating lawsuits in the judicial sphere. Moreover, parliamentary investigative commissions were established on issues such as violence against women, abortion, and human trafficking. Those commissions began to systematize their collaboration with civil society in drafting or redrafting public policies and in establishing regulations and passing legislation.

I refer to the most recent period (from 2000 to present) as a fourth wave of women's and feminist movements (Matos 2010). This wave has been characterized by, among other things, how it moves women's demands into hierarchical and institutional spaces within the state and into other institutions, such as political parties, unions, student movements, and universities. It should be noted that underlying these dynamics is a constant fear of cooptation and/or the loss of capacity for critical analysis, transformation, and emancipation. Some within these movements have chosen to step up their actions outside of government or have kept their distance from the state.

In complex and sometimes contradictory ways, the practices and the action agendas used by some social movements in Brazil have led to the state being seen increasingly as a reference point for action, whether for actions taken from the outside—pressuring the state—or for acting within the government by enlisting the bureaucracies, or by setting up partnerships, as suggested by feminist academics from public universities. Here we see the final form of possible state-society interaction: "*hybrid relations* or *close relationships*, in which activists demonstrate *multiple affiliations* . . . either in their movements or in their parties, universities, or other organizations; affiliations that, in different ways, lead back to the state. That is, an activist may at once be involved in a movement or in an area of struggle . . . while at the same time being active in a political party or working as a government employee" (Pinheiro 2010, 73).

Feminist and women's movements were apt at this repertoire, as they translated historic relationships with the PT into real influence. Several took on positions in state bureaucracy, effectively becoming "femocrats." Not only were long-time feminists appointed to the CNDM, but they also entered other state agencies. Their intersectional activism prepared prominent black feminist movement activists to head the Secretariat for the Promotion of Racial Equality. Given the longer trajectory of national organizing, feminists and women's movement activists used this strategy more than LGBTI* activists. Similar dynamics also occurred through legislative institutions, such as the "lipstick lobby," a group of female congressional representatives who may or may not come from previous trajectories of activism but often strategize together around gender justice. Due to the overwhelming difficulty of electing LGBTI*-identified representatives, alongside the fierce opposition to LGBTI* issues by religious right representatives, legislative coalitional work on sexuality has been more difficult. However, other parliamentary blocs have formed around such issues.

Throughout the expansion of strategic interactions, movements have continued to rely on the classic approach of *direct action* or *protests*. The ongoing activism of autonomous groups within these movements in mounting resistance and attempting to influence the state from the outside is particularly visible in the *marchas* (marches) that have taken place in Brazil over recent years: Marcha das Margaridas (March of the Daisies), Marcha das Vadias (Slut Walk), Marcha das Mulheres Negras (Black Women's March), and LGBTI* Pride parades, among others. Thus while elements of these movements paved the way for dialogue and engagement with the Brazilian state, other groups within those movements remained in the public space, pursuing direct-action contestation, holding marches, and mounting protests.

Many of those groups were, and continue to be, critical of the effective, yet contested, *close relationships*. A substantial subgroup have updated and reframed their demands, struggles, and grievances: the increased involvement of young feminists and the transfeminist movement are emblematic of this. They are critical of the ways that feminism, and the struggle against lesbo/homo/transphobia, have transformed as they have crossed the state's threshold and found their way into the government. Taken together, the wide range of strategic interactions that movements deployed in the 2000s resulted in substantial entrenchment of their goals in public policies, as shown by the data below.

Depatriarchalization and Deheteronormalization: How Far Have We Come? The Recent Democratizing Agenda of Gender and Sexuality Policies

This section offers an analysis of the main initiatives implemented by the Brazilian government to expand women's rights and the rights of LGBTI* persons during the longest continuously democratic period that Brazil has experienced. The data collected here focus on the two periods previously mentioned: (1) from 1988 to 2002, the post-CF/88 period, which also spans two PSDB administrations led by president Fernando Henrique Cardoso; and (2) from 2003 to 2016, the PT administrations of Luiz Inácio "Lula" da Silva and Dilma Rousseff.

Through extensive data collection from both on- and offline governmental sources[8] carried out in May/June 2015 and June 2016, my research team identified 797 initiatives as being relevant to the demands of women and LGBTI* groups for democratizing gender and sexuality relations. We classified the initiatives by issue type: that is, gender, sexuality, or both. We took into account that such policies could be of a further intersectional nature, including race/ethnicity, generational issues (notably children, adolescents, and the elderly), disability, indigeneity, and rurality. We also tracked reversals of such gains, resulting in a classification of the initiatives either as "progress" or "regression" in terms of the rights enjoyed by these groups. Such initiatives were further categorized by the various branches of government in which they originated.

TABLE 4.2 Examples of government initiatives in the database, according to date, type, and main proponent

Year	Statutes and laws/ proponent	Policy or program/ proponent	Institutional/ advocacy strategy/ proponent
1988	Public Law 7.670/1988: Disposition on the Granting of Employment and Survivor Benefits for HIV-Infected Persons, proposed by President José Sarney	The creation of the Brazilian Unified Health System (SUS), proposed by Congress	The Batom (Lipstick) Lobby and the Letter of the Brazilian Women to Constituents (1988), proposed by National Council for Women's Rights (CNDM)
1995	Bill 176/95: Mandatory Treatment in the Public Health System of Women Seeking to Terminate Pregnancy, proposed by MP José Genoíno	The creation of the quota system for women on party lists, proposed by MP Marta Suplicy	The preparation for the UN Beijing Conference, promoted by the UN and Brazilian feminist movements
2002	Public Law 10.406 of January 10, 2002, (Civil Code), a reform proposed by Congress	First response by the Brazilian State to CEDAW monitoring, promoted by the executive branch	Brazilian Platform of Political Rights for gays, lesbians, gender non-conforming people and bisexuals in elections, promoted by LGBTI* movements
2009	Public Law 11.970 of July 6, 2009: Mandatory Use of Protection in the Motor, Axis, and Moving Parts of Vessels (to prevent the scalping of women with long hair), proposed by the National Secretariat of Policies for Women (SPM)	National Health Policy of the Black Population (PNSIPN), proposed by Congress	Establishment of the General Coordinating Council for the Advancement of LGBTI* Rights, proposed by LGBTI* movements

(continued)

TABLE 4.2 Examples of government initiatives in the database, according to date, type, and main proponent

Year	Statutes and laws/ proponent	Policy or program/ proponent	Institutional/ advocacy strategy/ proponent
2013	Proposed Constitutional Amendment for Female Domestic Workers, bringing the employment rights of domestic workers in line with those of officially recognized employees, proposed by Congress	National Policy on Combating Human Trafficking, proposed by the National Secretariat of Policies for Women (SPM)	Creation of intersectoral committees to articulate local and regional actors dealing with violence against women (health, public safety, justice, education, social assistance, among others), proposed by the National Secretariat of Policies for Women (SPM)

Important initiatives from outside actors such as international organizations are also included here. Table 4.2 offers examples of the kinds of initiatives that were entered into the database from particular years.

As expected from the initial hypothesis, we noted that these initiatives expanded significantly under the PT administrations, rising from 315 to 482, or representing 60.5 percent of the total, as shown in table 4.3.

The greater concentration of proposals and initiatives in the second period (2003–16) reveals a greater level of attention to such goals by those administrations. The majority of initiatives seem to originate in the government branches, as shown in table 4.4.

TABLE 4.3 Gender and LGBTI* government initiatives in the two periods (1988–2002 and 2003–2016)

Periods	Number of initiatives	Percentage of total initiatives
The post-CF/88 period: 1988–2002	315	39.5
The PT administrations: 2003–2016	482	60.5
TOTAL	797	100.0

TABLE 4.4 Gender and LGBTI* government initiatives by branch and (overt) pressure type (1988–2016)

Branch of government or main instrument of pressure for the initiative	Number of initiatives	Percentage of total initiatives
Legislative	610	76.5
Executive	165	20.7
Judicial	11	1.4
External	11	1.4
TOTAL	797	100.0

In table 4.5, the role of PT administrations in this second period is clearly visible: 72.7 percent of the initiatives coming out of the executive branch occurred during that time (when there was a 160 percent increase, from 45 to 120 initiatives). This fact alone shows a pattern of greater responsiveness by PT administrations to civil society demands. It is also worth mentioning that, in terms of legislative initiatives, there were more here as well.

Even though the number of initiatives was low within the judicial branch, the pattern of interaction based on *judicializing* the demands was stronger in this second period as well, increasing from four to seven during the PT administrations. That detail shows us that, especially in this second period, Brazilian social movements perceived a greater openness to their rights agenda and pushed hard for its inclusion. Two cases stand out in this regard. In May 2011, the Brazilian Supreme Court ruled in favor of same-sex relationship recognition,

TABLE 4.5 Government initiatives by branch of government in the two periods (1988–2002 and 2003–2016)

Origin of the initiative	PERIODS OF BRAZILIAN REDEMOCRATIZATION		Total
	1988 to 2002	2003 to 2016	
Executive	45 (27.3%)	120 (72.7%)	165
Legislative	261 (42.8%)	349 (57.2%)	610
Judicial	4 (36.4%)	7 (63.6%)	11
External	5 (45.5 %)	6 (54.5%)	11
TOTAL	315 (39.5%)	482 (60.5%)	797

TABLE 4.6 Government initiatives by issue type in the two periods
(1988–2002 and 2003–2016)

	Period I	Period II	Total
Sexuality	11	28	39 (5% of total initiatives)
	28.2%	71.8%	100.0%
Gender	269	390	659 (82.6% of total initiatives)
	40.8%	59.2%	100.0%
Both	35	64	99 (12.4% of total initiatives)
	35.4%	64.6%	100.0%
TOTAL	315	482	797 (100% of total initiatives)

a decision affirmed two years later by the National Justice Council's vote to legalize same-sex marriage across the country. And responding to the long-sought demand of the feminist movement, the Court held in a November 2016 ruling that abortion should be decriminalized in the first trimester.

As these cases illustrate, the great majority of government initiatives taken on these issues by the executive, legislative, and judicial branches have their origins in the pressure exerted by movements in the distinct ways described in the previous section. However, to reliably identify the individual type(s) of strategic interactions between the state and the two social movements that gave rise to these demands would require a different research strategy, due to the way in which data are made available (especially in the case of data gleaned from websites and official documents).

Turning to the main topics covered by these public policy initiatives summarized by table 4.6, the ones connected with gender (82.6 percent) stand out, as those focusing on sexuality had a lower percentage (5 percent) and were even surpassed by other initiatives focusing on both of these categories (12.4 percent), for example, antitrafficking statutes, free HIV/AIDS diagnostic exams, and the like. This reflects the lengthy process, already under way in Brazil, of bringing women's demands into the state's institutions through the democratization of gender relations. But that same pattern appears to have been followed by segments of the LGBTI* community.

Figure 4.1 shows that in the second period reviewed there is a rise in the number of initiatives across all issues, the period of Brazilian redemocratization having been a fertile period for these agendas. In terms of disaggregating these two periods, table 4.6 shows that even though in absolute numbers, the gov-

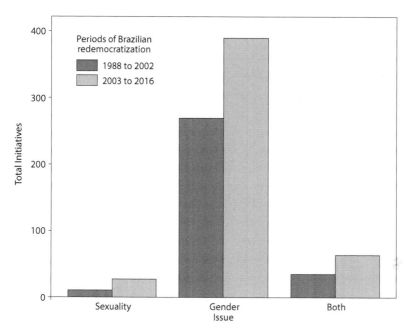

Figure 4.1 Total government initiatives by issue type.

ernment's commitment to initiatives dealing with sexuality and both gender and sexuality might seem low, in the second period the rate of increase picked up: by 71.8 percent for the former initiatives, and by 64.6 percent for the latter. Here it is worth noting again the importance of institutional engagement during this period, or the interaction that expert groups were able to have with the Brazilian government through consultative councils, public policy forums, and two national conferences on public policy—all of which actively sought to include the participation and perspectives of movement actors.

As for the distribution of these initiatives, figure 4.2 shows at least four spikes: the first spike occurs between 1989 and 1991, precisely when the Federal Constitution of 1988 was being implemented. The second spike occurs in 1995, with the onset of the FHC years. The third spike happens in 2002–3, when the PT years begin. And finally, the last spike is seen between 2012 and 2015, during Dilma Rousseff's second term. It should be noted that these final spikes took the initiative proposals back to the patterns that were seen at the beginning of Brazil's redemocratization, indicating that in Dilma Rousseff's second term the initiatives were intensifying. But, as discussed below, the reactionary agenda was also intensifying during this time. What stands out here is the effectiveness of social

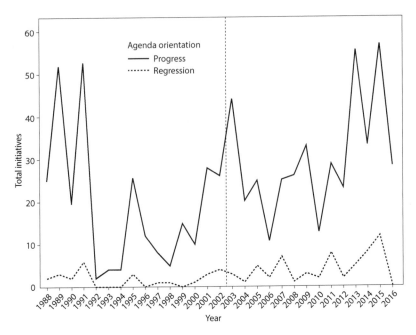

Figure 4.2 Chronology of government initiatives according to progress or regression of agenda (1988–2016).

movements of women, feminists, and the LGBTI* community, which increasingly sought to influence government projects through distinct relationships with the state—be they *institutional engagement, partnerships,* or *hybrid relations.*

After the adoption of CF/88, the beginning of the FHC years and the PT years, and Dilma Rousseff's second term were the moments of greatest openness to these goals. It is unequivocally clear that these issues were topics of interest on the agendas of two governments. But the issues were shaped by different features and informed by different motivations, as we will see: the first three terms represented progress, and there was also progress in the fourth term, but that is also where regression can be seen, especially in 2015.

These initiatives were evaluated based on whether they represent progress, in terms of an expansion of rights, or went in the direction of restricting rights or setting them back. The dominant pattern in these two periods is one of progress. As shown in table 4.7, of the 797 initiatives, 712 (or 89 percent) represented some form of rights expansion on the basis of gender and sexuality. There was, undoubtedly, progress on the rights agenda over the period of

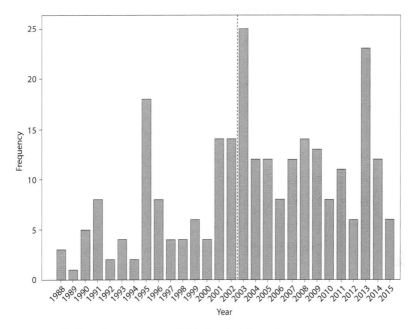

Figure 4.3 Progressive government initiatives (1988–2015).

Brazil's redemocratization, but that advance also set the stage for regression. The data show this dynamic.

In parsing out these "progress" initiatives by their respective years—that is, through this longitudinal study—the key peak moments for this rights agenda on progress and inclusion can be identified in figure 4.3.

For the period analyzed here, 1995, 2003, and 2013 registered peaks in the increase of state-inclusion initiatives moving these demands forward. In 1995, there are proposals favoring the decriminalization of abortion, as well as congressional funding for women candidates, and employment laws that made it illegal to fire pregnant female workers. At the beginning of the PT years, in 2013, examples of these advancements were the creation of several parliamentary lobbies (on sexual freedom of expression, on HIV/AIDS, and other issues), mandatory notification in cases of violence against women by public and private health providers, technical assistance for rural women, and support for family agriculture through the National Program for Food Access, among other initiatives. In 2013, we see an attempt to reserve seats in the legislature for women, the passing of the Proposal to Amend the Constitution for Domestic Workers, the National Program for Women to Live Free of Vio-

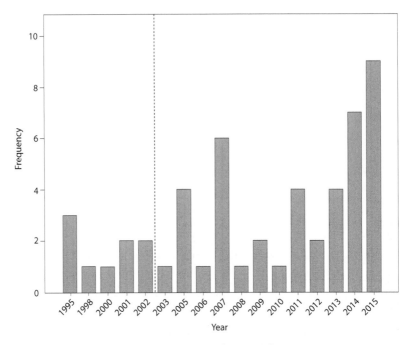

Figure 4.4 Regressive government initiatives (1995–2015).

lence, and the creation of the National System for Promoting Racial Equality, among other initiatives.

As for pushback on these initiatives, the peak moments of regression occurred in 1995, 2007, and 2014 and 2015, as shown in figure 4.4. For example, in 1995, the first constitutional amendment proposal was introduced with the purpose of changing the abortion laws in Brazil. In 2007, the Unborn Child bill was presented, as well as a bill proposing the chemical castration of rapists, and a debate erupted around the constitutionality of the antiviolence Maria da Penha Law. But the tendency toward backsliding was especially notable after 2011. That was the year when Congress was, in effect, hemmed in by the religious caucus within the legislature, which was opposed to women's and LGBTI* rights. It introduced bills such as the "rape fund," to financially support women who bear children resulting from rape, and the criminalization of doctors who perform abortions, among others. Figure 4.4 illustrates the pattern of increasing regression at the close of the long period analyzed here, and especially in 2014 and 2015.

To gain a sense of movement impact on governmental agendas, table 4.8 classifies the 797 initiatives at a more granular level, according to the respective areas of public life to which these policies were directed.

TABLE 4.7 Orientation of government initiatives in the two periods (1988–2002 and 2003–2016)

Issue types	Period I	Period II	Total
Regression	26 (30.6%)	59 (69.4%)	85
Progress	289 (40.6%)	423 (59.4%)	712
TOTAL	315 (39.5%)	482 (60.5%)	797

Reviewing the government's involvement in policy areas during the two periods reveals meaningful differences. In the post-CF/88 period, including during the administration of Fernando Henrique Cardoso, attention was focused in the following areas: international human rights legislation (62.5 percent), health (52.2 percent), employment and social security (51.9 percent), civil rights and justice (44.8 percent) and political enfranchisement and representation (26.3 percent). These areas manifest a universal or general policy agenda.

But for the PT administrations, the most notable areas were: human rights (87 percent), violence against women and LGBTI* persons (82.6 percent), education (78.9 percent), political participation and representation (73.7 percent), housing (60 percent) and employment and social security (48.1 percent). These are policy objectives that match the ideological platform of the PT administrations and that combine a universal agenda (human rights, education, employment, and social security) with more narrowly circumscribed agendas (violence, political enfranchisement and representation, and housing). Also noteworthy is the vital expansion of initiatives on education and on ending violence for both of these groups (women and LGBTI* persons). This comparison reveals that the inclusion of movement issues was oriented in distinct directions in the periods reviewed. This is no doubt due to the way in which movements engaged the PT administrations through *institutionalized participation* as well as *hybrid* relations.

As we can see in figure 4.5, some initiatives increased at different rates during these two periods, according to the priorities of the different administrations. With regard to gender, the priority of the PT administrations was to confront violence. In this second period, the focus for sexuality was on meeting goals in the areas of civil rights and justice, and there is even a notable increase in the intersectional goals of human rights, civil rights and justice, education, and employment and social security.

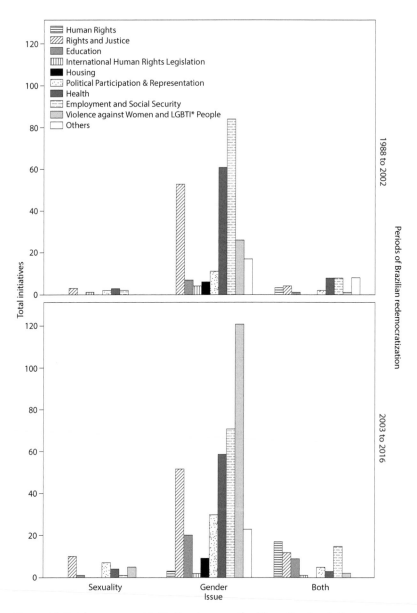

Figure 4.5 Total government initiatives by area of public policy in relation to gender and sexuality in the two periods (1988–2002 and 2003–16).

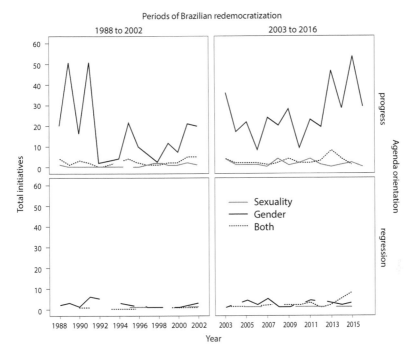

Figure 4.6 Total government initiatives by area of public policy in relation to issues and to patterns of progress and regression in the two periods (1988–2002 and 2003–16).

Figure 4.6 shows interesting findings in the patterns of progress and regression that reflect findings elsewhere in the volume, where gender-based rights tend to come under more direct attack than those achieved on the basis of sexuality. Gender is the most pronounced issue in building toward progressive gains during both these two periods; but in terms of regression, gender again is in the forefront.

Taken together, the data show how, or how much and in which direction, we are moving forward or falling back in terms of the demands made by women and members of the LGBTI* community for their respective rights and related public policies. What appears clear from these analyses is that the PT administrations made a more substantial effort to open their administrations to these two social movements' demands than had been done in previous periods. The result has been the transformation of many such demands into objectives on the government agenda.

TABLE 4.8 Government initiatives by area of public policy during the two periods (1988–2002 and 2003–2016)

Public policy areas	1988–2002	2003–2016	Total
Human rights	3 13.0%	20 87.0%	23 100.0%
Civil rights and justice	60 44.8%	74 55.2%	134 100.0%
Education	8 21.1%	30 78.9%	38 100.0%
International human rights legislation	5 62.5%	3 37.5%	8 100.0%
Housing	6 40.0%	9 60.0%	15 100.0%
Political participation and representation	15 26.3%	42 73.7%	57 100.0%
Health	72 52.2%	66 47.8%	138 100.0%
Employment and social security	94 51.9%	87 48.1%	181 100.0%
Violence against women and LGBTI* people	27 17.4%	128 82.6%	155 100.0%
Other miscellaneous demands	25 52.1%	23 47.9%	48 100.0%
TOTAL	315 39.5%	482 60.5%	797 100.0%

Conclusion

The above data unequivocally show that the processes of democratization already under way in Brazil's government institutions were advanced through various modes of interaction between social movements and the state. State institutions offer a complex and broad set of regulations, rules, and provision of services that, taken together, form a system of official and legal control. This chapter argues that it is possible to transform this system to achieve greater gender and sexual justice, through a process of entrenching the civil rights goals championed by movements for socio–political inclusion and rights expansion. This is the legacy and heritage of democratic contestation following the adoption of CF/88. And this is also, unarguably, the product of having women, men, feminists, and members of the LGBTI* community mobilized into social movements. As shown particularly under the Pink Tide governments of the PT, state and society can converge in a virtuous cycle that can become more stable. But as the movements that persist in focusing their energies on society remind us, public policies are only one arena for change. The daily struggle to transform culture, values, and mentalities, particularly given the regression at the national level, must continue.

Following the adoption of the new constitution in 1988, which reflected many of the demands of feminist, women's, and other movements, the governments of the ruling Partido do Movimento Democrático Brasileiro (Party of the Brazilian Democratic Movement, or PMDB) and its successor, the PSDB, implemented certain rights. However, given their focus on neoliberal governance, it was difficult for movements to advance their agendas. At this point the LGBTI* movement began to deploy the *judicializing* strategy, a key advance that would sustain them given how closed the legislature remained to their demands. Feminist and women's movements turned to *partnerships* through which, in some cases, the government transferred the responsibility for carrying out public policies to movement organizations.

With the inception of PT administrations, the movements gained more traction within the state, particularly via the executive branch, as well as through relations with supportive parties in the legislature. State-society relationships of *participatory institutions* and *close* or *hybrid relations* came to the fore. Under pressure from civil society, local, state, and federal governments built a complex network of institutions that focused on mainstreaming gender and sexuality issues, although many important programs had questionable impacts due to low budgets and low governmental priority. It should be noted that this process of approaching the state generated serious disagreements within the movements themselves, as many believed they would result in either cooptation and/or deactivation of the most transformative demands and disruptive actions of the movements. But it was undeniably a very rich moment of discovering the potential of state legitimacy, institutions, and resources.

In terms of progress on goals concerning gender and sexuality (issues that are interwoven not only throughout society but also across the institutions of the Brazilian government), the state can attempt to reorganize interests and demands (Skocpol 1985; Abers and von Bülow 2011). That conclusion is upheld by the actions of Brazilian administrations that came in during the post-CF/88 period, especially the PT administrations. The state also possesses other kinds of resources and discretionary powers that it can use to open up opportunities, and the various organized social groups are able to see, objectively, the need for empowering themselves through such victories and leaving a legacy. That is the only way of effectively consolidating these changes within the structures of state and of society itself.

The data presented here show a Brazil that, especially in the wake of the Pink Tide that swept Latin America, began highly complex processes of state depatriarchalization and deheteronormalization. And, despite some backsliding on these changes in other areas of politics and society, those changes are real vectors of progress under redemocratization. With the PT's assumption of the presidency in the 2000s, as redemocratization gained steam, the permanent pressure of the women's and LGBTI* movements finally pried open a window of opportunity for implementing a progressive agenda and making advances on civil rights and nondiscrimination issues for these groups.

In addition to trying to democratize state institutional patterns in terms of gender and sexuality—as well as other vectors, such as race and generation, which were not explored in depth here—the movements in question joined together with the executive and legislative branches in particular, and to a lesser degree, with the judicial branch, on relevant public policies. Moreover, an innovative series of democratic spaces for deliberation and interaction between the state and civil society were established in ways that Brazil had never seen before. This altered state institutions that had for many years served to maintain the privileges, elitism, and interests of society's dominant groups. And that fact is not trivial.

The gradual inclusion of oppressed groups in political life, as a result of the pressure exerted against the state by civil society (Dryzek 1996), is a core element of the redemocratization process. Through these many struggles, these ebbs and tides, these conflicts, contradictions, and controversies, that objective was being achieved in Brazil, especially in the second period discussed in this chapter.

As confirmed through the evidence presented here, and also affirmed by Rebecca Abers and Marisa von Bülow (2011), by Rebecca Abers, Lizandra Serafim, and Luciana Tatagiba (2014), and by Evelina Dagnino, Alberto Olvera, and Aldo Panfichi (2006), the state is a heterogeneous entity that possesses its own dynamism and a pluralistic nature, with a diversity of groups and projects in contestation through the state itself. These contestations are fiercer today, when historically conservative and privileged groups that had appropriated the government agenda for themselves took note of the progress that threatened, disturbed, disorganized, and changed patterns and structures upon which they depended. Thus, they began devoting their efforts to opposing the changes under way from the inside of the Brazilian state through a reactionary agenda.

There appears to be a reversal in the movement toward greater inclusion and more civil rights for historically marginalized groups, based on the project of publicly restoring democracy. Their movements appear not to have been able to definitively alter the historical patterns of gender, sexual, and political elitism that are so rooted in the traditions of Brazilian society. Centrist and center-right parties—PSDB and PMDB, for example—have recently moved clearly to the right of the political and ideological spectrum, forging alliances with other parties of the right and with ultraconservative segments of Brazilian society. Apart from the neoconservatism of Brazil's party politics, we can also identify moral and social dynamics within neoconservatism that have constituted themselves as threats to the advancement of Brazil's project of publicly participatory democracy and that are being disseminated and promoted by Brazil's mass media, which are oligopolies that foment a culture of hatred and intolerance.

Is Brazil now getting trapped once more in a short cycle of redemocratization, with authoritarian tendencies returning? A definitive answer to that is not possible, as it is not clear what lies on the horizon; but the events of the second half of 2016 would suggest that to be the case. Brazil's political elites—traditionally white, male, cis-gender, heterosexual, neoliberal, and conservative—are throwing their full weight into Brazilian state power in an authoritarian and markedly fascist way, with the result of the impeachment of the first female president.

However, making the PT governance legacy known and visible is a crucial contribution to the fight against the regressions that are now occurring. We need to know how to identify which strategies were most successful and why; and we need to recover, to the extent possible, our capacity to reopen the process of state dialogue. For there have indeed been victories in depatriarchalizing and deheteronormalizing the Brazilian state. Social movements, and society at large, must defend those victories, whether that means effectively implementing this complex array of government initiatives or monitoring and endorsing what has already been set in motion. Brazilian society, as well as the government, could see these processes give rise to a more profound form of democratization than when these changes began. And indeed, feminist and LGBTI* movements are experiencing a strong wave of renewal and reactivation in Brazil. Other movements, protests, and occupations have women and feminists in their leadership. But the scene today and what lies in store are, sadly, uncertain, if not clearly foreboding.

Notes

I would like to thank Elisabeth Jay Friedman for her thoughtful editing and great suggestions. Without her, this chapter would not have been completed. I also thank Nina Torres and Mauro Jerônimo, the research assistants who helped me build tables and graphs from the database, and warm thanks go out to Fernando Meireles for his fine teamwork and assistance with the online data collection.

1. Heteronormativity, or cis-heteronormativity, describes a socio-bio-political system that determines gender in relation to biological sex, and that presupposes the social ordering of all human beings according to heterosexuality, even before they are able to express their desires or their sexual orientation. In this way, anyone who strays from the cis-gender "hetero norm" is, to a greater or lesser degree, rejected. For example, homosexual men and women are thought of as "less of a man" or "less of a woman" or "less human" than heterosexual persons. The institutions of the state operate under the aegis of this normativity; deheteronormalization involves a struggle to dismantle such institutionalized norms from within state institutions.

2. In the acronym LGBTI*, L = Lesbians; G = Gays; B = Bisexuals; T = Transgender; and I = Intersex. The use of the asterisk (*) after these initials indicates that these acronyms are recognized as existing in multiple forms (even different from those shown here) for designating those segments of society; for example, TLBGI, BTGLI, GLTBI, and many others. More than simply privileging one letter arrangement over another, these acronyms lead to a better understanding of the specific demands that some groups consider of a higher priority than others. The asterisk (*) is used with the understanding that such diversity is to be celebrated, even though some of these groups are hierarchically ranked in the Brazilian constitution.

3. This is also where some activists "stand out for how they have positioned themselves in personal relationships that afford them a level of prestige" (Abers et al. 2014, 332).

4. See note 8 for more a more detailed description of methods and data.

5. The combination of AZT and Videx inaugurated the anti-AIDS cocktail in 1992, and in 1993 Brazil broke the AZT patent and started to produce it domestically.

6. During the National Constituents Assembly in 1988, civil society activists and organizations distinguished themselves in their struggles to craft a new state that would, finally, bring together popular direct-democracy participation with traditional forms of political representation. The drafting of the new Brazilian constitution was heavily marked, therefore, by that effort to bring the state closer to civil society. There were, for example, groups connected with health, education, and women's rights, among other goals, and those groups stood out in their effort to force open not only the public sphere but also state institutions.

7. Avritzer and Pereira (2005) call these "hybridized participatory institutions" to denote their intention to include non–state as well as state actors.

8. The online data collection was done through web scraping, a set of techniques for extracting data off of web pages (Haddaway 2015; Kumar, 2015; Vargiu and Urru, 2012). We used the same computer language used by the government (R language), as it provides considerable functionality and integration with several other languages, as well as being free and open-source. In addition, my research team also reviewed a wide range of national documents (including laws, bills, government agreements, policy executive bodies, parliamentary blocs and commissions, constitutional amendment proposals, regulatory resolutions, decrees, and the like) in a wide range of areas (health, education, employment, social security, insurance, food, violence against women and LGBTI* persons, political enfranchisement and representation, international human rights legislation, civil rights and justice, public assistance, children, adolescents, and the elderly, rural populations, and indigenous communities).

References

Abers, Rebecca, Lizandra Serafim, and Luciana Tatagiba. 2014. "Repertórios de interação Estado-sociedade em um Estado heterogêneo: A experiência na era Lula." *Dados* 57 (2): 325–57. Rio de Janeiro.

Abers, Rebecca, and Marisa von Bülow. 2011. "Movimentos sociais na teoria e na prática: Como estudar o ativismo através da fronteira entre Estado e sociedade?" *Sociologias* 13 (28): 52–84.

Alonzo, Ângela. 2009. "As teorias dos movimentos sociais: Um balanço do debate." *Lua Nova* 76:49–86. Accessed November 30, 2014. http://www.scielo.br/pdf/ln /n76/n76a03.pdf.

Alvarez, Sonia E., et al. 2003. "Encontrando os feminismos latino-americanos e caribenhos." *Revista Estudos Feministas* 11 (2): 541–75.

Alvarez, Sonia E., and Kia Lilly Caldwell. 2016. "Promoting Feminist Amefricanidade: Bridging Black Feminist Cultures and Politics in the Americas." *Meridians: feminism, race, transnationalism* 14 (1): v–xi.

Avritzer, Leonardo. 2002. *Democracy and the Public Space in Latin America*. Princeton, NJ: Princeton University Press.

Avritzer, Leonardo. 2007. "Sociedade civil, instituições participativas e representação: Da autorização à legitimação." *Dados* 50 (3): 443–64.

Avritzer, Leonardo, and Maria de Lourdes Dolabela Pereira. 2005. "Democracia, participação e instituições híbridas." Special issue, *Teoria & Sociedade*, March 2005: 16–41.

Bairros, Luiza, Sonia E. Alvarez, and Miriam Adelman. 2016. "Feminisms and Anti-Racism: Intersections and Challenges an Interview with Luiza Bairros, Minister, Brazilian Secretariat of Public Policies for the Promotion of Racial Equality (SEPPIR), 2011–2014." *Meridians: feminism, race, transnationalism* 14 (1): 50–69.

Carneiro, Sueli, and Regina Camargo. 2016. "Women in Movement." *Meridians: feminism, race, transnationalism* 14 (1): 30–49.

Dagnino, Evelina, Alberto J. Olvera, and Aldo Panfichi. 2006. *A disputa pela construção democrática na América Latina*. São Paulo / Campinas, Spain: Paz e Terra / Unicamp.

Doimo, Ana Maria. 1995. *A vez e a voz do Popular: Movimentos sociais e participação política no Brasil pós-70*. São Paulo: ANPOCS-Relume Dumará.

Dryzek, J. S. 1996. "Political Inclusion and the Dynamics of Democratization." *American Political Science Review* 90 (3): 475–87.

Gohn, Maria da Glória. 2011. *Teorias dos movimentos sociais: Paradigmas clássicos e contemporâneos*. 9th ed. São Paulo: Ed. Loyola.

Haddaway, Neal R. 2015. "The Use of Web-Scraping Software in Searching for Grey Literature." *Grey Journal* 11 (3): 186–90.

Kumar, Shyam Nandan. 2015. "World towards Advance Web Mining: A Review." *American Journal of Systems and Software* 3 (2): 44–61.

Laclau, Ernesto. 1986. "Os novos movimentos sociais e a pluralidade do social." *Revista Brasileira de Ciências Sociais* 2 (1): 41–47.

Matos, Marlise. 2010. "Movimento e teoria feminista: é possível reconstruir a teoria feminista partir do Sul global?" *Revista de Sociologia e Política* 18 (June Number 36): 67–92.

Matos, Marlise, and Clarisse Goulart Paradis. 2014. "Desafios à despatriarcalização do Estado brasileiro." *Revista Cadernos de Pagu* 43:57–118. Accessed August 12, 2015. http://www.scielo.br/scielo.php?script=sci_arttext&pid=S0104-83332014000200057&lng=en&nrm=iso.

O'Donnell, Guillermo. 2004. *Contrapuntos: Ensayos escogidos sobre autoritarismo y democratización*. Buenos Aires: Punto Sur.

Perry, Keisha-Khan Y. 2016. "Geographies of Power: Black Women Mobilizing Intersectionality in Brazil." *Meridians: feminism, race, transnationalism* 14 (1): 94–120.

Pinheiro, Marina Brito. 2010. *Os dilemas da inclusão de minorias no parlamento brasileiro: A atuação das frentes parlamentares e bancadas temáticas no congresso nacional*. PhD diss., PPGCP, Universidade Federal de Minas Gerais.

Pons Cardoso, Cláudia, and Miriam Adelman. 2016. "Feminisms from the Perspective of Afro-Brazilian Women." *Meridians: feminism, race, transnationalism* 14 (1): 1–29.

Santos, Boaventura de Sousa. 2002. *Democratizar a democracia: Os caminhos da democracia participativa*. Rio de Janeiro: Civilização Brasileira.

Skocpol, Theda. 1995. *Bringing the State Back In: Strategies of Analysis in Current Research*, 3–38. https://ediscipinas.usp.br/pluginfile.php/3141158/mod_resource/content/1/Skocpol_Bringing the state back in.pdf.

Young, Iris Marion. 1989. "Polity and Group Difference: A Critique of the Ideal of Universal Citizenship." *Ethics* 99: 250–74.

Vargiu, Eloisa, and Mirko Urru. 2012. "Exploiting Web Scraping in a Collaborative Filtering-Based Approach to Web Advertising." *Artificial Intelligence Research* 2 (1): 44.

CHAPTER 5

De Jure Transformation, De Facto Stagnation

The Status of Women's and LGBT Rights in Bolivia

SHAWNNA MULLENAX

Bolivia's significant political, economic, and social changes have created a unique opportunity for women's and lesbian, gay, bisexual, and transgender (LGBT) groups to increase their legal rights and quality of life. The election of Evo Morales, Bolivia's first indigenous president, and the Movimento al Socialismo (Movement toward Socialism, or MAS) party in 2005 marked a clear break with the neoliberal policies and right-leaning governments of the 1980s and 1990s. Morales and the MAS took office with the aim of creating equality, particularly for the marginalized indigenous population. An examination of law and practice since 2005 reveals that the new Bolivian state has allowed for greater legal recognition of many traditionally marginalized groups, but the extent to which these groups have been successful depends largely on their relationship to the state. Of the various women's and LGBT groups, the indigenous women's movement, due to its proximity to and support of the MAS, has benefitted the most from the return of the Left. Although several new laws and redistribution programs also address the demands of the nonindigenous women's movements, the MAS has created less space for these groups to influence policy. Until recently, the demands of the LGBT movement remained the most sidelined, as the restructuring of the state resulted in conflicting laws that simultaneously expanded and limited their rights. In early 2016, the administration addressed one of the movement's key goals, but only due to unrelenting pressure from LGBT activists.

In many ways, Bolivia embodies the challenges and changes of contemporary Latin America. Like other governments in the region, the Morales administration continues to struggle with the lingering effects of colonialism, dictatorship, and an unsteady transition to democracy. Years of neoliberal economic policies, elite hegemony, and marginalization of a majority of citizens pose contemporary political problems. Yet, the past decade has been one of rapid change and progress for the region, and Bolivia in particular. In 2014, Bolivia's economy grew faster than any other in South America (*Economist* 2015). A walk through the streets of La Paz, Bolivia's administrative capital, provides a glimpse of such growth. Government-funded construction projects fill the busy streets. A new cable car and public bus system carry passengers from the neighboring city of El Alto into downtown La Paz. Social changes are almost as apparent as the economic ones. A giant rainbow flag hangs from an office building downtown, reminding every resident of La Paz that the LGBT community is thriving. In another part of town, a large mural depicting Bolivian women of all types reads: "Tiempo de actuar: no mas violencia sexual alto a la impunidad" (Time to act: no more sexual violence stop the impunity). Bolivia is thriving, and women's and LGBT rights activists are seizing the opportunity created by the return of the Left to solidify their place in politics and society, and to guarantee their rights into the future.

This chapter evaluates whether Bolivia's left turn has been positive for the advancement of women's and LGBT rights. While I find that women's and LGBT legal rights in Bolivia have improved over the past decade, evidence suggests that law and practice remain disconnected. I begin by examining the politics of the past. The Left returned to power with a strong mandate to create equality for all citizens following years of dictatorship and uneven democracy. I then focus on the rich dynamics of women's rights and LGBT movements today, highlighting divisions and commonalities. The following section reviews state-society relations. I assess whether government institutions are inclusive and responsive to the desires of these marginalized groups. Finally, I evaluate how well the leftist government has implemented the progressive laws and policies they have passed since taking office. I end with a summary of the findings and predictions for the future of women's and LBGT rights in Bolivia. Many of the insights in this chapter are drawn from interviews with activists and NGO (nongovernmental organization) administrators working in the capital city of La Paz in July 2014, and repeated visits to the country since 2011.

Country Context

Political History: The 1952 Revolution
to the Election of Evo Morales

What qualifies as "left" governance in Bolivia? Like much of Latin America, Bolivia's Left formed in the mid-twentieth century in opposition to a wealthy ruling elite. A country rich in natural resources, Bolivia was controlled by an oligarchy of mine owners until the national revolution in 1952 unseated them. The center-left Movimiento Nacional Revolucionario (National Revolutionary Movement, or MNR), in alliance with the Central Oberera Bolivia (Bolivian Workers Central, or COB) labor movement, took office in a brief period of democratization and dramatic change in Bolivia. Among the government's many progressive actions was the extension of the right to vote to all women (Kohl and Farthing 2006). However, this period of leftist rule and democratization was short lived, brought to an end by a military coup in 1964. The dictatorships of René Barrientos Ortuño and Hugo Banzer Suárez lasted eighteen years and reversed many democratic advances made by the MNR (Kohl and Farthing 2006). In spite of these challenges, the political Left remained active, challenging the dictators to respect human rights and to return to democracy (Tapia 2008).

Women played a central role in leftist resistance movements during this time. In the early 1960s, a group of miners' wives joined together under the name El Comité de Amas de Casa de Siglo XX (The Housewives' Committee of Siglo XX, Bolivia's major tin mine) to fight the economic hardships stemming from rising inflation and decreasing tin prices. When male mining leaders were captured by the government in a protest against poor working conditions, it was a hunger strike led by the Housewives' Committee that set them free. As this group of women grew more militant, the Bolivian government came to see them as a real threat to state power (Miller 1991). When the resource-based economy began to collapse in the 1970s, the Banzer regime found itself under a number of pressures, but the breaking point came when the Housewives Committee staged a hunger strike that spread throughout the country. In the face of such opposition, the Banzer government could no longer ignore citizen cries for democracy, and conceded defeat in early 1978 (Kohl et al. 2011).

After several more years of political turmoil—including repeated coups and the threat of civil war—a coalition government composed of left-leaning political parties and nonparty groups took office in 1982. But the coalition's inability to alleviate the country's economic problems led to its swift downfall. Over the next two decades, right-leaning governments, in conjunction with the IMF and the World Bank, implemented a series of neoliberal reforms aimed at structural readjustment, economic liberalization, mass privatization, welfare state retrenchment, and decentralization. An IMF-led stabilization program that limited government spending and opened the economy plunged two million Bolivians into extreme poverty (Morales 2015). To survive this period of economic crisis, poor women again joined in community organizations to address collective problems, such as food shortages, and to participate in government-led work-for-food programs. Women also used these groups to organize protests against neoliberalism. During this time, neoliberal reforms made life difficult for many women, but also fostered the progress of the feminist NGOs formed under the dictatorships of the previous decades (Lind 2002). These organizations often took on contracts to carry out government-sponsored projects, as the state shed more and more responsibility for social development.

In 2000, citizen dissatisfaction with neoliberal policies finally boiled over when a US-based consortium lobbied to purchase and control Cochabamba's municipal water supply in exchange for financial support of the national government. Citizens violently clashed with police in what is known as the "Water War" (Olivera 2004). Two years later, President Gonzalo Sánchez de Lozada's unpopular decision to export Bolivian natural gas through Chile sparked widespread protests that led to an estimated seventy civilian deaths in the "Gas War." During the months following the Gas War, Bolivia's social movements continued to rail against the government until national presidential elections were scheduled for December 2005.

The Return of the Left

Evo Morales, an indigenous coca farmer turned labor organizer, won the 2005 presidential election with an unprecedented 54 percent of the vote, more than 20 percentage points ahead of the nearest candidate (Kohl and Bresnahan 2010). The Left's return to power was all encompassing. Not only did Morales win with more support than any president before him, but his MAS party members also swept the Senate and Chamber of Deputies, occupying 44 and 55 percent of the seats, respectively (Obarrio 2010). Morales was the candidate of the poor and middle class, the traditionally marginalized, and the ideologically Left. Morales and the MAS owed their success to support from a wide range of active social movements, including the indigenous women's movement, a faction of the feminist movement, and some groups in the LGBT community.

The Bartolinas, whose formal name is Federación Nacional de Mujeres Campesinas de Bolivia-Bartolina Sisa, or FNMCB-BS (National Federation of Peasant Women of Bolivia-Bartolina Sisa) were, and continue to be, a significant source of support for Morales and the MAS. Named after the wife of indigenous icon Túpac Katari, the Bartolinas began in 1980 as a complement to the male-dominated Confederación Sindical Única de Trabajadores Campesinos de Bolivia (Unified Syndical Confederation of Rural Workers of Bolivia, or CSUTCB). By the time of the 2005 election, they had established themselves as the largest women's group in Bolivia with their own unique political voice (Farthing and Kohl 2014). Part of the success of the Bartolinas lies in the group's ability to appeal to women in all nine of the country's political districts. Living at the intersection of two systematically disadvantaged groups, indigenous women were disproportionately affected by the late-twentieth-century neoliberal policies. The Bartolinas marched alongside their husbands and brothers in the CSUTCB during the Water and Gas Wars, and were an important force in the MAS political party from its early stages (Shakow 2014). Their support for Morales was, and remains, crucial to his success.

The Left also received support from feminist collectives or NGOs. Feminist NGOs are made up of mostly educated and middle-to-upper-class mestiza women who came together in the 1980s to promote women's issues (Alvarez 1999; Monasterios 2007; Rousseau 2011). Such groups formed across Latin America during the era of neoliberalism as part of the international development effort to both empower and work through civil society actors, and as a result, exhibit ideals and approaches in line with the global feminist movement (Alvarez 1999). Because the feminist NGOs formed during the neoliberal era are, in many ways, a product of globalization, their relationship with the Morales government is complex. Morales ran on a platform of anti-Westernism. He is known for fostering relationships with grassroots organizations over institutionalized NGOs (Boulding 2014), and has gone so far as to kick out some international NGOs (e.g., USAID) and requires domestic NGOs to register with the state if they receive international funding (*Economist* 2014). However, Morales also demonstrated a commitment to advancing the rights of women that resonates with many feminist NGOs. Although these groups did not mobilize for Morales to the extent of the Bartolinas, they tended to support him in the 2005 election and have continued to back him in the two subsequent elections.

Some members of Bolivia's LGBT community also saw opportunity in the election of Morales and the MAS. Until the mid-1980s, when the first case of AIDS was diagnosed in the country, Bolivian government and society treated homosexuality at best as something unmentionable, and at worst as punishable by abuse, torture, or death. Yet, just as globalization aided in the formation of feminist NGOs during the neoliberal period, the construction of AIDS clinics by Western countries brought the LGBT community into the open in Bolivia (Wright 2000). This movement was particularly liberating for gay men, and in the early 2000s, brought about the formation of a number of powerful groups, such as the Familia Galán and Colectivo Nacional TLGB, known as the Colectivo. These factions of the LGBT rights movement tend to support Morales because, while he did not directly advocate for the rights of LGBT persons, his overall platform as the representative of the traditionally marginalized and the progressive Left made him a more appealing choice for these groups than more rightist alternatives.

However, Morales and the MAS did not enjoy the support of Bolivia's anarchist-feminists. Mujeres Creando (Women Creating) leader María Galindo is one of Morales's fiercest opponents. In an interview with the *Economist* in 2016, she suggested the MAS is an "agglutination of caudillos' interests and does not represent progressive ideas at all." While also critical of the government, indigenous lesbian feminist Julieta Paredes, who leads Mujeres Creando Comunidad (Women Creating Community), also known as Feminismo Comunitario (Communitarian Feminism), admits that the Morales government has advanced the rights of marginalized groups. But she also acknowledges that her group's radical vision for the transformation of the Bolivian state is unlikely to be realized by the Morales administration.

Morales was also not well liked by groups on the right, such as the Catholic Church, wealthy landowners, and those who favor neoliberal policies. His promises of agrarian and education reform, as well as widespread nationalization, were, and continue to be, a threat to their power. Some right-wing extremists even went so far as to predict that the election of Bolivia's first indigenous president would spark a race war (Farthing and Kohl 2014). The main opponents of Morales and the MAS are largely located in the country's four lowland departments, where a majority of the population is light skinned and economically well off compared to citizens in the highlands.

During his campaign, Morales promised supporters that, if elected, he would oversee the rewriting of the constitution through an elected-representative constituent assembly. Due to pressure from feminists and other civil society leaders, party lists with gender alternation were used to ensure that a significant number of the assembly members were women. In the end, women made up 33 percent of the assembly, filling 88 of the 255 seats. Indigenous women constituted 45 percent of all female members. Although gender alternation on electoral lists aided in the election of women, some feminist NGOs had hoped for parity in representation and were disappointed that women filled only a third of the assembly seats (Rousseau 2011).

Although female assembly members were a minority, indigenous and feminist movements negotiated with each other and political parties to ensure that the new constitution addressed women's interests (Rousseau 2011). Representatives from NGOs and other women's organizations joined together under the label Mujeres Presentes en la Historia (Women Present in History, or MPH). The group advocated for a constitution that used nonsexist language and that addressed equality in employment, pay, landownership, and representation in political institutions. They also lobbied for antiviolence legislation and recognition of international human rights treaties (Rousseau 2011, 22). From the outset, the largest indigenous women's movement, the Bartolinas, allied with the predominantly male indigenous groups to form the Pacto de Unidad (Unity Pact). Despite their commitment to demonstrate a united front with their male counterparts, the Bartolinas also drew up a constitutional proposal calling for the recognition of many of the same issues the MPH addressed, such as equality of landownership, representation in political institutions, and criminalization of violence against women. They however diverged from their MPH peers in that they opposed, rather than supported, the inclusion of abortion rights (Buice 2013).

As these two groups exerted pressure on the constituent assembly from the outside, the women elected to the constituent assembly formed the Coordinadora de Unidad de Mujeres Constituyentes de Bolivia (Unity Coordination of Women Constituents of Bolivia). The purpose of this union was to craft a unified platform that combined the interests of both women's movements to incorporate into the new constitution. However, Rousseau's (2011) interviews with indigenous and feminist members of the Coordinadora revealed that the MAS hindered the strength of this group by insisting that male party leaders maintain control of the group. As Morales and the MAS leadership painted themselves as agents of gender equality, they stifled the voices of elected women by putting the party first. This kind of behavior has become characteristic of the Morales administration's handling of women's issues.

Activists in the LGBT community, such as El Colectivo Nacional TLGB president David Aruquipa, also lobbied for the inclusion of provisions that advanced their rights. Their goals included an antidiscrimination clause and the right to marry and adopt. The LGBT movement did not have its own representatives within the constituent assembly. Representatives from the feminist NGOs supported the aims of the LGBT movement, but were not willing to negotiate for LGBT provisions at the expense of their own primary objectives.

When the constitution was overwhelmingly passed by popular referendum on January 29, 2009, it was largely touted as a victory for Bolivia's marginalized groups. Much of the constitution advances the rights of indigenous citizens, and articles addressing women's and LGBT rights are also included. Article 14 prohibits discrimination based on sex, gender identity, or sexual preference. In addition to Article 14, the new constitution includes several issues that were of importance to both indigenous and feminist women's groups. Article 15 outlaws familial violence and violence against women, and Article 48 guarantees equal pay for men and women. The LGBT community views the constitution with mixed feelings. Activists celebrate the antidiscrimination clause but lament a new provision defining marriage as strictly between a man and a woman.

Movement Dynamics

Bolivia is a country of robust social movements (Boulding 2014; Farthing and Kohl 2014), and its women's and LGBT movements are no different. Although disparate visions of how to advance the status of women in Bolivia have, at times, hindered the advancement of women's rights (Monasterios 2007), the indigenous women's movement and the feminist women's movements overcame their differences during the constitutional assembly to ensure that some of their common goals were written into law. Interviews with women of both groups suggest that, in general, women in Bolivia desire many of the same outcomes, namely equality and safety.[1] Where women's groups tend to disagree is on reproductive rights and their approach to Bolivian women's empowerment. LGBT groups are somewhat divided in their aims, with gay men placing greater emphasis on marriage and adoption than lesbians. The following sections detail the dynamics of women's movements before turning to an analysis of the LGBT movement.

Indigenous Women's Movement

Of the indigenous women's movements in Bolivia, the largest and most powerful is the Bartolina Sisa. With over 100,000 members, the Bartolinas exercise influence across all levels of government and society, and enjoy a close relationship with the Morales administration. Organized indigenous women have always been an important force in Bolivian politics, acting to undermine and overturn the dictatorships of the 1960s and 1970s and neoliberal presidents of the 1980s and 1990s. However, it was women's involvement in the Water and Gas Wars of the early 2000s that solidified the importance of women in the broader indigenous rights movement and propelled them into formal politics (Buice 2013). Indigenous women of the Bartolina Sisa and similar groups were key participants and leaders of protests and roadblocks during the wars. They were crucial to the success of Morales and the MAS political party during the 2005 election, and received prominent positions in the government in return for their support.

Melissa Buice (2013) argues that the election of Morales allowed the Bartolinas to pursue a gendered political agenda in a way they could not under previous governments. Indigenous women used their position as key allies and members of the administration to advocate for gender equality and empowerment, and this strategy yielded gains for indigenous women in the form of enhanced citizenship rights, expanded electoral representation, and the institutionalization of their voice in the public policy process (Rousseau and Ewig 2017). For decades, indigenous women and men were united in the struggle for ethnic justice, indigenous autonomy, and cultural preservation. Following the election of Morales, indigenous women began to add gendered demands to those goals. They started to formally advocate for equality in political representation, landownership, and economic opportunity (Buice 2013; Monasterios 2007; Rousseau 2011). Indigenous women also prioritized legal protection from domestic violence, as well as guaranteed maternal care, respect for indigenous birthing practices, and autonomy in reproductive decisions. During this time, indigenous women's activism began to reflect their unique positions as women, grounded in traditional roles as caregivers, while remaining committed to indigenous sovereignty.

As manifest in the constituent assembly negotiations, the indigenous women's movement and the feminist NGOs share many goals, but diverge on the issue of legalized abortion (Rousseau 2011). While the Bartolinas advocate for reproductive freedom, they suggest abortion goes against their traditional values and cultural practices.[2] Additionally, the Bartolinas criticize feminism as hostile to men and in conflict with the Aymara principle of *chachawarmi*. Chachawarmi literally translated means man (*chacha*) and woman (*warmi*), and encompasses the notion that men and women are distinct yet equal, and their strengths are complementary (Maclean 2014). Due to the Bartolinas' privileged relationship with Morales and the MAS, women's rights progress in Bolivia has tended to reflect the principles, desires, and methods of indigenous women more than those of feminist NGOs. This is a key reason elective abortion was not addressed in the new constitution, and will likely continue to be illegal so long as the Bartolinas oppose legalization.

Feminist Movements

Bolivia's feminist women's movement has two factions. The first is an institutionalized women's movement known as the feminist NGOs (Rousseau 2011, 13).[3] This movement, composed of middle-class mestiza women either working in NGOs or in conjunction with NGOs, tends to approach gender inequality as a problem that can be solved by altering state institutions. Included in this group are many of the same organizations that formed the MPH during the writing of the new constitution (Rousseau 2011). They are aligned with the international women's rights movement and are guided by the principles of the 1979 Convention on the Elimination of all Forms of Discrimination against Women (CEDAW) and the 1995 Beijing Platform for Action.

The Coordinadora de la Mujer is the largest group in the feminist NGOs. Formed in 1984, it is made up of twenty-six NGOs throughout the country and headquartered in the capital city of La Paz. The group works closely with the intergovernmental organization International Institute for Democracy and Electoral Assistance (IDEA) to provide data and publications on the status of women in Bolivia. According to director Monica Novillo, the Coordinadora's key task is to use its research to assist politicians and activists in the struggle for women's rights. Although research is a key objective, many groups within the Coordinadora also provide services to empower and assist all women throughout the country. These services include jobs training, sexual assault prevention and assistance, health services, campaigns to inform women of their political rights, and support for political engagement.

Despite some differences, the groups in the Coordinadora now work more closely with the Morales administration than they have with past governments. Since some of the demands of the feminist women's movement have been successfully legislated, such as the electoral quota requiring gender parity in candidate lists and a 2013 antiviolence against women law, the focus of this faction of the women's movement has shifted toward reproductive issues.

What is notable about this faction of the feminist movement in Bolivia is that they are willing to work with existing government institutions, the international community, and the Morales administration to create change. While the indigenous women's movement tends to criticize the feminist NGOs for their close relationship with international allies, the more radical faction of the feminist women's movement is critical of their willingness to work within state institutions at all.

This second faction are the radical feminists. The radical feminists formed in the late 1980s under the name Mujeres Creando, and were the only highly visible lesbian activists in Latin America during the 1990s. During this time, they helped to mobilize autonomous feminist movements in Bolivia and the region. In the early 2000s, the cofounders separated. María Galindo kept the name Mujeres Creando while Julieta Paredes formed the group Mujeres Creando Comunidad (Daly 2011). Both groups are well known throughout Bolivia and internationally for their anarchic approach to combating patriarchy, homophobia, racism, and neocolonialism. The social base of the radical feminists tends to be mestizo and indigenous urban intellectuals. There is some intersection between the social bases of the radical feminists and the LGBT movement due to overlapping interests.

Mujeres Creando leader María Galindo is one of the harshest critics of the Morales government, often using the group's La Paz–based radio station as her outlet. She believes the government's inclusion of women in politics is nothing more than symbolic action and that adhering to "traditional politics does not transform reality" (Green and Lackowski 2012). The group also uses graffiti to critique the government, scrawling phrases such as "Evo no eres feminista, eres un machista impostor" ("Evo you are not a feminist, you are a macho imposter") on the streets of La Paz. Even though the average woman in Bolivia does not tend to identify with this group, Mujeres Creando helps to perpetuate the national conversation on women's issues.

Mujeres Creando Comunidad also remains a prominent organization in the radical feminist movement. Led by self-proclaimed Aymaran feminist lesbian Julieta Paredes, the group focuses on the intersectional experiences of being indigenous, female, and lesbian more than Mujeres Creando does. Paredes has become a well-known regional activist, emerging as a key figure at the Feminist Encuentro for Latin America and the Caribbean in 2014. The group's approach of "communitarian feminism" stresses the collective and community over the individualism it sees as espoused by Western-style feminists. Paredes is also a proponent of poetry and performance as tools for inclusion and societal change (Panoramas 2015).

Relationships among the Western-oriented feminist NGOs, organized indigenous women, and radical feminist groups can be quite strained. Although they desire many of the same outcomes, the radical feminists often accuse the other groups of being too moderate and complacent. Where the feminist NGOs supported legislative quotas based on a binary concept of gender (male/female), Mujeres Creando, in particular, wishes to challenge the entire conception of gender. María Galindo has also criticized the Bartolinas in opinion pieces, asking former leader Felipa Huanca why she continued to support the president when he turned a blind eye to sexism in the party, violence against women, rape in the Andean region, and "the other horrors that have been suffered by indigenous women along the way" (Galindo 2014). Feminist NGOs and indigenous women's movements suggest that the demands of the radical feminists are too disconnected from the reality of politics and public opinion to create pragmatic change. Yet, despite their differences, these organized groups have made women's rights a key political issue in Bolivia today, and one that is unlikely to fade from the national spotlight.

LGBT Movements

While it is still uncommon, if not dangerous, for LGBT people to be "out" in the rural areas of Bolivia, LGBT movements are robust and visible in the larger cities, especially La Paz. The country's first gay pride parade was held in the southeastern city of Santa Cruz in 2001, and the annual celebration has spread to highland cities such as Cochabamba and La Paz in the years since. Interviewees from the LGBT community reported that the general public grows more receptive of the parades each year, with people lining the streets to join in the celebration. This progress is due in large part to the Colectivo Nacional TLGB.

The Colectivo is Bolivia's largest LGBT activist group. They describe themselves as "a national and representative organization of the families, organizations, and independent people" who come together to create social and legal change (Colectivo TLGB Bolivia 2015). The social base of the Colectivo tends to be urban middle- and upper-class citizens with a variety of gender identities. As is the case in other Latin America countries (see Encarnación 2011, 2016), the Bolivian LGBT movement frames gay rights as human rights, and emphasizes similarities between the desires of the LGBT community and all citizens. This argument is particularly compelling in Pink Tide countries in which politicians were elected on promises of egalitarianism and respect for basic rights.

The Colectivo has a unified platform of six objectives and rights that guide their activism. First, the group calls for a right to equality and nondiscrimination. Second, they seek the right of transsexual and transgender persons to legally change their name or gender identity on all formal documents to reflect their self-determined identity. In the past decade, these two objectives have been addressed through national law, though not always completely. Bolivia's new constitution outlaws discrimination on the basis of sexual orientation or gender identity. Article 14 gives LGBT individuals a legal basis for discrimination claims, and is the foundation of the national ombudsman's current campaign to reverse a 1997 ban that prevents LGBT persons from donating blood (Defensoría del Pueblo 2016). Activists report that this law is helpful for legal purposes, but without recognition of some of their other rights, it seems somewhat hollow.

The second, remarkable victory for the LGBT community was realized in May 2016 when Bolivia became the fourth country in the world to implement a Gender Identity Law, as called for in the Colectivo's second objective. The law allows individuals to change their gender identity on all official identity documents, granting legitimacy to trans citizens (*Los Tiempos* 2016). While it may appear that the Morales government is at the forefront of advancing LGBT rights, the gender identity law is the result of a well-organized LGBT movement taking advantage of government scandal. Morales, like his Ecuadoran counterpart Rafael Correa, has provoked backlash over several sexist and homophobic comments during his presidency. In 2015, Morales speculated on the sexual orientation of his health minister, Ariana Campero, saying, in reference to her status as single woman, "I don't want to think she's a lesbian" (Tegel 2016). In an attempt to quiet outraged LGBT activists, the government entered into discussions with the Colectivo to work toward one of their main goals—the passage of a gender identity law. The story behind the recent gender identity law reveals the strength and resourcefulness of the Colectivo. Movement leaders used a negative comment toward one faction of their movement to advance the goals of the entire movement. It also exposes the Morales administration as less progressive on LGBT rights issues than it might appear at first glance.

Currently, the Colectivo continues to work toward their other goals of implementing a national plan to combat homophobia, transphobia, lesbophobia, and biphobia, and requiring sexual education courses in Bolivian schools to address issues of sexual orientation and gender identity. The community's fifth goal is a legal guarantee of the best level of health care possible. It is an open secret that in Bolivia many in the LGBT community are forced to seek medical care at special clinics. According to a 2013 publication by the Centro de Promoción y Defensa de los Derechos Sexuales y Reproductivos (Center for the Promotion and Defense of Sexual and Reproductive Rights, or PROMSEX), 41 percent of the LGBT population reported experiencing discrimination by their health care provider on the basis of their sexuality or gender identity. Finally, the Colectivo is in the process of lobbying the government for equal family rights. Under current law gays and lesbians have the right neither to marry nor to adopt children.

As with the feminists, there are divides within the LGBT movement, largely between radical lesbian feminists and gay men. Although they have worked together in the past, Mujeres Creando is critical of groups like the Colectivo that work within existing state structures to gain legal access to marriage and adoption. They view these traditional family structures as a product of patriarchy and a perpetuation of heteronormativity. Several interviewees also suggested that tensions arise between other lesbians and gay men in the movement. Gay men tend to dominate the institutionalized LGBT movement, and the push for legal marriage and the right to adopt children was largely led by these men. Yet, the radical lesbian feminists, all factions of the LGBT community, and feminist NGOs are united in their fight to end discrimination of all types.

State-Society Relations

Bolivia is unique in that the return of the Left marked a complete restructuring of the state. When Morales and the MAS were elected to office in late 2005, 16.9 percent of Bolivia's lower house, the Chamber of Deputies, were female, and only one of the country's twenty-seven senators was a woman (IPU 2016). Similarly, in his first term Morales appointed only five female ministers to his twenty-person cabinet. However, when the new constitution was passed in 2009, it reflected Morales's commitment to increasing the number of women in all areas of the Bolivian government.

The Executive Branch

Although there is no law requiring that the president select a gender-equal cabinet, pressure from the Bartolinas led Morales to appoint ten women to his cabinet following his reelection in 2009 (Htun 2016). The positions these women were granted were not limited to the less prestigious positions often given to women, such as culture, education, environment, family, health, and women's affairs (Escobar-Lemmon and Taylor-Robinson 2005). Instead, women were appointed to ministerial positions dealing with issues of justice, legal defense, and labor. Of these female cabinet members, three were indigenous, two of them high-ranking members of the Bartolinas. This step toward equality was praised by the director of the Coordinadora de la Mujer as a great victory for women in Bolivia (Chávez 2010).

Following his reelection for a third and final five-year term as president in October 2014, Morales chose to retain the existing cabinet, with only two minor changes. The woman in charge of the Ministry of Justice was replaced by another woman, and a Ministry of Sport was added. The Ministry of Sport position is currently filled by a man. While Morales has increased gender equality in the executive branch to a degree unseen in many countries, he has done nothing to increase the representation of the LGBT community in the executive branch.

The Legislative Branch

Although a gender quota law was in place when the Left returned to power in 2005, very few women were elected to the legislature; turning that around would take a concerted effort. Under pressure from the indigenous women's movement and feminist movements—and to some extent Morales himself—the constituent assembly amended the existing electoral law to require that one-half of all the candidates on party lists be women and candidates alternate by gender. Existing research suggests that progressive gender quota laws are often ineffective if they do not include strict sanctions for noncompliance (Schwindt-Bayer 2009). Article 107 of the Bolivian constitution warns that if parties fail to comply with the requirements of parity and alternation, the list will be rejected and the party given seventy-two hours to submit a list that complies with the rules (Quota Project 2016). This law applies to both the national and subnational levels and explains why the quota is so effective.

Bolivia's 2014 election was the first time that the new electoral law was put into practice. In terms of descriptive representation, the law was a stunning success. The Chamber of Deputies is now composed of a female majority, with 69 of the 130 seats being filled by women. Similarly, the Senate, which had only one female representative when Morales took office in 2006, is now 47 percent women. Bolivia is the world's second country to achieve a female majority in the legislature, after Rwanda.

However, these astounding gains in the descriptive representation of women in Bolivia may be hampered by the reality that, even with a majority of women, the gender norms that have defined Bolivian politics for so long are difficult to change. At the time of my interviews in July 2014, three months prior to the recent elections, roughly 30 percent of Bolivia's national representatives were women. While this is not parity, it is enough women to be considered a "critical mass," or the percentage of women needed to create real change in an institution (Dahlerup 2006). Despite the significant presence of women in government, many expressed the concern that the women in the government were merely "puppets" selected to run for office by the men in power because they could be easily controlled. On these grounds many suggested that the quota law was nothing more than a strategic move by the government to appear that they were working on women's issues, similar to the actions of the FSLN in Nicaragua. While such views are quite skeptical, one story in particular adds validity to the skepticism.

In June 2012, Rebecca Delgado, once president of the Chamber of Deputies, disagreed with the MAS on a number of issues, including the decision to allow Morales to run for a third term. She reported that when she began to disagree with the party she was threatened. When asked by a television host what she thought of all of the great legal steps the MAS had taken for women, Delgado reported that even though there were a substantial number of women in the legislature and in positions of power in the government, they were expected to be "accomplices" and follow the party line. Delgado has since left the MAS and become an outspoken critic of the Morales administration.

The LGBT community gained its first legislative representative in October 2014. Manuel Canelas made history when he became the first openly gay deputy to be elected in the history of Bolivia. As a representative of the MAS, Canelas's election was a victory for both the community and the party, which has failed to prioritize LGBT rights to the degree that many in the movement expected at the onset of MAS rule. Despite his historic victory, Canelas was quick to note in an interview following the election that LGBT issues would not be his primary focus in the legislature. He suggested that, while he supports the struggles of the LGBT movement, he does not intend to legislate on their behalf (Choque 2014). As with women in Bolivia, this case suggests that descriptive representation in the legislature does not guarantee substantive representation.

The Judiciary

The adoption of the new constitution in 2009 also included a significant change to Bolivia's judicial system. Bolivia became the first country in the world to select national-level justices through popular vote. Voters elect the justices in four of the country's most powerful courts.[4] As with candidate lists for the legislature, there must be gender parity and alternation on the ballot, and two-thirds of the legislature must approve each candidate (Driscoll and Nelson 2012). This change to the country's electoral law was led by the MAS, and is seen by some as reflective of Morales's commitment to making all of Bolivia's political institutions more inclusive.

However, the first elections, held in October 2011, were contentious. Bolivia's opposition parties openly opposed the elections, claiming that many of the selected candidates were too closely affiliated with the MAS. As a result, many voters chose to abstain from voting despite the country's compulsory voting law, or to submit spoiled ballots. Nevertheless, female candidates did fare well in the elections. Women were elected to over half of the seats in the Constitutional Tribunal, and three positions in the Agricultural and Supreme Court. It was an indigenous woman, Cristina Mamani Aguilar, who received the most votes of any candidate (Driscoll and Nelson 2012).

Despite these gains, few Bolivians trust the Supreme Court. In the Latin American Public Opinion (LAPOP) survey conducted in 2012, 15 percent of respondents reported that they do not trust the Supreme Court at all, while only 7 percent reported having the highest level of confidence in the court. When I asked interviewees if they felt that the increased representation of women in national courts is making a difference for women's rights policy, the consensus was that the status and treatment of women in the justice system has not changed.

Overall, Morales has delivered many of the institutional changes women's rights advocates lobbied for during the restructuring of the state. Thanks to gender parity laws for elected positions at all levels of government, Bolivia now has more women in politics than many developed countries. However, there is serious doubt among advocates for both women's rights and LGBT rights that the increased descriptive representation of women will lead to more progressive policies. Even indigenous women appointed by the MAS have found themselves sidelined when their political opinions or actions diverged from those of the MAS leadership. Unfortunately, despite an unprecedented number of women at all levels of politics, it remains difficult to achieve policy goals that are not readily supported by Morales or MAS elites.

Policy Issues

One of the key criticisms of Morales and the MAS is that laws and declarations intended to generate equality are largely symbolic. This section evaluates a number of national policies that address issues of bodily autonomy, identity recognition, and social redistribution. It is apparent that the priorities of the indigenous women's movements tend to receive the most attention, followed by those of the feminist NGOs. The desires of the LGBT movement and radical feminists are often seen as too progressive for state policies, although the Morales administration paid more attention to gender identity issues in the later years of their tenure.

Bodily Autonomy

While the return of the Left has led to many positive changes in women's representation, violence against women (an already severe problem) has also been on the rise in Bolivia. On March 9, 2013, the government took action to end violence against women by passing a comprehensive bill to guarantee women a life free from violence. The law, commonly referred to as Law 348, outlaws seventeen categories of violence, including physical and psychological violence, femicide, sexual violence, and spousal violence. Past legislation did not consider spousal rape a crime, or address femicide as a serious offense (Robinson 2013). Under the new law, the average sentence for violence against women is between twenty and thirty years, up from a maximum of ten in the past. The law also guarantees that women have equal opportunities regardless of their sexual orientation or ethnicity. The adoption of the law has been praised by all segments of the women's movement, the LGBT movement, and international organizations such as the United Nations.

However, a La Paz–based NGO, the Centro de Información y Desarrollo de la Mujer (CIDEM), reports that of the 206 reported femicides in Bolivia between January 2013 and November 2014, only eight men were convicted. The perpetrators range from teenagers to professors and public officials. The diversity of the offenders demonstrates that violence against women is not limited to one class or ethnicity, a point the director of CIDEM repeated during our interview. Violence against women is a problem that transcends class, ethnicity, region, and age. Yet, the new law has not significantly curtailed violence. Many suggest that this is because the government has not taken steps to properly fund the bill. Additionally, police are often the perpetrators of violence against women, and both indigenous and feminist activists lament the lack of police training on how to deal with these incidents. They claim that while the law is a step forward and has sparked a national conversation about violence against women, there will not be real change until the government provides the funding and the training necessary to prosecute offenders.

Although women's groups in Bolivia were unanimously supportive of curbing violence against women, the issue of decriminalizing abortion is more contentious despite the equivalent danger clandestine abortions pose to women. Research supported by CIDEM, Marie Stopes International, and the World Health Organization (WHO) suggest that, among sexually active women in Bolivia, 48 percent have had at least one unwanted pregnancy, and 13 percent at least one abortion (Aliaga Bruch et al. 2011). Although abortion remains illegal except in the case of rape, incest, or risk to the mother's health, activists suggest that this has done little to curb the abortion rate, and instead increases the number of women who die or become ill because of abortion. The WHO estimates that unsafe abortions are responsible for roughly 10 percent of maternal deaths in Bolivia. Even Bolivia's Ministry of Health acknowledges that abortions are a common occurrence in the country, with the safety of the abortion depending largely on economic factors. Women across all ethnicities and socioeconomic groups undergo abortions in Bolivia, but it is the poorest who tend to be the most at risk of dying from the procedure.

During the constitutional assembly, the Bartolinas openly opposed the full legalization of abortion on grounds that it conflicts with their cultural values (Rousseau 2011). For this reason, abortion remained largely illegal in the new constitution. However, in March 2013 Patricia Mancilla reopened the issue when she sued the Bolivian government over the criminalization of abortion in cases that did not meet the state-defined exceptions of the cases of rape, incest, or health risk. Mancilla, an indigenous MAS legislator, was an unlikely challenger to the state. She received support from feminist NGOs in her fight, but after two years of public debate that embroiled women's groups, evangelical groups, the Catholic Church, right-wing political parties, and the male leadership of the MAS, the Plurinational Constitutional Tribunal ruled against completely decriminalizing abortion in February 2014 (Fabricant and Gustafson 2015).

Although they did not achieve their overall goal of decriminalizing abortion, Mancilla and the feminist NGOs succeeded in persuading the court to remove the requirement that women seeking abortion services must receive court approval. This means that women who are seeking abortion for the permitted exceptions may now receive an abortion in a timely manner by avoiding Bolivia's inefficient judicial system. However, women still must file a report with the police in cases of abuse, and obtain a doctor's diagnosis in the cases of endangerment of women's health. International NGOs, such as Ipas and Marie Stopes, are training some police and health workers on how to handle issues of sexual violence so that the new provisions in the law can be fully utilized (Ipas 2014).

Identity Recognition

Article 14 of the Constitution prohibits discrimination based on sex, gender identity, or sexual preference. Colectivo Nacional TLGB president and prominent activist David Aruquipa says that this law has given LGBT individuals legal ammunition to fight discrimination. These laws clearly define the aggressor and the victim. The group is also celebrating two large victories in 2016: the reversal of a 1997 ban on blood donation by all LGBT persons and the legal right of transgender and transsexual individuals to match their legal identity to their self-determined identity, discussed earlier. These recent, hard-won victories suggest that the government may be opening to the advancement of LGBT equality, but there is a ways to go.

The movement's current goals are to achieve the legal right to marry and state recognition of all forms of families. Inspired by Argentina's legalization of gay marriage in 2010, Senator Hilda Saavedra introduced a bill to legalize gay marriage in August 2012. It was encouraging to LGBT activists that Saavedra was a member of the MAS, but despite her membership in the ruling party nothing ever came of the bill. Activists have not let this stifle their campaign for marriage equality, which may be working to slowly change the opinion of public officials in Bolivia. As recently as May 2015, the vice president, Álvaro García, said that "sooner or later" the state would address the issue of same-sex marriage. Furthermore, Senate president José Gonzales stated that he is in favor of discussing a legal framework for allowing same-sex marriage in Bolivia. However, leaders in the Catholic Church continue to be staunch opponents of such a provision (Paredes Tamayo 2015). As it stands, the Bolivian constitution still defines marriage as strictly between a man and woman.

In addition to lobbying for marriage equality, LGBT activists are fighting for the right to adoption, and for the state to recognize that families can come in many forms. At the time of my interviews in July 2014, the movement was hopeful that a new Código de Familias, or family code, would recognize diverse family forms and include legal rights to adoption for same-sex couples. However, when the new code was approved in November 2014, no such provisions were included (Corz 2014).

Social Redistribution

A conditional cash transfer program, Bono Juana Azurduy, was enacted by executive decree in 2009 with the goal of reducing maternal mortality and improving the nutrition and well-being of children younger than two years old. Pregnant women who enter the program can earn up to forty-five US dollars for attending prenatal checkups at an approved health center and giving birth in a hospital complete with a postpartum checkup. Once the child is born, mothers can earn another 214 US dollars over two years when they take the child to bimonthly checkups, complete all required vaccines, and attend education sessions on nutrition and health (UNFPA 2015).

The Bono Juana Azurduy has received diverse reactions from the various factions of the women's rights movement. The indigenous women's movement views this program as one of its major successes. A representative from the El Alto–based NGO Centro de Promoción de la Mujer (Center for Women's Advancement), Gregoria Apaza, works closely with many of the indigenous women who are beneficiaries of the program. In her experience, women are more educated about maternal and child health than they ever have been. This program is fulfilling the vision of women's reproductive freedom and education envisioned by the Bartolinas. Similarly, the director of CIDEM reported that, although data are not yet available about the success of the program, anecdotally it seems to have a positive impact on the lives of participants, even if only marginally. While the indigenous women's movement and the feminist NGOs tend to look favorably on the program, the radical feminists are outspoken critics. They believe that the Bono Juana Azurduy is a program imposed by the patriarchy to incentivize reproduction and reinforce traditional gender norms and family structure.

As successful as social redistribution programs like the Bono Juana Azurduy are, they come at a price. As Wilkinson (see chapter 8) notes of Correa in Ecuador, there is growing concern over Morales's use of natural resources to fund social redistribution, even among his most fervent supporters. Morales and the MAS campaigned on the platform of *vivir bien* (living well), an alternative vision of development that stresses respect for the earth and the minimization of capitalist models of economic growth (Gudynas 2013). Despite his critique of the extractive practices of the neoliberal governments before him,

Morales increased the extraction and production of minerals, natural gas, oil, iron, lithium, and soy to their highest rates ever (Gudynas 2013). This export-led growth model is volatile, subject to fluctuations in the international economy, and tends to create more male-dominated jobs than female ones.

Indigenous women are some of the harshest critics of these practices. Female leaders of the Confederación de Pueblos Indígenas de Bolivia (Confederation of Bolivian Indigenous Peoples, or CIDOB) and Consejo Nacional de Ayllus y Markas del Qullasuyu (National Council of Ayllus and Markas of Qullasuyu, or CONAMAQ), for example, were at the forefront of the 2011 protests in opposition to Morales's plans to build a highway through the Isiboro Sécure Indigenous Territory and National Park (TIPNIS) (Fabricant and Gustafson 2015). This 4,630-square-mile ecological reserve serves an estimated 8,000–12,500 indigenous citizens who rely on the park for subsistence fishing, hunting, and foraging (Achtenburg 2017). Proponents of the road argue that it will improve Bolivia's economy by facilitating intranational trade between the geographically divided Andean and Amazonian regions of the country and international trade with neighboring Brazil. Opponents, on the other hand, insist that the road will make the park vulnerable to logging, cattle farming, and other extractive industries that will ultimately strip it of its biodiversity and natural resources (Achtenburg 2011). Morales's formal stance on building a road through TIPNIS has oscillated between support and censure. In response to the 2011 protests, Morales legally banned the construction of a road through TIPNIS only to abolish that same law in August 2017 and, once again, call for the highway construction (Achtenburg 2017). The TIPNIS conflict highlights the toll that the development approach upon which the MAS has based its generous social redistribution programs may exact on the same citizens these programs are designed to help, and calls into question the government's *vivir bien* promises.

Further evidence that Morales may be losing support from key allies was the rejection of a constitutional amendment in early 2016 that would have allowed him to seek a fourth term in office. This practice of changing presidential term limits is not uncommon in the contemporary leftist populist governments of Latin America. Presidential term limits were abolished under Chávez in Venezuela and Ortega in Nicaragua. Term extensions like the one in Bolivia have been put forth most recently in Ecuador and Paraguay. In Bolivia, the amendment lost in a referendum 51.3 percent to 48.7 percent. While this margin is small, it is new territory for Morales, who has won all his presidential bids with well over 50 percent of the vote. Growing conflicts between the Morales government and his base are evidence that the progressive changes enacted since 2006 may be slowing as the MAS government struggles to fund its leftist transformation and support for Morales wanes.

Conclusion

Bolivia has undergone dramatic political and social changes since the return of the political Left in 2006. President Evo Morales and the governing MAS party oversaw the creation of a new constitution and the expansion of numerous social programs. Women's and LGBT movements used this restructuring of the state to expand their rights and solidify their place in politics. Unlike the situation in other Latin American countries, in Bolivia the indigenous women's movement, headed by the Bartolinas, enjoys a close relationship with the president and his MAS government. Many of their top leaders have been appointed to ministerial positions or elected to other positions in government. As a result, some of the key policies of the Bartolinas, such as the Bono Juana Azurduy and antiviolence law, were passed, while abortion remains illegal.

Although Morales is known for his propensity to avoid working with NGOs in favor of grassroots organizations, the feminist NGOs have managed to shape women's rights legislation since the return of the Left by capitalizing on the government's own promises to create equality for all citizens. Among their victories they can count the antiviolence law and the elimination of the need for court approval for abortions in extreme cases. Similarly, now that the constitution outlaws discrimination based on sexual orientation, LGBT persons have the legal power to fight against injustices. Trans-identified individuals also can legally change their identity, a right available in only a few other countries. The movement is continuing its fight for other rights, such as the right to marry and adopt.

When representatives of these groups were asked if their rights have improved since the return of the Left, the answer was always an emphatic "yes." They often added, however, that it was not the administration itself that created these positive changes. Instead, Morales and the MAS were more vulnerable to pressure for change than past governments due to their message of inclusive democracy and equality. Morales's promise to improve the lives of marginalized groups in Bolivia created a key opportunity for women's and LGBT groups to shape politics, but change in Bolivia has been uneven. In many ways society remains patriarchal, even as the country's laws have grown more equal. Recent signs of democratic backsliding—such as the attempt to extend presidential term limits and violent clashes with indigenous environmental protestors—

suggest that the era of Bolivia's progressive change may be slowing or ending. If Morales and the MAS want to continue to be seen as the champions of Bolivia's marginalized groups, they will have to provide greater financial support for their policies, meet more of the demands from the women's and LGBT community, and honor their commitment to environmental integrity. For Morales, this will also mean turning over his office to the next democratically elected president.

Notes

I thank Lorraine Bayard de Volo for recommending me as a potential author for this chapter, and the Department of Political Science at the University of Colorado Boulder for funding the fieldwork necessary for this study. I would also like to thank Elisabeth Jay Friedman the discussants and participants at LASA Congress 2015 and 2016, and the reviewers for their helpful feedback. A huge thank you to my friend and graduate school colleague Vania Ximena Velasco-Guachalla and her family for connecting me with crucial contacts in Bolivia. But most of all, thank you to the women's rights and LGBT activists in Bolivia who generously shared their time and insights with me.

1. This is an observation echoed by Rousseau's 2011 interviews with these groups.

2. While it may seem that the Bartolinas' opposition to abortion makes them natural allies of the Catholic Church, the Morales administration and the Church have a strained relationship. The loyalty of the Bartolinas tends to lie with Morales and the MAS rather than the Church. Although Maria Galindo suggests that the rise of evangelicalism in Bolivia, particularly in indigenous communities, is the key barrier to the legalization of abortion (*Economist* 2016), there is no evidence that religious concerns are what motivate indigenous opposition to abortion.

3. This faction of the feminist women's movement has also been called the "gender technocracy," a term coined by the radical feminist group Mujeres Creando and employed in Monasterios (2007).

4. These were the Bolivian Supreme Court, the Plurinational Constitutional Court, the Bolivian Judicial Council, and the Bolivian Agricultural Court.

References

Achtenberg, Emily. 2011. "Road Rage and Resistance: Bolivia's TIPNIS Conflict" *nacla Report on the Americas*. December 8. Accessed March 14, 2018. https://nacla.org/article/road-rage-and-resistance-bolivia's-tipnis-conflict.

Achtenberg, Emily. 2017. "Why is Evo Morales Reviving Bolivia's Controversial TIPNIS Road?" *nacla Report on the Americas*. August 21. Accessed March 14, 2018. https://nacla.org/blog/2017/08/22/why-evo-morales-reviving-bolivia's-controversial-tipnis-road.

Aliaga Bruch, Sandra, Ximena Machicao Barbery, Franklin Garcia Pimentel, and Louise Bury. 2011. *Embarazos no deseados y abortos inseguros en cinco ciudades de Bolivia*. La Paz: Organización Mundial de la Salud, Marie Stopes International Bolivia, and Centro de Información y Desarrollo de la Mujer.

Alvarez, Sonia E. 1999. "Advocating Feminism: The Latin American Feminist NGO 'Boom.'" *International Feminist Journal of Politics* 1 (2): 181–209.

Alvarez, Sonia E. 2009. "Beyond NGOization?: Reflections from Latin America." *Development* 52 (2): 175–84.

Boulding, Carew. 2014. *NGOs, Civil Society, and Political Protest*. Cambridge: Cambridge University Press.

Buice, Melissa Camille. 2013. "Indigenous Women, the State, and Policy Change: Evidence from Bolivia, 1994–2012." PhD diss., University of Tennessee. http://trace.tennessee.edu/utk_graddiss/1699.

Chávez, Franz. 2010. "Bolivia: Unprecedented Gender Parity in Cabinet." *Inter Press Service*, January 29. Accessed June 28, 2016. http://www.ipsnews.net/2010/01/bolivia-unprecedented-gender-parity-incabinet/.

Choque, Davo. 2014. "Primer legislador gay en Bolivia." *El Visor Boliviano*, November 14. Accessed July 17, 2016. http://www.elvisorboliviano.com/primer-legislador-gay-en-bolivia.

Colectivo TLGB Bolivia. 2015. "Colectivo TLGB Bolivia." Accessed April 28, 2015. https://es-la.facebook.com/colectivo.tlgbbolivia/.

Corz, Carlos. 2014. "Morales promulga Nuevo Código de Familias que aliliza divorcios y fija monto mínimo de asistencia familiar." *La Razón*, November 19. Accessed April 27, 2015. http://www.larazon.com/sociedad/Rige-Codigo-Familias-divorcios-asistencia_0_2165183548.html.

Dahlerup, Drude, ed. 2006. *Women, Quotas, and Politics*. London: Routledge.

Daly, Tara. 2011. "The Intersubjective Ethic of Julieta Paredes' Poetic." *Bolivian Studies Journal / Revista de Estudios Bolivianos* 15:237–63.

Defensoría del Pueblo. 2016. "Defensor busca revertir la prohibición a las personas con diferente orientación sexual de donar sangre." Accessed July 10, 2016. http://www.defensoria.gob.bo/sp/noticias_proc.asp?seleccion=2546.

Driscoll, Amanda, and Michael J. Nelson. 2012. "The 2011 Judicial Elections in Bolivia." *Electoral Studies* 31 (3): 628–32.

Economist. 2014. "Foreign Funding of NGOs." September 23. Accessed April 2, 2017. http://www.economist.com/news/international/21616969-more-and-more-autocrats are-stifling-criticism-barring-non-governmental-organisations.

Economist. 2015. "Third Time Unlucky." January 2. Accessed July 7, 2015. http://econ.st/1xYj548.

Economist. 2016. "Feminism v Faith." January 23. Accessed April 8, 2016. http://www.economist.com/news/americas/21688939-mar-galindo-fiery-feminist takes-christianity-feminism-v-faith?fsrc=scn/tw_ec/feminism_v_faith.

Encarnación, Omar G. 2011. "Latin America's Gay Rights Revolution." *Journal of Democracy* 22 (2): 104–18.

Encarnación, Omar G. 2016. *Out in the periphery: Latin America's gay rights revolution*. New York: Oxford University Press.

Escobar-Lemmon, Maria, and Michelle M. Taylor-Robinson. 2005. "Women Ministers in Latin American Government: When, Where, and Why?" *American Journal of Political Science* 49 (4): 829–44.

Fabricant, Nicole, and Bret Gustafson. 2015. "Revolutionary Extractivism in Bolivia?" NACLA *Report on the Americas* March 2. Accessed May 20, 2015. https://nacla.org/news/2015/03/02/revolutionary-extractivism-bolivia.

Farthing, Linda C., and Benjamin H. Kohl. 2014. *Evo's Bolivia: Continuity and Change.* Austin: University of Texas Press.

Galindo, María. 2014. "Felipa Huanca." *Pagina Siete*, December 3. Accessed July 15, 2016. http://www.paginasiete.bo/opinion/2014/12/3/felipa-huanca-40001.html.

Green, Sharyl, and Peter Lackowski. 2012. "Bolivian Radical Feminist Maria Galindo on Evo Morales, Sex-Ed, and Rebellion in the Universe of Women." *Upside Down World*, April 2. Accessed April 15, 2015. http://upsidedownworld.org/main/bolivia-archives-31/3549—bolivian-radical feminist-maria-galindo-on-evo-morales-sex-ed-and-rebellion-in-the-universe-of-women.

Gudynas, Eduardo. 2013. "Development Alternatives in Bolivia: The Impulse, the Resistance, and the Restoration." In NACLA *Report on the Americas,* April 16. Accessed April 8, 2014. https://nacla.org/article/development-alternatives-bolivia-impulse-resistance-and-restoration.

Htun, Mala. 2016. *Inclusion without Representation in Latin America: Gender Quotas and Ethnic Reservations.* Cambridge: Cambridge University Press.

Inter-Parliamentary Union (IPU). 2016. "World Average." http://www.ipu.org/wmn-e/world.htm.

Ipas. 2014. "Constitutional Court Issues Decision on Abortion Restrictions in Bolivia." Last modified February 19. http://www.ipas.org/en/News/2014/February/Bolivian-court-relaxes-abortion restrictions.aspx.

Kohl, Benjamin, and Rosalind Bresnahan. 2010. "Introduction: Bolivia under Morales Consolidating Power, Initiating Decolonization." *Latin American Perspectives* 37 (3): 5–17.

Kohl, Benjamin, and Linda C. Farthing. 2006. *Impasse in Bolivia: Neoliberal Hegemony and Popular Resistance.* London: Zed Books.

Kohl, Benjamin, Linda C. Farthing, and Félix Muruchi. 2011. *From the Mines to the Streets: A Bolivian Activist's Life.* Austin: University of Texas Press.

Lind, Amy. 2002. "Making Feminist Sense of Neoliberalism: The Institutionalization of Women's Struggles for Survival in Ecuador and Bolivia." *Journal of Developing Societies* 18 (2–3): 228–58.

Los Tiempos. 2016. "Promulgan la Ley de Identidad de Género." May 21. Accessed May 22, 2016. http://www.lostiempos.com/actualidad/nacional/20160521/promulgan-ley-identidadgeneo.

Maclean, Kate. 2014. "Chachawarmi: Rhetorics and Lived Realities." *Bulletin of Latin American Research* 33 (1): 76–90.

Miller, Francesca. 1991. *Latin American Women and the Search for Social Justice.* Lebanon, NH: University Press of New England.

Monasterios, Karin. 2007. "Bolivian Women's Organizations in the MAS Era." *NACLA Report on the Americas* 40 (March): 33–37.

Morales, Waltraud Q. 2015. "Bolivia." In *Politics of Latin America: The Power Game* 5, by Harry E. Vanden and edited by Gary Prevost, 481–505. New York: Oxford University Press.

Obarrio, Fernando Oviedo. 2010. "Evo Morales and the Altiplano: Notes for an Electoral Geography of the Movimiento al Socialismo, 2002–2008." *Latin American Perspectives* 37 (3): 91–106.

Olivera, Oscar. 2004. *Cochabamba! Water War in Bolivia*. Boston: South End Press.

Panoramas. 2015, 2015. "Julieta Paredes Brings Discussion of Communal Feminism to Pittsburgh." Accessed June 28, 2015. http://www.panoramas.pitt.edu/content /julieta-paredes-brings-discussion communal-feminism-pittsburgh#.dpuf.

Paredes Tamayo, Ivan. 2015. "El MAS se abre a debater la unión gay en el Legislativo." *El Deber*, May 24. Accessed June 28, 2015. http://www.eldeber.com.bo /bolivia/mas-abre-debatir-union-gay.html.

Quota Project. 2016. Accessed May 27, 2016. http://www.quotaproject.org/.

Robinson, Jessica. 2013. "New Law Mandates Harsh Penal Ties and Broad Services to Address Violence against Women in Bolivia." *Andean Information Network*, March 21. Accessed May 13, 2013. http://ain-bolivia.org/2013/03/new -law-mandates-harsh-penalties-and-broad-services-to-address-violence-against -woman-in-bolivia/.

Rousseau, Stéphanie. 2011. "Indigenous and Feminist Movements at the Constituent Assembly in Bolivia: Locating the Representation of Indigenous women." *Latin American Research Review* 46 (2): 5–28.

Rousseau, Stéphanie, and Christina Ewig. 2017. "Latin America's Left-Turn and the Political Empowerment of Indigenous Women." *Social Politics:* 24 (4): 425–51.

Schwindt-Bayer, Leslie A. 2009. "Making Quotas Work: The Effect of Gender Quota Laws on the Election of Women." *Legislative Studies Quarterly* 34 (1): 5–28.

Shakow, Miriam. 2014. *Along the Bolivian Highway: Social Mobility and Political Culture in a New Middle Class*. Philadelphia: University of Pennsylvania Press.

Tapia, Luis. 2008. "Bolivia: The Left and the Social Movements." In *The New Latin American Left: Utopia Reborn*, edited by Patrick S. Barrett, Daniel Chavez, and César A. Rodríguez Garavito, 215–31. London: Pluto Press.

Tegel, Simeon. 2016. "A Surprising Move on LGBT Rights from a 'Macho' South American President." *Washington Post*, July 17, 2016. https://www .washingtonpost.com/news/worldviews/wp/2016/07/17/a-surprising-move on-lgbt-rights-from-a-macho-south-american-president.

United Nations Population Fund (UNFPA). 2015. "Bono Juana Azurduy." Accessed April 27, 2015. http://bolivia.unfpa.org/content/bono-juana-azurduy.

Wright, Timothy. 2000. "Gay Organizations, NGOs, and the Globalization of Sexual Identity: The Case of Bolivia." *Journal of Latin American Anthropology* 5 (2): 89–111.

CHAPTER 6

Toward Feminist Socialism?

Gender, Sexuality, Popular Power, and the State in
Venezuela's Bolivarian Revolution

RACHEL ELFENBEIN

Four months before the October 2012 presidential election, Venezuelan gender machinery workers in the rural state of Falcón sent out text messages inviting the gender equality spokesperson of every communal council to attend a "meeting with the governor" in the state's capital.[1] The next day at midmorning, around three hundred poor and working-class women filed into an auditorium expecting to discuss their communities' needs for state assistance. Presidential campaign propaganda in support of Hugo Chávez and the Bolivarian revolution filled the auditorium. The main banner on the stage read: "Without the combative woman, the REVOLUTION does not exist!" A female MC entreated the participants to guarantee Chávez's victory. Some women responded by loudly chanting slogans in support of Chávez.

Falcón Governor Stella Lugo de Montilla, one of the first female governors in Venezuelan history, entered the auditorium to applause and ascended the stage, joined by the regional gender machinery leader and the regional presidential campaign director for women. They congratulated the crowd for their fundamental "protagonism" in the revolutionary process led by a "feminist man," Hugo Chávez. Acting together, Lugo claimed, the women's movement and Chávez had advanced women's constitutional and legal rights. The speakers asserted that state-based popular[2] women's organizing was testimony of Chávez's affirmation that women were the vanguard of the revolution. They were the ones who cared, the ones who loved, the ones who always saved others. Lugo urged the women present to "materializ[e] their love" through participating in Chávez's campaign.

The campaign director also invoked this revolutionary maternalism in her instructions on how those present should organize for the campaign. While asserting that their "protagonistic participation" should be endless, she also urged that it should be in equilibrium with their housework. They should follow the example of the governor, a head of state who continued to take care of her family, and "d[id] not stop being a woman." She likened their "electoral responsibility to defend the revolution" to their responsibility to shop for their families' needs. By completing this mission to guarantee Chávez's victory, she and the governor concluded, they would serve as liberators for Venezuela.

While these women believed they would meet with the governor to discuss their community work and needs, female state and party leaders dictated to them how to organize their communities for Chávez's reelection. These authorities invoked a discourse of feminism but made no mention of feminist demands for rights during the next presidential term. The focus of this campaign event with popular women was not about what Chávez and the revolution would do for their gender and sexuality rights and material needs but what they should do to defend Chávez and the revolution. These authorities invoked and promoted a gender normative and heteronormative model of women as altruistic mothers and resignified it in service of Chávez and the revolution.

This snapshot illustrates how the Bolivarian revolution, led by Hugo Chávez, articulated gender and sexuality. Using a range of qualitative research methods[3] that uncover and contextualize different women's, LGBTTI (lesbian, gay, bisexual, transgender, transsexual, and intersex), and state interests within Bolivarian Venezuela, I argue that the Chávez government incorporated poor and working-class women as central participants in reshaping the social contract between the Venezuelan state and society. As the Falcón state and party authorities' speeches attest, popular women became the backbone of the revolutionary process because of their positioning within social reproduction relations.

Under the new Bolivarian social contract promoting the inclusion of those marginalized by the previous political regime, women and their gender interests were recognized throughout the new constitution instituted in 1999. The state made women visible in its discourse, institutions, and laws and policies, including a range of new programs that recognized and/or lightened popular women's reproductive burdens and improved their welfare. As the revolution radicalized, President Chávez also framed feminism as central to Venezuela's construction of twenty-first century socialism. This popular political opening generated new opportunities for popular women's, feminist, and later LGBTTI organizing and their legitimation within the revolution. Not only did the state create new gender machinery, but new autonomous Bolivarian feminist and LGBTTI organizations, state-directed popular women's organizations, and articulations among these organizations emerged as well.

Yet state recognition and promotion of popular women's organizations also rendered their organizing vulnerable to appropriation, as shown in the Falcón event. Further, the Bolivarian government's maternalist framework explicitly linked poor women to the family and reproductive labor (Lind 2012, 542). This dominant framework was both gender normative, as it naturalized gender binaries, and heteronormative, as it ascribed reproductive heterosexuality as "universal and morally righteous" (Bedford 2009, xix–xx). The government framed "heteronormative social reproduction" as central to its postneoliberal development project (Lind 2012, 549), thereby generally rendering LGBTTI issues peripheral on its political agenda. While some policy gains were made for women's and LGBTTI bodily autonomy, identity recognition, and social redistribution, their implementation was often patchy and weak. Further, women and LGBTTI people often found their demands for rights in these areas subordinated or postponed by state and party authorities and imperatives to defend Chávez and the revolution.

Gender and Sexual Politics from Puntofijismo to the Bolivarian Republic's Inception

The Bolivarian regime supplanted Puntofijismo, the regime of democratic governance that ended ten years of military dictatorship in 1958 and lasted until 1998, and was premised on power sharing between Venezuela's political and economic elite. Puntofijismo promoted individual and collective welfare through state distribution of oil revenues (Coronil 1997, 228), and contained class conflict through centralized, political party-based, corporatist, and clientelist forms of interest mediation (Gómez Calcaño 1998; Grindle 2000; Hellinger 2003). Yet this elite-designed and -dominated regime fundamentally excluded large portions of the popular sectors, many of whom—including female activists—helped to bring down the dictatorship, from power sharing and representation.

As the Puntofijista regime consolidated, however, women's rights activists developed alliances and conjunctural coalitions across partisan and class lines and state and society spaces, which successfully lobbied for national gender machinery and legal recognition of some of women's gender interests (Friedman 2000). This cross-sectoral organizing by women from the 1970s to the 1990s did not extend to include LGBTTI interests. Gay rights organizations did emerge during this time, but they were small, tended to be dominated by men (Tovar 2010, 93), and focused more on social work than political mobilization (Fuentes and Janicke, 2005).

At the end of the 1990s, Puntofijismo underwent a legitimacy crisis, which was exacerbated by Venezuela's engagement with neoliberalism. Taking advantage of this crisis, Hugo Chávez rose to power by articulating popular-democratic demands unfulfilled by Puntofijismo under the broad rubric of Bolivarianism. In uniting a diverse range of social, political, and economic actors and forces against Puntofijismo, Chávez originally served as a populist leader without a definitive ideological agenda (Ciccariello-Maher 2013b, 236).

Chávez and the Movimiento Quinta República (Fifth Republic Movement, or MVR), the Bolivarian electoral bloc that supported him, centered his successful 1998 presidential campaign on the call for an Asamblea Nacional Constituyente (National Constituent Assembly, or ANC) to rewrite the constitution. They argued that an ANC was necessary to transform Venezuelan democracy from representative toward participatory and the state's economic role from neoliberal facilitator to social interventionist. Once Chávez assumed power, an ANC was elected and drafted the Bolivarian Constitution of Venezuela, ratified by the electorate in 1999.

During the 1998 presidential campaign, women from around Venezuela organized in support of a new constitution (Jiménez 2000, 20). Yet Chávez's campaign and election threatened previous women's movement gains vis-à-vis the state. Chávez showed very little interest in women's issues, employed a paternalistic gender-normative discourse, and initially named no women to his government. Moreover, his administration threatened to severely cut the budget of the national gender machinery—the Consejo Nacional de la Mujer (National Woman's Council, or CONAMU) (Rakowski 2003, 396–67). Nor did the MVR initially promote women's issues.[4]

The potential for retrogression in women's rights, institutions, and power spurred women's rights activists into a new phase of conjunctural coalition building across partisan and class divides (Rakowski 2003, 396). A core group of activists organized and proposed that María León, a long-proven activist in the Venezuelan Left and the women's movement, be named president of CONAMU. León's left background and recent activism within the MVR gave her political clout within the Bolivarian movement, and because of this,

Chávez appointed her CONAMU president in 1999 and restored the agency's funding. In 2000, he transformed it into the Instituto Nacional de la Mujer (National Woman's Institute, or INaMujer), strengthening it as a permanent state institution (Rakowski 2003, 397).

Exploiting the new political opening of rapid change, state upheaval and transformation, and popular participation, women's rights activists united to organize around the ANC as they would do in Bolivia a few years later—in spite of women's significant underrepresentation in the Venezuelan assembly (12 percent of all delegates elected). The dominant concept of participation within the ANC excluded the old elite and instead included sectors previously marginalized by them (García-Guadilla and Mallén 2012, 81), representing a master frame through which women's rights activists legitimated their demands. The ANC process was relatively open and transparent to women's pluralistic organizing and interventions. The few key women's rights activists in power incorporated the broader movement in crafting constitutional proposals.

Their coalition and agenda in the constituent process did not include LGBTTI activists and demands.[5] Lesbian and gay rights activists organized separately for the right to nondiscrimination based on sexual orientation (Fuentes and Janicke 2005; Tovar 2010, 98). Although Chávez's own constitutional proposal was thinner on gender-based rights than the women's movement's proposal, his included sexual orientation as a protected category. Yet lesbian and gay organizing did not have the organizational strength nor the political-institutional footholds that the women's movement possessed.

As a result of the women's movement's strategy and the relatively open political opportunity structure, the 1999 Constitution met almost all the rights demands made by the movement since the late 1970s (Rakowski 2003, 399). These new rights and obligations included affirmative action measures favoring vulnerable, discriminated, or marginalized persons or groups, especially people suffering sex-based discrimination (Article 21); sexual and reproductive health rights (Article 76); state obligation to guarantee reproductive health (Article 76); co-responsibility between fathers and mothers in child rearing (Article 76); gender equality and equity at work (Article 88); protection of maternity and paternity through the social security system (Article 86) regardless of the parent's marital status (Article 76); state obligation to protect maternity from the moment of conception (Article 76); and both the recognition of the socioeconomic value of housework and homemakers' right to social security (Article 88). The 1999 Constitution also employs a gender perspective throughout the text in its use of both masculine and feminine subjects.

However, conservative political forces and the Catholic Church blocked the lesbian and gay rights proposal for nondiscrimination based on sexual orientation before it even reached the ANC plenary. In a further setback to LGBTTI interests, the ANC established legal recognition and protection of marriages and civil unions between men and women (Article 77) and not for nonheterosexual relationships.[6] While the ANC constituted a political opening to contest and set a framework for restructuring gender power relations, it did not signify an opening to contest heteronormativity and advance LGBTTI interests because of conservative forces and the lack of LGBTTI organizational strength at the time.

The Nature of Bolivarian Governance under President Chávez

Under President Chávez, the Bolivarian government began to radicalize, triggering a strong backlash by the opposition. This dynamic generated a constantly shifting, conflictual political field for the remainder of Chávez's tenure. Along with the ANC process, political and economic moderation characterized Chávez's first years in office. But in 2001, he began to take anti-neoliberal executive actions, provoking opposition forces to unite against him and the Bolivarian project. Intense political polarization and conflict ensued for several years until the opposition's multiple tactics to bring down the regime were clearly defeated. This polarized political context prompted Chávez to centralize power in the executive branch. Boosted by high oil prices that enhanced state capacity to finance public goods and services for the popular sectors, he progressively articulated and fulfilled left demands within the Bolivarian movement. In 2005, this process culminated in Chávez declaring that he and his government would pursue twenty-first-century socialism—a form of socialism that would recognize and promote popular participation and direct democracy, as well as institute a new production model for Venezuela. Chávez radicalized his government in part by bypassing entrenched bureaucratic structures and modes of interest mediation and promoting, institutionalizing, and granting decision-making authority to local popular power organizations. As Chávez radicalized, so did Chavismo, the movement encompassing the dialectical relations between the Bolivarian government and popular forces aligned with Chávez.

The intense political conflict between Chavismo and the opposition closed down many possibilities for the advancement of women's and LGBTTI rights from 2001 to 2004. Yet, as Chávez and his coalition gained increasing control of the state from 2005 onward, possibilities for advancing women's and LGBTTI interests opened up. For example, the executive branch exercised complete control over the missions—the Bolivarian government's key social policy apparatus, largely targeting popular women (discussed below)—which were rolled out from 2004 onward, and they therefore did not fall victim to legislative contestation. Further, Chávez's and his government's gender and sexuality rhetoric and policies turned leftward: in 2007, he asserted "there is no socialism without feminism," while the gender machinery claimed to be forging a "new sexual contract" in Venezuelan society.

Yet the Bolivarian government's left turn during Chávez's tenure remained vague, contested, and in constant flux (Buxton 2009, 57–58). Even though persistent Chavista electoral victories signaled Puntofijismo's end, a new form of democracy did not consolidate. Instead, alongside the shift toward decentralization and popularization of power came a concomitant centralization of power, as state and party authorities tended to attempt to direct popular organizations and movements (Ciccariello-Maher 2013a, 7; Spronk and Webber 2011, 251), and resource disbursement to communal organizations was tied to the executive branch. In addition, the National Assembly legitimized Chávez's centralization of power as it periodically granted him legislative authority (enabling powers).[7] When he had such powers, he legislated as much as the legislative branch did, in addition to introducing bills for their consideration.

Executive centralization of power during Chávez's tenure both created and closed down opportunities to advance women's and LGBTTI interests. As the executive exerted increasing control over the state and the party in the context of persistent political polarization, channeling demands from the party's base up to leadership became difficult. Although President Chávez often espoused a religious discourse, unlike Correa in Ecuador and Ortega in Nicaragua, he did not align with conservative religious forces to maintain power, since the Catholic Church hierarchy in Venezuela sided with the opposition. Instead, Chávez employed a kind of liberation theology supportive of the popular forces that sustained him. Chávez's radical populist approach, centralization of power, evolving feminist discourse and discourse supporting lesbian and gay equality, and increasing support for gender machinery and policies made the executive the key government site for addressing women's and LGBTTI rights.

Gender, Sexuality, and Social Movements in the Bolivarian Social Contract

The 1999 National Constituent Assembly marked the beginning of "the Bo-livarian process," an ongoing political transformation of the state's multiple institutions, the people and popular sector social movements, and the inter-action among these forces. Further, it includes allies who defend the Bolivar-ian government but may act independently of it. For Bolivarian activists, the process also signifies a societal transformation beyond the struggle for legal rights. Key to the government's vision for reconfiguring state-society relations was the formation of local popular organizations to take on co-responsibility with the state. The process entails the construction of a new social contract from the standpoint of the popular sectors.

Venezuela's construction of a new social contract under Chávez pivoted on restructuring social reproduction relations. The development, diversification, and expansion of the forces of production were central to the socialist ide-als, but not the practices, of the revolution. Venezuela remained a petro-state heavily dependent on non-labor-intensive oil extraction and importation of essential goods. Similar to Bolivia's and Ecuador's dependence on unsus-tainable resource extraction to finance pro-poor redistributive policies (see chapters 5 and 8), extracting Venezuela's oil to fund social service expansion for the popular sectors was fundamental to the Bolivarian revolution's devel-opment and continuation. The revolution's legitimacy rested in large part on reconfiguring what Ruth Pearson (1997, 680) has termed (in relation to the Cuban revolution) "a reproductive bargain, . . . which ensured the continuity of social as well as aspects of human reproduction in the country." As Pear-son explains, such a reproductive bargain is political, in that the population offers the regime political support as long as the government continues to offer and/or improve upon a basic standard of living. The legitimacy of the Bolivarian revolution also rested on reconfiguring representation in terms of state acceptance and promotion of active popular sector social and political participation.

In this new social contract that privileged popular participation in com-munity service delivery and political mobilization, popular women, their labor, and their organization became central to the Bolivarian process's development. Popular women, who were largely *mestiza* and black, became the revolution's backbone because of their maternal gender role, their positioning within the gendered division of labor, and their ties to their households and communities. In its policy and program design and implementation supporting popular women's organization, the Bolivarian government drew upon these deeply entrenched and unquestioned gendered (and effectively racialized) assumptions about the availability and elasticity of their unpaid reproductive labor.

As the regime radicalized, the government envisioned that popular women would support the state, popular organizations, their communities and their families, and also mediate among them. From Chávez on down, state functionaries began to publicly recognize that the Bolivarian revolution had "a woman's face," as they were keenly aware that women were driving community organization, service delivery, and political mobilization supporting the government. They employed a discourse that resignified and praised popular mothers as revolutionary, protagonistic subjects. The government's promotion of revolutionary maternalism opened up possibilities for popular mothers to take on new political roles and activities (Fernandes 2007, 102), and many of them appreciated the government's maternalist discourse, policies, and programs.

Yet revolutionary maternalism was a gender-normative and heteronormative device for the government's general framework for inclusion and participation of popular women, as it promoted their empowerment through the exercise and amplification of their reproductive gender role rather than contesting it. By implication, non-gender-conforming and nonheterosexual people did not fit into this framework (Lind 2010, 653). For the Bolivarian state, popular women's reproductive labor was essential to sustaining the revolution, whereas LGBTTI subjects were not central to it. The state generally did not actively promote the queering of social and political participation, though it did not repress it.

At the same time, the reshaping of the social contract from the standpoint of the popular sectors, as Marcia Ochoa (2014, 246) notes, "transformed . . . the political imaginary of the most marginalized Venezuelan subjects," including LGBTTI subjects. The discourse of the inclusion of the previously excluded and popular power represented a "profound aperture" for LGBTTI people, as it hailed them too as "agents of claims on the state" (Ochoa 2014, 246). Chávez contributed to this change of political discourse on sexual diversity (Ochoa 2014, 236). On several occasions throughout his presidency, he publicly defended gay and lesbian equality and social inclusion (Fuentes and Janicke 2005;

Prensa ASGDRe 2011), stating in particular that the exclusion of gay and lesbian rights from the 1999 Constitution was a mistake (Fuentes and Janicke 2005).

This political opening generated new opportunities for feminist and later LGBTTI organizing and their legitimation within the revolution. Chávez's consistent assertion from 2007 onward that feminism was central to socialism enabled the popularization of feminist discourse and demands. Bolivarian-aligned feminist and LGBTTI activists appropriated concepts from the revolution's broader discourse, such as the government's socialist and feminist claims, and used them to legitimate their gender- and sexuality-based demands. This discursive tactic for radicalizing the revolution (or what activists often termed a "revolution within the revolution") enabled them both to align themselves with the government and to openly critique it.

New crosscutting coalitions of women's and LGBTTI organizations emerged inside Bolivarianism. For example, La Araña Feminista (The Feminist Spider) was a self-defined network "of revolutionary socialist feminist collectives and individuals" (La Araña Feminista, 2012b) that aimed to combat multiple, intersecting forms of discrimination (i.e., gender, ethnic, racial, class, sexual orientation, gender identity, nationality) (Carosio 2010). It included organizations of popular women, peasant women, academic women, afro-Venezuelan women, and LGBTTI activists from different regions of Venezuela who identified with Bolivarianism but who chose to "remain on the margins of the state apparatus" (Angeleri 2012, 2). The Araña also formed strategic alliances with state-organized women's groups in order to build a women's rights movement.[8] Due to its alliance with the process, the Araña gained regular access to state media, which helped to validate and popularize its ideas and demands. The Araña's organizing strategy enabled it to gain a leadership role within the umbrella Chavista social movement network, the Great Patriotic Pole, and insert a socialist feminist agenda within the alliance, the 2012 presidential campaign, and the 2013–9 government plan (Carosio 2014, 26–30).

However, ongoing political polarization hampered women's coalition building to advance their rights. This larger political context, coupled with constant elections,[9] rendered elections to be popularly interpreted as plebiscites on the regime (López Maya 2011, 6). The demand for partisan unity therefore was ever-present, and often turned the focus of women's organizing away from their specific gender interests toward actions for or against the government. State and party leaders viewed Bolivarian women's demands and organizing for gender and sexual rights as potentially divisive and vulnerable to appropriation by the opposition, and often encouraged them to delay their demands. Further, the increasing saliency of class and partisan divisions among women's rights activists rendered coalition building across such divides difficult (Rakowski and Espina 2010, 261).

After Chavismo clearly defeated the opposition in 2004, women from thirty organizations did come together across political divides as the Movimiento Amplio de Mujeres (Broad Women's Movement, or MAM). They formulated and submitted an agenda for legislative action to the National Assembly (García and Valdivieso 2009, 137). It included the primary demands of gender parity and alternation on electoral lists in national, regional, and local elections; regulation and implementation of homemakers' social security; abortion decriminalization; and gender violence law reform and implementation (UNIFEM, MAM, CEM, and UCV 2006).[10]

After 2000, more LGBTTI organizations began to appear and grow in their own right, many of them because the political climate under Chavismo encouraged popular organization and did not discourage LGBTTI organizing (Tovar 2010, 96–97). For example, the government provided permits for the first gay pride march in Venezuela—in Caracas—in 2000 (Tovar 2010, 103). At first, LGBTTI groups' work tended to be isolated from each other and from grassroots organizations (Tovar 2010, 103). In the later years of the Chávez regime, they began to unify across gender boundaries under the umbrella category of "sexual-gender diversity" and increasingly pressure the state to address sexual-gender diversity issues. In 2011, sexual-gender diversity networks joined forces to pressure the legislature to accept their "Basic Proposal for the Elimination of Legal Segregation against Persons for Sexual Orientation or Gender Identity Reasons in Venezuelan Legislation," which included demands for transversal sexuality- and gender identity-based nondiscrimination legislation, including a state institution to sanction such discrimination; penalization of homophobic and transphobic hate crimes; legal identity recognition for transsexual, transgender, and intersexual people; and legal recognition of marriage and stable unions between same-sex couples, including rights to social security benefits for same-sex partners (La Red LGBTI de Venezuela 2011).

During Chávez's presidency, feminist organizing was most successful when it was able to build alliances within the Bolivarian process and coalitions around issues that the government did not view as too challenging to the political and gender orders. Characterized by persistent political polarization for or against the government, this emergent political order under Chavismo meant that women's rights activists' long-standing strategy of coalition building was at times constrained and/or ineffective.

Gender and Sexuality in the Reconfiguration of State-Society Relations under Chavismo

During President Chávez's tenure, the Bolivarian government produced mixed results on representing women descriptively. Women's descriptive representation in the legislature increased minimally, while women experienced a significant increase in descriptive representation in executive-appointed positions, as Chávez's position toward women's leadership and representation within the state changed. For example, in the nine-year period preceding Chávez's presidency, 13 percent of ministers were women, whereas in the first nine years of his presidency, almost 20 percent of ministers were women (Aguirre et al. 2009, 323). By 2009, women occupied approximately 29 percent of national cabinet positions (García and Valdivieso 2009, 139). And in 2010, women headed four out of the five public powers: the legislative power, the judicial power, the citizen power, and the electoral power.

This gendered political opening in the Bolivarian process generated new opportunities for state incorporation of women's gender interests. The national gender machinery created a National Women's Rights Defender in 1999; a national toll-free hotline for women experiencing gender violence in 1999; and a citizenship school, providing gender mainstreaming and political training, in 2002 (Espina and Rakowski 2010, 191). The Bolivarian state established the Woman's Development Bank (BanMujer) in 2001, the Special Public Defender for Women's Rights in 2004, and district attorneys for violence against women in 2011.

Women activists inside and outside the state demanded that the government raise the profile of the national machinery by creating a ministry in the executive branch, and Chávez responded by establishing the Ministry of Woman's Popular Power and Gender Equality (MinMujer). MinMujer's mission was closely articulated with the government's larger vision for the revolution, as MinMujer Minister María León expressed, its role was to support the construction of feminist socialism within twenty-first century socialism (Alva and Castañeda 2009, 127). The work ambits of MinMujer's five vice-ministries contained an intersectional focus on gender, race, ethnicity, and class in terms of women's social, political, and economic inclusion and participation.[11]

As Rakowski and Espina (2010, 263) assert, "Once Chávez realized women's importance as voters and their organizational capacity, he charged María León with organizing them politically." The gender machinery progressively created a range of popular women's organizations through which it incorporated thousands of women across Venezuela into the revolutionary process.[12] Many of these new state-directed women's organizations provided social and economic assistance to popular women and new opportunities to engage with the state, other women, and their communities. These organizations also popularized feminism, as the state provided them education on gender issues.

These new forms of women's association and articulations with the state simultaneously rendered women's unpaid labor and organizing vulnerable to clientelistic use by the state. Popular women were more vulnerable to political direction and manipulation by state authorities when they depended on the state for resources, such as cash transfers, because the state could more easily control them, their organization, and their mobilization. In such instances, the Bolivarian government used social policy to organize and mobilize popular women, as happened in Nicaragua's "second" revolution (see chapter 7). As illustrated in the opening paragraphs, the gender machinery often mobilized the popular women it organized for marches and public events in support of the revolution rather than to contest gender power relations (Espina 2009, 71; Friedman 2009, 422), or to take advantage of opportunities to advance their rights during propitious political conjunctures.

The crosscutting relations that developed between feminist and sexual-gender diversity activists and organizations outside the state generally did not extend to incorporation of sexually gender diverse people and issues by the gender machinery and the Bolivarian state more broadly. No sexual-gender diverse descriptive representation existed in the national government, even though sexually gender diverse people were known to be there (Tovar 2010, 100). MinMujer's overarching intersectional focus did not include sexual orientation or gender identity. The only state organizations that existed specifically to address the issues that the sexually gender diverse community faced were local, situated in Caracas, and suffered from lack of political will to maintain them by both some Chavista sectors and the opposition (Divas de Venezuela No date-a; Tovar 2010, 96). For example, the Chavista Caracas metropolitan mayor Juan Barreto (2004–8) ran an office for the sexually gender diverse community, and the opposition mayor elected after him eliminated it (Tovar 2010, 96).

The Bolivarian government's overall peripheral incorporation of sexual-gender diversity issues was tied both to its maternalist, heteronormative approach to gender and sexuality issues and an underlying and sometimes explicit homophobia within the government. Some Bolivarian government and party authorities publicly used homophobic insults to discredit the opposition. As María Teresa Vera-Rojas (2014) explains, undermining the opposition through the invocation of a revolutionary moral discourse served both to reproduce heteronormativity and resignify it as tied to the values and aspirations of twenty-first-century socialism.

However, as the Bolivarian regime radicalized, Chávez and certain institutions in his government became more receptive to state incorporation of sexual-gender diversity issues and demands. For example, in the national governance plan of 2013–19, Chávez recognized the sexually gender diverse population as a vulnerable group and declared the objective of generating policies to guarantee respect for their rights and identities. From 2009 onward, the leadership of the Ministry of Popular Power for Communes and the public defender committed to working with the sexually gender diverse community to support their rights (Divas de Venezuela No date-b, No date-c).[13] And by 2007, the Chavista Caracas Mayor Barreto sponsored the gay pride march (Tovar 2010, 92).

The Bolivarian government's increase in women's descriptive representation in public power generally did not extend to legally mandating gender descriptive representation in the legislature. The government gave contradictory signs on gender parity in legislative bodies during Chávez's tenure. Just prior to the Bolivarian regime, voting law reform established political parties' obligation to include at least 30 percent female candidates in their electoral lists. Before the 2000 elections, the Consejo Nacional Electoral (National Electoral Council, or CNE) struck down this quota, arguing that it violated the constitutional right to equality, in spite of the recent constitutional enshrinement of affirmative action for groups suffering sex-based discrimination. The women's movement organized in response to this setback throughout Chávez's presidency, demanding gender parity and alternation on electoral lists. The CNE, in turn, issued a 2005 resolution in support of these demands. However, the CNE did not have the means to enforce its resolution, which was not respected in the 2005 elections (García and Valdivieso 2009, 147). In 2008, the CNE issued another resolution, obligating gender parity and alternation on lists for the regional and local elections that year. But the overwhelmingly Chavista-controlled National Assembly[14] counteracted CNE progress when it eliminated the gender parity electoral list obligation in the 2009 Organic Electoral Processes Law.

Without effective gender parity regulations, women emerged very under-represented in the first elections for the National Assembly (2000) that followed the enactment of the 1999 Constitution, making up only 9.6 percent of legislators. Their representation rose to 14.2 percent in the second term of the legislature in 2005, and then to 15.75 percent in the third term in 2010. Throughout these legislative terms, no sexual gender diverse descriptive representation existed.[15]

Nor did women enjoy forceful substantive representation within the National Assembly during Chávez's presidency. At its inception, the assembly created the Comisión Permanente de Familia, Mujer, y Juventud (Permanent Commission on Family, Woman, and Youth, or CPFMJ), which, although it linked women to the family, provided a stable institutional base through which activists could draft and lobby for women's rights within the legislature. Yet Chavista assembly deputies devalued the CPFMJ and its work, because of what former Chavista Deputy Marelis Pérez Marcano (2000–10) describes as their "very restricted and limited and unfortunately in some cases even condescending conception of what a women's rights commission meant."[16] Nor did the majority of opposition deputies view transforming gender power relations as a legislative priority. During the assembly's third term, the CPFMJ was renamed "Permanent Family Commission" and women's issues were dropped from its core focus, subordinating women's rights and gender equality.

The National Assembly generally proved even more resistant to incorporating sexual-gender diversity demands. No specific institutional base existed within the legislature to address these issues. In 2008, the CPFMJ did consult with sexually gender diverse organizations when it drafted the Gender Equality and Equity Organic Bill (Divas de Venezuela, No date-b). As a result, Chavista Deputy Romelia Matute proposed same-sex union legalization, transsexual identity recognition, and state obligation to finance sex reassignment surgery. Yet CPFMJ President Pérez Marcano struck those proposals from the bill (Tovar 2010, 99).[17] The advances in crosscutting gender and sexuality-based issues and alliances in social movements did not extend to the legislature. While the gendered political opening within the revolution enabled state incorporation of some women's gender interests, the Bolivarian government was very uneven and more closed to incorporating sexual-gender diversity demands.

Bodily Autonomy Policy Performance

During Chávez's presidency, the Bolivarian government did not prioritize the enforcement of women's and sexually gender diverse people's bodily autonomy. It did grant several new rights, yet it was not open to incorporating all demands in this area. Moreover, the implementation of new rights, policies, and programs was quite inconsistent. Venezuela therefore faced significant problems with maternal mortality, adolescent maternity, and state protection from gender violence.

Women's movement organizing was the most cohesive and strongest around violence against women (VAW), and the Bolivarian government was the most receptive to their demands in this area. The Supreme Court's 2003 declaration that protection orders issued via the 1998 VAW law were unconstitutional and therefore null compounded a preexisting lack of access to justice and state protection (Heredia de Salvatierra 2006). This decision provoked a new stage of conjunctural coalition building for a new anti-VAW law, which involved the MAM, state women's institutions, and the CPFMJ in an effective and public campaign (García and Valdivieso 2009, 137). They worked together to draft and lobby for the Organic Law of Women's Right to a Life Free from Violence (or the 2007 VAW law). The 2007 law broadly conceptualizes gender violence as it criminalizes nineteen types of violence against women.[18] But its definition of victims as women and aggressors as men potentially leaves sexually gender diverse victims of gender violence unprotected.

The application of justice for gender violence survivors as per the 2007 VAW law moved slowly during the remainder of the Chávez government. The law mandates the establishment of VAW courts, staffed by officials trained in VAW. Following the law's promulgation, the Supreme Court announced that it would create ninety-two VAW courts throughout the country (Rakowski and Espina, 2011, 169). By 2012, only forty-one VAW courts were established (La Araña Feminista 2012a). Women's rights activists and organizations observed somewhere between an 86 percent and a 96 percent archival or dismissal rate of VAW charges in 2009 (Mota Gutiérrez 2011; Observatorio Venezolano de los Derechos Humanos de las Mujeres 2011). As the Venezuelan Women's Human Rights Observatory (2010) notes, this lack of justice created a climate of "impunity for violence against women." The government did respond in 2010 to this level of impunity by creating a national commission to develop policies improving the justice system's response to VAW (Centro de Estudios de la Mujer de la Universidad Central de Venezuela et al. 2011, 5).

While statistical data on gender violence survivors' experiences with the state are difficult to access or do not exist (Mecanismo de Seguimiento Convención Belém do Pará 2012; Observatorio Venezolano de los Derechos Humanos de las Mujeres 2010), many survivors appear to have been unprotected, if not abused, by the state. At the outset of the Bolivarian regime, the gender machinery promised nation-wide shelter provision for women experiencing gender violence (Friedman 2009, 427). Yet, by 2011, only three women's shelters existed in Venezuela. The state ran two of the shelters, and a NGO ran one. The two state-operated shelters had very little space: MinMujer reported that they served eighty-eight women and children in total in 2010 (Ministerio del Poder Popular para la Mujer y la Igualdad de Género 2011, 159). UN-sponsored research with VAW survivors in five Venezuelan states found that many did not receive the help they needed from the police, judicial, and health sectors, and in some instances officials in these sectors acted in sexist, abusive, and/or insensitive ways (Jiménez García et al. 2013). As this study's authors observe, such officials turned the 2007 VAW law's application into an instrument to perpetuate violence against women (Jiménez García et al. 2013, 60).

Beyond the limited implementation of existing gender violence laws, the government left several demands for legal reform unaddressed. It did not reform the penal and civil codes according to the new constitutional framework of women's rights, and several blatantly discriminatory legal norms remained in effect. For example, rapists were exonerated from punishment if they married their victims, and sentences for perpetrators of gender violence crimes were reduced if their victims were sex workers. Further, the government did not incorporate the sexual-gender diversity movement demand for legal recognition and penalization of homophobic and transphobic hate crimes.

During Chávez's tenure, legislating reproductive autonomy suffered from both a lack of political will and uneven effort by women's movement activists. As sexual and reproductive health rights activist Magdymar León Torrealba states (2012, 96), demands for reproductive rights did not achieve the same political force as other areas of feminist struggle, because political parties tended to perceive sexuality and reproduction as private issues. This was born out in the key struggle to advance women's reproductive autonomy under Chavismo—the ongoing demand for decriminalization of voluntary abortion. Given that complications from abortion were the third leading cause of maternal mortality in Venezuela (Comité para la Eliminación de la Discriminación contra la Mujer 2006, 6), women's rights activists and organizations presented voluntary abortion decriminalization as a matter of legislative urgency. Yet their lack of consensus as a movement on the conditions under which abortion should be decriminalized, their lack of continuity in organizing, and their lack of public discussion of their proposals weakened their efforts (León Torrealba 2012, 14 and 110–11). Venezuela retained the policy from 1897: abortion was legal only when a pregnant woman's life was in danger.

In contrast, and in line with the Bolivarian government's maternalist framework, reproductive rights that support maternity and families were gained without contestation. For example, in 2007, the National Assembly passed two pieces of legislation proposed by the CPFMJ—the Protection of Families, Maternity, and Paternity Law and the Maternal Breastfeeding Promotion and Protection Law, both of which promote women's maternal roles.

In other areas of reproductive rights, the Bolivarian government advanced policies for women and sexually gender diverse people, yet their implementation and effectiveness was again inconsistent and feeble. For example, in 2003, the government established the Official Sexual and Reproductive Health Norm for the national health system, stipulating health institutions' duty to guarantee sexual and reproductive health rights, including contraception and family planning, without gender- and sexuality-based discrimination. The government asserted that it achieved free national contraception distribution by 2005 (Ministerio del Poder Popular para Relaciones Exteriores 2011). Yet later research indicated that family planning coverage reached no more than 30 percent of the sexually active female population (Beltrán Molina 2009, 25).

In spite of the legal establishment of youth sexual and reproductive health rights under the Chávez regime, the government often did not enforce these rights, and Venezuela experienced significant problems with adolescent maternity. The 2007 Organic Children's and Adolescents' Protection Law guarantees children's and adolescents' rights to sexual and reproductive health information, education, and services. The 2009 Youth Popular Power Law guarantees adolescent mothers the right to childcare during their studies and work. Yet research indicates that only 10 percent of sexually active adolescents used contraception (Centro de Estudios de la Mujer de la Universidad Central de Venezuela et al. 2011, 3). This low contraceptive usage contributed to Venezuela experiencing an adolescent maternity rate increase between 1993–2010, with 40 percent of women in 2010 having given birth to their first baby before the age of twenty—the highest adolescent maternity rate in South America (Naciones Unidas Fondo de Población 2011, 2; Centro de Estudios de la Mujer de la Universidad Central de Venezuela et al. 2011, 3). Further, young mothers encountered difficulties continuing their studies because educational institutions did not have childcare facilities, and 20 percent of adolescent mothers dropped out of school after giving birth (Centro de Estudios de la Mujer de la Universidad Central de Venezuela et al. 2011, 3). As the Central University of Venezuela Women's Studies Center, the Araña Feminista, and the Sexual Rights Initiative (2011, 3) conclude, this low schooling rate of adolescent mothers negatively affected their economic independence and labor market incorporation, thereby "reinforcing the cycle and feminization of poverty."

Venezuela also continued to experience high maternal mortality rates under Chavismo. Maternal mortality rates increased overall during the first half of the regime,[19] even though 98 percent of childbirths occurred in health institutions (Beltrán Molina 2009, 25). In response to these high maternal mortality rates and obstetric care problems, the Bolivarian government created two national programs to reduce maternal and infant mortality. Even with these new programs, infant mortality rates basically remained constant and maternal mortality rates increased overall between 2006 and 2010.[20]

Identity Recognition Policy Performance

Although the Bolivarian regime's dominant framework for gender and sexual relations was gender normative and heteronormative, during the last years of Chávez's presidency the government incorporated some identity recognition and equality demands for sexually gender diverse people. Yet the government's evolution on sexuality and gender identity was uneven, as some government sectors continued to treat LGBTTI people in marginalizing ways. Rights advanced on paper were not necessarily upheld in practice. Further, the Bolivarian government did not recognize the demands for marriage and family equality that were being won in various Latin American countries at the time.

Chávez's centralization of power during his last years as president proved beneficial for state incorporation of some demands for sexually gender diverse people's equality and protection as a class. For example, the 2010 Popular Power Organic Law established that a primary purpose of popular power is to strive for equal enjoyment of human rights without discrimination based on sex, sexual orientation, and gender identity and expression.[21] From 2010 to 2012, the government promulgated legislation and resolutions recognizing sexually gender diverse people's equality in banking, housing, policing, and employment. Further, the National Assembly passed the 2009 Civil Registry

Organic Law, which establishes the right to a name change when a name does not correspond with a person's gender.

Yet, as with VAW, the Bolivarian government often did not comply with these new rights. For example, the LGBTI Network (2011) reported that no state institution existed to guarantee the Popular Power Organic Law's nondiscrimination principle, and following the passage of the civil registry law, national identity registry institutions continued to refuse to allow name changes for transgender people.

Throughout Chávez's presidency, Venezuela remained without marriage and family equality for nonheterosexual couples and non-gender-conforming people, in spite of the sexual-gender diversity movement's demands. The Supreme Court ruled in 2008 that the 1999 Constitution protects homosexual individuals' rights and that recognition of their partnerships could be legislated (Merentes 2010, 221). Yet the Bolivarian government did not pass laws establishing equality for same-sex couples' partnerships following this ruling. Further, the Chavista-controlled National Assembly passed legislation establishing that only heterosexual couples could legally adopt (Asamblea Nacional de la República Bolivariana de Venezuela, 2007).

Social Redistribution Policy Performance

Bolivarian government policy performance in addressing social inequalities was strongest in the area of social redistribution. From 1998 to 2012, the poverty rate decreased from 43.9 to 21.2 percent, and the extreme poverty rate decreased from 17.1 to 6 percent (Instituto Nacional de Estadística 2014). The Gini coefficient measuring income inequality fell significantly during this time, making Venezuela the least income-unequal country in Latin America, besides Cuba (ECLAC 2013). These gains were made in large part because of increased public social spending,[22] which rapidly expanded welfare services in popular sector communities.[23] However, social redistribution largely occurred through redistribution of the country's oil revenues rather than a structural transformation of the economy.

The missions, a set of state oil company-financed social and economic programs, were one of the key policy measures that reduced poverty and inequality rates. The missions were able to quickly begin to meet popular sector social needs not only because of their oil financing but also because they bypassed the extant welfare state bureaucracy and relied upon popular community organization and participation for their rollout. The Bolivarian government aimed for them to promote both social equality and popular participation in public policy.[24]

Many of the missions either directly or indirectly targeted popular women, given their positioning in social reproduction relations. A number of the missions and other Bolivarian welfare programs recognized women's unpaid reproductive labor, and in some instances lightened and/or socialized their reproductive burdens. For example, the conditional cash transfer missions, Madres del Barrio (Mothers of the Barrio) and Hijos de Venezuela (Children of Venezuela), recognized popular women's unpaid reproductive labor, gave female beneficiaries some temporary income security, and contributed to improvements in their and their families' welfare. They may have also given some beneficiaries a newfound control over resources and household expenditure. Yet, by the time Chávez died, neither Madres del Barrio, Hijos de Venezuela, nor other missions and welfare programs such as Mi Casa Bien Equipada (My Well Equipped House), Amor Mayor (Elderly Love), Simoncitos, Bolivarian Schools, and popular cafeterias had become universally available for their target populations.[25]

Just as the missions did not restructure the economy, nor did they restructure gender relations. Indeed, as with similar social welfare programs for poor women across the region, the missions depended on entrenched unequal gender relations for their functioning. While these new public welfare programs were not designed to deliberately exploit popular women, their rollout largely relied on the deployment of popular women's unpaid or poorly paid labor and their community organizing (Elfenbein 2015; Espina and Rakowski 2010, 189). Their unpaid labor also filled in the gaps when these new programs did not reach portions of the popular sectors, as the Bolivarian welfare state apparatus was uneven and fragmented in its territorial penetration. Further, popular women's responsibilities within these social programs added to their workloads and, in some instances, conflicted with their paid labor (Elfenbein 2015; Espina and Rakowski 2010, 197).

In their respective studies of women-dominated Bolivarian social policy delivery in popular sector communities in Caracas, both Sujatha Fernandes (2010) and Sara Motta (2009, cited in Spronk and Webber 2011) conclude that such decentralized policy delivery marked a turn away from a neoliberal gendered division of labor that individualizes and depoliticizes social reproduction, because it politicized everyday life and relationships and opened them up to democratic decision making. Yet a further continuity with neoliberalism along gender lines occurred with social policy under Chavismo. Because of deeply rooted gender relations, decentralization tended to reinforce poor women's responsibility for social reproduction and their normative gender role as mothers. Simultaneously, and similar to Nicaragua's "second" revolution, wherein social policies targeted women and ended up reproducing the gendered division of labor and increasing women's workloads (see chapter 7), Bolivarian social policy intensified women's maternal role because they were expected to be responsible for their communities' welfare in addition to their families' welfare.

While the Bolivarian government promoted the intensification of popular women's traditional gender role and responsibilities, it also instituted a number of new laws, policies, and programs promoting their access to microcredit and participation in production. The government's "socioproductive" programs targeting popular women[26] were designed to fit into the broader national revolutionary project of supplanting capitalism and its organizing logics with a new production model fostering endogenous development and a solidarity economy. These programs granted microcredit[27] only to cooperatives and collective organizations led by women. However, women's experiences with cooperatives were largely unsuccessful (Centro de Estudios de la Mujer de la Universidad Central de Venezuela 2011, 31; Elfenbein 2015).

Even with their general economic failures, state-promoted women's socioproductive projects provided many popular women with new social and political opportunities. For example, created in 2001, BanMujer granted over 100,000 microcredits to women-led enterprises throughout Venezuela by 2010. Nearly half of BanMujer users self-reported achievement of economic independence through developing their socioproductive projects (Aguirre et al. 2009, 89). But the bank had extremely high loan default rates. It prioritized disbursing funds to poor women over loan recovery, indicating that "the social function of the bank" was "more important than its economic function" (Rakowski and Espina 2011, 190). BanMujer approached bank users not just as producers and debtors but also as social and political agents with rights, as it provided them with political and organizational education in addition to technical business training. Because of its holistic approach, BanMujer was widely recognized as one of the most successful Bolivarian government programs (Rakowski and Espina 2011, 176).

In spite of the government's promotion of popular women's productive participation, gender analysis reveals little social redistribution of the burden of poverty and reproductive labor during the Chávez regime. Women did increasingly enter the paid workforce, but predominantly in the least paid and most precarious positions in the informal sector (Martínez 2010; Richter 2007). The majority of women who remained outside the paid labor force (approximately half of working-age women [Sistema Integrado de Indicadores Sociales de Venezuela No date-e]) did so because of household and caring duties (Carosio 2010, 132; Llavaneras Blanco 2012, 81–83). Many women with preschool-aged children remained out of the paid labor market because they lacked childcare.[28]

At the end of Chávez's presidency, women's and sexually diverse people's labor rights and the struggle to redistribute care work were advanced when Chávez decreed the 2012 Organic Work and Workers Law. This law outlaws workplace discrimination based on sex, sexual orientation, and pregnancy. In addition, the law extends the protection period for mothers from being fired without due cause before and after childbirth (*inamovalidad*) from the initiation of pregnancy to two years after childbirth (rather than the previous Puntofijista-era stipulation of one year). Provision for pre- and postnatal leave was enhanced from a previous total of eighteen weeks to a total of twenty-six weeks. The law also grants fathers two-week paternity leave and two-year inamovalidad after their child's birth. The law grants permanent inamovalidad to both mothers and fathers of children with disabilities. It also specifically recognizes workers who work outside of an employment relationship as entitled to social security rights, yet it does not stipulate how these rights would be guaranteed.

Since the Bolivarian regime's inception, a primary arena for women's rights struggle for redistribution was the implementation of Article 88 of the 1999 Constitution, the first constitutional provision in the world to specifically recognize the socioeconomic value of unpaid housework and entitle homemakers to social security. This revolutionary article directly resulted from years of organizing by women across the political spectrum, and the 1999 National Constituent Assembly initiated by Chávez provided them the opportunity to successfully lobby for its constitutional enshrinement. Yet Article 88 was not immediately enforceable because a legal implementation framework was needed. Throughout Chávez's tenure, women's rights activists advanced a legislative proposal for elderly homemakers not covered by any pension regime to receive a pension equal to the minimum wage salary. However, state authorities consistently responded that this proposal would be too costly a burden on the state, because its subjects could not contribute monetarily to a pension fund. The National Assembly did include homemakers in two social security laws: the 2002 Social Security System Organic Law and the 2005

Social Services Law, entitling all elderly people sixty years and up without contributory capacity to an economic benefit, as well as homemakers of any age in "a state of need." Yet the Social Services Law was never implemented.

Women's rights activists in and outside the state continued to organize for Article 88's implementation, but no legislative enforcement occurred during the remainder of Chávez's presidency. However, on several occasions, President Chávez acted independently of the legislature, social security law, and women's movement demands by using state oil revenue to extend social assistance to some poor homemakers. In 2006, he decreed the creation of Madres del Barrio Mission, targeting a narrower band of homemakers—primarily working-age and not elderly homemakers—with a conditional cash transfer; while figures given by the state vary, they indicate that around 100,000 women were incorporated. In 2007, Chávez issued two separate decrees establishing "exceptional and temporary programs" granting pensions to 150,000 elderly people in total, with the second decree granting pensions to 50,000 poor elderly women in particular, some of whom were homemakers—but researchers could not find evidence of their enrollment (Rakowski and Espina 2011, 187). Chávez later decreed Amor Mayor Mission in 2011, which established a regime of pensions equivalent to the minimum wage salary not only for excluded homemakers but for all poor elderly adults. While Chávez promised that all poor elderly people would be included in this regime, most had not been incorporated by the time of his death in 2013,[29] leading to questions about the universality and sustainability of Amor Mayor.

Conclusion

The Bolivarian regime during Chávez's presidency reshaped state-society relations by fostering popular sector social, political, and economic participation in co-responsibility with the state to overcome poverty and social and political exclusion. Gender and sexuality were constitutive of this new social contract between the Venezuelan state and society, as popular women acting through heteronormative reproductive gender roles became key to advancement of the revolutionary process. As in Nicaragua's "second revolution," grassroots participatory democratic organizations both implemented government social policy and expanded the base, while in Venezuela popular women particularly became the backbone of such organizing. In this revolution that had a "woman's face," the state actively promoted the feminization of popular social and political participation.

During Chávez's tenure, popular women's organizing grew while cross-class organization among women declined as Venezuela increasingly polarized politically. Yet, unlike under neoliberalism, popular women's organization was often aligned with the government, and the government often promoted their organization materially and discursively. Chávez's position on gender and sexuality and mainstreaming feminism within a socialist project was progressive for the Left. Compared to the Ecuadorian and Nicaraguan Pink Tide governments, the Bolivarian government had relatively open relations with feminist and sexual-gender diversity activists and movements, and it did not repress independent gender and sexuality organizing. New feminist and sexual-gender diversity activists and coalitions emerged that were aligned with Bolivarianism. And progress was made in generating crosscutting gender and sexuality-based alliances, as well as popularizing feminism within social movements more broadly.

The Bolivarian state increasingly made women visible in positions of power, as women's descriptive representation in the executive grew during Chávez's tenure. Unlike the Ecuadorian and Nicaraguan governments' increasing hostility to state institutionalization of feminism, the Bolivarian government responded positively to women's movement demands for the maintenance and expansion of the national gender machinery. The gender machinery played an important role in the reconfiguration of state-society relations, as it facilitated women's conjunctural coalition building for the National Constituent Assembly and directly organized popular women within their communities under the new regime.

Yet, beyond the National Constituent Assembly, the women's and sexual-gender diversity movements struggled to harness the constantly shifting and conflictual political opportunity structure during Chávez's presidency to advance their rights. Persistent political polarization tended to detract from women's rights organizing, and the gender machinery increasingly tended to organize women to support the government and the revolution rather than to contest gender power relations. Chávez's ensuing radical populist hyperpresidentialism did make the executive the key, if inconsistent, site for gender and sexuality rights actions, unlike the more antifeminist hyperpresidentialisms of Correa and Ortega. But while Chávez's rhetoric legitimized feminism and sexual-gender diversity as important nodes of struggle for the Left, his position did not result in the dramatic material and cultural transformation that his government claimed on gender and sexuality issues. The government mostly did not mainstream feminism and gender and sexual diversity in policy design and implementation, as mandated by Chávez.[30] Venezuela lagged behind other Latin American countries, such as Bolivia, Ecuador, and Nicaragua, on mandating and increasing women's descriptive legislative representation, as women did not achieve gender parity, and sexually gender diverse people were not represented descriptively in national governance.

Without substantive political representation, women's rights advancements largely occurred when they fit into a maternalist framework that supported women's normative gender role. The government generally sidelined feminist demands to advance women's rights, especially rights that did not conform to traditional gender power relations but instead contested them. This is why no legislative debate occurred over the passage of laws promoting breastfeeding, but the government consistently suppressed the demand for decriminalization of voluntary abortion. Similarly, in spite of its rhetoric of social inclusion, the government prioritized the promotion of traditional gender relations over the incorporation of sexual-gender diversity demands for marriage and family equality.

Because of the government's maternalist approach toward poor and working-class women, instead of a general gendered redistribution of productive and reproductive labor, a continuity with neoliberalism occurred in spite of the government's rhetoric promoting feminist socialism. As with neoliberalism, women increasingly entered the paid labor force, mostly in more precarious positions, and they remained largely responsible for housework. This meant that many of them had to perform double shifts, or even add on a third shift of community work. Yet their community and political work was resignified: Bolivarian policies positioned popular women to perform, for little or no pay, much of the everyday labor to build and sustain the revolution. While the government championed popular women and rolled out social policies recognizing their reproductive labor, popular women remained vulnerable because most social policies were not universally implemented, nor was reproductive labor generally redistributed.

Using Venezuelan women's and sexual-gender diversity movements' own minimum agendas of demands as a basis to evaluate the Bolivarian government's performance on gender and sexuality rights shows that some progress was made during Chávez's tenure beyond the landmark ANC. For example, the National Assembly passed a new and more expansive anti-VAW law, and in the government's last years, the president and the legislature started promulgating legislation recognizing LGBTTI equality. In the case of the women's movement demand for gender parity and alternation on electoral lists, retrogression occurred when the Supreme Court and the National Assembly separately struck down gender quotas. Yet where women's and LGBTTI rights were advanced in law, in practice their implementation was patchy, weak, and/or unregulated.

The feminization of popular social and political participation during Chávez's presidency therefore entailed an unprecedented level of women's organization, but generally not for the advancement of their own rights as women. Bolivarian-aligned feminist organizations and networks did organize autonomously of state directives, yet they often heeded to state and party authorities' calls to hold back their demands when they felt they must act in unity in defense of President Chávez, his government, and the revolution in the broader context of ongoing political polarization. Thus, the revolution that hinged on popular women's participation did not hinge on the advancement of their gender rights. While the Bolivarian government enabled some gains to be made for women's and LGBTTI rights to bodily autonomy, identity recognition, and social redistribution, it simultaneously perpetuated heteronormative masculine domination.

Notes

I would like to acknowledge Elisabeth Jay Friedman for her dedicated and inspiring editing and mentoring throughout this project. I would also like to thank Amy Lind, Elizabeth Hutchison, and the reviewers for their helpful comments.

1. "Gender machinery" refers to state institutions that make and administer policy on gender-related issues. Communal councils are territorially based communal government organizations that were established under the Bolivarian regime and delegated legally binding decision-making authority. The law governing communal councils includes community work toward gender equality through "family and gender equality committees" as an ambit of the councils' work (Asamblea Nacional de la República Bolivariana de Venezuela, 2009).

2. This is a translation of the widely used Spanish term *popular*, connoting poor and working-class people. I use this term because, as the translators of Elizabeth Jelin's 1990 volume (10–11) note, informality and precariousness characterizes their living and working conditions, and "working-class" therefore does not accurately define their socioeconomic positions.

3. Participant observation of gender machinery and sixty-four semistructured interviews with popular women, feminist analysts and organizations, and gender machinery workers and leaders at national and sub–national levels conducted from July 2011 to October 2012, as well as archival and document analysis conducted from 2011 to 2015.

4. Marelis Pérez Marcano, interview with author, September 14, 2011, Caracas.

5. However, some prominent activists, such as Gioconda Espina, did raise these demands.

6. This constitutional provision signified a retrogression, as the 1961 (Puntofijista) Constitution did not specify that legally recognized and protected marriages were between men and women.

7. This practice of granting the president enabling powers was not unique to the Bolivarian government; rather, it constitutes a Venezuelan historical political practice that preceded Chávez, was utilized under Puntofijismo, was enshrined in the subsequent 1999 Constitution, and continued past Chávez's tenure.

8. Networks of women's rights activists and organizations not aligned with Bolivarianism, such as the Venezuelan Women's Human Rights Observatory, continued operating, yet mostly did not contribute directly to policy discussions developing women's rights because of political polarization.

9. Venezuela held eighteen elections between 1999 and 2010.

10. The MAM played a key role in achieving violence against women legal reform, as discussed below.

11. The five ministries were Gender Mainstreaming in the Public Powers; Socioeconomic Strategies with a Gender, Ethnic, and Class Perspective; Protagonistic Participation and Feminist Socialist Training; Gender, Afrodescendent, and Ethnic Equality and Equity; and Social Strategies for Gender Equality.

12. For example, through Encounter Points, Madres del Barrio (Mothers of the Barrio) Committees, BanMujer User Networks, the Bicentenary Women's Front, and Feminist Socialist Production Brigades. By 2008, INaMujer estimated that it had organized around a quarter million women in Encounter Points (Ministerio del Poder Popular para Relaciones Exteriores 2011, 11); and in 2010—the year it was created—the Bicentenary Women's Front counted thirty thousand members and organizational presence in all Venezuelan states (Ministerio del Poder Popular para la Mujer y la Igualdad de Género 2011, 7).

13. Also, according to Divas de Venezuela (No date-a), from 2006 on, sexual-gender diversity rights activists demanded the state create services addressing the trans community's specific needs. In 2011, the Bolivarian government responded by creating a rehabilitation center for homeless transgender women in Caracas. Yet this center soon suffered from poor public administration and was closed a few years after its opening.

14. Chavismo held over 90 percent of National Assembly seats at this time.

15. Open sexually and gender diverse candidates did run for the National Assembly but were not elected.

16. Marelis Pérez Marcano, interview with author, September 5, 2012, Caracas.

17. The National Assembly never passed this bill during Chávez's presidency.

18. These types include psychological violence, harassment, threats, forced prostitution, sexual slavery, workplace discrimination, economic violence, obstetric violence, forced sterilization, media violence, institutional violence, symbolic violence, and trafficking.

19. The maternal mortality rate was 51 per 100,000 in 1998 (Centro de Estudios de la Mujer de la Universidad Central de Venezuela et al. 2011, 2), when Chávez came to power; in 2002 it reached 68; and in 2005 it fell to 59.9 (Sistema Integrado de Indicadores Sociales de Venezuela No date-a).

20. The infant mortality rate was 4.2 per 1,000 live births in 2006, and 4.3 in 2010 (Sistema Integrado de Indicadores Sociales de Venezuela No date-b). The maternal mortality rate was 60.5 per 100,000 in 2006, and reached 69.3 in 2010 (Sistema Integrado de Indicadores Sociales de Venezuela No date-c).

21. Even though the National Assembly passed this law, it was part of a package of "socialist" bills that the executive presented to the outgoing (lame duck) assembly in 2010 (Margarita López Maya, interview with author, September 28, 2012, Caracas) and the assembly passed with little debate and without popular consultation (López Maya 2011, 7) just before its term ended. Thus, the inclusion of this article recognizing the equal rights of sexually gender diverse people can be attributed to the executive.

22. While Venezuela's reported public social spending increased from 18.6 to 21.4 percent of GDP from 2004 to 2011 (Sistema Integrado de Indicadores Sociales de Venezuela No date-d), its public social spending to GDP ratio fell below the ratio of Costa Rica for 2011, and far below that of Cuba (ECLAC 2013, 159).

23. For example, from 1998 to 2006, the number of primary care physicians working in the public health system increased twelvefold from 1,628 to 19,571; and from 1999/2000 to 2006/2007, the number of public schools in Venezuela increased by over 55 percent (Weisbrot 2011, 201).

24. By 2013, the year President Chávez died, the government had enacted thirty-eight missions.

25. Barrio Adentro (a mission providing free, community-based primary health attention) and the public health system more broadly, and Mercal (a mission distributing and selling low-cost basic food products) became universally available. However, Mercal was not universally accessible. In my ethnographic fieldwork with popular women in 2012, they described lines for Mercal in their communities lasting for hours, and they said they did not have time to wait in such lines given their family caregiving duties (Elfenbein 2015).

26. For example, BanMujer, Madres del Barrio cooperatives, and Feminist Socialist Production Brigades.

27. These programs attached differing terms to credit, ranging from interest-free loans to low-interest loans.

28. While the Bolivarian government significantly increased public education and daycare services for children three to five years old, public child care services for children zero to three years old remained insufficient (Llavaneras Blanco 2012). In the 2008–9 school year, approximately 70 percent of children three to five years old received early education or day care services (public and private services combined). In the ten-year period between 1998–99 and 2008–9, the rate of (public and private) education and daycare service coverage for children zero to two years

of age increased from 5.5 to 16 percent (Llavaneras Blanco 2012, 97–98). Households remained the primary childcare provider for infants and toddlers (Llavaneras Blanco 2012). The paid labor market inactivity rate of mothers of young children also indicates that, within households, women were primarily assuming responsibility for filling in gaps in public childcare services.

29. By the beginning of 2012, the state counted 1,097,487 elderly people as registered for Amor Mayor (Instituto Venezolano de los Seguros Sociales 2012). From 2011 to 2012, 321,482 elderly people began to receive state economic assistance, and from 2012 to 2013, 19,146 elderly people began to receive state economic assistance (Sistema Integrado de Indicadores Sociales de Venezuela No date-a).

30. For example, President Chávez responded to women's movement demands in 2005 by issuing an administrative mandate to incorporate gender-sensitive budgeting in the national budget (Llavaneras Blanco 2011, 142). This mandate was deepened in 2009 when all national public institutions were instructed to include at least one project dedicated to gender equity in their annual plans. Yet, according to Masaya Llavaneras Blanco (2011, 146), the majority of the Bolivarian government's 163 self-declared gender equity programs in 2009 proposed measures that reproduced existing gender relations.

References

Aguirre, Virginia, Luisa Bethencourt, and Pablo Testa. 2009. *Políticas públicas dirigidas hacia las mujeres, resultados 1999–2009*. Caracas: Ministerio del Poder Popular para la Mujer y la Igualdad de Género.

Alva, María Elena, and Nora Castañeda. 2009. "Feminismo y socialismo: Aportes teórico-prácticos en Venezuela (1999–2009)." *Revista Venezolana de Estudios de La Mujer* 14 (33): 119–32.

Angeleri, Sandra. 2012. "La Araña Feminista: Estableciendo los parámetros para el estudio de una experiencia de articulación feminista y socialista." Paper presented at Encuentro de Investigación en Feminismos, Estudios de la Mujer y Género, Centro de Estudios de las Mujeres, Universidad Central de Venezuela, Caracas, June 13–14.

Asamblea Nacional de la República Bolivariana de Venezuela. 2007. *Ley Orgánica para la Protección de Niños, Niñas y Adolescentes.*

Asamblea Nacional de la República Bolivariana de Venezuela. 2009. *Ley Orgánica de los Consejos Comunales.*

Bedford, Kate. 2009. *Developing Partnerships: Gender, Sexuality, and the Reformed World Bank*. Minneapolis: University of Minnesota Press.

Beltrán Molina, Luz. 2009. *Informe sobre Venezuela que se presenta al CEDAW 2008: Artículo 12: Salud*. Caracas: Observatorio Venezolano de los Derechos Humanos de las Mujeres.

Buxton, Julia. 2009. "Venezuela: The Political Evolution of Bolivarianism." In *Reclaiming Latin America: Experiments in Radical Social Democracy*, edited by Geraldine Lievesley and Steve Ludlam, 57–74. London: Zed Books.

Carosio, Alba. 2010. "Tejiendo la red de colectivos de mujeres en Venezuela."
Correo del Orinoco, December 14.

Carosio, Alba. 2014. "Crónicas de la Araña." In *La Araña Feminista Opina*, edited
by Alba Carosio, Alejandra Laprea, and Akaida Orozco, 14–33. Caracas: Tinta
Violeta.

Centro de Estudios de la Mujer de la Universidad Central de Venezuela. 2011.
Informe de la situación de género en Venezuela. Caracas.

Centro de Estudios de la Mujer de la Universidad Central de Venezuela, Araña
Feminista, and Iniciativa por los Derechos Sexuales. 2011. *Informe sobre la
República Bolivariana de Venezuela: 12° Ronda del Examen Periódico Universal—
Septiembre de 2011*.

Ciccariello-Maher, George. 2013a. "Constituent Moments, Constitutional Processes,
Social Movements and the New Latin American Left." *Latin American Perspectives* 20 (10): 1–20.

Ciccariello-Maher, George. 2013b. *We Created Chávez: A People's History of the
Venezuelan Revolution*. Durham, NC: Duke University Press.

Comité para la Eliminación de la Discriminación contra la Mujer. 2006. *Obser-
vaciones finales del Comité para la Eliminación de la Discriminación contra la
Mujer: República Bolivariana de Venezuela*. New York: United Nations.

Coronil, Fernando. 1997. *The Magical State: Nature, Money, and Modernity in Venezuela*. Chicago: University of Chicago Press.

Divas de Venezuela. No date-a. "DIVAS DE VENEZUELA Y MISIÓN NEGRA HIPÓLITA."
Accessed December 2014. https://divasdevenezuela.wordpress.com/a-c-divas-de
-venezuela-y-mision-negra-hipolita/.

Divas de Venezuela. No-date-b. "Gestiones (Historial)." Accessed December 2014.
https://divasdevenezuela.wordpress.com/gestiones-historial/.

Divas de Venezuela. No date-c. "NOTICIAS sexo-género diversas y feministas." Accessed December 2014. https://divasdevenezuela.wordpress.com/articulos-de
-prensa-sexo-genero-diversas-y-feministas/.

Economic Commission for Latin American Countries (ECLAC). 2013. *Social Panorama of Latin America 2012*. Santiago: United Nations.

Elfenbein, Rachel. 2015. *They Want Our Work, but Not Our Power: Popular Women,
Unpaid Labor, and the Making of the Bolivarian Revolution*. PhD diss., Simon
Fraser University.

Espina, Gioconda. 2009. "Feminist Activism in a Changing Political Context: Venezuela." In *Feminist Agendas and Democracy in Latin America*, edited by Jane S.
Jacquette, 65–80. Durham, NC: Duke University Press.

Espina, Gioconda, and Cathy A. Rakowski. 2010. "Waking Woman Up? Hugo
Chávez, Populism and Venezuela's 'Popular' Women." In *Gender and Populism
in Latin America: Passionate Politics*, edited by Karen Kampwirth, 180–201.
University Park: Pennsylvania State University Press.

Fernandes, Sujatha. 2007. "Barrio Women and Popular Politics in Chávez's Venezuela." *Latin American Politics and Society* 49 (3): 97–127.

Fernandes, Sujatha. 2010. "Gender, Popular Participation, and the State in Chávez's Venezuela." In *Gender and Populism in Latin America: Passionate Politics*, edited by Karen Kampwirth, 202–21. University Park: Pennsylvania State University Press.

Friedman, Elisabeth. 2000. *Unfinished Transitions: Women and the Gendered Development of Democracy in Venezuela, 1936–1996.* University Park: Pennsylvania State University Press.

Friedman, Elisabeth Jay. 2009. "Gender, Sexuality and the Latin American Left: Testing the Transformation." *Third World Quarterly* 30 (2): 415–33.

Fuentes, Frederico, and Kiraz Janicke. 2005. "Struggling for Gay and Lesbian Rights in Venezuela." *Green Left Weekly*, December 5.

García, Carmen Teresa, and Magdaleno Valdivieso. 2009. "Las mujeres venezolanas y el proceso Bolivariano: Avances y contradicciones." *Revista Venezolana de Economía y Ciencias Sociales* 15 (1): 133–53.

García-Guadilla, María Pilar, and Ana L. Mallén. 2012. "El momento fundacional de la Venezuela bolivariana: El problema de la legitimidad en la Asamblea Nacional Constituyente venezolana de 1999." *Revista Politeia* 35 (49): 65–98.

Gómez Calcaño, Luis. 1998. "Redefining the State's Social Policies: The Case of Venezuela." In *The Changing Role of the State in Latin America*, edited by Menno Vellinga, 213–37. Boulder, CO: Westview Press.

Grindle, Merilee Serrill. 2000. *Audacious Reforms: Institutional Invention and Democracy in Latin America.* Baltimore, MD: Johns Hopkins University Press.

Hellinger, Daniel. 2003. "Political Overview: The Breakdown of Puntofijismo and the Rise of Chavismo." In *Venezuelan Politics in the Chávez Era: Class, Polarization, and Conflict*, edited by Steve Ellner and Daniel Hellinger, 27–53. Boulder, CO: Lynne Rienner.

Heredia de Salvatierra, Isolde. 2006. "¿Es la violencia de género y el acceso a la justicia un asunto de derechos humanos?" *Revista Venezolana de Estudios de La Mujer* 3 (1): 99–112.

Instituto Nacional de Estadística. 2014. *Pobreza por línea de ingreso, 1er semestre 1997–2do semestre 2013.* Caracas: Instituto Nacional de Estadística.

Instituto Venezolano de los Seguros Sociales. 2012. "Van 1.097.487 adultos mayores registrados en Amor Mayor." Accessed January, 2014. http://www.ivss.gob.ve/.

Jelin, Elizabeth. 1990. "Introduction." In *Women and Social Change in Latin America*, edited by Elizabeth Jelin, 1–11. London: Zed Books.

Jiménez García, Morelba. 2000. "Las mujeres en el proceso constituyente." In *Mujeres protagonistas y proceso constituyente en Venezuela*, edited by Morelba Jiménez García, 17–29. Caracas: Embajada Británica, Unifem, Programa de las Naciones Unidas para el Desarrollo, and Editorial Nueva Sociedad.

Jiménez García, Morelba, Jessie Blanco Freites, Susana Medina Salas, and Rosalba Gómez Lozano. 2013. *Ruta crítica de las mujeres afectadas por violencia de pareja en Venezuela.* Caracas: Fondo de Población de Naciones Unidas, Universidad

Central de Venezuela, Universidad Católica Andrés Bello, and Universidad Católica Cecilio Acosta.

La Araña Feminista. 2012a. "25 de Noviembre de 2012: Día Internacional de la No Violencia Contra las Mujeres." Accessed December 2014. http://encuentrofeminista.weebly.com/declaraciones-y-solidaridad.html.

La Araña Feminista. 2012b. "Araña Feminista . . . y socialista." Accessed March 17, 2013. http://encuentrofeminista.weebly.com/nuestra-red.html.

La Red LGBTI de Venezuela. 2011. "Propuesta básica de eliminación de segregación legal contra las personas por razón de orientación sexual o identidad de género en la legislación Venezolana."

León Torrealba, Magydmar. 2012. *Temas centrales en el debate sobre el aborto en Venezuela y argumentos teóricos para su despenalización.* Caracas: Universidad Central de Venezuela.

Lind, Amy. 2010. "Gender, Neoliberalism and Post-Neoliberalism: Re-Assessing the Institutionalisation of Women's Struggles for Survival in Ecuador and Venezuela." In *The International Handbook of Gender and Poverty: Concepts, Research, Policy,* edited by Sylvia Chant, 649–54. Cheltenham, UK: Edward Elgar.

Lind, Amy. 2012. "'Revolution with a Woman's Face'? Family Norms, Constitutional Reform, and the Politics of Redistribution in Post-Neoliberal Ecuador." *Rethinking Marxism: A Journal of Economics, Culture & Society* 24 (4): 536–55.

Llavaneras Blanco, Masaya. 2011. "Los presupuestos sensibles al género como herramienta para la justicia de reconocimiento y redistribución: Análisis de la experiencia venezolana." In *Aportes al debate del Desarrollo en América Latina: Una perspectiva feminista,* edited by Norma Sanchís, 135–50. Buenos Aires: Red de Género y Comercio.

Llavaneras Blanco, Masaya. 2012. *Análisis de la demanda de cuidados de los hogares con niñas y niños de 0 a 6 años en Venezuela desde una perspectiva de género: Principales características y mecanismos públicos y de mercado a los que se accede para su satisfacción.* Caracas: Universidad Central de Venezuela.

López Maya, Margarita. 2011. "Venezuela entre incertidumbres y sorpresas." *Nueva Sociedad* 235:4–16.

Martínez, Ángel. 2010. "Determinantes de la participación laboral femenina en Venezuela: Aplicación de un modelo probit para el año 2005." *Revista Venezolana de Estudios de la Mujer* 15 (35): 17–44.

Mecanismo de Seguimiento Convención Belém do Pará. 2012. *Informe final sobre Venezuela. Análisis de la respuesta del gobierno de Venezuela al cuestionario para la evaluación de la implementación de la Convención Interamericana para Prevenir, Sancionar y Erradicar la Violencia contra la Mujer "Convención de Belém do Pará."* Washington, DC: Organización de los Estados Americanos.

Merentes, Jose Ramon. 2010. "Gay Rights in Venezuela under Hugo Chávez, 1999–2009." In *The Politics of Sexuality in Latin America: A Reader on Lesbian, Gay, Bisexual, and Transgender Rights,* edited by Javier Corrales and Mario Pecheny, 220–23. Pittsburgh, PA: University of Pittsburgh Press.

Ministerio del Poder Popular para la Mujer y la Igualdad de Género. 2011. *Memoria y cuenta 2010*. Caracas: Ministerio del Poder Popular Para la Mujer y la Igualdad de Género.

Ministerio del Poder Popular para Relaciones Exteriores. 2011. "Informe nacional Cairo +15: Evaluación de los avances en la implementación del Programa de Acción de la Conferencia Internacional Sobre Población y Desarrollo a 15 años de su firma." Caracas: Gobierno Bolivariano de Venezuela.

Mota Gutiérrez, Gioconda. 2011. "Acto en contra de la violencia hacia la mujer." *Ciudad CCS*, November 25.

Motta, Sara C. 2009. "Venezuela: Reinventing Radical Social Democracy from Below?" In *Reclaiming Latin America: Experiments in Radical Social Democracy*, edited by Geraldine Lievesley and Steve Ludlam, 75–90. London: Zed Books.

Naciones Unidas Fondo de Población. 2011. *Encuesta demográfica de Venezuela 2010: Primeros resultados*. Caracas: Naciones Unidas Fondo de Población.

Observatorio Venezolano de los Derechos Humanos de las Mujeres. 2010. *Violencia contra las mujeres en Venezuela: Informe alternativo sobre el derecho de las mujeres a una vida libre de violencia*. Caracas: CISFEM and Observatorio Venezolano de los Derechos Humanos de las Mujeres.

Observatorio Venezolano de los Derechos Humanos de las Mujeres. 2011. *Informe sobre la República Bolivariana de Venezuela—Duodécima sesión del Examen Periódico Universal—Octubre 2011 (Período 2007–2010)*.

Ochoa, Marcia. 2014. *Queen for a Day: Transformistas, Beauty Queens, and the Performance of Femininity in Venezuela*. Durham, NC: Duke University Press.

Pearson, Ruth. 1997. "Renegotiating the Reproductive Bargain: Gender Analysis of Economic Transition in Cuba in the 1990s." *Development & Change* 28: 671–705. The Hague: Institute of Social Sciences.

Prensa ASGDRe. 2011. "El presidente Chávez aboga por la inclusión de homosexuales en espacios para la juventud bicentenaria." Accessed December, 2014. http://asgdre.blogspot.com/2011/07/el-presidente-chavez-aboga-por-la.html.

Rakowski, Cathy. 2003. "Women's Coalitions as a Strategy at the Intersection of Economic and Political Change in Venezuela." *International Journal of Politics, Culture and Society* 16 (3): 387–405. Springer US.

Rakowski, Cathy, and Gioconda Espina. 2010. "Women's Struggles for Rights in Venezuela: Opportunities and Challenges." In *Women's Activism in Latin America and the Caribbean: Engendering Social Justice, Democratizing Citizenship*, edited by Elizabeth Maier and Nathalie Lebon, 255–72. New Brunswick, NJ: Rutgers University Press / Tijuana: El Colegio de la Frontera Norte A.C.

Rakowski, Cathy, and Gioconda Espina. 2011. "Advancing Women's Rights from Inside and Outside the Bolivarian Revolution, 1998–2010." In *The Revolution in Venezuela: Social and Political Change under Chávez*, edited by Thomas Ponniah and Jonathan Eastwood, 155–92. Cambridge, MA: Harvard University Press.

Richter, Jacqueline. 2007. "Segmentadas y segregadas: Las mujeres en la fuerza de trabajo en Venezuela." *Revista Politeia* 39 (30): 151–85.

Sistema Integrado de Indicadores Sociales de Venezuela. No date-a. "Atención integral al adulto mayor / Población atendida en atención económica." Accessed January 2015. http://sisov.mppp.gob.ve/indicadores/AS1400700000000/.

Sistema Integrado de Indicadores Sociales de. No date-b. "Disponibilidad y oferta de trabajo / Tasa neta de actividad por sexo." Accessed January 2015. http://sisov.mppp.gob.ve/indicadores/MU0400200000000/.

Sistema Integrado de Indicadores Sociales de. No date-c. "Reducción de la mortalidad infantil / Tasa de mortalidad postneonatal." Accessed January 2015. http://sisov.mppp.gob.ve/indicadores/MM0400300000000/.

Sistema Integrado de Indicadores Sociales de. No date-d. "Salud reproductiva / Tasa de mortalidad materna." Accessed January 2015. http://sisov.mppp.gob.ve/indicadores/SA0300200000000/.

Sistema Integrado de Indicadores Sociales de. No date-e. "Total / Inversión pública social como porcentaje del PIB." Accessed January 2015. http://sisov.mppp.gob.ve/indicadores/GA0100800000000/.

Spronk, Susan, and Jeffrey R. Webber. 2011. "The Bolivarian Process in Venezuela: A Left Forum." *Historical Materialism* 19 (1): 233–70.

Tovar, Marianela. 2010. "Marianela Tovar, Contranatura." In *Venezuela Speaks! Voices from the Grassroots*, edited by Carlos Martinez, Michael Fox, and Jojo Farrell, 92–105. Oakland, CA: PM Press.

UNIFEM, MAM, CEM, and UCV. 2006. *Agenda de las mujeres para el trabajo parlamentario y legislativo, 2006–2011.* Caracas.

Vera-Rojas, María Teresa. 2014. "En nombre del amor: Políticas de la sexualidad en el proyecto socialista bolivariano." *Cuadernos de Literatura* 18 (36): 58–85.

Weisbrot, Mark. 2011. "Venezuela in the Chávez Years: Its Economy and Influence on the Region." In *The Revolution in Venezuela: Social and Political Change under Chávez*, edited by Thomas Ponniah and Jonathan Eastwood, 193–223. Cambridge, MA: Harvard University Press.

CHAPTER 7

Nicaragua and Ortega's "Second" Revolution

"Restituting the Rights" of Women and Sexual Diversity?

EDURNE LARRACOECHEA BOHIGAS

In 2007, after sixteen years of being in opposition, the Frente Sandinista de Liberación Nacional (Sandinista Front for National Liberation, or FSLN) returned to power and Daniel Ortega was reelected president of Nicaragua. President Ortega and the FSLN presented themselves as the legacy of the Sandinista revolution of the 1980s, branding Ortega's three subsequent terms in office "the second period of the revolution." The president claims to have "restituted the rights" of all Nicaraguans, including those of women and the LGBT[1] population. Contrary to Ortega's claims, this chapter argues that during his presidency there has been a rollback in citizens' rights, in particular those of women and LGBT people.

Ortega's government has been examined as part of the Latin American Pink Tide (Cameron 2009; Cannon and Hume 2012; Levitsky and Roberts 2011; Panizza 2009; Weyland 2013). However, voices at home and abroad have warned against labeling today's FSLN as a representative of the Latin American "new Left": they argue that the party no longer possesses a "leftist" agenda (Kampwirth 2008; MAM 2009; Torres-Rivas 2007). In fact, many agree that, since 2007, Ortega's Frente has followed a cynical, pragmatic, and clientelistic way of doing politics, far from the revolutionary ideals it claims to represent.

Despite impressive numbers of women in elected positions, which have catapulted Nicaragua nearly to the top of international gender equity rankings, Ortega and first lady Rosario Murillo have pursued a baldly antifeminist agenda: harassing and persecuting feminist organizations, banning abortion in all cases, and defending the "unity of the family" above the right of women to live free from violence. As for LGBT rights, while initially appearing to favor a progay agenda through the removal of an antisodomy article from the Penal

Code and the creation of a Special Ombudsperson for Sexual Diversity, the presidential couple has made clear that heteronormativity[2] is central to their social project.

As this chapter will show, Ortega's gender and sexuality agenda has entailed directly attacking feminists and women's organizations, creating divisions between LGBT organizations and the women's movement, and co-opting sexual diversity leaders and part of the community. However, Ortega's administration has engaged in "pinkwashing"[3] strategies, trying to partially veil the setbacks regarding women's rights by advancing women's descriptive representation and appearing to be friendly to LGBT organizations and demands in order to improve the president's international credentials as a modern leftist leader. The international audience is particularly relevant to Nicaraguan politics. Although the country's extreme dependence on international aid has been reduced from an average of nearly 40 percent of its GDP between 1990 and 2009, by 2015 international funds still represented 8.7 percent (Avendaño 2010, 4; Banco Central de Nicaragua 2016, 5). Thus, external validation is a central factor that does not affect other countries examined in this volume to the same degree.

To explain how these developments have come about, I argue that Ortega's rule since 2007 has brought together two heretofore separate historical phenomena: the classic *caudillismo* (rule by an authoritarian, often highly self-promoting, leader) of Nicaragua's dictatorial past, and the Latin American Marxist Left's subordination of gender and sexuality to political rights and socioeconomic justice. This long-standing tension that the Marxist Left set up as a zero-sum game between class and cultural issues was already at the center of gender and sexuality policies during the Sandinista revolution in the 1980s. But the increasingly centralized and authoritarian Frente under Ortega has exacerbated the hostility toward feminists and their autonomous work for women, even as the administration has sought international approbation of its pinkwashing actions. However, this chapter also shows that an analysis of the lives and struggles of Nicaraguan women and LGBT populations demonstrates that denying rights in one sphere has effects across all of them; that is, sexual and gender rights are indivisible from other aspects of social justice.

Thus, the point of departure of my analysis is to go beyond the divisions among redistributive measures, political participation, and gender and sexuality policies. Even though the organization of this chapter follows, to some extent, the logic it is trying to avoid, I coincide with Silke Heumann's view (2014a, 307) that the "shortcomings" of Ortega's administrations already identified by various authors from a feminist and sexual rights perspective (see

Kampwirth 2011), cannot be compensated by "achievements" in, for instance, reducing poverty rates among poor women through redistributive and social policies. In other words, an assessment of any regime from a feminist and sexual rights perspective implies precisely assessing sexual and gender rights as inherent in and inseparable from social justice.

This chapter draws most directly on qualitative research carried out during the second half of 2014, the beginning of 2015, and July 2016, when I conducted in-depth interviews with twenty key informants, mostly LGBT and feminist activists, but also with the Special Ombudswoman for Sexual Diversity and a member of the Movimiento Renovador Sandinista (Sandinista Renovation Movement, or MRS)'s Red de Mujeres (Women's Network). It is also based on an exhaustive academic literature search together with a review of recent on-line media, government documents, and legislation. In addition, my research is informed by my personal experience living in the country for a total of eight years between 2004 and 2013. During this period I worked with several feminist organizations and was an active member of the feminist movement in the northern city of Matagalpa. My account is directly influenced by the discussions, conversations, and engagement I have had with my fellow activists of the Red de Mujeres de Matagalpa (Women's Network of Matagalpa), as well as my own experience as a feminist activist in the country during the time that I examine.

Contextual Reflections

The "Left" Returns to Power: From Sandinismo to Orteguismo

The FSLN, founded as a guerrilla organization in 1961, was not originally an authoritarian vehicle for Ortega's domination of the state. It spent its first eighteen years fighting and finally overthrowing the Somoza family dictatorship (1936–79). The Sandinista-led insurrection was followed by a decade of revolutionary transformation based on three main principles: political pluralism, mixed economy, and nonalignment (Vanden and Prevost 1993, 95). During the 1980s, the Frente became the hegemonic actor and there was a progressive fusion of the party with the state, which was reinforced by the party's conception of itself as a "vanguard" (Martí i Puig 2010, 83). For a decade, the Sandinista revolutionary project was under attack from a CIA-sponsored counterrevolutionary force, the Contra, which heavily influenced the revolution's development and its electoral demise in 1990. During the 1990s and 2000s, the FSLN remained the second largest political force in Nicaragua, transforming from a "cadre" to an electoral party (Martí i Puig 2010, 79). The process of transformation took place amid several internal conflicts that led to a split in the party and the subsequent creation of the dissident MRS. In addition, this process was characterized by a growing exaltation of Ortega's leadership and the concentration of power in his hands and that of his circle, which has come to be known as Danielismo or Orteguismo.

The return of Ortega and the FSLN to the presidency in November 2006 was mostly the result of an exclusionary pact staged between caudillos: in January 2000, then-president Arnoldo Alemán and Daniel Ortega had signed "el Pacto." Here, Ortega's hostility to women's demands was foundational: while his counterpart was looking for immunity to protect himself against corruption charges, Ortega sought to preserve his parliamentary immunity to avoid standing trial after being accused of sexual abuse in 1998 by his stepdaughter, Zoilamérica Narváez. The Pacto resulted in, among other things, a "forced 'two-party' system" (Yllescas and Montenegro 2003, 3), an electoral reform, the division of important government positions between Liberals and Sandinistas, and the protection of both leaders from criminal prosecution (Close 2004, 11). One element included in the pact, and the key to understanding Ortega's return to power, was the lowering of the percentage of votes necessary to win the presidency without going to a second round of voting.

The FSLN won the presidency in the first round with only 38 percent of votes, running against a divided Right and a weakened Left opposition after the sudden death of the MRS Alliance's popular presidential candidate, Herty Lewites. Thus, the return of "the Left" in Nicaragua was not the result of a change in voting patterns but rather the outcome of very strategic changes made to the electoral law and the division of the Right into two tickets partly fueled by the very same Frente.

After a decade in office, the Frente has managed to enlarge and consolidate its power, aided by its absolute control of political institutions including the Supreme Electoral Council, the use of social policies mostly financed by Venezuelan petrodollars to enlarge its political base (Pérez-Baltodano 2013, 33), the adoption of illegitimate methods,[4] and the 2014 reforms to the constitution that further reinforced Ortega's leadership and the Frente's hegemony. Whereas during his first administration the FSLN ruled with a minority in the National Assembly, during Ortega's second and third consecutive terms, the Sandinistas ruled with a majority in the National Assembly, after internationally and nationally questioned landslide victories in both 2011 and 2016 national elections.[5]

Ortega's Economic, Political, and Social Model: How Left Is This "Left"?

The FSLN returned to power with a discourse of reversing the damages inflicted by sixteen years of neoliberal governance by "restituting the rights" of the people, especially those of the poor. This rhetoric became central to the self-proclaimed "Christian, Socialist and Solidarity" government. Ortega claimed to be implementing an economic model based on redistribution policies for the poor majority, a political model based on direct and participatory forms of democracy, and a social model based on the "unity of the family." But his party, which replaced its traditional socialist red and black colors with bright pink, was far from the Frente that had left government in 1990. Ortega strengthened his control over the FSLN, based on strong personalism and nepotism, while supporting economic policies for the wealthy. For example, he and his powerful wife, Rosario Murillo, became friends with the Frente's historical foe, cardinal Miguel Obando y Bravo. The FSLN also endorsed the complete ban of abortion in the country,[6] siding with the most conservative forces and directly contravening women's basic rights.

Turning to the economic model, Ortega's discourse of social redistribution was embodied through targeted pro-poor social policies and ensuring access to free healthcare and primary and secondary education. Despite the accusations of clientelism surrounding Ortega's social policies, these have had some positive impact in reducing poverty.[7] Nonetheless, Nicaragua continues to be one of the Latin American countries with the lowest Index of Human Development (UNDP 2016), and poverty remains high.

But the neoliberal economic model has changed very little since the Frente came to power. Despite Ortega's anticapitalist and antiimperialist rhetoric, he has managed to keep the IMF and the World Bank content "with growth levels above the average for Latin America and the Caribbean" (World Bank 2016),[8] while protecting the interests of the national economic elites. The president ratified the Central American Free Trade Agreement (CAFTA); maintained an inequitable tax system full of exemptions and exonerations that favor big businesses (Acevedo 2012); promoted a resource extraction economic model of development—in line with the kind of model pursued by other Latin American "leftist" leaders (Cannon and Hume 2012, 7; Lind and Keating 2013), such as Morales in Bolivia, Chávez and Maduro in Venezuela, and Correa in Ecuador—and openly supported the construction of an interoceanic canal to be built by a Chinese company, in spite of warnings about the damage that this infrastructure would cause in terms of indigenous and environmental rights.

As for the political model, Nicaragua's concentration of power in the executive defines the extreme end of the spectrum of hyperpresidentialist cases within the Pink Tide, alongside Venezuela and Ecuador. Ortega and Murillo reflect a political culture based on top-down leadership and caudillismo inherited from the colonial past, strengthened by more than forty years of Somoza dictatorship, and not transformed by the revolutionary decade (Contreras 2011; Close 2016; Colburn and Cruz 2012; Martí i Puig 2016). Moreover, Ortega and Murillo have established a regime based on the coalescing of state, government, party, and their family, resulting in what Edward Banfield termed as "amoral familism" (Martí i Puig 2016, 256). In 2007, Murillo was officially appointed president of the Secretary of Communication and Citizenship Council. From this specially tailored position, Murillo became the most powerful person in the government after Ortega, often acting as his voice and public representative. Although Ortega came to power under the promise of direct democracy implicit in the *pueblo presidente* and *poder ciudadano* (people as president; citizen power) mottos, he has established an exclusionary model, led by Murillo, based on paraparty and parastate structures at all levels, from community to national, with the Citizen Power Councils (CPCs, conservatively rebranded Cabinets of the Family, Community, and Life). This "direct democracy-participatory" model contradicts the mechanisms of citizen participation already established in Nicaraguan legislation. CPCs have been critical in the implementation of Ortega's social policies and the enlargement of his electoral base (Bay 2010; Stuart 2009). To further consolidate the "family dynasty,"[9] in 2016, Daniel and Rosario registered as the FSLN's presidential and vice-presidential candidates for November's elections, an act of nepotism that came as no surprise to most Nicaraguans. Although I argue here that the overwhelming influence of the presidential couple on Nicaraguan politics has had a negative impact on gender and sexual rights, ironically, Ortega presented Murillo's candidacy as a further recognition of women's rights (Chamorro 2016). In January 2017, Ortega was invested president for a third consecutive term, while first lady Murillo was officially inaugurated as vice president of Nicaragua, institutionalizing personalism and caudillismo even further.

Finally, the FSLN has promoted a mostly heteronormative conservative social agenda, which has been severely detrimental to women's and LGBT rights. The rhetoric of the "unity of the family" has been concomitant with the omnipresence of religious discourse, illustrated by one of Ortega's mottos,

Cumplirle al pueblo es cumplirle a Dios (To deliver to the people is to deliver to God), and by the inclusion of references to God and Christianity in the reformed constitution. Religious fundamentalism impregnates the practice and discourse of Ortega and Murillo in appeals to both Catholics and Protestants. As former Sandinista guerrilla commander and former deputy Mónica Baltodano observes, "State institutions are operating as reproducers of religious beliefs to emphasize that everything that happens in the country is 'God's will,' thus establishing that Chayo [Rosario Murillo]-Orteguista's authority comes from divine will, just as in the old absolutist monarchies the power of the kings came directly from God" (2014).

Movement Dynamics

Women, Feminists, and Sexual Diversity
before Ortega's "Second Revolution"
In order to understand the relationship between Orteguismo and both the women's movement and LGBT groups[10] during the period we are examining, it is necessary to go back to the revolutionary decade. Understanding the 1980s-Frente policies toward gender and sexuality, the origins of the women's movement, and the repressed attempts of organization by lesbians and gays under Sandinismo will shed light on movement dynamics during Nicaragua's "Second Revolution."

Despite the existence of an early feminist movement (González 2001; Whisnant 1995), the rise of the Nicaraguan women's movement is usually seen as one of the unintended consequences of the revolution (Jubb 2014, 293; Kampwirth 2014, 325; Montenegro 1997, 379; Murguialday 1990). Its history is closely tied to the FSLN and its mass organizations, yet, as Jennifer Bickham Méndez (2005, 27) notes, there is a fundamental paradox in Nicaraguan oppositional politics: "For many participants in the revolution, particularly women, the FSLN was a source of self-determination and political empowerment, but ultimately also a constraining and even oppressive force in their lives as political actors."

During the 1980s, women were mobilized by the Frente according to an integrationist strategy, which Maxine Molyneux described as "Mobilization without Emancipation" (1985), following the Marxist Left logic that a revolution would automatically end gender oppression. Thus, the goal of the women's mass organization Asociación de Mujeres Nicaragüenses Luisa Amanda Espinoza (Luisa Amanda Espinoza Nicaraguan Women's Association, or AMNLAE) was to liberate women by integrating them into the overall revolutionary process

(Criquillion 1995, 212; Randall 1994, 25). However, during the second half of the 1980s, discomfort began to grow among women who resented the control of the party over AMNLAE and feminists who felt that the revolution had made insufficient advances for women. By the end of the decade, women's organizing had started to take different forms, from autonomous women's organizations to women's secretariats in unions.

The politics of this period made organizing on the basis of sexuality even more daunting, although not ultimately impossible. In the last decades of the Somoza dictatorship, Managuan gay nightlife began, and closeted lesbians and gay men were allowed into the Somozas' party ranks (Babb 2012, 313; González 2014, 78). However, when the Sandinistas came to power, they sought to "restitute morality" (González 2014, 78). Although they did not have an official policy on homosexuality, FSLN leaders associated homosexuality with the decadence of the Somoza dictatorship, and, therefore, believed that it clashed with notions of morally correct revolutionaries (Lancaster 1992). The Sandinista leadership depicted homosexuality and lesbianism as a foreign, middle-class, minority issue—the same words that it used to discredit feminists—and thus as incompatible with the revolution (Heumann 2014a, 304).

In 1985, a group of gays and lesbians active in the revolutionary process began to meet to discuss the particular forms of discrimination they faced as sexual minorities. However, the Frente persecuted the group, accusing its members of being an antirevolutionary "deviation" (Babb 2003, 308; Heumann 2014a, 298). People were detained, interrogated, and admonished by the Ministry of the Interior, and the group subsequently disbanded. Gay and lesbian activists not only ceased their activities, but "out of their sense of commitment to the revolutionary project and loyalty to the Sandinista State" decided to remain silent about this repressive experience for many years (Heumann 2014b, 299).

A few years later, however, "AIDS served as both catalyst to and cover for gay and lesbian organization" (Thayer 1997, 400) when the minister of Health officially integrated gays and lesbians into HIV prevention brigades. This opened up opportunities for organization, offered an official and legitimate arena in which to meet (Heumann 2010, 59), and some limited forms of visibility for LGBT issues. But it also tied the work of the community to HIV-AIDS prevention rather than advancing their own rights.

With the Sandinistas' electoral defeat in 1990, both the women's movement and the incipient gay and lesbian movement gained new opportunities and greater independence. Karen Kampwirth argues that for the women's movement, the FSLN's defeat was a "blessing in disguise" (2000, 7). After a decade of controlled mobilization, the women's movement—feminists in particular—began to incrementally distance themselves from the FSLN (Bickham Méndez 2005, 27; Cuadra and Jiménez 2010, 70; Montenegro 1997, 409). Autonomy, a principle that is at the core of the Nicaraguan women's and feminist movement,[11] came to be understood mostly as autonomy from the FSLN (Lacombe 2014, 284). This was concomitant with a rapid process of "NGOization," which paralleled that of most Latin American women's movements (Alvarez 1998; Ewig 1999).[12] Since 1990, the country's movement became one of the most robust and combative in the region (Kampwirth 2011, 7).

In the years that followed the Sandinista loss, the relationship between the Frente and the women's movement was characterized by, on the one hand, a growing sense of disillusionment and betrayal among many women,[13] and, on the other, the FSLN's open hostility toward feminists in particular. Besides the movement's quest for autonomy, the major issues that marked this relationship were the widely publicized sexual abuse accusations against Ortega by his stepdaughter in 1998; the Liberal-Sandinista Pacto in 2000; and the FSLN's support for the abolition of therapeutic abortion, as well as part of the movement's alliance with the left opposition, MRS, during the electoral campaign in 2006. I return to the last two issues below.

The women's movement in Nicaragua's semiautonomous Atlantic regions—a multiethnic region that represents 50 percent of the national territory, but only 9.5 percent of the population (Palenzuela 2004, 266)—has had a different history from that of the rest of the territory. During the 1980s, the Caribbean Coast was the site of widespread armed resistance against the ethnocentric modernization project of the Sandinista government, and many among the Indigenous population (mostly Miskitus) joined the Contra counterrevolutionary forces (Baracco 2011; Palenzuela 2004, 268).[14] Women were key actors in achieving peace in the region, which led to the establishment of a semiautonomous form of governance in 1987 (Dixon and Gómez 2009, 13; Herlihy 2011, 228). During the 1990s, the Caribbean Coast women's organizations predominantly focused their efforts on advancing regional autonomy and defending Afro and Indigenous rights (Blandón et al. 2011, 39), whereas the national women's movement focused on its quest for autonomy mostly from the FSLN. But in the 2000s, Caribbean Coast organizations brought women's rights into the center of their efforts, even as Indigenous (Miskitu, Mayagna, and Rama), Afro (Creole and Garifuna), and Mestiza women tended to maintain distinct organizational spaces (Blandón et al. 2011, 38).

The relationship between the Coastal women's movement and the Pacific women's movement has been characterized, to a large extent, by lack of communication and mutual unawareness (Blandón et al. 2011, 43). On the one hand, the national women's movement has been criticized for not having integrated the voices of Afro and Indigenous women into its agenda (Blandón et al. 2011, 58). On the other, the disconnection between feminists from the Coast and the Pacific since Ortega's 2006 election may be due to fears by Atlantic organizations of potential governmental repression if they were to associate with the antigovernmental Pacific feminist movement, as well as the dangers of internal division between those who oppose or sympathize with the government (Blandón et al. 2011, 46).[15] Given the dominance of the Pacific women's movement in national politics, the rest of this chapter will focus on them.

As was the case with the national women's movement, the nascent gay and lesbian movement also gained new opportunities and greater autonomy with the Frente's electoral defeat (Babb 2003, 309; Thayer 1997, 402). This was despite the fact that most sexual diversity activists "were (or had been) Sandinista supporters and continued to identify with the party's revolutionary goals" (Thayer 1997, 393). However, this development occurred in the context of neoliberal politics with a very conservative gender and sexuality agenda. In 1992, the government of Violeta Barrios de Chamorro passed an antisodomy article (Article 204) within the Penal Code that converted Nicaragua into the only country in the region that outlawed homosexuality (Heumann 2010, 115). Although this article was not widely applied, "its existence served as a threat to anyone, or any organization, that dared to 'promote' or discuss homosexuality or lesbianism. It was a tool of intimidation and surveillance that could be drawn upon by individuals or the state" (Howe 2013, 169).

At the beginning of the 1990s, a lesbian collective, a gay collective, and two LGBT NGOs—both of which worked with gays and lesbians, offering self-help groups and HIV-AIDS prevention—emerged from those previously organized around the HIV brigades. Many of the LGBT groups founded during the 1990s were in alliance with, and had the protection of, the emerging feminist movement (Babb 2003; Kampwirth 2011, 2014). Between 1992 and 2008, defying the criminalization of homosexuality, several women's organizations helped create gay rights groups, offered space for lesbian groups, ran support groups for gays and lesbians, and participated in organizing gay and lesbian pride events (Babb 2003; Welsh 2014, 43). LGBT groups and the women's movement shared a history rooted in the revolutionary past and were "natural" allies in their struggle for transforming gender and sexual politics.

Movement Dynamics with Ortega's Return to Power

Since Ortega took office in 2007, there has been an important difference between the Frente's clearly oppositional attitude toward the women's movement and its more open attitude toward LGBT groups. The women's movement is one of the most—if not the most—openly critical voices against Orteguismo and as such is seen as a major threat to the FSLN's hegemonic vision of civil society. As already mentioned, two of the main issues that have had a major impact in the mutual hostility between Orteguismo and feminists occurred during the 2006 national electoral campaign. First, the Movimiento Autónomo de Mujeres (Autonomous Women's Movement, or MAM), an "umbrella" space established in late 2004 that brought together feminists from across the country, signed an alliance with the MRS left opposition party. The decision to sign an alliance with a political party came after an analysis in which the potential victory of the Frente with Ortega as its undisputed leader was identified as the "worst-case scenario" (Lacombe 2014, 280). Not everyone at MAM agreed on this analysis and the electoral alliance. This disagreement finally led to the expulsion of some members from MAM and a split within the women's movement that still has tangible consequences. The FSLN did not appreciate the open support for MRS by some of the most visible faces of feminism in Nicaragua and by former Frente supporters.

Second, the other major issue that led to the final breakup of the movement and the FSLN was the party's support for the ban of therapeutic abortion in the midst of the 2006 campaign. After a few weeks of debate in the National Assembly and a massive march organized by the Catholic Church, therapeutic abortion was abolished from the Penal Code with the support of the FSLN. Initially, many observers interpreted the Frente's support as a political strategy to win the votes of the hardcore Catholic electorate and reaffirm its new friendship with the Catholic Church (Kampwirth 2011, 15). Nonetheless, when just a few months after taking office Ortega's FSLN backed a new Penal Code ratifying the previous abolition of therapeutic abortion, it became evident that the Sandinista support for its ban had not simply been a "pragmatic and spontaneous response to the 'pro-life' campaign" (Heumann 2014a, 305). Whereas AMNLAE had remained loyal to the party in spite of

Ortega's stepdaughter's accusations of sexual abuse and the Frente's growing antidemocratic and caudillistic tendencies, the ban of therapeutic abortion finally led the Sandinista women's organization to break with the party line. AMNLAE joined the rest of the movement in criticizing the complete ban of abortion. As a result, first lady Murillo impugned the leadership, which was forced to resign in 2008.

Despite conflicts over the agenda, strategy, and leadership that led to divisions and even expulsions within the movement, as a well-known Managua-based feminist puts it, under Ortega's administration "the women's movement has been forced to articulate around a common problem: the Ortega-Murillo government."[16] As the foregoing illustrates, Ortega and Murillo have tried to both intimidate and discredit the women's movement and feminists in particular. Moreover, in 2008–9, the Sandinista-controlled judiciary system launched a persecution of nine feminist leaders—most of them former FSLN members—and two feminist organizations (as well as other national and international NGOs).[17] Besides legal persecution, the Ortegas also tried to undermine the women's movement with the creation, in 2008, of a parallel officially sanctioned movement, following the "defection" of AMNLAE over the issue of therapeutic abortion: the Blanca Aráuz Women's Movement.[18] Despite the publicity the new "movement" received, it failed to gain momentum and soon disappeared.

Whereas the women's movement was dismayed at Ortega's return to power, the sexual diversity community viewed some of his initial political moves—mostly the decriminalization of homosexuality—with enthusiasm. Once the new Penal Code came into effect in 2008, groups and organizations[19] that worked from a human rights perspective and self-identified as LGBT proliferated (Welsh 2014, 42). This was partly as a result of new international funding. The new groups openly worked on LGBT issues and essentially responded to three identities: gay, lesbian, and female transgender. While the 1990s generation of LGBT activists and feminists had a strong bond, some of the new groups founded after 2008 did not know or acknowledge the central role that feminists played in supporting the organization of the LGBT community and placing the issue of sexual diversity rights on the national agenda (GEDDS 2010, 4).

In this context, soon it became clear that the Frente's "gay friendliness" was a simultaneous effort to burnish the government's international credentials through pinkwashing, that is, showing a gay-friendly face to mask antifeminist actions, while controlling movement organizing. Paradoxically, the same

Penal Code that outlawed therapeutic abortion also abolished the antisodomy article in place since 1992. This was the first sign of Ortega and Murillo's pink-washing. Another effort staged for international community observers was the creation of a sexual diversity movement within the Sandinista Youth in 2010 (Kampwirth 2014, 325), which, apart from a few appearances in progovernment media, has had a low profile. Its leaders had no history of LGBT activism, and a veteran gay activist referred to it as "the red and black puppet of sexual diversity" in allusion to the FSLN's traditional colors. Many believed that behind this "smokescreen"—as a feminist activist and researcher put it[20]—was the presidential couple's efforts to weaken the traditional alliance between the women's movement and historic LGBT groups while co-opting a younger generation of sexual diversity activists (also see González 2014; Heumann et al. 2017; Kampwirth 2014). In doing so, "the FSLN is fostering new memories and new identities for a generation that has no personal recollections of the sexual persecution some lesbian, bisexual, and gay Sandinista militants experienced during the revolution" (González 2014, 84).

Also during the first years of Ortega's return, an NGO directed by Zoila-mérica Narváez, Murillo's daughter (who by then had reconciled with her family), was in charge of administering the largest project on LGBT rights in the country, funded by the Norwegian Embassy. Thus, during Ortega's first term, the organizations that worked with Zoilamérica's internationally connected NGO benefited from a close relationship with a person well connected to the ruling party (Kampwirth 2014).[21]

Feminists were initially surprised to see some of their old allies "flirting" with the government. Nonetheless, during Ortega's second term, initial optimism among many LGBT activists faded. While some activists and organizations remained close to the FSLN, by 2014 some of the activists that I interviewed believed that the government was just offering *caramelitos* (candies) but not rights.[22] In fact, since 2012, the FSLN's heterocentric exclusion of nonheterosexual families from the new Family Code, which I will discuss below, led some LGBT organizations to mobilize publicly against the Frente's stance. This brought some sexual diversity organizations and women's groups closer (Kampwirth 2014, 320). Nonetheless, while the women's movement, and feminists in particular, continued to actively denounce the Ortega-Murillo regime's abuses, most LGBT groups focused on their sexual diversity agenda.

State-Society Relations

Women's and LGBT's Descriptive Representation:
Do Numbers Matter?

In a striking contrast to Ortega and Murillo's antifeminism, Nicaragua leads international rankings on women's political participation. In March 2017, women headed nine out of the sixteen executive ministries; held nearly half of seats in the National Assembly; led institutions such as the National Police and the Supreme Court of Justice; and the government claimed that 50 percent of mayors and vice-mayors were female. Surprisingly, the government's "gay friendliness" did not translate into the participation of LGBT in formal spaces of governance. There was only one exception to that: the sexual diversity ombudsman, the only public servant representing the LGBT community. In the introduction to this volume, Elisabeth Jay Friedman and Constanza Tabbush argue that the term "pinkwashing" "can also be used to consider how states trade off different gender-based rights, such as offering evidence of women's political leadership to distract from the rejection of women's right to control their own bodies." The Nicaraguan case is a clear example of this form of pinkwashing as well, in which the high numbers of women in formal politics has been used to mask the government's antifeminist agenda to the international community.

Since the FSLN came to power, the legal framework for women's formal political participation dramatically improved. The Ley de Igualdad de Derechos y Oportunidades (Law of Equal Rights and Opportunities, or LIDO), which mandates parties to introduce a gender quota, was approved in February 2008, just a few months after the abortion ban. Four years later, symbolically on International Women's Day, the president introduced an urgent reform to the Law of Municipalities, which, among other things, included the requisite to incorporate 50 percent women on all electoral lists. This came to be known as the "50–50 Law." Two months later, this was reinforced with the reform of the Electoral Law, including parity not only for municipal elections' lists but also for those of the national and Central American parliaments.

The improvement of the legal framework for women's political participation was accompanied by a significant increase in the numbers of women in both elected and appointed positions. When Ortega became president in January 2007, 46 percent of the ministers appointed were women (Larracoechea 2008, 44). Ten years later, women headed over 56 percent of ministries, including the Ministries of Defense, Labor, and Natural Resources. Parity in the number of cabinet positions has been a constant under Ortega.

As for the legislative branch, as a result of the FLSN's adoption of a gender quota and the passing of the 50–50 Law and electoral law reforms, the Nicaraguan Parliament has one of the highest proportions of women in the world: 42.39 percent during the 2012–16 term, and 45.7 percent in the assembly inaugurated in 2017.[23] In addition, in 2013, the assembly approved its own gender equity policy, and an Institutional Group of Deputies for the Promotion of Gender Equity was created (Asamblea Nacional 2014). Women's participation in other areas of governance was also significant. For instance, at the local level, the FSLN claimed that 50 percent of mayors and vice-mayors were female (*La Voz del Sandinismo* 2012), although the Supreme Electoral Council never published official results for the 2012 elections.[24]

In contrast with the impressive figures for women's formal representation, the LGBT community was absent from the formal political arena. Despite having a sexual diversity group within its youth structure, the FSLN has never included an openly LGBT candidate in its lists.[25] Descriptive representation of the LGBT constituency is not yet an issue on the national political agenda, as it would entail confronting religious hierarchies and conservative Nicaraguan society.

Parity has been a historic demand of feminists, in Nicaragua and elsewhere, and some regard the remarkable percentages of women's formal political participation as an advance in women's rights. In particular, the high number of women in formal politics has helped Nicaragua climb in international gender-equity rankings and, like some of Ortega's actions on LGBT rights, has contributed toward consolidating Ortega's international image as a "progressive" leader. However, as a feminist from the northern city of Matagalpa asked, "What's the point in having this bunch of deputies if they cannot have their own voice in Parliament? It is purely symbolic," she replied, "it is showpiece representation."[26] Moreover, the rapid rotation and instability in appointments held by women (Kampwirth 2011, 13) has led feminist activist Violeta Delgado to label them "recyclable women" (Miranda Aburto 2012). As this chapter argues, the high proportion of women in elected positions and the institutionalization of "gender equity" within the Sandinista state have not resulted in an improvement in women's rights. To the contrary, there has been a rollback in women's substantive rights.

Institutionalization of Gender and Sexual Diversity: An "Empty Shell"

Like its promotion of parity, the Sandinista government's institutionalization of gender equity from the local to national level has been heralded by an international audience. But here again, critics argue that this is purely ornamental, an "empty shell"—in the words of a feminist from Matagalpa.[27] The government has also created the Sexual Diversity Ombudsperson, the first of this kind in the region. However, feminist activists and some LGBT leaders complain that both the national women's agency and the sexual diversity institution do not have strong mandates, work with very little budget, and divide rather than unite movements. On the whole they have not been the staunch allies for feminist and LGBT movements that similar ministries (or ministers) have been in countries such as Brazil, Chile, Argentina, and Ecuador.

Although the Ministry of Women, formerly known as Institute of Nicaraguan Women (INIM), has always had a low profile, once the Frente took office, it went completely quiet. For a while, the only news from INIM was the frequent rotation of its directors: between 2007 and 2012, seven women were appointed. At the beginning of 2013, it was announced that the institute would become a ministry by presidential decree. However, its absence from the political arena continued to be noticeable, and feminists complain that its work is "nearly clandestine" and "invisible" (Miranda Aburto 2013).

Besides the ministry and the existence of a special ombudswoman of women since 2000, Ortega's executive has promoted the creation of women's units, offices and secretariats at all levels, from ministries to local governments, but with very few resources and nearly divorced from civil society activism. Their ill-defined functions mean that, as in Venezuela, they frequently end up working on issues unrelated to gender equity, such as implementing the government's social programs or campaigning for the FSLN during elections. Local institutions have been instructed by the executive not to coordinate with women's organizations, and interaction between the national women's agency and the women's movement has virtually disappeared. Only in some municipalities do local women's groups still enjoy a good relationship with institutions such as the public prosecutor or the Forensic Institute around the struggle against gender violence, but these are exceptions to the rule.

As for the institutionalization of LGBT rights promotion, one of the most publicized prosexual diversity moves of the government was the appointment of lesbian activist Samira Montiel as Special Ombudswoman for Sexual Diversity in 2009. The creation of this position was announced in 2008 by the human rights ombudsman at a Central American Forum for Sexual Diversity held in Managua, and its nomination involved the participation of the most active LGBT organizations at the time. As Kampwirth notes, this was an impressive turnaround. Just two years earlier, even advocating for LGBT rights was punishable with prison time (2011, 20). However, critics (including feminists) saw the creation of the special ombudsman as part of the Frente's triple strategy aimed at international pinkwashing, monitoring and controlling emerging LGBT groups, and dividing sexual diversity organizations from feminists.

Five years later, the initial widespread optimism within the sexual diversity community about the significance of the new institution has largely dissipated. Several LGBT activists I interviewed believed that it had not served the interests of the community. In fact, a gay activist claimed that Montiel had been co-opted and only served the interests of the ruling party.[28] Moreover, others criticized that she was working mainly from the older health perspective on HIV-AIDS issues, rather than from a human rights-based approach to LGBT rights.[29] Besides, little state funding was made available for her work. By 2014, the Norwegian Embassy was the main sponsor of this institution. Nonetheless, despite criticisms, and unlike the Women's Ministry distance from the women's movement, Montiel maintained an open relationship with LGBT groups and organizations.

While the women's movement has found nearly all governmental institutions, both local and national, to be closed, some LGBT organizations have managed to secure spaces for dialogue with local institutions, the legal system, the Ministry of Health and the national police. For instance, as a result of a transgender organization's advocacy work, by 2014 four municipal governments had approved a declaration condemning discrimination based on sexual orientation. However, as a member of this organization noted, the declarations had no legal application and merely depend on the will of the incumbent mayor.[30]

Policy Issues

Bodily Autonomy Policies: Pinkwashing in Action and Legislating the Social Order

As already discussed, the first sign of Ortega and Murillo's pinkwashing efforts came during Ortega's first year in office, with the approval of the new Penal Code. This simultaneously represented an enormous step back for women's rights and some advancement in LGBT rights. The approval of the new Penal Code established severe punishments for those having an abortion and for those performing or aiding in abortions, especially medical professionals.[31] In this way, Nicaragua became the sixth country in Latin America and the Caribbean to completely ban abortions,[32] despite having the highest adolescent pregnancy rate in the region (UNFPA 2013). Whereas therapeutic abortion was criminalized, the new code abolished the antisodomy Article 204, thus decriminalizing homosexuality in the country. In addition, it introduced a series of articles that addressed discrimination based on sexual orientation. Women's rights worsened under Ortega's second term in office, when the administration sought to promote the Catholic Church's vision of family unity as a response to gender-based violence despite vociferous protest by the women's movement.

Penal Code politics demonstrated how far state-society relations had deteriorated. The only political party to oppose the abolition of therapeutic abortion was the MRS. Former guerrilla leader-turned-Sandinista dissident Mónica Baltodano became the most critical voice against its complete ban. Besides the MRS Alliance, two deputies from the conservative Right also opposed its derogation on medical grounds. On the day that the ban was voted on in the assembly, the numerous female FSLN representatives were absent. Whereas the abortion ban was approved despite the mobilization of the women's movement—which for months held weekly demonstrations in front of the Court of Justice as well as introduced several constitutional challenges—and part of the international community, the decriminalization of homosexuality was not the result of LGBT activism. As gay activist and poet Héctor Avellán argued at the time, the removal of Article 204 had been the result of "hidden and obscure negotiations under the table in the National Assembly," rather than a victory of LGBT activism. Many feminists and human rights activists, like Avellán himself, believed this was a political decision to sow divisions between the women's movement and sexual diversity organizations (Avellán 2007; Kampwirth 2014, 325; Welsh 2014, 44).

The second legislative setback for the women's movement took place during Ortega's second administration. An advanced law on violence against women, the Integral Law on Violence Against Women (Law 779),[33] approved in 2012 with a unanimous majority vote from FSLN deputies and seen as a victory by the movement, received a major blow. As feminist Ruth Marina Matamoros puts it, "The assault [on the law] occurred with a three-punch combination: a reform, a regulation, and a set of instructions" (2016). Once more, the president evidenced his absolute control of the FSLN bench in the National Assembly, his disrespect for the rule of law, his alliance with religious hierarchies, and his open hostility toward the women's movement.

Almost immediately after its approval, the Catholic Church launched an advocacy campaign against Law 779, arguing that it contravened the unity of the family and attacked men. Within the Supreme Court of Justice, Sandinista Rafael Solís led those who were against the law and promoted a reform to introduce family mediation as a primary response to cases of gender violence. The women's movement mobilized against this reform, arguing that the introduction of mediation promoted male perpetrators' impunity and the reprivatization of violence against women (Jubb 2014, 289), and thus would lead to an increase in the number of femicides (Matamoros 2016). Despite several prominent FSLN figures[34] also publicly speaking out against the "family values" reform, in September 2013 the parliament approved it with only four members against and the FSLN's bench unanimously in support (Jubb 2014, 289).

Then, in July 2014, in the midst of widespread mobilization of the women's movement condemning the increase in the number of femicides, President Ortega issued an illegal regulation of Law 779 by presidential decree.[35] The objective of the law was changed from combating violence against women to "strengthening" the Nicaraguan family. In addition, the decree also changed the categorization of femicide to include only murder in the private sphere, namely, committed by a man who was or had been the partner of the victim, thus contravening the regional Belém do Pará convention.[36] Finally, it introduced new steps in women's path to justice, as women must now attend community-level family counseling—made up of religious and community leaders—for mediation, instead of reporting to women's police offices. In the following months, the women's movement, together with human rights organizations, filed more than a hundred constitutional challenges.

Feminists interpreted this final blow to Law 779 as a result of religious sectors' pressure, but also part of Ortega-Murillo's attempt to legislate a social order based on the centrality of the family. As Nadine Jubb noted after the 2013 reform, Ortega and Murillo "managed to impose their moral order and construct consent for it" (2014, 299). In addition, the change in the categorization of femicide allowed the government to reduce femicide incidence statistics (Matamoros 2016), supporting its claim that Nicaragua is the safest country in Central America.[37] Despite the extreme distortion of Law 779, Ortega and Murillo would still be able to parade the existence of a law against gender violence in front of their international audience.

Identity Recognition Policies: Heteronormativity, Promises, and Pageants

Regarding identity recognition policies, the government has engaged in yet another pinkwashing trade-off, here between LGBT recognition on the one hand

and the legislation of heteronormativity on the other. The government developed a much-desired Gender Identity Law and sponsored the celebration of beauty pageants and sexual diversity carnivals. At the same time, it imposed its heterocentric vision of the Nicaraguan family through a Family Code that further legislated the social order established by the decree of Law 779.

The assembly had begun to discuss a new Family Code (Law 879) in 2012. The women's movement and LGBT organizations maintained that the proposal emphasized the conservative and interventionist orientation of the Nicaraguan state, signaling that it severely conflicted with the constitution, the Children and Youth Code, Law 779, and even the Law of People with Disabilities (Blandón 2012). Some of the stronger criticisms launched against the code were the fact that it did not recognize nonheterosexual unions or families (the code clearly states that unions or marriages between "men and women") and used the term "domestic violence" instead of "violence against women." Thus, several LGBT and feminist organizations mobilized against the code, organizing weekly demonstrations in front of the assembly and several fora to discuss its content. A committee of LGBT activists even managed to meet with representatives from the National Assembly to present their position. As a lesbian activist who was at the meeting explained, they were told that "if we wanted to introduce a change to the code we would need to wait at least for another thirty years, because Nicaraguan society was not ready to talk about other types of family yet."[38] This is a similar argument to the one that has been repeatedly used to postpone discussions on abortion.

The Family Code as approved reinforced that view of Nicaraguan society, advancing a model of a heterosexual nuclear family with reproductive ends and without acknowledging the diversity of Nicaraguan family forms. But as scholar Kampwirth notes, not only was "this version of the Family Code . . . considerably more conservative than the family legislation of the 1980s," it was "so conservative that it sometimes seems it was written for another society" (2014, 330). In a similar vein, feminist lawyer and activist Juanita Jiménez maintains, "If we accept that the law must be adjusted to a society's real situation, this Code is far removed from ours" (2015). This law is an obstacle toward legalizing same-sex marriages or partnerships, as well as adoption by nonheterosexual couples and individuals. In addition, Jiménez (2015) claims that the code "has a profound skew imposed by the current regime, which combined authoritarian political elements with conservative religious ones, intensifying discrimination and restricting rights in its desire to promote a Christian, socialist, and solidary family model." She adds, "The discourse and propaganda around the Family Code, presenting it as progressive legislation that guarantees rights, is yet another of the current government's efforts to falsify reality."

As the Family Code was being discussed in the National Assembly in 2012, LGBT Ombudswoman Montiel announced that a bill for a Gender Identity Law was being developed with the assistance of three female transgender organizations. This law aimed at allowing transgender people to officially register as the gender of their choice. Transgender associations also hoped that it would include the right to free sex-changing hormonal treatments. However, by 2014 discussions on the proposal had been indefinitely postponed. The fact that this law has not materialized confirms the impression of feminists and some within the LGBT community that the development of this bill at exactly the same time as the National Assembly was drafting an heteronormative and discriminatory Family Code was just a way to distract and appease the sexual diversity community, especially transwomen groups, by promising a sought-after law.

Instead of legal recognition and appropriate health care, one of the most visible and publicized moves of the government to support sexual diversity and recognize transgender women was the sponsorship of Miss Gay Nicaragua; its name notwithstanding, this is a beauty pageant for transgender women. In 2012, first lady Murillo, together with the National Institute of Culture, sponsored the event and opened the doors of the traditional national theatre, Rubén Darío, to stage the pageant. In a similar manner, through the National Institute of Culture the Frente has sponsored sexual diversity carnivals and local fairs. For many transwomen, this is proof of Ortega's support: these events promote recognition and visibility, two basic demands of the LGBT community, and of transgender people in particular. However, for other sexual diversity activists, this showed the government's support for LGBT entertainment but did not entail an extension of their rights (Kampwirth 2014, 321). As a Managua-based feminist activist and journalist told me in an August 2014 interview, this kind of cultural event recognizes the right to publicly demonstrate one's identity, but "it has not solved basic problems such as the identity issue or the quality of healthcare they receive in public health centers."

Social Redistribution Policies: Maternalism and Clientelism

Ortega has made the Frente's social redistribution policies central to his socioeconomic model, in keeping with the quintessential goal of the Latin American Left of eliminating class inequality. To both internal and international audiences, President Ortega and first lady Murillo publicized programs such as

Zero Hunger or Zero Usury as key successes of their government and pivotal in reducing poverty rates. Since women were the direct beneficiaries of such policies, they claimed that these were yet another way in which they contributed toward women's empowerment and to "restituting their rights." However, these programs offer yet more evidence of the Ortega-Murillo merging of caudillismo and conservative values, relying on women's traditional roles in supporting their families and the state. As Silke Heumann maintains, "The discourse of the revolution has been used to render the exclusion of gender and sexuality issues as an acceptable (if not correct) prioritization of social justice issues" (2014a, 307). Thus, the emphasis on social justice and the limited success of these pro-women social policies have been used to justify abuses in women's rights (or at least downplay them). However, this discourse seems to ignore that the beneficiaries of Nicaraguan social policies are exactly the same women who suffer the consequences of the complete ban of abortion or of a law against violence that protects the interests of the "family" at women's expense.

One of the best publicized of such social policies is Zero Hunger, launched in 2007. By 2013, this program had reached more than 100,000 families. The direct beneficiaries are women who receive a set of assets—a "bonus"—that typically includes a pregnant cow, a pig, a hen, and five chickens; some construction materials to build corrals; some seeds; and technical assistance and training. Besides the assets and the training that women receive, women are supposed to save 20 percent of the total value of the "bonus." For this, beneficiaries are organized in groups of twenty-five to thirty women (Larracoechea 2011, 2014). Zero Usury and Roof Plan are also well-known policies of Ortega's administration. The former is a microloan program aimed to enable women to become small entrepreneurs and organize in small self-help groups. The latter consists of the distribution of zinc sheets among poor families to replace old roofs. As with Zero Hunger, these two policies have women as their direct beneficiaries.

Without a doubt, these policies have had some positive impacts on the lives of poor families, in terms of improved diet or housing, and poor women, in terms of an increased self-esteem and access to monetary resources that improve their negotiating capacity within the family. However, this has been at the cost of reproducing the sexual division of labor—men are, in fact, absent from the design of such policies—and of increasing the workload of female members of the household (Larracoechea 2011, 2014). Women are seen in their roles as mothers and caretakers, always in the service of others. As the literature has pointed out about similar programs and policies in Latin America—CCTs in particular—and as nearly every chapter of this volume attests, rather than including them as subjects of rights, women are seen as efficient "channels" to meet programs' targets and reach children and the family as a whole (Molyneux 2007, 37), including them in instrumental terms. As Amy Lind (2012, 452) notes, this "maternalist" discourse of economic development characterizes both neoliberal and postneoliberal agendas throughout Latin America, and we can find its origins in the early twentieth century.

Besides being criticized for their "maternalist" approach, Ortega's social policies have been plagued with accusations of clientelism (Kampwirth 2011; Larracoechea 2011, 2014; Quirós 2011), as paraparty and parastate structures have played a key role in the selection of beneficiaries and the distribution of assets. In addition, since the presidential couple failed to organize popular women through their Blanca Aráuz Women's Movement back in 2008, weak organization of poor rural and urban women through these social policies has been used to mobilize poor urban and rural women to show massive support for the government on dates such as International Women's Day, Mother's Day, or the 19th of July—the day of the victory of the revolution—alongside female civil servants. Similar mobilizational uses have been made of poor women in the Venezuelan case, but through much more robust forms of organization.

In addition to poor women, the LGBT population has also been targeted by clientelistic policies. In particular, LGBT working-class and poor youth— especially transwomen—have benefited from scholarships, housing, and meeting spaces (González 2014, 79; Kampwirth 2014). This sector has traditionally been the most discriminated against and marginalized in both the health and education public systems, as transwomen continue to face high illiteracy rates, exclusion from the education system, and abuse by public health professionals (GEDDS 2010; Pizarro 2012, 193; Welsh 2014, 5).[39] Thus, this sector of the population feels some recognition for having been included in the distribution of benefits, in much the same manner as poor rural women do (Larracoechea 2014, 36). However, being included in clientelistic networks comes at a cost for the LGBT population, "in that the FSLN has limited the sorts of demands that the movement can make" (Kampwirth 2014, 328) when faced with problems such as the unfulfilled promise of the Gender Identity Law. This is especially the case for transwomen's organizations.

Conclusions

In October 2014, just three months after President Ortega gave a mortal blow to Law 779 on violence against women, the *Global Gender Gap Report*, published by the World Economic Forum, was released; Nicaragua was ranked sixth in terms of gender equity, after countries such as Norway and Sweden, leaving first lady Murillo overjoyed and Nicaraguan feminists startled. This example underscores the success that Ortega's Frente has had in presenting itself as a modern leftist representative of the Latin American Pink Tide to an international audience, thus disguising the real face of the "second stage" of the Nicaraguan revolution.

However, the FSLN's gender and sexuality policies demonstrate that the twenty-first-century Frente has not promoted a modern leftist agenda, or at least not a progressive one. Modern-day caudillo Ortega and his wife have used their concentration of power to, among other things, follow the traditional Marxist Left in its subordination of gender and sexuality to social and political rights. Using the deceptive discourse of a "rights' restitution," the FSLN has in fact inflicted a setback in the population's rights, including women and the LGBT community.

Regarding gender justice, despite the government's promotion of parity at all levels of governance, an analysis of its relationship with the women's movement and of the policies and legislation that it has promoted—or hindered—shows that Ortega's project is not feminist but rather antifeminist. Paradoxically, the high numbers of women in office have been used to mask this outcome through one type of pinkwashing. This chapter contends that beyond the historic hostility between the feminist movement and the FSLN, the refusal of Nicaraguan feminism to be silent in the face of the presidential couple's centralization of power and conservative social policies has resulted in Nicaragua's "new Left" being more blatantly antifeminist than nearly all other Latin American Lefts, with the possible exception of Correa's Ecuador. In addition, the Nicaraguan case shows that when high levels of women's formal political participation comes through highly centralized and nondemocratic parties with an antifeminist agenda, in the context of absolute disrespect for the rule of law and democratic institutions, this can contribute to a setback in women's substantive representation.

As for LGBT rights, during the first years in government, the FSLN made a few significant gains—first and foremost the decriminalization of homosexuality. However, at this point, many consider these measures, again as in Correa's Ecuador, to be mere tokens aimed at coopting and controlling LGBT organizations and their leaders; creating divisions between the LGBT community and one of Ortega's and Murillo's public enemies, the feminist movement; and advancing another form of pinkwashing, that is, improving the party's international profile as part of the Latin American Left despite the FSLN's opposition to women's substantive rights. The sexual diversity community is more visible than it was a few years ago. But besides the appointment of the special ombudsperson, the LGBT population has not gained much space for political representation, with their legal rights stymied. Instead, the Frente passed legislation that further reinforced and institutionalized heteronormativity and Ortega-Murillo's vision of family unity.

At the beginning of this chapter, I stated that my point of departure for analyzing the Nicaraguan case would be to go beyond the divide among redistributive measures, political participation, and gender and sexual policies. I argued that sexual and gender rights are inherent to social justice. This contradicts Ortega and Murillo's claim, as leftists have traditionally held worldwide, that gender-specific demands—such as the right to abortion—are irrelevant to poor women (Kampwirth 2011, 9). However, this disarticulation of social justice issues does not work for people. As Heumann asks, do people actually "manage to separate their gendered, sexual, and reproductive bodies, and their personal and public or political lives in the ways that this discourse suggests?" (2014a, 307). In other words, are beneficiaries of Zero Hunger not the same women who die of illegal abortions due to the complete ban? Are transwomen who participate in Miss Gay Nicaragua with the sponsorship of the government not the same women who do not have their right to identity recognized by the state?

Taken as a whole, the arenas covered in this chapter reveal that Ortega and Murillo's project has been one of "rights' seizure" rather than "rights' restitution." Despite advancement in the formal representation of women, the abolition of antisodomy legislation, the institutionalization of an LGBT ombudswoman, and the reduction of poverty rates resulting from social policies focused on women, since 2007 there has been a rollback in women's and LGBT rights.

Notes

I would like to thank feminists and LGBT activists in Nicaragua who shared their ideas and time with me. Considering the current political climate in Nicaragua, I decided to maintain the anonymity of my informants, but this chapter could not have been written without their generosity.

1. This chapter uses the terms "LGBT" and "sexual diversity" as rough synonyms. The second is the term most widely used in Nicaragua. However, activists do also use "LGBT"—although they often use the more encompassing "LGBTI" (lesbian, gay, bisexual, transgender, and intersex) or even LGBTTI (lesbian, gay, bisexual, transgender, transsexual, travesti, and intersex).

2. In this chapter I use Bedford's definition of heteronormativity: "institutions, structures and practices that normalize dominant forms of heterosexuality as universal and morally righteous" (in Lind 2012, 539).

3. According to Victoria González, "pinkwashing" consists of "the promotion of LGBT rights in order to veil other non-LGBT-related human rights abuses (in this case the prohibition of abortion in all cases and Daniel Ortega's alleged rape of his stepdaughter)" (2014, 85). I will discuss this further in the next sections.

4. For instance, in 2009 a ruling of the Supreme Court that many considered a "legal obscenity" (Pérez-Baltodano 2010, 406), Ortega was allowed to seek a third term. In addition, since 2008 the Sandinista-controlled Supreme Electoral Council has repeatedly banned opposition parties and candidates from elections.

5. Note that the first administration mentioned here was actually Ortega's second term as president of Nicaragua, since he had already been president between 1984 and 1990. In November 2011, the FSLN won with 62.6 percent of votes and in 2016 with 72.5 percent. Both elections were characterized by irregularities and accusations of fraud, and in November 2016, despite claims by the Supreme Electoral Council that participation had been at 68.2 percent, data from volunteer observers indicated abstention above 70 percent (Peraza 2016).

6. Abortion has always been a crime in Nicaragua, but since 1837, abortion for medical reasons, or therapeutic abortion, had been legal.

7. According to independent institute FIDEG, between 2009 and 2015 poverty was reduced by 5.7 percent, from 44.7 percent to 39 percent (FIDEG 2016). However, government official statistics report that poverty dropped by 13 percent between 2009 and 2014, from 42.5 to 29.6 percent (INIDE 2016).

8. After record growth rates of 6.2 percent in 2011, GDP growth rates between 2012 and 2015 fluctuated between 5.6 percent and 4.5 percent (Banco Central de Nicaragua n/d).

9. The sons and daughters of Ortega and Murillo have also gained powerful positions within the state (Salinas 2016).

10. This chapter is mostly based on central and Pacific Nicaragua. The Caribbean Coast has a particular history and a regional form of political organization with a certain degree of autonomy. Both the women's movement and LGBT groups in the Atlantic Regions also have a different history from that of the Pacific, as briefly discussed below. Whereas we can easily identify the existence of a robust women's movement in Nicaragua, there is a shared understanding among the sexual diversity community that there is no "LGBT movement" as such but rather sexual diversity groups and organizations.

11. In this chapter, I take the view of a well-known feminist director of a Managua-based feminist NGO who explains that the distinction between the Nicaraguan feminist and women's movements should be seen as "a continuum, rather than as a dichotomy" (feminist activist, interview with author, September 22, 2014, Managua). The feminist movement is very strong within the broader movement.

12. As Ewing (1999) notes, while this allowed the movement to grow, the resulting imbalance of funds among women's NGOs led to power struggles and internal divisions. More than two decades later, the women's movement is mainly comprised of women's NGOs that are heavily dependent upon international funding, and the withdrawal of historic international aid from the country since 2007 has posed an enormous challenge for many of these organizations' long-term sustainability.

13. However, during this period organizations such as AMNLAE remained loyal to the FSLN.

14. In 1982, the forced evacuation of the Miskitu population from the Coco River, known as "Red Christmas," generated a vicious circle of trauma, discontent, and mistrust. According to Baracco, "The trauma involved in the removal of the Miskitu from the centre of their ancestral homeland was wholly counterproductive, significantly increasing the number of recruits to MISURASATA [a Miskitu organization that joined the Contra]" (2011, 131).

15. During the 2006 electoral campaign, YATAMA (a regional Indigenous party led mostly by Miskitus) signed an electoral alliance with the FSLN that lasted until 2014. As García Banini (2014) explains, "While the agreement never had the sympathy of the Yatama's [sic] grassroots, due to historic mistrust, the leaders on both sides viewed it from a pragmatic standpoint. . . . The FSLN attempted to improve its national image, especially in the Coast itself, by projecting an appearance of reconciliation and consensus. Meanwhile Yatama saw it as a path to access arenas of power and publicly legitimize itself as a key counterpart in the Coast."

16. Feminist activist, interview with author, September 22, 2014, Managua.

17. The nine feminists had helped nine-year-old "Rosita" get an abortion after being raped, back in 2003 when therapeutic abortion was still legal. A few months later, eight national and international organizations were accused of triangulation and money laundering. Feminist organizations were particularly targeted.

18. The "Movement" was named after Blanca Aráuz, César Sandino's wife. In its foundational declaration, the new movement stated its support for Ortega, Murillo, and their family and questioned the legitimacy of other women's groups, which, according to the declaration, "exercise a belligerent opposition from the extreme right in women's name" (Movimiento por la Dignidad y Derechos de las Mujeres, "Blanca Aráuz" 2008).

19. A report by FED-HIVOS in 2010 identified the existence of eighteen Sexual Diversity groups (CEJIL 2013, 187). According to the LGBT ombudswoman, the number rose from ten organizations or groups in 2008 to nearly sixty in 2014 (Samira Montiel, LGBT ombudswoman, interview with author, August 20, 2014, Managua), whereas two of the LGBT activists interviewed for this chapter mentioned the existence of over thirty organizations (interviews with author, August 21 and November 14, 2014, Managua).

20. Interviews with author, August 21 and September 22, 2014, Managua.

21. Later in 2013, Zoilamérica was again isolated from the Ortega-Murillo clan, when the government launched corruption and embezzlement charges against her

NGO (Miranda Aburto and Enríquez 2013). Among those LGBT activists interviewed, many believed this to be an indirect threat to the nascent LGBT movement, which was becoming too strong.

22. Interviews with author, August 20, 22, and October 19, 2014, Managua.

23. Data from the Inter-Parliamentary Union website shows that Nicaragua ranks fifth in the world classification (IPU 2017).

24. CEPAL reports 40.1 percent of female mayors after 2012 municipal elections (CEPAL 2016).

25. Nor has the MRS, the only party that defended LGBT rights during the discussion of the 2014 Family Code. However since 2014, this party has a Sexual Diversity Network to formally integrate the LGBT rights agenda within the party's (MRS 2017).

26. Feminist activist, interview with author, August 18, 2014, Matagalpa.

27. Feminist activist, interview with author, August 18, 2014, Matagalpa.

28. Interview with author, August 21, 2014, Managua.

29. Interviews with author, August 20 and 21, 2014 Managua.

30. Transgender activist, interview with author, August 20, 2014, Managua.

31. Between 2008 (when the new Penal Code came into effect) and 2011, the National Police and Women's Police offices registered that 132 people were denounced and/or detained for abortion-related crimes (Pizarro 2012, 150). Fortunately, unlike in El Salvador, there is no evidence of anyone having been jailed for them.

32. The other countries are Chile, Dominican Republic, Haiti, Honduras, and El Salvador.

33. For the first time, femicide was recognized as a crime; moreover, the law established the creation of specialized courts and prohibited the use of mediation for all cases of violence against women.

34. Among them were Alba Luz Ramos, president of the Supreme Court of Justice; Deborah Grandinson, the Women's Special Ombudswoman; and the secretary of the National Assembly.

35. Besides not following established legal procedures, the regulation was illegal because it changed the law's original intention, spirit, and objective (Matamoros 2016; MRS n.d.).

36. The 1994 Belém do Pará Inter American Convention to Prevent, Punish, and Eradicate Violence against Women was claimed as a major advance by the region's women's movements and is one of the key legal referents in the struggle against violence in Latin America. Nicaragua ratified the convention in 1995.

37. For instance, from January to November 2014, the women's movement reported sixty-five cases of femicide, whereas official statistics recognized only thirty-one (Observatorio Nacional de las Mujeres, email, December 9, 2014).

38. Interview with author, Managua, August 22, 2014.

39. This is despite the fact that in 2009 the Ministry of Health issued Charter Number 249, subsequently updated in 2014, aimed at promoting the end of discrimination for sexual orientation reasons in public and private health services. However, the charter was not disseminated, and most health staff are unaware of its existence.

References

Acevedo, Alfredo. 2012. "Reforma tributaria: ¿Tanto secreto para tan pocas nueces?" *Correo para Ciegos*, November 29. Accessed October 18, 2014. http://www.correoparaciegos.com/reforma-tributaria%25BFtanto-secreto-para-tan-pocas-nueces-n292.html.

Álvarez, Sonia. 1998. "Latin American Feminisms 'Go Global': Trends of the 1990s and Challenges for the New Millennium." In *Cultures of Politics / Politics of Cultures*, edited by Sonia Álvarez, Evelina Dagnino, and Arturo Escobar, 293–324. Boulder, CO: Westview Press.

Asamblea Nacional. 2014. "Primera evaluación 'Grupo institucional de diputadas y diputados para la promoción de la equidad de género.'" January.

Avellán, Héctor. 2007. "Un triunfo de nadie, el principio de la lucha." *Situación de los homosexuales en Nicaragua*. Accessed April 13, 2015. http://extranomd.blogspot.com.ar/2007/11/ante-la-noticia-de-la-despenalizacin.html.

Avendaño, Néstor. 2010. *Montos y destinos de la cooperación internacional en Nicaragua, 1990–2009*. Managua: Estado de la Región.

Babb, Florence E. 2003. "Out in Nicaragua: Local and Transnational Desires after the Revolution." *Cultural Anthropology* 18 (3): 304–28.

Babb, Florence E. 2012. *Después de la revolución*. Managua: IHNCA-UCA.

Baltodano, Mónica. 2014. "¿Qué régimen es éste? ¿Qué mutaciones ha experimentado el FSLN hasta llegar a lo que es hoy?" *Envío*, 382. Accessed October 26, 2014. http://www.envio.org.ni/articulo/4792.

Banco Central de Nicaragua. n/d. "Anuario de cifras macroeconómicas 2015." Accessed March 27, 2016. http://www.bcn.gob.ni/publicaciones/periodicidad/anual/anuario_estadistico/anuario_estadistico_2015.pdf.

Banco Central de Nicaragua. 2016. "Informe de Cooperación Oficial Externa 2015." April. Accessed March 27, 2016. http://www.bcn.gob.ni/publicaciones/periodicidad/semestral/cooperacion/2015/ICOE_2.pdf

Baracco, Luciano. 2011. "From Developmentalism to Autonomy: The Sandinista Revolution and the Atlantic Coast of Nicaragua." In *National Integration and Contested Autonomy: The Caribbean Coast of Nicaragua*, edited by Luciano Baracco, 117–46. New York: Algora Publishing.

Bay, Kelly. 2010. "The Return of the Left in Nicaragua: Citizen Power Councils, Pro Poor Social Services and Regime Consolidation." Paper presented at the annual meeting of the Political Sciences Association, Washington, DC on September 5, 2010.

Bickham Méndez, Jennifer. 2005. *From the Revolution to the Maquiladoras*. Durham, NC: Duke University Press.

Blandón, María Teresa. 2012. "El código de la familia tal como está es interventor, conservador y neoliberal." *Envío*, 363. Accessed October 26, 2014. www.envio.org.ni/articulo/4533.

Blandón, María Teresa, Clara Murguialday, and Norma Vázquez. 2011. *Los cuerpos del feminismo nicaragüense*. Managua: Programa Feminista La Corriente.

Cameron, Maxwell. 2009. "Latin America's Left Turns: Beyond Good and Bad."
    Third World Quarterly 30 (2): 331–48.

Cannon, Barry, and Mo Hume. 2012. "Central America, Civil Society and the 'Pink
    Tide': Democratization or De-democratization?" In *Democratization, iFirst*: 1–26.

Centro por la Justicia y el Derecho Internacional (CEJIL). 2013. "Diagnóstico sobre
    los crímenes de odio motivados por la orientación sexual e identidad de género:
    Costa Rica, Honduras y Nicaragua." San José: CEJIL. Accessed July 24, 2016.
    https://www.cejil.org/sites/default/files/legacy_files/El%20Caso%20de%20Nica-
    ragua.pdf.

Comisión Económica para América Latina y el Caribe (CEPAL). 2016. "Poder local:
    porcentaje de mujeres alcaldesas electas." Accessed July 29, 2016. http://oig.cepal
    .org/es/indicadores/poder-local-porcentaje-mujeres-alcaldesas-electas.

Chamorro, Carlos F. 2016. "La memoria histórica de la dictadura." *El Confidencial*,
    August 3. http://confidencial.com.ni/la-memoria-historica-la-dictadura/.

Close, David. 2004. "Undoing Democracy in Nicaragua." In *Undoing Democracy:
    The Politics of Electoral Caudillismo*, edited by David Close and Kalowatie De-
    onandan, 1–16. Oxford: Lexington Books.

Close, David. 2016. *Nicaragua: Navigating the Politics of Democracy*. New York:
    Lynne Rienner.

Colburn, Forrest D., and Arturo Cruz S. 2012. "Personalism and Populism in Nica-
    ragua." *Journal of Democracy* 23 (2): 104–18.

Contreras, Félix. 2011. *Déficits de institucionalidad democrática en Nicaragua y su
    impacto en el desarrollo económico, político y social*. Managua: Fundación Fried-
    rich Ebert.

Criquillion, Ana. 1995. "The Nicaraguan Women's Movement: Feminist Reflections
    from Within." In *The Politics of Survival: Grassroots Movements in Central America*,
    edited by Minor Sinclair, 209–37. New York: Monthly Review.

Cuadra, Elvira, and Juana Jiménez. 2010. *El movimiento de mujeres y la lucha por
    sus derechos en Nicaragua*. Managua: CINCO.

Dixon, Bernardine, and Núria Gómez. 2009. *Participación política y liderazgo de las
    mujeres indígenas en América Latina: Estudio de caso Nicaragua*. Mexico City:
    PNUD.

Ewig, Christina. 1999. "The Strengths and Limits of the NGO Women's Movement
    Model: Shaping Nicaragua's Democratic Institutions." *Latin American Research
    Review* 34 (3): 75–102.

Fundación Internacional para el Desafío Económico Global (FIDEG). 2016. *Informe
    de resultados de la encuesta de hogares para medir la pobreza en Nicaragua:
    Informe de resultados 2015*. Managua: FIDEG.

García Babini, Salvador. 2014. "Caribbean Coast Elections: Between Conspiracy
    and Responsibility." *Envío*, 394. Accessed April 17, 2017. http://www.envio.org.ni
    /articulo/485.

González Rivera, Victoria. 2001. "Somocista Women, Right-Wing Politics, and
    Feminism in Nicaragua, 1936–1979." In *Radical Women in Latin America: Right*

and Left, edited by Karen Kampwirth and Victoria Rivera González, 41–78. University Park: Pennsylvania State University Press.

González Rivera, Victoria. 2014. "The Alligator Woman's Tale: Remembering Nicaragua's 'First Self-Declared Lesbian.'" *Journal of Lesbian Studies* 18:75–87.

Grupo Estratégico por los Derechos Humanos de la Diversidad Sexual (GEDDS). 2010. *Una mirada a la diversidad sexual en Nicaragua.* Managua: GEDDS.

Herlihy, Laura Hobson. 2011. "Rising up? Indigenous and Afro-Descendant Women's Political Leadership in the RAAN." In *National Integration and Contested Autonomy: The Caribbean Coast of Nicaragua,* edited by Luciano Baracco, 221–42. New York: Algora Publishing.

Heumann, Silke. 2010. "Sexual Politics and Regime Transition: Understanding the Struggle around Gender and Sexuality in Post-Revolutionary Nicaragua." PhD diss., University of Amsterdam.

Heumann, Silke. 2014a. "Gender, Sexuality and Politics: Rethinking the Relationship between Feminism and Sandinismo in Nicaragua." *Social Politics* 21 (2): 290–314.

Heumann, Silke. 2014b. "The Challenge of Inclusive Identities and Solidarities: Discourses on Gender and Sexuality in the Nicaraguan Women's Movement and the Legacy of Sandinismo." *Bulletin of Latin American Research* 33 (3): 334–49.

Heumann, Silke, Ana V. Portocarrero, and Camilo Antillón Najlis. 2017. "Dialogue: Transgendered Bodies as Subjects of Feminism: A Conversation and Analysis on the Inclusion of Transpersons and Politics in the Nicaraguan Feminist Movement." In *Bodies in Resistance: Gender and Sexual Politics in the Age of Neoliberalism,* edited by Wendy Harcourt, 163–87. Netherlands: Palgrave.

Howe, Cymene. 2013. "Epistemic Engineering and the Lucha for Sexual Rights in Postrevolutionary Nicaragua." *Journal of Latin American and Caribbean Anthropology* 18 (2): 165–86.

Instituto Nacional de Información de Desarrollo (INIDE). 2016. *Encuesta de medición de nivel de vida: EMNV 2014.* Managua: INIDE.

Inter-parliamentary Union (IPU). 2017. "Women in National Parliaments." Accessed March 26, 2017. http://www.ipu.org/wmn-e/classif.htm.

Jiménez, Juanita. 2015. "The Family Code Is the Final Link in a Project of Social Control." *Envío,* 406. Accessed July 31, 2016. http://www.envio.org.ni/articulo/5024.

Jubb, Nadine. 2014. "Love, Family Values and Reconciliation for All, but What about Rights, Justice and Citizenship for Women? The FSLN, the Women's Movement, and Violence against Women in Nicaragua." *Bulletin of Latin American Research* 33 (3): 289–304.

Kampwirth, Karen. 2000. "Incest Strikes the Revolutionary Family." Paper presented at the International Congress of the Latin American Studies Assoc., March 16–18.

Kampwirth, Karen. 2008. "Abortion, Antifeminism, and the Return of Daniel Ortega: In Nicaragua, Leftist Politics?" *Latin American Perspectives* 35:122–36.

Kampwirth, Karen. 2011. *Latin America's New Left and the Politics of Gender: Lessons from Nicaragua.* New York: Springer.

Kampwirth, Karen. 2014. "Organising the Hombre Nuevo Gay: LGBT Politics and the Second Sandinista Revolution." *Bulletin of Latin American Research* 33 (3): 319–33.

Lacombe, Delphine. 2014. "Struggling against the 'Worst-Case Scenario'? Strategic Conflicts and Realignments of the Feminist Movement in the Context of the 2006 Nicaraguan Elections." *Bulletin of Latin American Research* 33 (3): 274–88.

Lancaster, Roger. 1992. *Life Is Hard: Machismo, Danger, and the Intimacy of Power in Nicaragua.* Oxford: University of California Press.

Larracoechea, Edurne. 2008. "Informe Nicaragua." In *Democracia en Centroamérica: Más mujeres en el poder, más hombres asumiendo las tareas domésticas,* 21–70. San Salvador: Alianza Feminista por la Transformación de la Cultura Política Patriarcal.

Larracoechea, Edurne. 2011. *¿Ciudadanía cero? El Hambre Cero y el empoderamiento de las mujeres.* Matagalpa, Nicaragua: Grupo Venancia.

Larracoechea, Edurne. 2014. *Hambre Cero cuatro años después.* Matagalpa, Nicaragua: Grupo Venancia.

La Voz del Sandinismo. 2012. "Cuenta el país con más mujeres alcaldesas." November 30. Accessed July 28, 2016. http://www.lavozdelsandinismo.com/nicaragua/2012-11-30/cuenta-el-pais-con-mas-mujeres-alcaldesas/.

Levitsky, Steven, and Kenneth M. Roberts, eds. 2011. *The Resurgence of the Latin American Left.* Baltimore, MD: Johns Hopkins University Press.

Lind, Amy. 2012. "'Revolution with a Woman's Face'? Family Norms, Constitutional Reform, and the Politics of Redistribution in Post-Neoliberal Ecuador, Rethinking Marxism." *Journal of Economics, Culture & Society* 24 (4): 536–55.

Lind, Amy, and Christine Keating. 2013. "Navigating the Left Turn." *International Feminist Journal of Politics* 15 (4): 1–19. Accessed April 12, 2015. https://www.academia.edu/4301829/Navigating_the_Left_Turn_Sexual_Justice_and_the_Citizen_Revolution_in_Ecuador.

Martí i Puig, Salvador. 2010. "The Adaptation of the FSLN: Daniel Ortega's Leadership and Democracy in Nicaragua." *Latin American Politics and Society* 52 (4): 79–106.

Martí i Puig, Salvador. 2016. "Nicaragua: desdemocratización y caudillismo." *Revista de Ciencia Política* 36 (1): 239–58.

Matamoros, Ruth Marina. 2016. "Three Mutilating Blows to the Law against Violence to Women." *Envío,* 417. Accessed July 30, 2016. http://www.envio.org.ni/articulo/5171.

Miranda Aburto, Wilfredo. 2012. "La maldición del INIM." *Confidencial,* June 19. Accessed November 7, 2014. http://www.confidencial.com.ni/articulo/7015/.

Miranda Aburto, Wilfred. 2013. "Ministerio de la Mujer nace bajo sombras." *Confidencial,* March 9. Accessed March 29, 2017. https://confidencial.com.ni/archivos/articulo/10681/ministerio-de-la-mujer-nace-bajo-sombras.

Miranda Aburto, Wilfredo, and Octavio Enríquez. 2013. "Zoilamérica: esto es una guerra personal." *Confidencial,* June 26. Accessed July 28, 2016. http://www

.confidencial.com.ni/archivos/articulo/12449/zoilamerica-039-esto-es-una
-guerra-personal-039.

Molyneux, Maxine. 1985. "Mobilization without Emancipation? Women's Interests,
the State, and Revolution in Nicaragua." *Feminist Studies* 11:227–54.

Molyneux, Maxine. 2007. *Change and Continuity in Social Protection in Latin America: Mothers at the Service of the State?* Gender and Development Programme
Paper 1. Geneva: United Nations Research Institute for Social Development
(UNRISD).

Montenegro, Sofía. 1997. "Un movimiento de mujeres en auge, Nicaragua." In
Movimiento de mujeres en Centroamerica by Aguilar et al., 339–446. Managua:
La Corriente, Centro Editorial de la Mujer.

Movimiento Autónomo de Mujeres (MAM). 2009. "30 años después el enemigo
sigue siendo el mismo." Last modified July 17. Accessed December 9, 2014.
http://movimientoautonomodemujeres.org/pr5.php.

Movimiento por la Dignidad y Derechos de las Mujeres, "Blanca Aráuz." 2008.
"Pronunciamiento de Constitución." September 22. Unpublished. Accessed
November 8, 2014. www.nicaraguatriunfa.com/DOCUMENTOS%202008
/SEPTIEMBRE/DECLARACION.pdf.

Movimiento Renovador Sandinista (MRS). n.d. "Cuadro comparativo Ley 779 y
Decreto 42–2014 (Reglamento de la Ley 779)." Accessed November 8, 2014.
http://partidomrs.org/files/Cuadro%20Comparativo%20Ley%20779%20y%20.

Movimiento Renovador Sandinista (MRS). 2017. "Red de la diversidad sexual: documentos constitutivos." Accessed June 11, 2017. http://partidomrs.org/index.php
/2016-02-05-21-12-44/2016-02-19-21-25-23/documentos-constitutivos.

Murguialday, Clara. 1990. *Nicaragua, revolución y feminismo, 1977–1989*. Madrid:
Editorial Revolución.

Palenzuela, Pablo. 2004. "Autonomía pluriétnica y autoridades indígenas en la
Costa Caribe de Nicaragua." In *Etnicidad, descentralizacion, y gobernabilidad en
América Latina Salvador*, edited by Martí Puig and Josep M. Sanahuja, 263–79.
Salamanca, Spain: Ediciones Universidad de Salamanca.

Panizza, Francisco. 2009. "Nuevas Izquierdas y democracia en América Latina."
Revista CIDOB d'Afers Internacionals 85–86:75–88.

Peraza, José Antonio. 2016. "This Time They Committed the Perfect Fraud." *Envío*,
424. Accessed March 27, 2017. http://www.envio.org.ni/articulo/5283.

Pérez-Baltodano, Andrés. 2010. "Nicaragua: se consolida el Estado por Derecho y se
debilita el Estado de Derecho." *Revista de Ciencia Política* 30 (2): 397–418.

Pérez-Baltodano, Andrés. 2013. *Postsandinismo*. Managua: IHNCA-UCA.

Pizarro, Ana María. 2012. *Cairo+20-Nicaragua: diagnóstico nacional, 1994–2012*.
Managua: Sí Mujer.

Quirós, Ana. 2011. *Hambre Cero: avances y desafíos. Tercer informe de evaluación del
Programa Productivo Agropecuario Hambre Cero*. Managua: IEEPP.

Randall, Margaret. 1994. *Sandino's Daughters Revisited: Feminism in Nicaragua*.
New Brunswick, NJ: Rutgers University Press.

Salinas, Carlos. 2016. "El círculo familiar del poder en Nicaragua." *El País*, August 4. Accessed August 28, 2016. http://internacional.elpais.com/internacional/2016/08 /04/america/1470268415_587452.html.

Stuart Amendáriz, Roberto, coord. 2009. *Consejos del Poder Ciudadano y gestión pública en Nicaragua*. Managua: CEAP.

Thayer, Millie. 1997. "Identity, Revolution and Democracy: Lesbian Movements in Central America." *Social Problems* 44 (3): 386–407.

Torres-Rivas, Edelberto. 2007. "Nicaragua: el retorno del sandinismo transfigurado." *Nueva Sociedad* 207:4–10.

United Nations Development Program (UNDP). 2016. *Human Development Report 2016: Human Development for Everyone*. New York: UNDP. Accessed June 10, 2017. http://hdr.undp.org/sites/default/files/2016_human_development_report .pdf.

United Nations Population Fund (UNFPA). 2013. *Motherhood in Childhood: Facing the Challenge of Adolescent Pregnancy*. Accessed July 22, 2016. https://www .unfpa.org/sites/default/files/pub-pdf/en-swop2013.pdf.

Vanden, Harry, and Gary Prevost. 1993. *Democracy and Socialism in Sandinista Nicaragua*. Boulder, CO: Lynne Rienner.

Welsh, Patrick. 2014. "Homophobia and Patriarchy in Nicaragua: A Few Ideas to Start Debate." *IDS Bulletin* 45 (1): 39–45.

Weyland, Kurt. 2013. "The Threat from the Populist Left." *Journal of Democracy* 24 (3): 18–32.

Whisnant, David. 1995. *Rascally Signs in Sacred Places: The Politics of Culture in Nicaragua*. Chapel Hill: University of North Carolina Press.

World Bank. 2016. "Nicaragua: Overview." Accessed September 16, 2016. http:// www.worldbank.org/en/country/nicaragua/overview.

World Economic Forum. 2014. *Global Gender Gap Report*. Accessed December 1, 2014. http://reports.weforum.org/global-gender-gap-report-2014/.

Yllescas, Martha, and Sofía Montenegro. 2003. *Feminismo y globalización: apuntes para un análisis político desde el movimiento*. Managua: Comité Nacional Feminista.

CHAPTER 8

Ecuador's Citizen Revolution 2007–17

A Lost Decade for Women's Rights and Gender Equality

ANNIE WILKINSON

There is this [thing] called *gender ideology* . . . that one has the right, the freedom even, to choose if one is a man or a woman. . . . Please! This doesn't hold up to the most basic analysis. It's a barbarity that goes against everything! . . . I insist. We are struggling for *equal rights* between men and women, but it's another thing, these *feminist fundamentalist* movements that look for men and women to be totally the same [*igualitos*], and I insist: this ideology is *extremely dangerous*, and they are teaching it to our youth. . . . They aren't theories [but] pure and simple ideology . . . that destroy the *basis of society*, which continues to be *the conventional family*.
—PRESIDENT RAFAEL CORREA, December 28, 2013

In December 2013, Ecuadorian president Rafael Correa railed against "fundamentalist feminists" in his weekly national television broadcast, denouncing the spread of their "extremely dangerous" ideas about gender and equality. He argued that this "gender ideology"—a catchphrase stemming directly from conservative religious discourse—threatens the conventional family, the "basis of society," and therefore the nation. This is not a matter of left or right, he insisted, but simply consists of "moral questions" (Secretaria Nacional de Comunicación 2013).

Correa's direct attack on feminist scholars and activists underscores the relevance of gender and sexuality for understanding and evaluating Ecuador's so-called turn to the Left—synonymous with Correa's election in 2006 and the ostensibly postneoliberal national project he initiated: the Citizen Revolution. Correa's construal of feminists as threatening to this project exposes the antagonism that developed between the Correa administration and feminist movements over the past decade. Further, this rhetoric points to an increasingly authoritarian governance style and reveals the enduring influence of conservative Catholicism, specifically the unquestioned centrality of the heteropatriarchal family in political discourse and social policy. And it alludes to the resultant setbacks—especially in terms of women's rights—that contradict the equal rights rhetoric of Ecuador's "New Left."

Correa went on to preempt the reaction to his speech: "[They will say that] I'm conservative. I'm no longer part of the Left. . . . Whoever does not ascribe to these things, is not [part] of the Left" (Secretaria Nacional de Comunicación, YouTube, 2013). In this Correa got one thing right: the Citizen Revolution's status within the Left faces broad questioning and growing resistance—including from feminists—and challenges conventional political typologies. But rather than an attempt at evaluating the authenticity of Correa's belonging to the so-called Left, I offer a feminist analysis of how the Citizen Revolution itself has engaged with gender and sexual politics during Correa's decade in office (2007–17). In doing so, I take as a measure the degree to which it has contributed to transforming heteropatriarchal power relations as an approximation of Ecuadorian feminist agendas. This examination of the Ecuadorian case through the lens of gender and sexuality provides the basis for challenging the presumption that leftist agendas necessarily incorporate feminist demands. Instead, it suggests that the self-declared New Left has not overcome its historically uneven and often contentious relationship to feminist movements and demands in Latin America (Friedman 2009). This chapter reveals that it can—and in this case, has—set them back.

After contextualizing the emergence of the Citizen Revolution, I make four interrelated arguments, echoed elsewhere in this volume, about the impact of Ecuador's return to the Left on the realization of feminist agendas in terms of both gender and sexuality. First, the Citizen Revolution's flagship socioeconomic gains have benefited many Ecuadorians, including many women. However, as in Venezuela and Bolivia, the government's aggressive reliance on extractive-led development has not only rendered these gains economically contingent and unsustainable but has also achieved them at high environmental, economic, and social costs. While women have borne these costs in specifically gendered ways, certain women have experienced them disproportionately. Second, while the Citizen Revolution initially opened opportunities for increased political participation and representation—which were seized by feminist and LGBT groups to implement key aspects of longstanding agendas in the 2008 constitution—increased formal representation of women, while celebrated internationally, has not facilitated feminist agendas, again similar to developments in Nicaragua and Bolivia. Third, this trend paralleled an increasingly contentious relationship between the Correa administration and social movements marked by a growing authoritarian, personalist, and hyperpresidentialist style of governance, much as happened in Nicaragua under President Ortega and First Lady Murillo. While alienating and weakening feminist movements, the Correa administration also engaged in "pinkwashing" strategies that deflected attention from setbacks faced by women, among others, by endorsing moderate gains for sexual minorities. This trend is fueled and sustained by organized conservative religious movements, which have strengthened during this period and evidenced their profound influence on government discourse and policy. Finally, I argue that not only do the notable achievements in Ecuador's legal framework—particularly its celebrated 2008 constitution—remain far from fully implemented but those rights most directly affecting women have eroded as well. As in Nicaragua, they have been replaced by a resurgent heteropatriarchal family values discourse whose mark on law, policy, and practice deepened over the course of the Correa administration.

In each section, I examine how the Correa administration used contingent gains in each area—impressive economic growth, increased formal women's representation, a vibrant LGBT movement, and an internationally celebrated constitution—to justify its overall project in ways that mask the notable overall setback in advancing transformative feminist agendas. Ultimately, as the Correa administration deprecated its progressive challengers more generally, feminist actors have been unable to overcome the overwhelming alliance between conservative Catholicism and the consolidated political power of an unfriendly presidential administration. Nor have they been able to shift the political weight generated by the Correa government's impressive macroeconomic growth and undeniable institutional stability.

In analyzing each of these trends in succession, I draw extensively from social movement productions, media sources, government documents and reports, and academic literature, as well as interviews and participant observation conducted with LGBT and feminist activists online and in person between 2009 and 2016.[1] In conformity with many other chapters in this volume, the Ecuadorian case suggests that despite moderate alleviation of longstanding economic inequalities, ostensibly postneoliberal or new leftist Latin American governments are as capable as both conservative governments and their historical leftist challengers of resisting feminist demands to transform heteropatriarchal power relations—and even reversing them.

Ecuador's "Turn to the Left": Contextualizing the Citizen Revolution

Years of political instability, acute economic crisis, crushing foreign debt, and a discredited political system provided the political vacuum that facilitated Rafael Correa's election to office (Conaghan 2011). Neoliberal restructuring and market-led development throughout the 1980s and 1990s had left Ecuadorians—and especially women—in conditions of greater poverty, debt, and unemployment than before (Lind 2005; Prieto 2005). A series of economic and political crises and rampant corruption fostered a series of protest-fueled presidential oustings leading to five different governments between 1997 and 2004 and a demoralized electorate. Correa's successful navigation of these conditions in his campaign, including an exceptional communications strategy broadcasting rhetoric featuring hope, renewal, progress, and modernity, ensured his electoral success in 2006 (Conaghan 2011). In the second round of elections he was able to assemble a weak but sufficient alliance among those within the deeply fragmented Left, including Ecuador's powerful indigenous movements, who feared the seemingly likely reelection of the historically entrenched conservative political elite.

Correa succeeded in winning the cautious support of many—though certainly not all—women and feminists due to a number of factors. Above all, women from both popular and institutionalized women's movements alike offered their reticent support to ensure that a conservative, neoliberal government and old economic elite "would absolutely *not* win" again (Varea 2016; Aguinaga 2014). Second, Correa claimed his platform "had a woman's face" and appealed specifically to poorer women, promising in the second round of elections to significantly expand and extend the traditional cash transfer programs as well as microcredit and housing subsidy programs upon which many of them relied (Lind 2002; Conaghan 2011). To the hopeful reception of many, he promised his female supporters that eradicating violence against women, providing equal opportunities, and ensuring access to health care, education, employment, and social security was at the heart of his agenda. Third, despite a wary stance in the face of a long and contentious history with both the Right and the Left (Friedman 2009), many feminists saw key convergences between Correa's platform and their long-standing agendas and the possibility of political openings in which to pursue them, especially in the opportunity to redraft the constitution (Aguinaga 2014; Vasquez 2016).

At the same time, Correa assured his victory by placating the traditionally conservative Catholic electorate, consistently reaffirming his devout Catholicism as part of what he called the "Christian humanist left" (Conaghan 2011). Correa vehemently reiterated his opposition to abortion, which many feminists conceded as expected given Ecuador's ranking among nations in the region with the lowest levels of popular support for abortion (Pew Research Center 2014). Nevertheless, Correa had won not only the votes of many women and feminists but also their hopes. As one of Ecuador's leading feminist activists commented to me in 2009, registering her early doubts, "We believed in Correa. Even I voted for him."[2]

Once elected, Correa brought together a broader political base eager to take part in the rewriting of the constitution. Correa began consolidating political power from the outset, ensuring a constitution that deeply favored executive power (Ellner 2012; Vasquez 2016). The 2009 constitution reflected widespread national participation and became one of the most rights granting in the world. It was ratified in September 2008 by a large majority of voters. Correa claimed the victory as a mandate for his Alianza PAIS[3] (AP) party's postneoliberal platform, the Citizen Revolution. He was reelected to a first term under the new constitution in 2009 and reelected to a second in 2013. In both cases, he won by wide margins to become Ecuador's longest serving and one of its most popular presidents.[4] Following the Correa administration's ten years in office, Ecuadorians voted on April 2, 2017, to elect vice president Lenin Moreno, who only narrowly defeated his far-right conservative contender, Guillermo Lasso, but whose administration this analysis does not address.[5]

Correa's popularity declined precipitously after 2015, and anti-Correa sentiment grew not only in response to Ecuador's stalling economy—a situation precipitated in part by falling oil prices—but also in opposition to Correa's steady consolidation of presidential power, extensive exertion of control over the judiciary and supermajority in the legislature, increasingly personalist politics and authoritarian governance style, and growing repression of the media, social movements, academic institutions, unions, and human rights defenders. Even so, Correa's visible and enduring investments in infrastructure and social programs and their returns ensured the retention of a strong baseline of supporters. As a result, even while domestic approval ratings fell steeply in his final two years in office, they still remained among the highest in the region.

Despite rising opposition from both Right and Left and falling popularity, Correa's grasp on executive power remained firm. In a fiercely criticized move, Correa bypassed constitutional stipulations to push through the removal of term limits. While he ultimately did not run in the 2017 election, the change allows for his potential reelection in the future. Although Correa justified his excessive power as protective against a conservative opposition that sought to destabilize the government, it earned his administration characterizations of hyperpresidentialism (Andrade 2016), delegatory democracy (Polga-Hecimovich 2013), continued *caudillismo* (Basabe-Serrano 2009), high-intensity, middle-class populism (Svampa 2016), and a plebiscitary presidency running a permanent campaign (Conaghan and de la Torre 2008)—conditions that are neither compatible with nor amenable to the pursuit of feminist agendas, as will become evident in the analysis that follows.

Cracks in Correísmo: Economic and Gender Equality at Odds

Ecuador's past decade of economic growth and poverty reduction has been dubbed by some "the Ecuadorian miracle." The Correa administration renegotiated petroleum contracts, restructured foreign debt, and revamped the taxation system, among other strategies enacted to increase revenue. This helped Correa double social spending between 2006 and 2012, elevating Ecuador to lead Latin America in terms of public investment as a proportion of GDP in 2012 (Ghosh 2012). Enrollment in the Bono de Desarrollo Humano (Human Development Credit) cash transfer program expanded by 25 percent, while housing assistance and the budget proportion allocated to education doubled (Grugel and Riggirozzi 2012). The number of people living in poverty fell by 10 percent between 2005 and 2012 (Grugel and Riggirozzi 2012), and unemployment fell to its lowest level on record since 2007 (Ray and Kozameh 2012).

As a result, the Citizen Revolution has undoubtedly resulted in impressive short-term economic gains that have benefited some women. However, when viewed through a feminist analytical lens, these achievements' lack of long-term economic and environmental sustainability, lack of clear benefit for *all* women, and significant costs for *some* women called into question the Citizen Revolution's redistributive successes. This is of particular importance when considering that the Correa administration routinely pointed to socioeconomic success to justify and distract from the negative consequences of the neoextractive development model (Gudynas 2010) that underwrites this economic growth as well as Correa's ever more blatant abuses of executive power. Both of these are detrimental to women in three specific ways.

First, the economic policies and development model of the Citizen Revolution are neither environmentally nor economically sustainable, a fact acknowledged by the 2008 constitution itself. Yet Correa consistently justified an extractive-led development model and its costs as necessary for long-term development and economic stability, much as President Morales and vice president García Linera have in Bolivia. As Eduardo Gudynas (2010) has argued, "neoextractivism" as practiced by Latin America's new Left modified but did not break entirely with the previous neoliberal form of extractivism. What primarily distinguishes neoextractivism from earlier models is that the state plays a more active role, capturing and redistributing a greater proportion of surplus to the population, particularly through social programs. While this generates a "progressive stamp" and greater legitimacy for the state, it also contributes to pacifying local demands and weakens avenues for contestation (Gudynas 2010, 3). Meanwhile, the negative environmental and social impacts of extractivism as well as its service orientation to global markets are left unaltered and even exacerbated, as with new mining exploits in Ecuador. As a result, in Left Latin America as well as across the globe, extractivism is highly correlated with the "increasing marginalization" of indigenous people—despite the expansion of legal instruments recognizing their rights (Sawyer and Gomez 2012, 6).

As Correa regularly phrased it, the nation "can't sit like beggars on the sack of gold," and thus, exploiting natural resources to fund growth and development has been construed as the government's duty, even a matter of national security, a feature characteristic of neoextractivism (Gudynas 2010, 10). But studies cast doubt on whether the cost of cleaning up the environmental damage caused by extractive industry surpass generated revenues (Valencia 2015), and some economists question the justificatory link between extractive-led development and redistributive equality as both unsupported and misleading (Dávalos 2014). Correa's failure to concomitantly ensure economic diversification and build reserves has left the economy and national budget exposed to the volatility of global commodity prices. Thus, while world petroleum prices boomed, this model "[bore] fruit" (Grugel and Riggirozzi 2012). But when world oil prices began to sharply fall in 2015, Ecuador sank into its worst economic position since Correa took office (Escandón 2016). In essence, the country's previous neoliberal model of economic development has had a change of face but little change of pace under Correa's leadership (Dávalos 2014; Lind 2012b). While the Citizen Revolution has certainly generated economic growth and some material redistribution, it has not necessarily transformed in the long term the political, economic, and social structures cultivated by preceding neoliberal governments that generate poverty and inequality. Further, these advancements have remained dependent on both natural resources and foreign creditors and investors (Valencia 2015).

Moreover, the neoextractive development model has been implemented at great human cost to those deemed expendable, an example of what Maristella Svampa labels "maldevelopment" (Svampa 2016). Extraction projects under the Correa administration—as with earlier governments—routinely bypassed the constitutional right to free, prior, and informed consent of directly affected peoples, ignored environmental assessments, did not always compensate displaced communities, and routinely caused significant environmental damage and contamination incompatible with human health and inhabitance (Valencia 2015; Riofrancos 2015). The Correa administration also aggressively rolled back constitutional rights to land, water, and resources in indigenous territories to facilitate expansions of extractive industry, which brought it into the worst conflict with indigenous movements in recent decades and invited the condemnation of the Inter-American Court of Human Rights (IACHR) in 2012 (Becker 2015; Novo 2014). In short, to oppose resource extraction rendered one an enemy of the state (Riofrancos 2015). While all of these affect women generally, they also face particular gendered consequences, to which I return below.

Second, among those who have gained from Correa's redistributive policies, not all Ecuadorians—nor all Ecuadorian women—have benefited evenly. For example, while urban unemployment among women saw one of the steepest declines in the region in recent years, such job growth has not benefited women in rural areas nor in agriculture, and neither the nature, the quality, nor equitable compensation of women's traditionally exploited labor has improved (Wappenstein and Villamediana 2013). Women's time burdens, gendered labor patterns at the household level and economy as a whole, the major wage gap, and women's overrepresentation in the informal economy have all remained largely unchanged (Wappenstein and Villamediana 2013). These data are suggestive of the fact that without transforming heteropatriarchal power relations, material redistribution does not itself lead to gender equality. The Citizen Revolution has alleviated poverty for some women but has thus far failed to fundamentally redistribute economic or social power from men to women or significantly affect women's attainment of economic justice.

Third, while the Correa administration has justified its extractive-led development model by promoting its economic benefits for women—especially for poor and indigenous women—these same women are among those who lose the most from aggressive extractive-led development (Colectivo Miradas Críticas del Territorio desde el Feminismo 2014a). Assessments of extractive industry that consider material equality alone overlook potential detriments to other forms of equality as well as how different dimensions of equality themselves "are often interconnected and reinforce each other" (Valencia 2015, 3). In practice, Correa's neoextractivist model puts economic inclusion and gender equality at odds, even when that economic inclusion yields material benefits for some women. For example, empirical evidence reveals that women at extractive sites face elevated workloads, increased sexual and domestic violence, and environmental health problems—including those related to reproductive and maternal health, obstacles to political participation, and heightened exploitative sex trafficking (von Gall 2015; Colectivo Miradas Críticas del Territorio desde el Feminismo 2014b; Oxfam 2009; Coalición Nacional de Organizaciones de Mujeres 2014). Further, while some economically benefit from natural resource rents, extractive industry tends to disrupt women's dominant sources of livelihood in informal sector employment, including agriculture and tourism, while offering male-oriented formal sector jobs (Valencia 2015). This is so despite the fact that these industries employ the largest number of rural women and surpass extractive industry's contribution to GDP (Radcliffe 2013). Such a dynamic in turn strengthens male power in households and divides families and loyalties within communities—often along gender lines (Valencia 2015). As long as the administration's development model justifies growth at any cost, one of those costs will be gender equality.

Massive mobilizations in opposition to extractive industry attest to the fact that material gains for some, including women, do not erase, compensate, nor legitimize setbacks in the recognition or respect of their or others' rights. Even while underrepresented at leadership levels, women have been at the forefront of this resistance (Valencia 2015). For example, women from every region affected by extractive industry joined together to organize the Women and Extractivism gathering in October 2014, a national effort that aimed to demand government accountability, articulate a common agenda, and strategize and forge alliances with urban-based feminist movements (Colectivo Miradas Críticas del Territorio desde el Feminismo 2014b). In another example, a large contingent of indigenous women marched to Quito to stage demonstrations during the nationwide protests of August 2015, centering on their rights to water, land, and self-determination *as* women (*La Hora* 2016). However, actions such as these helped to generate yet another cost borne by those women defending their territories, resources, and rights: becoming targets of the Correa administration's increasingly repressive tactics directed at opponents, a topic examined in more detail below.

Behind the "Woman's Face" of the Citizen Revolution: The Politics of Women in Politics

In addition to economic indicators of growth and poverty reduction, the Correa administration consistently marketed women's increased formal political representation as proof that women had advanced under the Citizen Revolution. In his weekly national broadcast in 2013, Correa boasted that Ecuador was at the "vanguard" with respect to women's political participation, citing the only gender parity constitutional court in the world, with one of the highest proportions of female representatives in the region (Secretaria Nacional de Comunicación 2013). Indeed, the number of women in the National Assembly increased by 54 percent between 2009 and 2016, and the body currently remains led by three women in the positions of president and vice president (Alexis 2016). Correa even appointed an openly lesbian minister of Public Health in 2012, Carina Vance.

In light of these achievements, Ecuador attracted the approval of an international audience, much as Nicaragua did for its efforts on descriptive representation. In 2015, Ecuador was given the annual award of the Women in Parliaments (WIP) Global Forum, which praised its achievement of gender parity in cabinet positions, a National Assembly of 42 percent women, a recently passed law mandating gender parity in multiparty elections, and its success in "reducing gender inequality in the country" (Agencia Efe 2015). Through a variety of channels, the Correa administration broadly circulated the news, prominently announcing these statistics as major achievements of the Citizen Revolution (CNIG 2015). At the awards ceremony, Alianza PAIS assemblywoman Ximena Ponce attributed the prize to the political will and efforts of Correa and the Citizen Revolution.

However, increased formal political representation of women under the Citizen Revolution, as in Nicaragua's "Second Revolution," has not facilitated the advancement of feminist agendas. Many of those joining public office do not pursue gender agendas, do not count on significant independence or decision-making power, and do not compensate for the deinstitutionalization of Ecuador's women's state agency under Correa's leadership. Instead, as the WIP prize makes clear, government claims and international accolades serve to obscure and deflect attention from the overall setback in women's rights and from the dismantling of the state women's institution specifically.

First, just as this case demonstrates that counting does not equate with consciousness with regard to political representation (Friedman 2009), so too it reveals that quality does not necessarily proceed from quantity (Alexis 2016). Of the 329 bills proposed in the National Assembly between May 2013 and July 2016, only eighty-nine (27.1 percent) were proposed by women (despite constituting 42 percent of the legislature), and of these, only two passed, both by AP "oficialistas," and neither of which related to women or gender (Alexis 2016). Despite the initial inclusion of feminists in the Correa administration, there remain few women in public office, including among the vastly AP-dominated legislature, who are connected to feminist movements or who pursue feminist proposals independent of the "oficialista" AP party platform (Varea 2016). This includes the three female leaders of the National Assembly who maintained definitive political loyalties to Correa throughout his tenure (Alexis 2016). Many vocal AP feminists were pushed out or defected to the leftist opposition after being sidelined, particularly in relation to disagreements over women's reproductive rights. María Paula Romo, of the leftist political movement Ruptura 25, is a well-known example who left the AP party in 2011 citing presidential abuse of power (Buendía and Calapaqui 2016). Still other women appointed by Correa—especially in his latter term— have pushed staunchly antifeminist agendas. For example, as discussed below in more depth, Correa tapped Mónica Hernandez, who holds self-admitted former ties to Opus Dei (Varea 2015; Morales 2015), to design and lead Plan Familia, as an ultraconservative national strategy for addressing reproductive and sexual health and education.

Second, the ability of women in public office to promote feminist proposals or a gender agenda has been significantly hampered by limits imposed on the decision-making power under the Correa administration. Correa's extensive control over the legislature and AP party discipline more generally accentuated this. As assemblywoman Mae Montaño pointed out, the Correa administration "made an effort to have more women authorities, but their decision-making power is not there; there is only one force, which is that of one man [Correa]" (Alexis 2016). Correa's unilateralism was especially evident in response to proposals and policies favorable to progressive gender agendas and women's reproductive rights. The most powerful example occurred during the redrafting of the Penal Code in 2013. After three assemblywomen proposed to decriminalize abortion in all cases of rape, they were suspended for a month after Correa called them "traitors" and threatened to personally resign from office in order to block the measure (Morales 2015).[6] They withdrew their proposal, voted the party line, and did not raise the issue again. As Correa lambasted them in his national broadcast like a "disciplining father" (Chaher 2014), the other nineteen assemblypeople who had supported them were effectively warned against contradicting Correa (Buendía and Calapaqui 2016).

Correa has curtailed feminist opposition through other means as well. His consistent sexualized comments and gendered attacks—chiefly directed at women who leave or oppose his administration—further deterred, delegitimized, and constrained women's political participation (Buendía and Calapaqui 2016). Feminists have documented the gendered nature of dozens of these frequent assaults, which ranged from comments about the physical attractiveness of assemblywomen to instructions to "shut up" to the use of derogatory gendered terms to refer to women (Buendía and Calapaqui 2016).[7] After María Paula Romo left the AP to become the only woman to lead a political party, she became one of Correa's most frequent targets. Undeterred, Ruptura 25 ran an opposition candidate against Correa in 2013. In June 2014, Correa's Consejo Nacional Electoral (National Electoral Council) bent campaign rules to disqualify Ruptura 25 from fronting candidates, effectively extinguishing its only feminist leftist political party opposition (Buendía 2014). While blocking Ruptura 25–affiliated individuals from employment anywhere within the administration, AP invited back willing previous defectors, such as assemblywoman Alexandra Ocles, who had been left without prospects for employment or a political career after the Correa administration destroyed the Ruptura 25 party (Vasquez 2016).

Third, the increase in women holding political office was severely offset by the dismantling of one of the women's movement's hard-won "triumphs"— the Consejo Nacional de Mujeres (National Women's Council, or CONAMU) (Chaher 2014). Institutionalized as a women's state agency in the 1990s, CONAMU gave activists a crucial foothold within the state to promote feminist and gender agendas at a time when few women active in state politics had activist roots. The agency allowed women's movements to bypass the exclusion they experienced elsewhere in politics—including political parties—to access the halls of national government and influence laws, policies, research, and programming (Radcliffe 2008). Despite CONAMU's symbolic, historical, and strategic importance for Ecuador's women's movement, the 2008 constitution mandated its replacement with the Consejo Nacional de Igualdad de Género (National Gender Equality Council, or CNIG). The new entity would constitute one of five permanent councils mandated to address inequalities according to a mainstreaming logic and organized by axes of inequality—gender, ethnicity, generation, interculturality, and disability and human mobility— rather than by specified identity-based groups—such as women, youth, or indigenous people (Constitución Política de la República del Ecuador 2008). This shift rendered CONAMU a "transition commission," effectively handicapping the agency as it awaited reinstitutionalization while eliminating its mandate to address the specific needs of women.

After seven years of legal and institutional limbo, in May 2014 CNIG became the last of the councils to be set up. However, the reconstituted agency's funding and its linkages to the women's movement were significantly diminished. Consuelo Bowen, who was appointed to lead the council in April 2016, focused her attention on advertising the Citizen Revolution's "ten years of advancements for women" and Correa's rendering of "the struggle for gender equality . . . [as] a flagship" issue (*El Ciudadano* 2016). While the agency produced colorful reports and pamphlets about the Citizen Revolution's achievements for women, it accomplished little of substance in its first two years (CNIG 2015). The disintegration of CONAMU represents one of the most profound setbacks for women since 2007. Its weak replacement has meant the persistence of "a wide institutional gap with regard to gender equity policies, laws, and education, and an absence of mechanisms to address issues concerning sexual orientation and gender identity" (Lind 2012b, 258), and the increase in women's political representation under the Correa administration has come nowhere close to bridging that gap.

Assets, Adversaries, and Pinkwashing: Social Movement Dynamics of the Citizen Revolution

The Citizen Revolution platform emphasized participatory democracy as a core tenet. While the Constituent Assembly of 2008 incorporated broader participation than ever before, in its latter years, the Correa administration came to obstruct the effectiveness and participation of a broad range of social movements, the media, and academic institutions through a variety of means, including cooptation, defunding, legal harassment, and direct repression (Picq 2013; Vasquez 2016; Elwood et al. 2016). Largely to their detriment, "Correa and others have sought to reposition the state as the interlocutor of social movements" (Lind and Keating 2013, 4), disrupting women's movements while instrumentalizing LGBT movements.

In this section, I examine the dynamics among women's movements, LGBT rights movements, growing conservative movements, and the Correa administration. What began as a cautious relationship between feminists and the Correa administration deteriorated into a contentious one. Feminists are among those who have been hindered by the Correa administration's intense destabilization efforts directed at social movements. While Correa's tenure partly enabled—or at least did not hinder—the growth of a vibrant LGBT movement, it also successfully wielded two interrelated strategies that worked together to undermine the mobilization of feminist LGBT agendas: cooptation and pinkwashing. Ultimately, while both movements have forged creative alliances among themselves and with other social movement actors to maintain a strong presence, they have been unsuccessful at institutionalizing coalitions robust enough to mount a significant and sustained challenge to the influence of conservative groups pushing heteropatriarchal discourses and policies. Thus, while both external interference and a lack of internal institutional capacity remain important factors in explaining the setback in women's rights, this points to a third and crucial factor: the steady growth and influence of conservative religious movements in this period.

Ecuadorian feminist movements are composed of diverse agendas and political tensions along ethnic, class, and ideological lines (Aguinaga 2014). Though they have never reached the same ability to extract concessions from the state as Ecuador's powerful indigenous movements, they expanded, diversified, and institutionalized significantly in the 1990s and successfully established a number of foundational gains in this decade.[8] These included the institutionalization of CONAMU, a national quota law and legislation on violence against women (Law 103), and the repeal of several discriminatory laws (Lind 2005). A nascent LGBT movement also grew out of the 1990s, after the decriminalization of homosexuality in 1997 allowed for open political organizing[9] and led to a groundbreaking sexual orientation antidiscrimination clause in the 1998 constitution. This movement has grown in the 2000s in ways analogous to that of women's movements in the 1990s and remains similarly divided along the lines of gender, geography, class, and politics.

The Correa administration partly enabled the expansive growth of the nascent LGBT movement—or at least did not hinder what has been a broader regional growth trend. Yet it further polarized and weakened women's movements through a variety of strategies. These range from stoking existing tensions and controlling nongovernmental women's organizing spaces to obstructing women's organizing by threatening or silencing critical individuals and organizations as part of a larger repressive trend against social movements. The exclusion of non-AP loyalists in government and dismantling of CONAMU severed linkages between feminists working inside and outside the state. In another example I observed, progovernment instigators hijacked the strictly nongovernmental 2011 Encuentro Feminista (Feminist Encounter), a key national feminist organizing space, disrupting critical discussion and strategic organizing efforts. Meanwhile, Correa regularly and aggressively discredited and verbally attacked feminist critics, including social movement leaders.[10]

Of most concern was the deployment of state-sponsored and increasingly repressive tactics of targeted legal harassment, arbitrary detention, and excessive punishment reserved for those women human rights defenders who were most vocal against government violations related to land, water, and extractive industries. For example, Rosaura Bastidas was sentenced to three years in prison for sabotage and terrorism for mobilizing a defense of her territory (Buendía and Calapaqui 2016), and the administration detained and deported Manuela Picq, a critical journalist, academic, and partner of national indigenous opposition leader Carlos Pérez Guartambel, allegedly for participating in and documenting nationwide protests in 2015 (Viteri 2016). Both are examples of the increasing criminalization of protest under the Correa administration and of "lawfare"—the abuse of the law as a weapon to discredit and justify state action against political opponents (Picq 2013), including national security claims and labeling dissidents "terrorists," a tactic replicated elsewhere in the region (Richards 2010). Some organizations, such as Defensoras de la Pachamama (Women Defenders of Mother Earth), have faced only threats or frivolous investigations (Valencia 2015). But the most vocal organizations, such as ecofeminist group Acción Ecológica (Ecological Action), were shut down under the pretense of violating Presidential Decree 016 (CONAMU 2014). Issued in June 2013 as perhaps the most repressive act against social movements undertaken during the Correa administration, Decree 016 mandated the creation of a database to track civil society organizations and forbade them from engaging in "political" activity—a vague concept that easily included unwelcome criticism of the administration (Montúfar et al. 2014).

After ten years and growing hostility—as evidenced by this chapter's opening quote—the Correa administration retained the support of only a few loyalist women's groups, such as Foro de la Mujer (Women's Forum) and antichoice Mujeres por la Vida (Women for Life), while alienating, weakening, and dividing most organized women and feminists. The division and debilitation of women's and feminist movements does not entirely result from external interference. Disagreements over priorities, strategies, and approach to state engagement, interpersonal rifts, competition over resources, capacity issues, and race and class chasms are also ever-present factors, as they are in all social movements. Regardless, it is clear that the Correa administration has contributed to weakening rather than strengthening the capacity of women's movements, and that "there is more divisiveness now than during the previous neoliberal period (1980–2007)" (Lind 2012a, 550). This has worked to prevent activists' effective mobilization against the rollback of their rights, which I review in the final section of this chapter.

Correa's strategic alliance with some sectors of the LGBT movement displayed a different pattern. The administration's pinkwashing efforts served to position the Citizen Revolution as modern and pro-LGBT, while at the same time its cooptation of sectors of the movement divided and undermined it. The growing influence of homonationalist discourse globally—which praises nations for the descriptive recognition of LGBT rights and catalogues this as a marker of progress and modernity—paralleled Correa's entry into office and his own emphasis on social equality. This had the effect of opening opportunities for advancing LGBT rights agendas on one hand, but given that LGBT movements and the government alike stood to benefit, it enabled conditions for "pinkwashing" on the other—that is, the promotion of highly visible, strategic, and often nominal concessions or rhetoric favorable to sexual minorities as a means to foster perceptions of progressive modernity or detract from other failures or rights violations. While pinkwashing is not unique in the region (see chapter 7), in this case it draws attention away from the administration's systematic violations of indigenous people's rights, social movement repression, and—quite ironically—the setbacks in women's rights that it fostered.

This pinkwashing approach has been successful. The Correa administration received widespread recognition for its support of LGBT rights. Correa's ministry appointment of openly lesbian Carina Vance made international news,[11] and Ecuador was celebrated on the global stage for joining the ranks of nations granting some form of same-sex partnership recognition and for being among the few with constitutional protections for both gender identity and sexual orientation. Correa even received a special plaque by vocal trans activist and now AP National assemblywoman, Diane Rodriguez, of the LGBT rights organization Asociación Silueta X (Buendía and Calapaqui 2016). The award—given supposedly "on behalf of the LGBT community"—recognized Correa as the president who has done the most for LGBT Ecuadorians (Buendía and Calapaqui 2016). Such praise gives undue credit to Correa for these achievements while obscuring Correa's contributions to blocking more substantive advancements, including same-sex marriage and adoption rights, the universal recognition of gender, and the implementation of newly recognized rights, as I further detail in the next section.

But pinkwashing as a strategy has depended on another interrelated and divisive one: cooptation. The Correa administration built an exceptionally strong and mutually beneficial alliance with transgender-focused Asociación Silueta X. Correa accepted the organization's request for a meeting in December 2013, extending verbal support and opening an unprecedented channel between LGBT activists and the state. Correa praised Rodriguez on national television as a courageous activist, apologized to the LGBT community for his own homophobic social conditioning, and pointed to his support of Rodriguez as an example of his administration's commitment to diversity and inclusion (Ramos 2013). Correa named Rodriguez his official liaison to the LGBT community and supported the establishment and funding of a new national umbrella organization, the Ecuadorian Federation of LGBT Organizations, with Rodriguez as the federation's president. Asociación Silueta X's ability to secure these political inroads were followed by an elevated profile within the international LGBT movement, which brings with it donor funds and related opportunities, and provided Correa with an expansive international audience for Rodriguez's praise of the Citizen Revolution. In return for AP support for Rodriguez's candidacy for assemblywoman—which she ultimately won in 2017 to become the country's first openly transgender assemblywoman—Rodriguez agreed to support the administration's LGBT policies and its interventions in the LGBT movement (Vasquez 2016). This effectively rendered her at least partially an instrument of the state within the LGBT movement, a role she implemented effectively.

The Correa administration's returns on its investment in this alliance exceeded Rodriguez's public accolades. The federation took on a policing role in the LGBT community, admonishing other LGBT leaders in meetings who criticized the Correa administration and labeling them "divisive" (Federación Ecuatoriana LGBT 2016). In August 2015, massive nationwide demonstrations protesting the Correa administration garnered international concern. The protests were led by indigenous peoples protesting the administration's systematic violations of their rights, social movements and union leaders protesting the crackdown on rights to free speech and association, and feminist and LGBT leaders protesting presidential authoritarianism and Correa's efforts to restrict reproductive rights. Amid this widespread national opposition, Rodriguez released an open letter "on behalf of the LGBT community" in which she declared solidarity with Correa and—echoing administration rhetoric—

condemned the protests as illegitimate conservative opposition movements efforts aimed at destabilizing the government (Asociación Silueta X 2016b).

The Correa administration's selective and exclusive support of Rodriguez's candidacy and organizations—and her reciprocated and unqualified support of Correa—have caused enormous tensions and divisions within the broader LGBT activist community. These tensions peaked when Rodriguez split from a nationwide LGBT lobbying coalition in 2016 to strike a deal with Correa's team directly to approve adding "gender" to national ID cards, resulting in the passage of a significantly weakened law (detailed in the next section). A large and growing proportion of the LGBT activist community vehemently rejects her claims to represent them and critiques her actions for supporting pinkwashing and acting as a mouthpiece for the administration. She has responded by delegitimizing long-standing organizations as "partisan" and denouncing their criticisms as "spreading hate" in an ironic rhetorical reversal (Federación Ecuatoriana LGBT 2016). This discussion not only illustrates the interdependency of strategies of cooptation and pinkwashing but also points to one factor explaining why LGBT agendas seem to have advanced in moderate ways: the valued currency of homonationalist LGBT rights discourse that underwrites pinkwashing and masks setbacks in reproductive rights and more transformative interpretations of LGBT rights.[12]

At the same time, conservative family values discourses have also taken on renewed weight in Ecuador among both Correa himself (as evidenced in this chapter's opening quote) and broader conservative movements in a reflection of global trends (Wilkinson 2013; Varea 2015; Vasquez 2016; AWID 2016). Transnational manifestations of this trend include the ex-gay and pro-family movements, which coordinate efforts to promote heteropatriarchal discourses promoting family values and demonstrate significant traction and growth in Ecuador and globally (Varea 2015; Wilkinson 2013, 2017). Globally, family values discourse has proven particularly powerful for reframing policies to recenter the family and for influencing governments around the world who "don't want to be seen as 'against' the family" (AWID 2015). And in Ecuador, research has documented an analogous steady growth and rise in influence of such groups over the past two decades, noting their specific success in raising funds, influencing discourse, and mobilizing membership, especially among conservative young people and women on the issue of abortion (Varea 2015). The concept on which Correa's defensive discourse draws—"gender ideology"—has come to operate as a marker of these movements, acting as an omnibus metonym for antiabortion and anti-LGBT stances combined with missionary support for traditional heteronormative gender roles. The term, which Correa regularly employed when addressing topics of sexual and reproductive rights, exclusively derives from organized religious movements and is regularly invoked by the Vatican and conservative actors across Latin America, and entered into Ecuadorian discourse through Catholic antiabortion activists (Varea 2015; Wilkinson 2017). Successful alliances between the Correa administration and these strengthening conservative groups—which remain a critical electoral block—ensured that many in government positions, including some of Correa's closest advisors, were active members of these movements. This includes those tasked with overseeing policy and programs on gender and sexuality, such as Mónica Hernandez. Feminist groups have not been successful at warding off the generous uptake of these discourses, whose influence on policy is evident.

Responses to both LGBT and conservative religious constituencies led the Correa administration to tack back and forth between what Amy Lind and Christine Keating (2013) call homoprotectionist and homophobic logics: "Whereas the homophobic state secures heterosexist power and privilege, the homoprotectionist state challenges it" (Lind and Keating 2013, 6). While seemingly contradictory, both logics have served to consolidate support for Correa and the Citizen Revolution. Just as with economic growth or political representation statistics, the homoprotectionist approach "can be used to justify the consolidation, extension and centralization of state authority" (Lind and Keating 2013, 6). This helps to explain why Correa stated that it is the government's duty to "respect the intrinsic dignity of everyone, of every human being, independent of their . . . sexual preference" when expressing support for same-sex unions (Xie and Corrales 2010) at the same time that he vehemently vowed to reject same-sex marriage and adoption and ridiculed transgender people. While the Correa administration's instrumentalization of LGBT movements left room for some successes, its blockage or undermining of progressive feminist movement agendas led to setbacks in terms of women's rights, as I examine in the next section.

One Step Forward, Two Steps Back: Setbacks in Laws, Policies, and Practice

Correa claimed that the overwhelming passage of Ecuador's 2008 constitution expressed a mandate for his presidency. Indeed, he asserted that he had "won elections, but not [yet] power" in 2006, and that "the mother of all battles" was the new constitution (Conaghan 2011, 271). Ecuador's 2008 constitution was heralded globally as one of the most rights-granting and progressive constitutions in the world. With *buen vivir*[13] centered as its guiding force, it recognized the rights of nature for the first time, declared Ecuador a plurinational, intercultural, and secular state, and incorporated international law as binding. In terms of gender and sexuality, it offered tremendous transformational potential (Villagómez 2013). Women's movements won incorporation of thirty-four of their thirty-six demands, and observers noted that 360 articles were in some way favorable for women (Lind 2012b; Buendía and Calapaqui 2016). Ecuador's became one of the first constitutions in the world to add discrimination protections for gender identity, ban hate speech, guarantee affirmative action for sexual minorities, affirm rights to sexual and reproductive health information and services, and grant civil partnerships to any two people (Constitución Política de la República del Ecuador 2008).

Its most transformational potential perhaps lies in its unprecedented resignification of the family. A creative alliance between indigenous and transfeminist Constituent Assembly participants succeeded in ensuring that plurality be taken into account when understanding what it referred to as the primary "nucleus of society" (Lind 2012a). As a result, the constitution spawned the legal concept of "diverse families," which went beyond the family as defined solely by blood or marriage to theoretically accommodate not only Ecuador's recently massively expanded population of transnational families as well as diverse indigenous family forms, but also queer forms of kinship, women-led households, and nonpatriarchal family forms (Lind 2012b), in addition to the "traditional" or "natural" nuclear family celebrated in family values discourse. The potential of this concept for transforming heteropatriarchal power relations cannot be overstated. This revision "challenges the state's historical role in regulating intimate and familial arrangements through biological reproduction and/or marriage" (Lind 2012b, 257).

However, despite an impressive expansion of constitutional rights and guarantees early in Correa's tenure, and the recognition of some rights important to sexual minorities, the past ten years have produced an overall erosion of women's rights in practice and reduced potential for transforming heteropatriarchal power relations. Limitations and contradictions in the constitution itself generate significant constraints, and its transformational potential has been implemented only partially or in ways that actually derogate or limit rights while appearing to advance them. The potential of its resignification of the family lies largely dormant as trends point to a deepening, rather than a whittling away, of the heteropatriarchal family—entrenched in law, policy, and practice.

The de facto setbacks faced by women did not necessarily come as a result of a change in approach by the Correa administration, even if Correa's attitudes seemingly radicalized over the course of his tenure (Varea 2016). From the beginning, Correa vehemently and regularly insisted that he would never approve abortion or same-sex marriage. This not only reflected the personal moral convictions so well articulated in this chapter's opening quote and the strength of Correa's alliance with powerful conservative constituencies, it also anticipated that on these issues, conservative religious constituencies would hold significantly more influence over the Correa administration than would feminists. These limitations began with specific and newly introduced concessions embedded in the constitution and guaranteed by Correa: the definition of marriage as between a man and a woman, a "right to life since conception," and a ban on adoption by same-sex couples. All of these clauses cemented new obstacles to decriminalizing abortion or gaining full equal marriage rights while forestalling later efforts to undo them and reinscribing the primacy of the heteropatriarchal family into the constitution. And though the constitution declared Ecuador to be secular—a change from the 1998 constitution—conservative groups won the explicit mention of God in the preamble (Morales 2015). These moves helped to secure enough conservative support to ensure the constitution's passage, but also created deeply rooted contradictions both within the document itself and between its more radical rights-granting aspects and their implementation.

Furthermore, while the constitution guaranteed Ecuadorians expansive rights, much like others in the region, it also bestowed significant power to the president and made fulfillment of rights significantly contingent upon executive political will and discretion even while it supposedly elevated the constitution as supreme (Villagómez 2013). As Correa's authoritarianism grew alongside expanding conservative influence, feminists saw the ever more forceful and blatant obstruction of those rights that contradicted Correa's conservative moral political nexus through varying forms of unilateral executive action. These included Correa's disruption of efforts to decriminalize abortion in all cases of rape in 2013 and the closure of Acción Ecológica. But in other instances as well, Correa relied on presidential decrees and vetoes to reverse or weaken feminist efforts.

In one of the most prejudicial examples, Correa issued a presidential decree in November 2014 to terminate the Estrategia Intersectorial de Prevención del Embarazo Adolescente y Planificación Familiar (National Intersectorial Strategy on Family Planning and the Prevention of Adolescent Pregnancy, or ENIPLA). Though its roots preceded Correa, the program's launch in 2010 had represented one of the few clear feminist policy achievements under the Correa administration and had been praised as a model by the UN (Viteri 2016). The strategy operationalized constitutional rights to comprehensive sexuality education and reproductive health services, provided free contraception (including emergency contraception for the first time), addressed gendered power relations through its curriculum and a national public health campaign, and responded to the country's alarming rates of adolescent pregnancy, which had risen significantly between 2002 and 2010 to over 20 percent, ranking second only to Venezuela in the South American region (Ministerio Coordinador de Desarrollo Social 2011; Pertierra 2015). For its first four years, supporters insisting on the right to a secular approach overpowered vocal conservative critics, and Ecuador achieved some of the highest reductions in adolescent pregnancy in the world between 2010 and 2013 (González 2015). But a conservative Catholic and Evangelical coalition mounted a steady lobbying effort to end the program. Correa commissioned Mónica Hernandez, who had joined Correa's advisory team in 2013, to spearhead a report evaluating ENIPLA (Varea 2015). In April 2014, Hernandez presented a report that fiercely critiqued ENIPLA on both moral and performance grounds. Six months later and without consulting its managing team, including Public Health minister Carina Vance, Correa abruptly terminated the program. He appointed Hernandez to draft a new plan titled the Plan Familia Ecuador (Plan for the Strengthening of the Family) and shifted oversight of the program to him personally (Pertierra 2015).

The overpowering influence of conservative family values in Correa's reasoning over that of constitutional secularism, feminist concerns, or constitutionally stipulated plural conceptions of the family were evident in his commentary. Correa claimed that Plan Familia would "rescue the role of the family as the basis of society," and specifically that moral "values" and the institution of the family would be the basis for the prevention of pregnancy (*La República* 2015). Parents and families, not health centers, would be properly tasked with sexuality education, he argued (*La República* 2015). Instead of deconstructing the gender stereotypes that underlie gender-based violence as ENIPLA did, Plan Familia instead reinforces gendered stereotypes based on romanticized, heteronormative notions of "love" that prescribe monogamy, heterosexuality, marriage, and abstinence, returning the heteropatriarchal family to the center of reproductive and sexual health policy.

Hernandez's public attacks extended even further, criticizing ENIPLA for promoting the now infamous "dangerous gender ideology" that Correa had warned against a few months earlier. She defended discredited faith-based abstinence approaches and criticized ENIPLA for "leav[ing] open or directly mention[ing] that homosexuality is something natural" (Pertierra 2015). She asserted that "gender" is a mere "invention of the dangerous ideology of gender," arguing that it is proven that "in societies in which there is not this unnatural influence there are not these divergences among sex and gender" (Pertierra 2015). Further, she argued, as the only kind of "gender" that exists is the grammatical one, the state should not "espouse as natural or normal that there are persons that have a different gender identity with respect to their biological sex and different sexual orientation" (Pertierra 2015), a claim made in direct contravention to the 2008 constitution's groundbreaking guarantees against discrimination on the basis of gender identity.

The clear influence of this discourse against gender—backed by a powerful, transnational network of conservative religious actors, including the Vatican—revealed itself again in 2016 when Correa gutted the proposed gender identity law via partial presidential veto. In 2012, a broad-based coalition of eighteen LGBT and allied feminist groups overcame their differences to jointly campaign for a long-standing collective goal based upon the expanded constitutional rights to identity and nondiscrimination: the "universal right to gender identity." The coalition demanded the adoption of "universal gender," proposing to *replace* the civil category "sex" with that of "gender" on national identification cards and to allow anyone to change one's official gender at will. The group drafted the proposed law led by lawyer Elizabeth Vásquez, extensively lobbied assemblypersons, and led a public campaign with the mottos "*My* Gender on *My* ID Card" and "Everyone has gender, [so] gender for everyone."

The proposal initially faced the onslaught of conservative backlash from the usual suspects. Using language bearing the influence of their regional and global profamily movement counterparts, conservative groups such as Vida, Familia, y Libertad (Life, Family, Liberty), Familias Unidas (United Families), Red Pro Vida y Familia (Pro-Life and Family Network), and 14 Millones (14 Million) argued that this was a quintessential example of the dangerous imposition of "gender ideology" aimed to destroy the family and a ploy to enable workarounds to allow same-sex marriage and adoption (Wilkinson 2017). After submitting a petition of 42,000 signatures protesting the idea, this opposing alliance secured assurances from Correa that he would stand against the proposal (*El Universo* 2015).

Committee debates rendered the proposed "gender" replacement optional rather than universal and stipulated that altered cards would be made pink, moves that not only increased—rather than decreased—the potential for discrimination but also eviscerated the transformative potential and intent of the proposed law. Correa gutted the remainder, vetoing the majority of its articles and insisting that "sex" continue to be registered at birth and remain unchanged except in cases of "error," referring to intersex cases. His proposal allowed sex to be replaced with gender only once after age eighteen, by judicial order only, and on identification cards but not birth certificates—a provision that would surely stave off the feared attempts to "bypass" same-sex marriage and adoption bans. He further mandated that requestors procure two witnesses, and—redundantly—reiterated that adoption be allowed only between opposite-sex couples, which resulted in newly codifying a ban on adoption by single mothers (*El Universo* 2016).

While the coalition advocated for the restoration of universality, Asociación Silueta X's Rodriguez launched a spin-off group, Revolución Trans, to support Correa's proposal in an effort to ensure its passage. She argued that Correa's proposal to require witnesses was intended to protect transgender people from nontrans individuals such as criminals who might abuse the law to fake or mask their identity. With the pretense of backing from the LGBT community behind him, Correa's version was adopted in its entirety in January 2016. Later, Rodriguez claimed the victory as her own. When the identification cards became available in August 2016, hers was the first to be issued.

Ultimately, while the trans community gained "crumbs" in the form of nominal legal gender identity recognition, the final product reversed the original intent of the law by swapping one form of discrimination for another. Those who wished to access the benefits of identification that conformed with their gender presentation—critical for improving sorely needed access to education, housing, employment, and medical care among trans persons—did so at the cost of calling further attention to their status. One activist pointed to two factors in lamenting and explaining the loss: "It so happens that conservative forces are very well organized and have a lot of representation inside the executive, despite that a majority of the Legislature supported our proposal. And it is also the case that the fracturing and cooptation of the [LGBT] movement bore fruit" (comment on Pacto Trans Ecuador Facebook page, January 29, 2016, translated by author).

In addition to the de jure contradictions in the constitutional rights of women and sexual minorities and the de facto contingencies in their implementation detailed in this section so far, legal advancements have in some respects disguised setbacks and derogations of rights—those both newly enshrined in the constitution and those predating it—in substantive ways. In particular, the most important gains of the women's movement of the 1990s—violence against women legislation, the state women's agency, and legislation protecting pregnancy and mothers—have been progressively dismantled or weakened. For example, while the legal constitution of CNIG in 2014 appeared to operationalize the constitution's commitment to ensuring gender equality, in reality it served as the final nail in CONAMU's coffin. While feminists were able to maintain the debated text of another of the women's movement's key gains of the 1990s—the Ley de Maternidad Gratuita y Atención a la Infancia (Free Maternity and Infant Attention Law), which established key protections related to women's sexual and reproductive rights—the law was severed from its budget source leaving it intact on paper but utterly defunct in practice (Buendía 2015).

Violence against women, a long-standing target of women's and feminist movements, remains epidemic. A 2010 national prevalence survey found that seven out of ten women nationwide experienced violence (including physical, sexual, and psychological), most commonly at the hands of their partners (Chaher 2014). Yet violence against women protections have weakened since the women's movement pushed through groundbreaking Law 103 in the 1990s. This law had criminalized violence against women, designated funds and support to police units devoted to responding to this type of violence, and provided immediate protection to victims. In the process of revising Ecuador's Penal Code in 2013, Law 103 "had its teeth removed" as one activist put it (Maldonado 2015). As in Chile and elsewhere, the paradigm of "violence against women" that women had fought for was changed to "intrafamily violence," placing violence against women once again in the private sphere of the heteropatriarchal family. The change also stripped the immediate victim protections provided by Law 103, and expanded sentences—seemingly strengthening the law—rather served to further disincentivize access to justice (Buendía 2014).

Relatedly, while the crime of femicide was finally codified during these same debates—a long-standing feminist demand—it lacked sufficient mechanisms for enforcement and gave substantial favor to aggressors (Buendía 2014). In 2011, new legal units were set up to process and respond to cases of violence against women, replacing those set up in the 1990s by Law 103. While the Correa administration touted these as among its greatest successes for women, the change in fact did away with nearly two decades of institutional experience, leaving significant gaps in training and geographical coverage (Buendía 2014; Coalición Nacional de Organizaciones de Mujeres 2014).

As new constitutional definitions and silenced debates have thwarted and set back efforts to decriminalize abortion, feminist activists report that in recent years, women have actually faced increased prosecution for suspected abortions under previously unenforced laws (Varea 2016; Buendía and Calapaqui 2016). Feminist observers have gathered over 150 such cases between 2009 and 2015 and in this time period registered the first known incarceration of a woman for abortion (Colectivo Salud Mujeres 2016). The spike in charges against women followed the Penal Code's increased criminalization of licensed medical providers for performing illegal abortions and public radio campaigns encouraging the public to report suspected illegal abortions (Colectivo Salud Mujeres 2016). With unsafe abortions remaining the second leading cause of death among women of reproductive age (Buendía 2014), the backlash against abortion is deadly.

Meanwhile, outcomes for sexual minorities have been more mixed. The obstacles sexual minorities faced over the past ten years were distinct from the frontal attacks launched at women's reproductive rights. The former often manifested as a lack or uneven implementation of laws or policies that appear to deliver on LGBT rights priorities but achieve only a modicum of their intent or potential, as demonstrated in the case of the 2016 Gender Law. In another example, while the constitution provisioned civil partnerships for same-sex couples with the same rights and responsibilities as marriage, it guaranteed rights and responsibilities only once achieved—not in the process of procuring the status itself. The fine print made it available to those "who form a de facto couple [hogar], since the time and under the conditions and circumstances specified by law" (Constitución Política de la República del Ecuador 2008, 32, translated by the author). In reality this meant that the required waiting period and expensive fees, something that marriages—free and instant—do not require, left many lesbians and gay men unable to access civil partnerships. This was not the only hurdle. The Civil Registry refused to process them due to unresolved legal contradictions. Correa waited until September 2014 to order the Civil Registry to officially include civil partnerships as a valid civil status, and so the first civil unions were finally registered only six years later. Still other barriers remain: as of 2014, only a few notaries in the country provided the required first step, and a lack of perceived legitimacy has created conditions for discrimination and extortion. For example, one same-sex couple alleged that a notary attempted to charge them seven times the stated fee (Jaramillo and Paucar 2014).

In the end, the promises of recognition for "diverse families" and the equal rights to marriage guaranteed by the constitution have resulted in sorely uneven outcomes. Even though a woman was granted access to her same-sex partner's pension upon her death in 2011 for the first time (Lind and Keating 2013), by 2016 another lesbian family had unsuccessfully fought for more than five years since the birth of their daughter to secure the legal recognition of both mothers' parental rights, with significant consequences for the family (Fundacion Causana 2016). While the transformational potential of the 2008 constitution—most especially the resignification of the family—is both groundbreaking and alive, efforts over the last decade to transform the heteropatriarchal power relations on which gender inequality rests have taken one step forward and two steps back.

Conclusion

The Citizen Revolution, which Correa claimed to have awakened Ecuador from the lost decade of its "long neoliberal night," has put feminist aspirations of transformative gender and sexual justice to rest and resulted in a lost decade for women's rights and gender equality. Its tenure has marked a decade of failure to implement feminist agendas to transform heteropatriarchal power relations. With feminist agendas positioned as a traitorous and dangerous threat to the Citizen Revolution, it is unsurprising that women faced setbacks so significant that some named the Correa administration the worst government for women since before Ecuador's return to democracy in the 1980s (Buendía and Calapaqui 2016). Women's long-term economic equality remains insecure while short-term gains have not led to gender equality and have even undermined current and future attempts to address it. At particular expense to rural and indigenous women, the neoextractive development model pursued by Correa continues to operate under the false premise—and false promise—that redistributing wealth automatically resolves other forms of inequality, including gender inequality, no matter its costs.

After ten years, the ability to advance feminist agendas is weaker despite the increased formal political representation of women. Women's movements are more divided than before, social movements and women human rights defenders have recently faced the worst repression in three decades, and the unprecedented legal gains of the women's movement in the 1990s were progressively dismantled—leaving women worse off in some ways under the "New Left" than they were under earlier conservative neoliberal governments. Under the Correa administration, women were more subject to the Citizen Revolution than subjects of the Citizen Revolution. While sexual minorities gained undeniably important protections, they too stopped short of significantly transforming the heteropatriarchal power relations that underlie and reproduce gender and sexual inequalities and pointed to a contradictory rather than clearly pro-LGBT administration.

What gained momentum over the past decade were the consolidation of presidential power and the presence of the heteropatriarchal family in political discourse and social policy. As I have shown in this chapter, despite the constitution's transformative resignification of the family, the Correa administration mounted a consistent defense of the "conventional" heteropatriarchal family as the "nucleus of society." This materialized in law, policy, and practice. Thus, while the Citizen Revolution brought about the return of the state, it trafficked with it the return of the heteropatriarchal family, ensuring that it became as entrenched at the center of the state as Correa did himself.

As with Ortega and Murillo in Nicaragua, Correa made clear that his government had not broken with the historical left's Marxist legacy of demoting feminist concerns to the status of detractor rather than finding them integral to achieving material equality itself. "Gender ideology," he challenged, is not even a matter of ideology at all—which is "based above all upon material conditions, the mode of production"—and simply doesn't deserve "so much discussion" (Secretaria Nacional de Comunicación 2013). To the extent that the self-proclaimed "New Left" under the Citizen Revolution in Ecuador has derogated feminist aspirations for gender equality, it is neither new where the left is concerned, nor alone, as many of the chapters in this volume attest.

Notes

Epigraph: Secretaria Nacional de Comunicación 2013.

1. This includes participant observation during extensive fieldwork between 2010 and 2012 while affiliated with the Program in Gender and Cultural Studies at

FLACSO-Ecuador, as well as informal and formal interviews with LGBT and feminist activists and researchers between 2014 and 2016.

2. Executive director, Ecuadorian feminist organization, personal communication with author, August 10, 2009, San Francisco, United States.

3. Alianza Patria Altiva y Soberana (Proud and Sovereign Homeland Alliance). The acronym PAIS also means "country." Alianza PAIS was formally constituted on top of a series of previous movements and organizations and in initial coalition with an array of political actors, including the Ecuadorian Socialist Party and the Communist Party of Ecuador, and later other political parties, though it did not emerge with or ever fully consolidate a broad national base.

4. Correa held approval ratings of 70 percent in official polls in 2012 (Ghosh 2012) and was elected in the first round by nearly 57 percent of the vote in the 2013 elections (Freidenberg 2013).

5. The 2017 presidential race was hotly contested, bearing the scars of the significant loss of popular support suffered by the Correa administration in its final years. But ultimately, an electorate still reluctant to return a neoliberal conservative to power narrowly voted to continue Alianza PAIS' Citizen Revolution under uncertain circumstances.

6. The proposal to decriminalize abortion in all cases of rape was a response to the fact that 65 percent of Ecuadorians support the decriminalization of abortion in cases of rape (Pertierra 2015). Correa called the assemblywomen traitors when he stated that "anything that challenges life from the moment of conception is quite simply, treason" (Ruptura and International Network of Human Rights n/d, 6, translated by author).

7. For example, "Gordita horrorosa, cállate majadera, coloradita, mediocre, mafiosa, tirapiedras, malcriadas, tipas, ¡qué minifaldas!, ¡qué piernas!, etc." These roughly translate to: horrible little fatty (condescending connotation if not overtly negative); shut up, ignorant woman; little colored woman; mediocre; gangster; rock thrower; rude or unrefined; that "type" (objectifying connotation); what miniskirts!; what legs!, etc. (Buendía and Calapaqui Tapia 2016, 5).

8. For an overview of the history and development of the Ecuadorian women's movement, see Lind 2012a, 2005; Radcliffe 2008.

9. For a brief history of these events see Lind and Keating 2013.

10. For dozens of meticulously documented cases, see Buendía and Calapaqui 2016.

11. Though the administration denied a link, Vance was appointed amid international outcry regarding Ecuador's burgeoning crisis over private forced sexual conversion abuses (see Wilkinson 2013).

12. For detailed discussion of various forms of discourse on sexuality, rights, and social change, including critiques of liberal nationalist discourses of LGBT rights, see Jasbir Puar's analysis of homonationalism (Puar 2007).

13. *Buen vivir* (good living)—or *sumac kawsay* in its original Kichwa form—is a broad concept derived from the worldview of many Andean indigenous peoples

that refers to a balanced and harmonious relationship between people and the natural world, in both material and spiritual terms.

References

Agencia Efe. 2015. "Ecuador, premiado por sus políticas para lograr la igualdad de género." *El Comercio*, March 24. Accessed July 8, 2016. http://www.elcomercio .com/actualidad/ecuador-premiado-politicas-igualdad-genero.html# .VRLVU9K05-w.facebook.

Aguinaga Barragán, Alba. 2014. "Análisis feminista de coyuntura del gobierno de Rafael Correa y la dinámica política del movimiento de mujeres y feminista, 2010–2012." BA thesis, Universidad Central del Ecuador. http://www.dspace.uce .edu.ec/handle/25000/2248.

Alexis González, Mario. 2016. "De 89 proyectos propuestos por mujeres, solo dos se aprobaron." *El Comercio*, July 20. http://www.elcomercio.com/actualidad /proyectos-mujeres-asambleistas-genero-politica.html.

Andrade, Pablo Roberto. 2016. "Post-Correa Ecuador? 2017 Scenarios and Beyond." Presentation at the International Congress of the Latin American Studies Association , May 27–30.

Asociación Silueta X. 2016a. "Hoy transexuales cambiaron su sexo por género en la cédula en Ecuador." *Plataforma Revolucion Trans Ecuador*, August 3. https:// revoluciontrans.com/2016/08/03/hoy-transexuales-cambiaron-su-sexo-por -genero-en-la-cedula-en-ecuador/.

Asociación Silueta X. 2016b. "LGBT RECHAZAMOS PARO NACIONAL—BOLETÍN DE PRENSA / LGBT REJECT NATIONAL STRIKE—PRESS RELEASE." Accessed July 13, 2017. https://groups.google.com/forum/?hl=de#!topic /asociacionsiluetax/I9c7et9SI7k.

Association for Women's Rights in Development (AWID). 2015. "'Protection of the Family': What It Means for Human Rights." *AWID Blog*. December 9. http:// www.awid.org/news-and-analysis/protection-family-what-it-means-human -rights.

Association for Women's Rights in Development (AWID). 2016. "The Devil Is in the Details: At the Nexus of Development, Women's Rights, and Religious Fundamentalisms." Toronto, Canada: AWID. http://www.awid.org/sites/default/files /atoms/files/final_web_the_devil_is_in_the_details.pdf.

Basabe-Serrano, Santiago. 2009. "Ecuador: Reforma constitucional, nuevos actores políticos y viejas prácticas partidistas." *Revista de Ciencia Política (Santiago)* 29 (2): 381–406.

Becker, Marc. 2015. "Ecuador's New Indigenous Uprising." *Upside Down World*, August 12. http://upsidedownworld.org/main/ecuador-archives-49/5422-ecuadors -new-indigenous-uprising.

Buendía, Silvia. 2014. "Las leyes que caminan para atrás ¿Por qué las mujeres ecuatorianas tienen menos derechos que antes?" *GKillCity*, October 27. http:// gkillcity.com/articulos/fuck-you-curuchupa/las-leyes-que-caminan-atras.

Buendía, Silvia. 2015. "Ecuador aprueba una ley que discrimina a mujeres solas, a lesbianas y a trans." *20 Minutos*, December 11. http://blogs.20minutos.es/1-de -cada-10/2015/12/11/reforma-registro-civil-ecuador/.

Buendía, Silvia, and Karla Calapaqui Tapia. 2016. *Rafael Correa: 9 años de violencia contra las mujeres*. Malcriadas.org. https://malcriadasdotorg.files.wordpress.com /2016/03/9anios_-violencia.pdf.

Chaher, Sandra. 2014. "El presidente Correa tiene una fuerte convicción cristiana frente a los temas de género." *Comunicar Igualdad*, November 27.

Coalición Nacional de Organizaciones de Mujeres para la elaboración del Informe Sombra al Comité de la CEDAW. 2014. "Informe sombra al Comité de la CEDAW Ecuador 2014." Quito. http://media.wix.com/ugd/273e4d_8109bbb4e95042f7938 8c7e102fb9600.pdf.

Colectivo Miradas Críticas del Territorio desde el Feminismo (CMCTF). 2014a. "La vida en el centro y el crudo bajo tierra: El Yasuní en clave feminista." Quito: Colectivo Miradas Críticas del Territorio desde el Feminismo. https:// miradascriticasdelterritoriodesdeelfeminismo.files.wordpress.com/2014/05 /yasunienclavefeminista.pdf.

Colectivo Miradas Críticas del Territorio desde el Feminismo (CMCTF). 2014b. "Encuentro de mujeres frente al extractivismo y al cambio climático." Quito: Colectivo Miradas Críticas del Territorio desde el Feminismo. https:// territorioyfeminismos.org/2014/10/15/encuentro-de-mujeres-frente-al -extractivismo-y-al-cambio-climatico/.

Colectivo Salud Mujeres. 2016. Representative of Colectivo Salud Mujeres, personal interview, Bahia, Brazil, September 8, 2016.

Conaghan, Catherine. 2011. "Rafael Correa and the Citizen Revolution." In *The Resurgence of the Latin American Left*, edited by Steven Levitsky and Kenneth M. Roberts, 260–82. Baltimore, MD: Johns Hopkins University Press.

Conaghan, Catherine, and Carlos de la Torre. 2008. "The Permanent Campaign of Rafael Correa: Making Ecuador's Plebiscitary Presidency." *International Journal of Press/Politics* 13 3:267–84. doi:10.1177/1940161208319464.

Consejo Nacional de Igualded de Genero (CNIG). 2015. "CNIG Logros." http://www .igualdadgenero.gob.ec/images/saladeprensa/ok-cnig_Logros20de%20la%20 Revolucin.pdf.

Constitución Política de la República del Ecuador, 2008. October 20. Accessed February 21, 2018. http://www.refworld.org/docid/3dbd62fd2.html.

Dávalos, Pablo. 2014. *Alianza PAIS, o, La reinvención del poder: Siete ensayos sobre el posneoliberalismo en el Ecuador*.

El Ciudadano. 2016. "Bowen: La lucha de la equidad de género ha sido una bandera de este gobierno y se debe mantener." June 14. http://www.elciudadano.gob.ec /bowen-las-mujeres-durante-estos-anos-hemos-podido-actuar-antes-eramos -usadas-como-figuras/.

Ellner, Steve. 2012. "The Distinguishing Features of Latin America's New Left in Power: The Governments of Hugo Chavez, Evo Morales, and Rafael Correa."

Latin American Perspectives, January 17. http://venezuelanalysis.com/analysis
/6754.

Elwood, Sarah, Patrick Bond, Carmen Martínez Novo, and Sarah Radcliffe. 2016.
"Learning from Postneoliberalisms." *Progress in Human Geography*. 41, no. 5
(October 2017): 676–95. doi:10.1177/0309132516648539.

El Universo. 2015. "Cambios en cédula de identidad a debate final." October 20.
http://www.eluniverso.com/noticias/2015/10/20/nota/5194559/cambios-cedula
-debate-final.

El Universo. 2016. "Molestia en AP por parte de veto a Ley de Identidad." January 19.
http://www.eluniverso.com/noticias/2016/01/19/nota/5354944/molestia-ap-parte
-veto-ley-identidad.

Escandón Guevara, Francisco. 2016. "¿La década ganada? Un año atrás el sim-
bolismo." Accessed July 11, 2016. https://www.facebook.com/photo.php?fbid
=10208504067734728&set=a.1960129878444.114238.1098703843&type=3.

Federación Ecuatoriana LGBT. 2016. "Rechazo a encuentros donde se convoca
a líderes LGBTI con el fin de adoctrinarlos bajo el odio." AsociaciónSiluetaX,
August. https://siluetax.files.wordpress.com/2016/08/rechazo-a-encuentros
-donde-se-convoca-a-lideres-lgbti-con-el-fin-de-adoctrinarlos-bajo-el-odio-2
.jpg.

Freidenberg, Flavia. 2013. "Ecuador 2013: Las claves del éxito de la revolución ciudadana." Fundación Alternativas, Memorando OPEX, 185. http://works.bepress
.com/flavia_freidenberg/75/.

Friedman, Elisabeth Jay. 2009. "Gender, Sexuality and the Latin American Left:
Testing the Transformation." *Third World Quarterly* 30 (2): 415–33.

Fundacion Causana. 2016. "Boletín de prensa audiencia familia Bicknell Rothon."
Fundacion Causana, March 28.

Ghosh, Jayati. 2012. "Could Ecuador Be the Most Radical and Exciting Place on
Earth?" *Guardian*, January 19.

González, Mario Alexis. 2015. "Ecuador reduce los índices de embarazos adolescentes." *El Comercio*, November 11. http://www.elcomercio.com/tendencias/ecuador
-indices-embarazosadolescentes-salud-educacion.html.

Grugel, Jean, and Pía Riggirozzi. 2012. "Post-Neoliberalism in Latin America:
Rebuilding and Reclaiming the State after Crisis." *Development and Change* 43
(1): 1–21.

Gudynas, Eduardo. "The New Extractivism of the 21st Century: Ten Urgent Theses
about Extractivism in Relation to Current South American Progressivism."
Amercias Policy Program, January 21, 2010.

Jaramillo, Elena, and Andrés Paucar. 2014. "La unión de hecho constará en la
cédula como un estado civil." *El Comercio*, September 14.

La Hora. 2016. "Las 'Mujeres del levantamiento' siguen en la 'pelea.'" Accessed
July 11, 2016. http://lahora.com.ec/index.php/noticias/show/1101853869/-1
/Las_%E2%80%98Mujeres_del_levantamiento%E2%80%99_siguen_en_la
_%E2%80%98pelea %E2%80%99.html.

La República. 2015. "Correa propone la abstinencia como alternativa para reducir el embarazo adolescente." February 28.

Lind, Amy. 2002. "Making Feminist Sense of Neoliberalism: The Institutionalization of Women's Struggles for Survival in Ecuador and Bolivia." *Journal of Developing Societies* 18 (2–3): 228–58.

Lind, Amy. 2005. *Gendered Paradoxes: Women's Movements, State Restructuring, and Global Development in Ecuador*. University Park: Pennsylvania State University Press.

Lind, Amy. 2012a. "'Revolution with a Woman's Face'? Family Norms, Constitutional Reform, and the Politics of Redistribution in Post-Neoliberal Ecuador." *Rethinking Marxism* 24, no. 4 (October 2012): 536–55. https://doi.org/10.1080/08935696.2012.711058.

Lind, Amy. 2012b. "Contradictions That Endure: Family Norms, Social Reproduction, and Rafael Correa's Citizen Revolution in Ecuador." *Politics & Gender* 8 (2): 254–61.

Lind, Amy, and Christine ("Cricket") Keating. 2013. "Navigating the Left Turn: Sexual Justice and the Citizen Revolution in Ecuador." *International Feminist Journal of Politics* 15 (4): 515–33.

Maldonado, Sarahí. 2015. Member of Colectivo Salud Mujeres, personal interview online, September 21.

Ministerio Coordinador de Desarrollo Social. 2011. "Estrategia Intersectorial de Prevención del Embarazo Adolescente y Planificación Familiar (ENIPLA)." Accessed May 11, 2017. http://www.desarrollosocial.gob.ec/wp-content/uploads/downloads/2015/04/Proyecto_enipla.pdf.

Montúfar, César, Enrique Herrería, Carlos Pérez Guartambel, and Delfín Tenesaca. 2014. "El derecho a reunirnos en paz: El decreto 16 y las amenazas a la organización social en el Ecuador." Quito: Fundamedios.

Morales Alfonso, Liudmila. 2015. "Claroscuro: Voces y silencios sobre el aborto en la Cuba revolucionaria y el Ecuador de la Revolución Ciudadana." MA diss., FLACSO Ecuador. http://repositorio.flacsoandes.edu.ec/handle/10469/8424.

Novo, Carmen Martínez. 2014. "Managing Diversity in Postneoliberal Ecuador." *Journal of Latin American and Caribbean Anthropology* 19 (1): 103–25. doi:10.1111/jlca.12062.

Oxfam. 2009. "Women, Communities and Mining: The Gender Impacts of Mining and the Role of Gender Impact Assessment." Carlton, Australia: Oxfam Australia. https://policy-practice.oxfam.org.uk/publications/women-communities-and-mining-the-gender-impacts-of-mining-and-the-role-of-gende-293093.

Pertierra, Irina. 2015. "La 'Revolución Ciudadana' en Ecuador y los derechos de las mujeres." *Pikara Magazine*, April 29. Accessed June 15, 2017. http://www.pikaramagazine.com/2015/04/la-revolucion-ciudadana-en-ecuador-y-los-derechos-de-las-mujeres/.

Pew Research Center. 2014. "Religion and Morality in Latin America." *Pew Research Center's Religion & Public Life Project*. Accessed July 25, 2016. http://www.pewforum.org/interactives/latin-america-morality-by-religion/.

Picq, Manuela Lavinas. 2013. "Lawfare: Ecuador's New Style of Governance?" *Upside Down World*, October. http://www.upsidedownworld.org/main/ecuador -archives-49/4515-lawfare-ecuadors-new-style-of-governance.

Polga-Hecimovich, John. 2013. "Ecuador: Estabilidad institucional y la consoli- dación de poder de Rafael Correa." *Revista de Ciencia Política (Santiago)* 33 (1): 135–60.

Prieto, Mercedes, ed. 2005. *Mujeres Ecuatorianas: Entre las crisis y las oportuni- dades, 1990–2004.* Quito: CONAMU, FLACSO, UNIFEM, UNFPA.

Puar, Jasbir K. 2007. *Terrorist Assemblages: Homonationalism in Queer Times.* Dur- ham, NC: Duke University Press.

Radcliffe, Sarah A. 2008. "Women's Movements in Twentieth-Century Ecuador." In *The Ecuador Reader: History, Culture, Politics*, 284–96. Durham, NC: Duke University Press.

Radcliffe, Sarah A. 2013. "Gendered Frontiers of Land Control: Indigenous Terri- tory, Women and Contests over Land in Ecuador." *Gender, Place and Culture: A Journal of Feminist Geography* 21 (7): 854–71.

Ramos, Zuania. 2013. "Rafael Correa, Ecuadorian President, Apologizes to Gay Community during Reelection Speech." *Huffington Post*, February 22. http://www .huffingtonpost.com/2013/02/22/rafael-correa-gay-community_n_2743906.html.

Ray, Rebecca, and Sara Kozameh. 2012. "Ecuador's Economy Since 2007." Washing- ton, DC: Center for Economic and Policy Research.

Richards, Patricia. "Of Indians and Terrorists: How the State and Local Elites Construct the Mapuche in Neoliberal Multicultural Chile." *Journal of Latin American Studies* 42, no. 1 (February 2010): 59. https://doi.org/10.1017 /S0022216X10000052.

Riofrancos, Thea. 2015. "Beyond the Petrostate: Ecuador's Left Dilemma." *Dissent Magazine*, summer. https://www.dissentmagazine.org/article/riofrancos-beyond -petrostate-ecuador-left-dilemma.

Ruptura, and International Network of Human Rights. "Alternative Report on Civil and Political Rights Submitted to the 6th Periodic Report of Ecuador Human Rights Committee (CCPR), 117 Session. June 20–July 15, 2016," http://tbinternet .ohchr.org/Treaties/CCPR/Shared%20Documents/ECU/INT_CCPR_CSS_ECU _24068_E.pdf.

Sawyer, Suzana, and Edmund Terence Gomez, 2012. "Transnational Governmental- ity in the Context of Resource Extraction." In *The Politics of Resource Extraction: Indigenous Peoples, Multinational Corporations, and the State*, edited by Su- zana Sawyer and Edmund Terence Gomez, 1–8. International Political Economy Series. New York: Palgrave Macmillan: United Nations Research Institute for Social Development, 2012.

Secretaria Nacional de Comunicación (SECOM). 2013. "Enlace Ciudadano Nro. 354 desde Guayaquil, Guayas." *Enlace Ciudadano, Presidencia de la República del Ec- uador*. Filmed December 28, 2013. YouTube video. 3:31:15. Accessed July 21, 2016. https://www.youtube.com/watch?v=ODXFdqtGsyo.

Svampa, Maristella. 2016. *Debates latinoamericanos: indianismo, desarrollo, dependencia y populismo*. Buenos Aires: Edhasa.

Valencia Vargas, Areli S. 2015. "Women and the Deconstruction of the Promise of 'Inclusive Equality' in the Context of Extractive-Led Development: The Case of Ecuador." Presentation at the International Congress of the Latin American Studies Association, May 29–30.

Varea Viteri, María Soledad. 2015. "Actores del aborto: Estado, iglesia católica y movimiento feminista." PhD diss., FLACSO Ecuador. http://repositorio .flacsoandes.edu.ec/handle/10469/7871.

Varea Viteri, María Soledad. 2016. Academic researcher, personal interview, online, July 15, 2016.

Vasquez, Elisabeth. 2016. Director of Casa Trans, personal interview, Bahia, Brazil, September 11, 2016.

Villagómez Weir, Gayne. 2013. "La Revolución Ciudadana y las demandas de género." In *El correísmo al desnudo*, edited by Juan Cuvi, 54–69. Quito: Montecristi Vive.

Viteri, Maria Amelia. 2016. "Gender, Sexuality, Human Mobility, and Academic Freedom in Ecuador." *LASA Forum* 47 (2): 3.

von Gall, Anna. 2015. "Policy Paper: Litigation (Im)possible? Holding Companies Accountable for Sexual and Gender-Based Violence in the Context of Extractive Industries." Policy Paper, Berlin. Accessed July 19, 2016. https://www.boell.de/en /2015/09/08/policy-paper-litigation-impossible-holding-companies-accountable -sexual-and-gender-based.

Wappenstein, Susana, and Virginia Villamediana. 2013. "Estudio regional de las políticas públicas en el eje de género." In *Políticas sociales en América Latina y el Caribe: Escenarios contemporáneos, inversiones y necesidades*, edited by Adrián Bonilla Soria, Isabel Álvarez Echandi, and Stella Sáenz Breckenridge, 281–309. Quito: FLACSO.

Wilkinson, Annie. 2013. *"Sin sanidad, no hay santidad": Las prácticas reparativas en Ecuador*. Quito: FLACSO Ecuador.

Wilkinson, Annie. 2017. "Latin America's Gender Ideology Explosion." *Association for Queer Anthropology Section News*. March 21. http://www.anthropology-news .org/index.php/2017/03/21/latin-americas-gender-ideology-explosion/.

Xie, Selena, and Javier Corrales. 2010. "LGBT Rights in Ecuador's 2008 Constitution." In *The Politics of Sexuality in Latin America: A Reader on Lesbian, Gay, Bisexual, and Transgender Rights*, edited by Javier Corrales and Mario Pecheny, 224–29. Pittsburg: University of Pittsburgh Press.

Maneuvering the "U-Turn"

Comparative Lessons from the Pink Tide

and Forward-Looking Strategies for Feminist

and Queer Activisms in the Americas

SONIA E. ALVAREZ

This unprecedented, richly detailed collection analyzes some important advances in women's and queer/LGBT rights under governments of the Pink Tide, but the overall policy and political results of nearly two decades of Left and Center-Left rule are shown to be at best mixed, at worst disturbingly regressive. It's hard for the reader invested in gender/sexual justice not to walk away from it disheartened, indeed, disillusioned. Today, when the Pink Tide is clearly ebbing and a veritable right-wing tsunami is crashing in on much of the region, however, it is more critical than ever to assess what went wrong *and* what went right under governments of the "Left Turn" so as to envision strategies that might help feminists, queers, and other progressive forces to maneuver the sharp political "U-turn" under way in the Americas as whole.[1]

In addition to brazen, boldfaced class warfare, the U-turn represents a visceral reaction to the perceived successes of feminist, queer, antiracist, indigenous, human rights, and environmental movements under the Pink Tide. The multiple limitations and contradictions detailed in this volume's chapters don't seem to have assuaged the trans-homophobic, misogynist, racist Right's wrath. The U-turn has, in effect, ushered in what I call a "postneoliberal Right." Brazil's Michel Temer and his cronies, as well as their reactionary counterparts elsewhere in the Americas, do not merely represent a return to 1990s-style neoliberalism. Many neoliberals are/were "liberal," after all, in the classic sense of promoting individual rights or recognition that would facilitate more effective integration into the market—remember "neoliberal multiculturalism" (Hale and Millamán 2006)—and make the gender and racialized poor less dependent on the state.

Today's postneoliberal Right still adheres to many of the economic doctrines that have driven neoliberalism for decades (that's why it's "post"), but it also promotes a selectively active state, one that would again intervene in the interests of its cronies/constituents who lost privileges under the Left—like the elite, white monopoly of the university, in the case in Brazil. Seeking a return to righteous white, Western, Christian heterofamily values, it is a moralistic, often religiously fundamentalist, and, if you will, "intersectional" Right, one that wages open warfare against feminists, queers, transpeople, Afro-descendants, indigenous people, and other "others."

Feminists and other others are already working to turn this right-wing offensive around. In response to conservative leaders' efforts to criminalize abortion by making it difficult for health professionals in the national health service to assist women seeking abortions, for instance, Brazil's "Feminist Spring" brought tens of thousands of (mostly young, often queer and trans) women into the streets in November 2015. The misogynist attacks spearheading the right-wing's efforts to impeach President Dilma Rousseff were also central in spurring these mass mobilizations of women, the first public protests to condemn the opposition's ultimately successful drive to secure a legislative coup (M. Matos 2017; Veloso et al. 2017).

Feminists today have taken the lead in reimagining Left opposition and are prominent among emergent actors who position themselves to the left of Left-Turn governments and parties. These include autonomist, anarchist, and neo-Leninist political groups; variegated feminist-queer-transgender formations; as well as a variety of recent protest movements that claim to be redefining democratic practices and social justice agendas. Feminists and queer activists struggle to make gender, race, and sexual politics central to this post-Left-Turn Left and to a reconstituted Left more generally. In so doing, they perhaps would be well advised to heed some of the lessons offered in this book as to what worked and what didn't under Pink Tide governments.

One clear takeaway is the importance of coalition building across institutional arenas, engaging civic and state actors. Creating a "dense network among feminist NGOs, grassroots women's groups, women in trade unions and political parties, and female legislators" that was "multinodal" as well as "multisited" was found to be critical for Uruguayan feminists' relative success, for instance (chapter 1). And "issue networks" comprised of activists, professionals, and government representatives, along with judicial activism, were essential for pushing forward gender and sexual justice demands in Argentina, according to Constanza Tabbush, María Constanza Díaz, Catalina Trebisacce, and Victoria Keller (chapter 2).

The greatest policy gains were evident in cases such as that of Uruguay, where feminists organized "autonomously" within the ruling FA coalition, a kind of "auto-organização" or self-organization strategy similar to that enacted by the World March of Women and other organized feminist groupings active within the PT, the PCdoB, and other progressive/Left social movements and parties in Brazil. Moreover, feminists and queer activists appear to have been most successful where they had engaged in long-term advocacy within progressive parties or party coalitions that had been building social constituencies for a number of years, even decades, prior to gaining the presidency, as was the case with the PT in Brazil and the Socialists in Chile. They faced greater obstacles where their partisan activism was necessarily shorter-lived, in contexts where the Pink Tide coalition or party that came to power was emergent, or younger, as was the case with Chávez's Bolivarianism or Morales's MAS.

While the MAS granted "greater legal recognition of many traditionally marginalized groups," Shawnna Mullenax's chapter 5 shows that "the extent to which these groups have been successful depends largely on their relationship to the state." Proximity to the ruling coalition did not necessarily lead to policy gains, moreover, as many among the significant number of women in government were mere "'puppets' selected to run for office by the men in power because they could be easily controlled." Indeed, seeking to elect women or LGBT folks to office as a key to advancing movement goals would appear to be a common strategy in need of significant reconsideration. As Elisabeth Jay Friedman and Constanza Tabbush suggest in their introduction, the case studies in this volume "reveal a lack of correlation between high levels of women's descriptive representation and positive outcomes for women's rights."

This volume innovates in bringing gender and sexuality policy and state-society relations during the Pink Tide into sharp relief as never before. Seizing "political opportunities" opened by the Left and counting on "state allies" in a "framework of institutionalized political interactions," Friedman and Tabbush suggest, were essential to promoting feminist and queer policy agendas. But the chapters' almost exclusive focus on advocacy processes and policy outcomes may be at least part of the reason the book's overall political balance sheet tilts toward the side of mixed results or outright failures. In the past decade or so in particular, many queer and feminist innovations arguably occurred outside/beyond the state, beyond institutionalized interactions, in the streets, in the realms of media, culture, meanings, and representations. These novel efforts have (re)focused beyond the halls of governance to spaces and places of societal transformation. Started during the Pink Tide, their radical agendas and innovative strategies have expanded and intersected in reaction to the U-turn.

A (still cautiously) optimistic picture emerges when we look beyond policy and institutions to the realms of (trans)formative cultural and social change. *Feminismos callejeros*, or "street feminisms," for instance, also took advantage of the Left's political and cultural openings and flooded the sometimes staid, socially conventional and conservative Pink Tide with splashy and flashy, often ludic protests and performances. They founded hundreds of new *colectivas* throughout the region, many organized by young women, gay men, and trans folks in secondary schools and universities, others grounded in youth popular culture, in hip hop, rap, skate, capoeira, graffiti, and other interventions in the urban peripheries and in Afro and indigenous communities (Gonçalves et al. 2013; C. Matos 2017; Zanetti and Souza 2008). Decolonial feminist thought spread to many corners of the continent and further "decentered" the patriarchal, heteronormative premises that continued to inform the Left Turn (Costa 2016; Segato 2010).

Brazil's "Marchas das Vadias" and Spanish-speaking Latin America's "Marchas de las Putas," regional translations of the now global "Slut Walk" phenomenon, have mobilized tens of thousands of young women, transfeminists, and solidary gay and straight young men in dozens of cities since their first editions in 2011. Literally embodying their feminisms by emblazoning gender nonconforming, queer, antiracist, prosocial justice, and trans-inclusive slogans on their bodies, the Putas'/Vadias' rebellious public defiance of gender and sexual norms brazenly enacts a radical cultural politics (Carr 2014; Ferreira 2013; Name and Zanetti 2013). Feminists and queers have been on the frontlines of many recent pro-democracy, pro-social-justice protest movements throughout the region as well—from Mexico's Yo Soy 132 to Chilean student movements of the 2010s to Brazil's June 2013 uprisings and anti–World Cup, anti–Olympic organizing (Balaguera 2015; Larrabure and Torchia 2015; Mattos 2014).

Since its first massive (300,000-strong) march in Buenos Aires and other Argentine cities in June 2015 to condemn femicide, Ni Una Menos has spread like a veritable tidal wave to other countries in the region (Friedman and Tabbush 2016). Brazil's 2015 Black Women's March against Racism and Violence and for Living Well made cultural politics the centerpiece of its nationwide organizing, featuring Afro-religiosity, musicality, performance, social-interactive community events, hip hop, and a wide mix of ludic expressions to draw in women "who never went to hegemonic feminist meetings to engage in 'building the *Marcha*'" from wherever they were situated. The process explicitly called upon the full range of expressions of organized and heretofore unorganized sectors of Afro-Brazilian women and their allies (of whatever genders and races) to join them in loudly proclaiming black women as subjects of their own lives, of a transformed racially and gender conscious citizenship (Alvarez and Costa 2018). Afro-descendant feminists in Colombia also have organized numerous protest actions to challenge gendered racism and denounce black displacement by generalized but always racially gendered violence. Cyber-queer feminisms and black feminist cyberactivists such as Brazil's Blogueiras Negras or Cuba's Negra Cubana Tenia Que Ser have helped propel these protests, diffuse the messages that inspired them, and disseminate the post–Left-Turn Lefts' political imaginary more widely than ever before.[2]

Many among the *feministas, callejeras, anarcas, populares, negras, indígenas, decoloniales*, and queer political formations work in broad-based coalitions and engage in organizing around a wide range of social, racial, sexual, and social justice issues—matters that extrapolate the now "conventional" feminist and LGBT rights agendas. We must develop research strategies to probe the dynamics of such coalitions in an effort to contribute to their efficacy. Future research might also further explore the relationship between feminist and queer protest and performance and policy and electoral outcomes. Finally, in turning back the U-turn, we should identify and theorize the most effective ways of confronting right-wing and religious cultural politics with our own. To achieve the policies feminists and LGBT movements have long advocated requires not only policy advocacy directed at state institutions and their incumbents, but also building broader feminist- and queer-friendly constituencies through transformative social and cultural action.

Notes

1. On the Right's ascendance in Latin America, see especially NACLA's special issue, "Right Turn: The New and the Old in Latin America's Right-Wing Revival," vol. 48, no. 4 (March 2017).

2. See "African Descendant Feminisms in Latin America, Part I: Brazil," and "Afro-descendant Feminisms in Latin America, Part II: South and Central America and the Spanish-Speaking Caribbean," coedited by Sonia E. Alvarez, Kia Lilly Caldwell,

and Agustín Lao-Montes, special issue of *Meridians: feminism, race, transnationalism* 14 (1–2). For Brazil's Blogueiras Negras, see http://blogueirasnegras.org/. For Cuba's Negra Cubana Tenia Que Ser, see https://negracubanateniaqueser.com/.

References

Alvarez, Sonia E., Kia Lilly Caldwell, and Agustín Lao-Montes, eds. 2016. "African Descendant Feminisms in Latin America, Part I: Brazil" and "Afro-descendant Feminisms in Latin America, Part II: South and Central America and the Spanish-Speaking Caribbean." Special issue of *Meridians: feminism, race, transnationalism* 14 (1–2).

Alvarez, Sonia E. and Claudia de Lima Costa. 2018. "Turning to Feminisms: Re-Visioning Cultures, Power, and Politics in Latin America." In *New Approaches to Latin American Studies: Culture and Power*, edited by Juan Poblete, 161–78. New York: Routledge.

Balaguera, Martha. 2015. "Student Activism in Mexico from 1968 to Yo Soy 132: Transnationalism, Memory and Protest Temporalities." Paper delivered at the University of Texas Austin Lozano Long Conference "Nuevas Disidencias: Youth Culture, Transnational Flows, and the Remaking of Politics in the Americas," February 19–20.

Carr, Joetta L. 2014. "The SlutWalk Movement: A Study in Transnational Feminist Activism." *Journal of Feminist Scholarship* 4 (spring): 24–38.

Costa, Claudia de Lima. 2016. "Gender and Equivocation: Notes on Decolonial Feminist Translations." In *The Palgrave Book on Gender and Development*, edited by Harcourt, Wendy, 48–61. New York: Palgrave MacMillan.

Ferreira, Gleidiane de S. 2013. "Feminismo e Redes Sociais na Marcha das Vadias no Brasil." *Revista Artemis* 15 (1): 33–43.

Friedman, Elisabeth J. and Constanza Tabbush. 2016. "#Ni Una Menos: Not One Woman Less, Not One More Death!" NACLA *Report on the Americas*, November 11. https://nacla.org/news/2016/11/01/niunamenos-not-one-woman-less-not-one-more-death.

Gonçalves, Eliane, Fátima Freitas, and Elismênnia Oliveira. 2013. "Das Idades transitórias: As 'jovens' no feminismo brasileiro contemporâneo, suas Ações e seus dilemas." *Revista Feminismos* 1 (3).

Hale, Charles R., and Rosamel Millamán. 2006. "Cultural Agency and Political Struggle in the Era of the *Indio Permitido*." In *Cultural Agency in the Americas*, edited by Doris Sommer, 281–304. Durham, NC: Duke University Press.

Larrabure, Manuel, and Carlos Torchia. 2015. "The 2011 Chilean Student Movement and the Struggle for a New Left." *Latin American Perspectives* 42 (5): 248–68.

Matos, Carolina. 2017. "New Brazilian Feminisms and Online Networks: Cyberfeminism, Protest and the Female 'Arab Spring.'" *International Sociology* 32 (3): 417–34.

Matos, Marlise. 2017. "Violência Política Sexista: As reconfigurações no campo de controle politico das mulheres na América Latina." Paper presented at the International Congress of the Latin American Studies Association, April 29–May 1.

Mattos, Amana. 2014. "On Sluts, Teachers, and Black Blocs: The Street and the Construction of Political Dissent in Brazil." *Signs* 40 (1): 69–74.

Name, Leo, and Julia Zanetti. 2013. "Meu Corpo, Minhas Redes: A Marcha das Vadias do Rio de Janeiro." Anais da ANPUR.

"Right Turn: The New and the Old in Latin America's Right-Wing Revival." 2017. NACLA *Report on the Americas*, March (48) 4.

Segato, Rita Laura. 2010. Género y colonialidad: En busca de claves de lectura y de un vocabulario estratégico descolonial. In *La cuestión descolonial*, edited by Aníbal Quijano and Julio Mejía Navarrete. Lima: Universidad Ricardo Palma—Cátedra América Latina y la Colonialidad del Poder.

Veloso, Ana Maria Conceição, Fabíola Mendonça de Vasconcelos, and Laís Ferreira. 2017. "As Duas Faces do Sexismo na Mídia: Como Marcela Temer e Dilma Rousseff (PT) são retratadas pela *Veja* e *Istoé.*" *Revista Observatório* 3 (1): 58–83.

Zanetti, Julia, and Patricia Souza. 2008. "Jovens no feminismo e no hip hop na busca por reconhecimento." Paper presented at the 26th Reunião Brasileira de Antropologia. June 1–4, Porto Seguro, Bahia, Brazil.

CONTRIBUTORS

SONIA E. ALVAREZ is director of the Center for Latin American, Caribbean and Latino Studies and Leonard J. Horwitz Professor of Latin American Politics and Society at the University of Massachusetts–Amherst. She is author or coeditor of *Engendering Democracy in Brazil: Women's Movements in Transition Politics*; *The Making of Social Movements in Latin America: Identity, Strategy, and Democracy*; *Cultures of Politics / Politics of Cultures: Re-visioning Latin American Social Movements*; *Translocalities/Translocalidades: Feminist Politics of Translation in the Latin/a Américas*; and *Beyond Civil Society: Activism, Participation and Protest*. She has published extensively, in Spanish and Portuguese, as well as English, with many essays written collaboratively, on topics including social movements, feminisms, NGOs, civil society, race/racism, transnational activism, and democratization. She is presently engaged in research on women/gender/sexuality in contemporary protest and co-coordinates an international research-action network on the global politics of protest.

MARÍA CONSTANZA DIAZ is a PhD student in anthropology at the Interdisciplinary Institute of Gender Studies, University of Buenos Aires. She has worked extensively with community-based women's groups and feminists in Buenos Aires as a consultant and community developer. She also teaches undergraduate courses on anthropology, gender, and sexuality, and supports activist-oriented research as part of the collective AntropoSex of the University of Buenos Aires. Her research areas include gender, sexuality and social movements, and lesbian and feminist activism. Currently, she is doing ethnographic research on Argentine lesbian and feminist movements. Her work has been published in edited volumes such as *Feminism, Lesbianism, and Motherhood in Argentina*, edited by Mónica Tarducci (2015).

RACHEL ELFENBEIN has a PhD in sociology from Simon Fraser University in Vancouver. She was a Fulbright scholar to Venezuela, where she undertook her dissertation fieldwork. Rachel also works as a popular and participatory educator, researcher, facilitator, and counselor with civil society organizations in southern Africa and North America on issues of youth, gender violence, HIV/AIDS, occupational health and safety, organization building, and children's, women's, and workers' rights.

ELISABETH JAY FRIEDMAN is professor of politics and Latin American studies at the University of San Francisco. She has published extensively in the area of gender politics, as well as on sexuality politics, in Latin America and globally. Her published works include *Interpreting the Internet: Feminist and Queer Counterpublics in Latin America* (2017); *Sovereignty, Democracy, and Global Civil Society: State-Society Relations at UN World Conferences*, with Kathryn Hochstetler and Ann Marie Clark (2005); *Unfinished Transitions: Women and the Gendered Development of Democracy in Venezuela, 1936–1996* (2000); and articles in journals including *Politics & Gender, Latin American Politics and Society, Signs, Women's Studies International,* and *Comparative Politics.* She is currently serving as an Editor-in-Chief of the *International Feminist Journal of Politics.*

NIKI JOHNSON has a PhD in politics and an MA in Latin American area studies from the University of London. She is a lecturer and researcher at the Institute of Political Science, Faculty of Social Sciences of the Universidad de la República (Uruguay), where she coordinates the Gender and Diversity Politics Research Area and the Postgraduate Diploma in Gender and Public Policy. Her research and publications cover issues in gender politics relating to political representation, candidate selection, gender quotas, legislative activity, and gender mainstreaming in public policy. Her most recent publications in English include "Marginalization of Women and Male Privilege in Political Representation in Uruguay," in *Gender and Representation in Latin America* (Leslie Schwindt-Bayer, ed., 2018) and articles in *Government and Opposition* and *Parliamentary Affairs.*

VICTORIA KELLER is a feminist researcher focused on gender and sexuality issues in health policy. She holds an MA in women and gender studies from the University of Toronto and currently works at the National Health Ministry on adolescence and sexual and reproductive rights. Her published work on gender and sexuality appears in book compilations such as *The Global Trajectories of Queerness: Re-thinking Same-Sex Politics in the Global South* (2015) as well as local health policy documents.

EDURNE LARRACOECHEA BOHIGAS was awarded her PhD in political science by the Institute of Latin American Studies, University of London in 2007. Since then she has lived in Nicaragua, where she has worked extensively with the local feminist movement as a consultant, teacher, and researcher. Some of the topics she has worked on in Nicaragua are women's political participation, gender analysis of local budgets, religion and feminism, the influence of religion in public secondary schools, and gender analysis of social policies. She teaches in the Gender and Development Masters degree of Universidad Centroamericana (UCA) in Managua.

AMY LIND is Mary Ellen Heintz Professor of Women's, Gender, and Sexuality Studies at the University of Cincinnati. Her areas of scholarship include feminist and queer studies, critical development studies, global political economy, postcolonial studies, transnational feminisms, social movements, and studies of neoliberal governance. She is the author of *Gendered Paradoxes: Women's Movements, State Restructuring, and Global Development in Ecuador* (2005), and editor of four volumes, including *Development, Sexual Rights and Global Governance* (2010) and *Feminist (Im)mobilities in Fortress North America: Rights, Citizenships, and Identities in Transnational Perspective*, coedited with Anne Sisson Runyan, Patricia McDermott, and Marianne Marchand (2013). Currently she is working on her new book *Decolonial Justice: Resignifying Nation, Economy, and Family in Ecuador* (with Christine Keating).

MARLISE MATOS is associate professor of political science at the Federal University of Minas Gerais and Director of the Women's Studies Program and of the Center for Feminist and Gender Interests. Her research is in the areas of gender relations, public policy evaluation, political representation and participation, social movements and minorities, and women's political activity. She also has experience in the areas of sociology and politics of gender relations, social inequalities, planning, evaluation and monitoring of public policies, human rights, and citizenship. Her publications include "Social Justice and Democratic Representation: Is It Possible to Democratically Include in Brazil? The Case of Female Political Candidates" in *Region and Power: Representations in Flux* (2010) and "Emergence of Intersectional Activist Feminism in Brazil: The Interplay of Local and Global Contexts," with Solange Simões, in *Global Currents in Gender and Feminisms: Canadian and International Perspectives*, edited by Glenda Tibe Bonifacio, (2017).

SHAWNNA MULLENAX holds a PhD in political science from the University of Colorado Boulder. Her research interests include gender politics, political attitudes and behaviors, inequality, and global development. Her dissertation examined the disconnect between rising gender egalitarian attitudes in the mass public and government accountability for improving gender equality. Her coauthored paper on the gendered networking patterns of Brazilian legislators was published in *Legislative Studies Quarterly*.

ANA LAURA RODRíGUEZ GUSTá has a PhD in sociology from the University of Notre Dame. She is a researcher at Consejo Nacional de Investigaciones Científicas y Técnicas in Argentina. She is a faculty member of the Schools of Politics and Government at the Universidad Nacional de San Martín. Her research and publications focus on gender and organizations and gender mainstreaming in public policy, with a comparative emphasis on Latin America.

DIEGO SEMPOL graduated in history from the Instituto de Profesores Artigas (IPA), and has a postgraduate degree in contemporary history from the CLAEH University Institute, and a PhD in social sciences from the Universidad Nacional General Sarmiento-IDES (Argentina). He is a lecturer and researcher at the Institute of Political Science, Faculty of Social Sciences of the Universidad de la República (Uruguay). His research interests include the recent past, state violence, gender and sexuality, social movements, and public policy and heteronormativity. Among his most recent publications in English are "Violence and the Emergence of Gay and Lesbian Activism in Argentina, 1983–1990" in *The Sexual History of the Global South. Sexual Politics in Africa, Asia, and Latin America*, edited by Saskia Wieringa and Horacio Sívori (2012); and "The Creation of Civil Partnerships in Uruguay" in *Same-Sex Marriage in Latin America. Promise and Resistance*, edited by Jason Pierceson, Adriana Piatti-Crocker, and Shawn Schulenberg (2012).

CONSTANZA TABBUSH is research specialist at UN Women and is currently on leave from her position as research associate at Consejo Nacional de Investigaciones Científicas y Técnicas and the Interdisciplinary Institute of Gender Studies, University of Buenos Aires. Her lines of research focus on gender, poverty, and social protection, and on social movements and social policies in Argentina. She has collaborated in *The Gendered Impacts of Liberalization* (2008), and her research has been published in *Signs, Oxford Development Studies, Journal of International Development*, and *Global Social Policy*.

GWYNN THOMAS is an associate professor in the Department of Global Gender and Sexuality Studies at the University at Buffalo, State University of New York. Her first book, *Contesting Legitimacy in Chile: Familial Ideals, Citizenship, and Political Struggle, 1970–1990* (2011), examines the mobilization of familial beliefs in Chilean political conflicts. Her published work on gender and politics, women's political leadership and participation, and feminist institutionalism appears in *The Journal of Women, Politics and Policy, The International Feminist Journal of Politics, Gender & Politics, The Journal of Latin American Studies*, and *The Annals of the American Academy of Political and Social Science*. She received the Elsa Chaney Award in 2007 from the Gender and Feminist Studies section of the Latin American Studies Association. She is currently working on projects examining institutional innovations promoting gender equality in Chile and Costa Rica, and electoral reforms and party change in Chile.

CATALINA TREBISACCE is a postdoctoral research fellow working at the Interdisciplinary Institute of Gender Studies, University of Buenos Aires. She received her PhD in anthropology from the University of Buenos Aires in 2014. Her research areas are feminist activism during authoritarian rule and feminism and left-wing movements. She has done fieldwork and archive research on Argentine feminists of the 1970s and plans to conduct further research on feminist activists of the 1980s. Her work has been published in journals such as *Sexualidad, Salud y Sociedad*, and *Estudos Feministas*.

ANNIE WILKINSON is an anthropology PhD student at University of California, Irvine, focused on gender and sexuality issues. Her research interests include gender and sexuality politics and transnational social movements in Latin America and globally. She holds an MA in social science from FLACSO-Ecuador and and has supported women's and LGBT rights activists around the world in her former roles at the Global Fund for Women and Benetech. She is the author of *Sin sanidad, no hay santidad: Las prácticas reparativas en Ecuador* (Cleanliness Is Holiness: Reparative Practices in Ecuador, 2013) and "Transgressing Transgenders: Exploring the Borderlands of National, Gender, and Ethnic Belonging in Ecuador" in *Queering Paradigms*, IV, edited by Elizabeth Sara Lewis, Rodrigo Borba, Diana de Souza Pinto, and Branca Falabella Fabrício (2014).

INDEX

Abers, Rebecca, 145, 168

abortion rights, 3, 7, 16; in Argentina, 4, 82, 84, 86–87, 88–89, 92–94, 97–101, 106; in Bolivia, 179, 182, 191–92, 195, 196n2; in Brazil, 158, 162; in Chile, 131, 136–37; decriminalization of, 3–4, 31, 32, 33, 34, 49, 67–69, 86, 97–98, 100, 103–4, 131, 158, 161, 210, 216–17, 225, 279, 289, 294, 297n6; in Ecuador, 289–90; in Nicaragua, 31, 239, 245–46, 251–52, 259; in Uruguay, 32, 33, 49, 52, 60, 66–69, 75; in Venezuela, 216–18, 225

adoption by same-sex couples, 71–72, 192–93, 219, 284–85

Afro-Latinx, 8, 14

Agrupación de los Familiares de los Detenidos y Desparecidos, 122

Aguilar, Cristina Mamani, 189

Aguirre, Rosario, 70

AIDS. *See* HIV/AIDS

Albornoz, Laura, 136

Alemán, Arnoldo, 238

Alessandri, Jorge, 122

Alianza PAIS (Ecuador), 273, 278, 279

Alianza por Chile, 115, 133

Allende, Salvador, 121

Alvear, Soledad, 126–27, 136

Amnesty International, 93

AMNLAE. *See* Asociación de Mujeres Nicaragüenses Luisa Amanda Espinoza (Nicaragua)

Amor Mayor Mission (Venezuela), 223

ANC. *See* Asamblea Nacional Constituyente (Venezuela)

ANPS. *See* Non-Punishable Abortions (Argentina)

AP. *See* Alianza PAIS (Ecuador)

Araña Feminista, La (Venezuela), 209, 218

Área de Denuncias e Investigación (Uruguay), 62

Área de Salud Sexual y Reproductiva (Uruguay), 69

Argentina: abortion rights in, 4, 82, 84, 86–87, 88–89, 97–101, 106; executive branch vs. Catholic Church in, 87–90, 103–4; feminist movement in, 86–87, 102; gender identity recognition in, 4, 82, 83, 86, 89, 91, 101–2; gender/sexual justice in, 83–84, 94–106; issue networks in, 99–101; judicial activism in, 101–3; legislative process in, 90–94; LGBT rights in, 87; poor women, ratio of, 19; reproductive rights in, 83, 103–4; same-sex marriage in, 4, 82, 83, 86, 89, 90–91, 96–97, 99–100, 101; sexual politics in, 82; social policies in, 85–86; women's rights laws in, 85. *See also* Kirchnerism (Argentina); Partido Justicialista (Argentina)

Aruquipa, David, 180, 192

Asamblea Nacional Constituyente (Venezuela), 203–4

Asociación de Mujeres Nicaragüenses Luisa Amanda Espinoza (Nicaragua), 241–42, 245–46

Asociación Nacional de Mujeres Rurales e Indígenas (Chile), 125

Asociación Silueta X (Ecuador), 284–85, 292

Augsburger, Silvia, 91

Avellán, Héctor, 252

Aylwin, Patricio, 118, 126

Kirchner, Néstor, 22, 82, 84
Kirchnerism (Argentina), 10; on marriage equality, 99; on neoliberal policies, 84; Perón legacy and, 84, 85, 105; public image of, 104; social policies under, 85–86; women's rights laws under, 85, 98–99
Kirkwood, Julietta, 123

labor: gendered division of, 6, 15, 17–18, 20–22, 70, 208, 220–21; reproductive, 15, 22, 202, 208, 220, 221–22, 225; unpaid women's, 12, 18, 22, 23, 36–37, 69–71, 128, 208, 212, 220, 222
Lagos, Ricardo, 128, 133
Lasso, Guillermo, 273
Latin America. *See* Pink Tide; specific countries
Law of Municipalities (Nicaragua), 248
Left: LGBT relationship with, 6; meaning in national context, 9–10; as reactionary on sexuality, 6. *See also* Pink Tide
León, María, 203–4, 211
León Torrealba, Magdymar, 216
Lewites, Herty, 238
Ley de Igualdad de Derechos y Oportunidades (Nicaragua), 248
Ley de Maternidad Gratuita y Atención a la Infancia (Ecuador), 293
LGBT movements/rights, 2, 5, 6, 8, 33; affirmative action for, 4; alliance with feminism, 3–4, 57–59, 244–45; on bodily autonomy, 30–33; in Bolivia, 173–74, 178, 180, 184–86; in Brazil, 146, 149, 150, 151, 158, 169–70; Catholic Church on, 10; in Chile, 122–23, 127, 130, 132–33; in Ecuador, 282, 284–87; legislative representatives in, 153; in Mexico, 14; in Nicaragua, 235–36, 242–43, 244, 246–47, 249, 250–51, 257, 258–59; state-society collaboration and, 34–35; in Uruguay, 34, 48–50, 56–60, 58, 68, 71–72, 71–74, 75; in Venezuela, 201–2, 203, 204–5, 208–9, 218–19, 225. *See also* gender identity recognition; homosexuality, decriminalization of; same-sex marriage; sexual orientation

liberal democracy, 9
LIDO. *See* Ley de Igualdad de Derechos y Oportunidades (Nicaragua)
Lind, Amy, 257, 287
Lindner, Marisa, 64
Lugo de Montilla, Stella, 200–201

Madres del Barrio Mission (Venezuela), 223
MAM. *See* Movimiento Amplio de Mujeres (Venezuela)
Mapuche indigenous movement, 134
Marcha das Margarida (Brazil), 153–54
Marcha das Mulheres (Brazil), 153–54
Marcha das Vadias (Brazil), 153–54
marginalization: of feminism, 50; of indigenous populations, 5, 189–90; sexual orientation and, 31; of social groups, 5
Maria da Penha Law, 162
marriage equality. *See* same-sex marriage
Marriage Equality Law (Argentina), 86, 88–89, 96–98
Marshal, Maria Teresa, 123
MAS. *See* Movimiento al Socialismo (Bolivia)
masculinity, 6, 122, 226
Matamoros, Ruth Marina, 252
Matute, Romelia, 214
Mazzotti, Mariella, 56, 61
Mercal (Venezuela), 228n25
Mexico, LGBT movement in, 14
Ministerio de Educación y Cultura (Uruguay), 62
Ministerio del Interior (Uruguay), 54, 64
Ministerio de Salud Pública (Uruguay), 64
Ministry of Popular Power for Communes (Venezuela), 213
Ministry of Women (Nicaragua), 250
Ministry of Women's Popular Power and Gender Equality (Venezuela), 211, 216
MinMujer. *See* Ministry of Women's Popular Power and Gender Equality (Venezuela)
Ministerio de Trabajo y Seguridad Social (Uruguay), 61
Miss Gay Nicaragua pageant, 255, 259

MNR. *See* Movimiento Nacional Revolucionario (Bolivia)

Molyneux, Maxine, 11, 39–40n14, 241

Montiel, Samira, 251, 255

Morales, Evo, 7–8, 173–74, 176–80, 181, 185, 186–87, 193–94, 195–96

Moreira, Constanza, 67–68, 75–76

Moreno, Lenin, 273

Motta, Sara, 220

MOVILH. *See* Movimiento de Integración y Liberación Homosexual (Chile)

Movimiento al Socialismo (Bolivia), 7–8, 173, 181, 189, 195–96

Movimiento Amplio de Mujeres (Venezuela), 210

Movimiento de Integración y Liberación Homosexual (Chile), 133, 136

Movimiento Feminista (Chile), 123

Movimiento Nacional Revolucionario (Bolivia), 175

Movimiento por la Diversidad Sexual (Chile), 133

Movimiento Quinta República (Venezuela), 203–4

Movimiento Renovador Sandinista (Nicaragua), 237–38, 245, 252

MPH. *See* Mujeres Presentes en la Historia (Bolivia)

MRS. *See* Movimiento Renovador Sandinista (Nicaragua)

Mujer Ahora (Uruguay), 64

Mujeres Creando (Bolivia), 183, 184, 186

Mujeres Creando Comunidad (Bolivia), 183–84

Mujeres Jefas de Hogar (Chile), 128

Mujeres Presentes en la Historia (Bolivia), 179, 182

Mujica, José, 23–24, 32, 52, 60–61; on abortion, 67

MUMS Chile, See Movimiento por la Diversidad Sexual (Chile)

Murillo, Rosario, 31–32, 239; on AMNLAE leadership, 246; antifeminist agenda of, 235, 246, 247, 248, 258–59; on gender equity report, 31–32, 257–58; on hetero-

normativity, 235–36, 253, 259; nepotism under, 239, 240, 247, 260n9; pinkwashing by, 236, 246–47, 248, 251–53, 258–59; political culture of, 240; poverty programs of, 255–56; religious fundamentalism, use of, 241; sponsorship of transgender beauty contest, 255

MVR. *See* Movimiento Quinta República (Venezuela)

Narváez, Zoilamérica, 238, 243, 245–46, 247, 261–62n21

National Assembly (Venezuela), 213–14, 218–19

national identity, 14

National Plan for Equal Opportunities and Rights (Uruguay), 61

National System of Care, 24

National Women's Rights Defender (Venezuela), 211

nation building, 6, 11

neoliberalism: gendered division of labor under, 20–21, 220, 225; policies, critiques of, 8, 115–16, 134, 147–48, 176, 205; on same-sex marriage, 5

Nicaragua: abortion rights in, 31, 239, 251–52; attack on women's rights in, 3, 137–38, 235, 246, 247, 248, 258–59; Catholic Church in, 245, 252–53; decriminalization of homosexuality in, 246–47, 252, 258; feminist/women's movement in, 235, 241–44, 245, 247, 250–51; gender identity recognition in, 254–55; gender/sexual justice in, 236–37, 249–51, 258; heteronormativity in, 235–36, 253, 259; international aid dependency, 236; LGBT movement/rights in, 235–36, 242–43, 244, 246–47, 249, 250–51, 254, 257, 258–59; nonheterosexual unions in, 254; pinkwashing in, 236, 246–47, 248, 251–53, 258–59; political representation in, 26, 248–49; social movements in, 241–45; social programs, 22; social redistribution in, 239, 255–57; state-society relations in, 248–49; transformation claims vs. reality,

Nicaragua (continued)
10; violence against women in, 252–53.
See also Frente Sandinista de Liberación
Nacional (Nicaragua); Murillo, Rosario;
Ortega, Daniel
#NiUnaMenos (slogan), 29
Non-Punishable Abortions (Argentina), 98,
100, 102, 106, 107–8n12
Novillo, Monica, 182
Nueva Mayoría (Chile), 115, 116, 118, 135,
136, 138

Obando y Bravo, Miguel, 239
Ochoa, Marcia, 208
Ocles, Alexandra, 280
OECD. *See* Organisation for Economic Co-
operation and Development
Oficina de Denuncias y Asesoramiento
(Uruguay), 62
Olvera, Alberto, 168
Organic Children's and Adolescents' Protec-
tion Law (Venezuela), 217
Organic Electoral Processes Law (Venezuela),
213
Organic Law of Women's Right to a Life
Free from Violence (Venezuela), 215
Organic Work and Workers Law (Venezuela),
222
Organisation for Economic Co-operation
and Development (OECD), 6–7
Ortega, Daniel: attack on women's rights
by, 3, 137–38, 235, 245, 246, 247, 248, 252,
258–59; caudillismo of, 236, 240, 256, 258;
criminalization of abortion under, 31;
on decriminalization of homosexuality,
246–47; governing style, 239–41; governing style of, 10, 237–38; on heteronormativity, 235–36, 253, 259; nepotism under,
239, 240, 247, 260n9; pinkwashing by,
236, 246–47, 248, 251–53, 258–59; political
culture of, 240; poverty programs of,
255–56; religious fundamentalism, use
of, 241; return to power, 245–47; sexual
abuse case, 238, 243, 245–46; on social
redistribution, 239; vote percentage

change by, 238; women's representation
under, 26
Ovejas Negras, 56, 62, 72, 74

Pacto de Unidad (Bolivia), 179
Panfichi, Aldo, 168
Paredes, Julieta, 183–84
Partido Colorado (Uruguay), 59, 67, 71
Partido Comunista (Chile), 115
Partido da Social Democracia Brasileira
(Brazil), 148, 167, 169
Partido Demócrata Cristiano (Chile), 115,
127, 136. *See also* Concertación de Parti-
dos por la Democracia (Chile)
Partido do Movimento Democrático
Brasileiro (Brazil), 167, 169
Partido dos Trabalhadores (Brazil), 7, 34,
144, 146–47, 163
Partido Independiente (Uruguay), 68
Partido Justicialista (Argentina), 7; move-
ments within, 9–10
Partido Nacional (Uruguay), 59, 67, 71
Partido por la Democracia (Chile), 115.
See also Concertación de Partidos por la
Democracia (Chile)
Partido Radical (Chile), 115. *See also* Con-
certación de Partidos por la Democracia
(Chile)
Partido Socialista (Argentina), 91
Partido Socialista (Chile), 115. *See also* Con-
certación de Partidos por la Democracia
(Chile)
Partido Socialista (Uruguay), 53–54
Partido Socialista Unido de Venezuela, 7–8
PC. *See* Partido Colorado (Uruguay)
PDC. *See* Partido Demócrata Cristiano
(Chile)
Pearson, Ruth, 207
Pecheny, Mario, 40n16
Peña, Susana, 123
Penal Code reform of 2013 (Ecuador), 29
Percovich, Margarita, 67, 71
Pérez Marcano, Marelis, 214
Peronism, 84, 85, 105. *See also* Partido Justi-
cialista (Argentina)

welfare programs. *See* social welfare programs

women: bodily autonomy of, 1, 12, 30–33, 74, 130–32, 136–37, 190–92, 215–18, 251–53; maternalism in social welfare policies, 120–21; men's power over, 11, 12; poor/working-class, 7, 14–15, 17–21, 127–28, 201, 208, 218, 221, 225, 236–37; reproductive labor of, 15, 22, 202, 208, 220, 221–22, 225; reproductive rights of, 10, 12, 66–69, 83; rights of, 2, 5, 30–33, 48, 49, 63–69, 83, 117, 120–21, 206, 211; unpaid labor of, 12, 18, 22, 23, 36–37, 69–71, 128, 208, 212, 220, 222.

See also feminist/women's movements; political representation; violence against women (VAW)

Women and Extractivism gathering (Ecuador), 277

Women's Development Bank (Venezuela), 211, 221

World Economic Forum, 31–32

Xavier, Mónica, 67–68

Youth Popular Power Law (Venezuela), 217

Zero Hunger (Nicaragua), 256